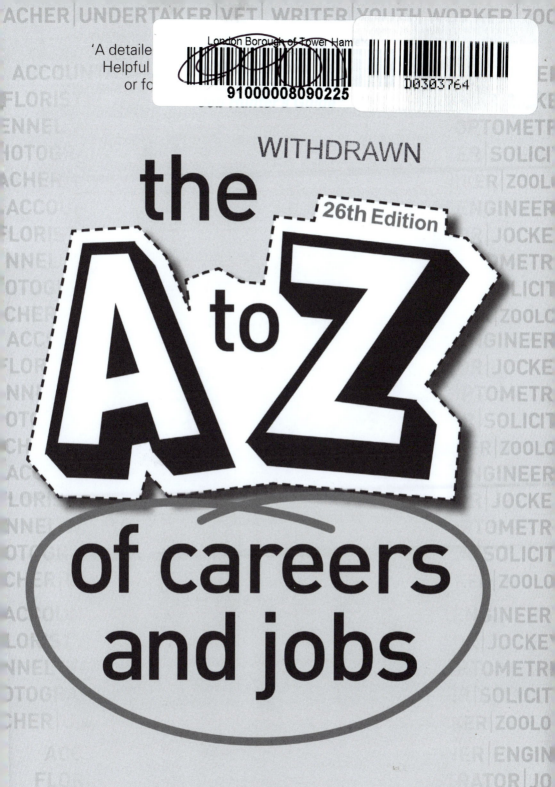

'A detaile...
Helpful ...
or fo...

WITHDRAWN

the

26th Edition

A to Z

of careers and jobs

'Recognized as the most dependable career guide available.'
Job Scene

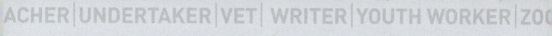

the A to Z of careers and jobs

26th Edition

KoganPage

First published in Great Britain in 1984 by Kogan Page Limited
Twenty-sixth edition published in Great Britain and the United States in 2021

2nd Floor, 45 Gee Street	122 W 27th St, 10th Floor	4737/23 Ansari Road
London	New York, NY 10001	Daryaganj
EC1V 3RS	USA	New Delhi 110002
United Kingdom		India

www.koganpage.com

Kogan Page books are printed on paper from sustainable forests.

© Kogan Page 1984, 1986, 1988, 1991, 1992, 1994, 1995, 1997, 2000, 2002, 2004, 2005, 2006, 2007, 2008, 2009, 2010, 2011, 2012, 2013, 2014, 2015, 2016, 2017, 2018, 2021

ISBNs

Hardback   978 1 78966 461 4
Paperback 978 1 78966 458 4
Ebook   978 1 78966 459 1

British Library Cataloguing-in-Publication Data

A CIP record for this book is available from the British Library.

Library of Congress Cataloging-in-Publication Data

Names: Kogan Page (Firm), editor.
Title: The A-Z of careers and jobs / Kogan Page, editor.
Description: 26th Edition. | New York : Kogan Page Inc, 2020. | Revised
   edition of The A-Z of careers and jobs, 2018.
Identifiers: LCCN 2020033158 (print) | LCCN 2020033159 (ebook) | ISBN
   9781789664584 (paperback) | ISBN 9781789664614 (hardback) | ISBN
   9781789664591 (ebook)
Subjects: LCSH: Occupations. | Professions. | Vocational guidance.
Classification: LCC HF5381 .A92 2020 (print) | LCC HF5381 (ebook) | DDC
   331.702–dc23
LC record available at https://lccn.loc.gov/2020033158
LC ebook record available at https://lccn.loc.gov/2020033159

Typeset by Integra Software Services, Pondicherry
Print production managed by Jellyfish
Printed and bound by CPI Group (UK) Ltd, Croydon CR0 4YY

How to use this book

With a seemingly infinite number of jobs and career paths available, whether you're entering the workforce for the first time or hoping to change careers, this book is an informative guide to over 300 of the jobs and careers available in the United Kingdom and a valuable tool to get you through 'choice overload'. The A–Z of *Careers and Jobs* is the definitive tool to help you on your way to that dream job.

Discover new careers

If you're looking for inspiration, browse the pages to discover jobs that you may not have known existed. Each section has a 'Personal attributes' heading to help you discover how each job would suit your personality along with a section to find out how much you might expect to earn.

Continue your education

If you want some ideas for the different ways you could apply your qualifications, or if you're interested in further study and want to know where it could take you, go to the 'Entry, qualifications and training' heading under each section to find out about what qualifications are needed for each career, or where your current qualifications could take you.

Plan your path

Do you already have a dream job in mind? Look up the entry directly, and find out more about how to get to your goal. You can find out if the job is what you thought it was, discover more about the entry requirements usually needed, and be signposted to further in-depth information on your specific dream job.

Abbreviations

A level	Advanced level
Edexcel	Edexcel Foundation
GCSE	General Certificate of Secondary Education
H grade	Higher grade (SCE)
HNC/HND	Higher National Certificate/Higher National Diploma
NC/ND	National Certificate/National Diploma
NVQ	National Vocational Qualification
SQA	Scottish Qualifications Authority
SVQ	Scottish Vocational Qualification
T Level	Technical Level
UCAS	Universities and Colleges Admissions Service

Qualifications

In England, the GCSE grading system has changed. Since 2017, English and maths have been graded from 1 to 9, with 9 being the top grade. Grades 9 to 4. or 5 equate to the previous system's A* to C. By 2019, all exams were graded by the 1 to 9 system, but most exam boards switched before that deadline. This guide refers throughout to grade 4 as equivalent to grade C.

Technical Levels (T Levels), first taught in September 2020, are an option following GCSEs and equivalent to three A Levels. These are two-year courses that prepare students for work. To ensure the content meets the needs of industry, T Levels have been developed in collaboration with various businesses and employers. As they are being finalised at the time of publication they are not widely referred to in the entry requirements for roles.

Scottish readers should be aware that, in order to simplify the text, the editor has referred to qualifications required in terms of GCSEs, A levels and NVQs or equivalent. NVQs are directly equivalent to SVQs but Scottish National and Higher Qualifications are not equivalent to GCSEs and A levels. The Advanced Higher does equate to A level. Full details of all Scottish qualifications can be found on the SQA website. The easiest way to compare the points awarded for A levels and Highers is to use the Universities and Colleges Admissions Service (UCAS) tariff calculator.

UCAS points were revised in 2017 and the new points system is used throughout this book. The UCAS tariff calculator can be used to calculate the UCAS points of your qualifications.

Overseas international qualifications

The National Academic Recognition Information Centre (comparability of international qualifications) (NARIC) can provide a letter outlining how your overseas qualifications equate to UK qualifications. There is a charge for this service: £59.40 for awards certified in English; £95.40 for awards certified in languages for which translation into English is required. They offer other services such as career path reports – check their website for charges, options, etc: **www.naric.org.uk**.

Useful points of contact

www.cityandguilds.com
City & Guilds awards a wide range of qualifications across nearly 30 industries in the United Kingdom.

www.gov.uk/government/organisations/disclosure-and-barring-service
The Disclosure and Barring Service (DBS) carries out the necessary checks on anyone who has applied to work with children, young people or vulnerable adults. Only employers and licensing bodies can request a DBS check. Job applicants can't do a criminal records check on themselves. Instead, you can request a basic disclosure from Disclosure Scotland (you don't have to be from Scotland to do this).

www.ucas.ac.uk
Provides information about, and processes applications for, higher education courses. UCAS also provides information about postgraduate courses. It offers advice on funding your studies.

Apprenticeships are offered for a huge range of jobs; for example, a PE assistant in a secondary school or a software developer in an IT company.

Apprenticeships combine practical experience in a job with study. They are available at different levels, from Intermediate (Level 2, the equivalent of GCSE) right through to degree (Levels 6 and 7, the equivalent of a bachelor's or a Master's degree).

Apprenticeships are administered slightly differently according to whether you live in England, Northern Ireland, Scotland or Wales. Each has its own web pages, giving advice:

England – **www.gov.uk/apprenticeships-guide**
Northern Ireland – **www.nidirect.gov.uk/campaigns/apprenticeships**
Scotland – **www.gov.scot/Topics/Education/Work-based-Training**
Wales – **http://gov.wales/topics/educationandskills/skillsandtraining/apprenticeships**

Not Going to Uni (**www.notgoingtouni.co.uk**) is a website that was set up by a student in 2008, to give options for school leavers who do not want to go to university. It includes lots of useful information about apprenticeships, as well as employer-advertised opportunities.

Sector Skills Councils (SSCs) provide a range of career and training information in different industries and are frequently listed in the information boxes under individual career entries.

BESA (Building Engineering Services Association) – design, installation, maintenance and management of heating and ventilation in buildings: **www.thebesa.com**

CITB (Construction Industry Training Board) – the construction industry: **www.citb.co.uk**

Cogent Skills – skills for science industries: chemical, pharmaceutical, healthcare, environmental technologies: **www.cogentskills.com**

Create with code – as coding becomes an increasingly important skill, there are many organisations that offer opportunities to learn to code. This is one example: **www.create.withcode.uk**

Creative & Cultural Skills – art, crafts, culture and heritage, music literature, performing arts: **www.ccskills.org.uk**

IMI (Institute of the Motor Industry) – retail motor industry: **www.theimi.org.uk**

Instructus Skills (formerly Skills CFA) – skills for business: **www.instructus-skills.org.**

Lantra – agriculture, animals, forestry, land, natural environment: **www.lantra.co.uk**

National Skills Academy for Food & Drink – food and drink manufacturing: **www.nsafd.co.uk**

National Skills Academy Nuclear – nuclear power station design and management, decommissioning and waste management: **www.nsan.co.uk**

People 1st – hospitality, passenger transport, retail, travel and tourism: **www.people1st.co.uk**

PHSP (Plumbing and Heating Skills Partnership): **www.phsp.org.uk**

Screen Skills – works with the UK's screen-based creative industries: film, TV and games: **www.screenskills.com**

SEMTA – engineering and advanced manufacturing technologies: **www.semta.org.uk**

SkillsActive – sport and fitness, hair and beauty, playwork, outdoors recreation: **www.skillsactive.com**

Skills for Care & Development – childcare and social care: **www.skillsforcareanddevelopment.org.uk**

Skills for Health – healthcare: **www.skillsforhealth.org.uk**

Skills for Justice – law enforcement, fire and rescue policing, custodial care: **www.sfjuk.com**

Skills for Logistics – haulage, supply chain, logistics: **www.skillsforlogistics. co.uk**

TESP (The Electrotechnical Skills Partnership) – electrical design, installation and engineering: **www.the-esp.org.uk**

Tech Partnership Degrees – information technology, telecommunications and business: **https://www.tpdegrees.com**

www.careerconnect.org.uk
Career Connect is a charity providing high quality careers advice.

The National Minimum Wage

From April 2020, the National Minimum Wage hourly rates are £8.20 if you are aged 21 to 24, £6.45 if you are aged 18 to 20, and £4.55 if you are under 18.

In April 2016, a minimum wage for workers aged over 25 was introduced called the National Living Wage; it currently stands at £8.72 an hour. It is difficult to express pay for jobs paid at the National Minimum Wage or National Living Wage rate as an annual salary, as the amount will vary according to the number of hours worked a week. Often these jobs are not full time. This guide refers to 'the minimum wage' to cover both the National Minimum Wage and the National Living Wage.

The minimum wage for apprentices aged under 19 or at any age in the first year of their apprenticeship is £4.15 an hour. Apprentices aged 19 and over who have completed the first year of their apprenticeship must be paid at least the minimum wage for their age.

All figures given for pay, minimum or otherwise, are guidelines only.

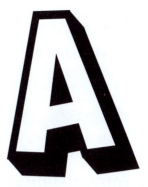

ACCOUNTANCY

Members of the accounting professions work on many financial matters for business, public bodies and private individuals.

Accountant

Accountants work with, and have expert understanding of, a wide range of financial questions, issues and procedures. They work in many settings, including small high street accounting firms, local and central government departments, management consultants and for the finance departments of commercial and industrial organisations, from small businesses to global corporations. They deal with matters such as taxation, business forecasting, monitoring financial performance, advising on investments, acquisitions and mergers, and good daily financial management. They also audit the paperwork and digital records of organisations to make sure that all financial transactions are accounted for and comply with the law.

Because accountants work in such a range of situations, they train and work in one of four accountancy professions. There is, however, crossover between these professions, so one qualifying route does not necessarily restrict you to one type of work.

Chartered accountant

As a chartered accountant you are likely to play a strategic role in your organisation, which could be an accounting firm, an industrial or commercial business, the public or the not-for-profit sectors. Your work could include auditing, financial reporting, taxation, forensic accounting or business recovery. Generally your role is to help your organisation maximise profitability.

Chartered certified accountant

As a chartered certified accountant you could undertake a variety of accountancy services including developing and maintaining financial and accounting systems, financial forecasting, auditing financial records and investigating financial anomalies. You can work in many sectors including private practice, public sector, financial services or the corporate sector. Rather like a chartered accountant, your main role is to maximise profitability and efficiency and ensure value for money.

Chartered management accountant

As a chartered management accountant working in commerce and industry you would work with a company monitoring and planning budgets, preparing information for external auditors, overseeing credit control, monitoring financial performance and suggesting future business developments. You would work closely with other members of the management team.

Chartered public finance accountant

As a chartered public finance accountant your role would be to control and assess the efficiency of public spending. Working, for example, in health trusts, local authorities, universities and central government departments, chartered public finance accountants examine the cost-effectiveness of policies, manage budgets, conduct internal audits and advise on policy.

Knowing in what kind of environment you would work and what specialist knowledge you wish to apply will help you choose which of the branches of accountancy is most appropriate for you.

Entry, qualifications and training

Each professional body offering training has slightly different entry requirements, but with much similarity. As an applicant you not only have to satisfy your prospective employer, but ensure that you meet the entry requirements of the accountancy body with which you wish to train.

Training places in accountancy are fiercely competed for. While smaller firms may accept you with good A levels or an HND, it is very much a graduate profession. Any degree is acceptable, but business-, finance- and mathematics-based subjects may be preferred and may offer you some exemptions from sections of your professional training. Many companies taking on people to train as accountants will expect 104 to 120+ UCAS points as well as a good degree (2.1). Some firms will allow people who have qualified as accounting technicians (see next entry) to go on and train as accountants. Another useful stepping stone if you don't have the appropriate qualifications is to study for a Certificate in Finance Accounting and Business (CFAB), which is available as a part-time modular programme. All the accountancy bodies do offer alternative entry routes for mature applicants with other qualifications and relevant experience.

Management accountants do not have to be graduates, but a good honours degree in a mathematical or business subject may offer exemptions from some of the professional examinations.

Accountants qualified with any of the professional accountancy bodies can work in the public sector, but the most relevant organisation is the Chartered Institute of Public Finance and Accountancy (CIPFA). If you don't have another accountancy qualification you must have three GCSEs grades 9–4 and two A levels. You must have maths and English at either GCSE or A level.

All the accountancy professions offer similar training routes where you have to complete three years' supervised work and take professional exams at two levels.

Training contracts are popular and you face a lot of competition for every opening. Some firms offer work experience during summer vacations and if you can obtain one of these positions this will also help your cause.

Personal attributes

Accountants have to be good at working with numbers but they must also be very good communicators. They have to be able to understand complex information and also to explain complicated information to people who don't have detailed financial knowledge. They must be able to use their own initiative, be persistent, and assertiveness is as important as tact and discretion.

Earnings

Starting salaries depend on location, size of firm and field of accountancy, but are around £18,000 to £30,000 for trainees in London and the South East; £16,000 to £25,000 is more typical elsewhere. On qualifying, salaries increase significantly – £40,000 to £55,000 with a few years' experience. Salary packages often include benefits such as pay bonuses, share options, and pension and private health plans. The professional bodies conduct regular salary surveys and you can obtain further information from them.

Info

Chartered Institute of Management Accountants (CIMA)
020 8849 2251
www.cimaglobal.com

Chartered Institute of Public Finance and Accountancy (CIPFA)
020 7543 5600
www.cipfa.org

Association of Chartered Certified Accountants (ACCA)
ACCA Connect 0141 582 2000
www.accaglobal.com

Institute of Chartered Accountants England and Wales (ICAEW)
01908 248250
www.icaew.com

Institute of Chartered Accountants Scotland (ICAS)
0131 347 0100
www.icas.com

Accounting technician

Accounting technicians work in a variety of roles, often alongside professionally qualified chartered accountants. As an accounting technician you would be concerned with the day-to-day practical work of accounting and finance, including the preparation of information and accounts and the interpretation of digital information, such as audit, tax and payroll. Accounting technicians are widely employed in public finance, industry and commerce, and in private practice. Their roles range from accounts clerks to finance managers. A growing number of accounting technicians provide a range of services direct to the public and manage their own practice. Many go on to qualify with the senior chartered accountancy bodies.

Entry, qualifications and training

Entry qualifications vary, but many employers expect you to have four GCSEs grades 9–4 including maths and English. It is also useful to have some office experience and good IT skills, especially spreadsheet and database software. Many accounting technicians start work as accounts clerks and this may be an alternative entry route if you don't have appropriate qualifications. The Association of Accounting Technicians (AAT) and the Chartered Institute of Certified Accountants (ACCA) offer accounting technician qualifications for which you can study part time at college or through work-based training. It is also worth checking the Government's apprenticeships website (under business, administration and law) for details of accounting apprenticeships which are offered at intermediate, advanced and higher levels.

Personal attributes

You must be thorough and methodical and enjoy working with figures. Good IT skills and the ability to work as part of a team are also very important. Excellent verbal communication skills are important, and some positions involve considerable responsibility and/or the pressure of deadlines.

Earnings

In London and the South East trainees earn £20,000 to £24,000; in the regions £15,000 to £17,000 – less during an apprenticeship. Qualified technicians earn from £17,000 to £32,000.

Info

Association of Chartered Certified Accountants (ACCA)
0141 582 2000
www.accaglobal.com

Association of Accounting Technicians (AAT)
020 3735 2468
www.aat.org.uk

ACTOR

(see Performing Arts)

ACTUARY

Actuaries use their knowledge of mathematics, statistics, economics and business to assess financial risks and probabilities. Traditionally their work is mainly concerned with the issue of pensions, plus life assurance and other types of insurance, but they may also work in investment and other business areas where major financial risks are involved.

They create statistical and mathematical models to analyse past events and predict the financial outcome of different situations. For example, in insurance they may study accident rates or medical data to develop and price new insurance policies, making sure that there are sufficient funds to cover liabilities but allow the company to remain profitable.

Around 45 per cent of actuaries work for consultancies, with the job title of actuarial consultant, providing specialist actuarial services to businesses of every kind. They advise on business recovery, acquisitions and employee benefit schemes. Central government also has its own actuarial departments, which provide actuarial support and information across central government, its agencies and the National Health Service.

Entry, qualifications and training

To qualify as an actuary you must become a student member of one of the professional bodies – either the Faculty or Institute of Actuaries – referred to collectively as the Actuarial Profession. Minimum entry qualifications are three GCSEs grades 9–4 including English and two A levels, one of which must be maths at grade B, though if your degree is in maths or actuarial science you do not need A level maths. This is a highly competitive profession and most entrants have a 2.1 or first class degree. Favoured subjects include maths, economics, statistics, actuarial science, physics, chemistry and engineering.

Having completed your professional training, study and examinations you become a Fellow of either the Institute or Faculty. To qualify as a Fellow of the Faculty or Institute of Actuaries, you must pass 15 professional examinations. After one year's work experience and appropriate examinations you should reach associate membership and after three years' work experience and appropriate exams you should reach fellowship.

If you have a degree or postgraduate qualification in actuarial science, statistics or economics, you may be exempt from some or all of the exams at the Core Technical Stage and some at the next stage. Please contact the Institute of Actuaries for further details of exemptions.

The profession has also introduced a new career of Certified Actuarial Analyst aimed at school leavers with A levels, graduates and people already working in insurance or other financial areas.

Personal attributes

You need excellent maths and statistical and analytical skills and must be able to understand and explain complex information. The ability to think clearly using reasoning and logic is important, as well as using your judgement to make decisions. You should have a thorough understanding of business and economics, be a great communicator and be aware of the bigger picture while paying attention to fine detail.

Earnings

Trainee actuaries start on around £30,000. This rises to between £35,000 and £45,000 for part-qualified associate actuaries. Qualified actuaries with at least five years' experience can earn between £55,000 and £80,000 and some salaries in the profession reach more than £150,000.

Info

The Actuarial Education Company
01235 550005
www.acted.co.uk

The Association of Consulting Actuaries
020 3102 6761
www.aca.org.uk

Institute and Faculty of Actuaries
www.actuaries.org.uk

ADVERTISING

Persuading people to buy a product, develop brand loyalty, choose a service provider, donate to a charity or subscribe to an idea is what the advertising industry is all about. This sector has changed enormously with the impact of social media – the internet, Facebook, Twitter, Instagram and instant messaging to mobile phones. Advertisers also use all their traditional media of television, radio, newspapers, magazines and poster campaigns. Advertising agencies help their clients, who may be from business, government, charities or pressure groups to identify, target and engage with suitable markets. Whatever your role in advertising, your work will be concerned with some aspects of these activities.

Account executive

As an account executive you are responsible for a particular client or group of clients. You interpret the client's wishes and coordinate and supervise others working on ideas for the campaign, such as creatives, account planners, copywriters and scriptwriters. You then present the ideas most likely to meet with the client's approval to that client. If the client is happy you continue to coordinate the project through to its completion.

Account planner

As an account planner you consider the client's brief and work to identify the target audience and optimum method of getting the client's message across. You analyse market research and other data and provide the creative team with information to help them develop the most effective campaign. You may work on forward planning for your agency, identifying likely future clients based on market research data.

Art editor/executive director

This position involves coordinating the work of the creative department, which converts the client's original intentions into a visual form for approval. Others, including copywriters, may elaborate upon this.

Copywriter and scriptwriter

The writers in the agency produce headings, text, jingles and copy for articles in journals, and scripts for films and commercials. Copywriters often work closely with the other professionals who have developed the basic ideas on which the copy- and scriptwriters are working.

Media executive

Media executives work as media buyers and media planners to ensure that advertising campaigns reach their target audiences. Media planners work out where advertising will be most effective – television, radio, posters, newspapers, magazines, mobile and online media. They must keep abreast of the changing market; the growth in mobile and online advertising is a prime example of this. Media buyers try to get the best possible deals for their clients when placing advertising with this wide variety of media.

Entry, qualifications and training

Many people want to work in this highly competitive sector. Most successful applicants have either a degree or an HND. Any subject is acceptable, but related subjects, including advertising, business studies, marketing, English or consumer science could give you the edge. Smaller agencies may take you without a degree, particularly if you have relevant work experience. Work experience is really valuable: it shows you how agencies work and shows you are keen, but this experience is hard to come by. You could consider voluntary work for an agency. Some agencies offer formal work placement schemes. Details of these appear on the Institute of Practitioners in Advertising (IPA) website. There are many courses in marketing, communications and media studies at many levels but they won't necessarily make you more employable. There are a few highly respected postgraduate courses in advertising, for example including a diploma in art direction and copywriting and a postgraduate diploma in creative advertising.

Most training is on the job, learning from colleagues, and you are usually considered to be a trainee for about two years. The IPA offers induction courses and continuing professional development courses, and the Chartered Institute of Marketing (CIM) offers a range of part-time and distance-learning courses for those who are already working in the sector.

A few schools and colleges offer vocational diplomas in creative and media studies. These can be taken at foundation, higher or advanced level. These courses combine academic study and training with an employer.

Personal attributes

Excellent communication skills at every level are essential. Being able to deal with people, think quickly, write clearly and work creatively are all essential. Many roles require you to be persuasive and tactful, and to be a media planner you need to be highly numerate. Advertising is a highly pressured business so you have to be thick-skinned and keep calm when chasing deadlines.

Earnings

Starting salaries range from £18,000 to £25,000 depending on your role. Trainee account executives often earn more than trainee media planners and buyers. Salary also depends on the size of the agency. Many agencies are based in London and the South East. In the regions, starting salaries range from £15,000 to £20,000. Senior account executives can earn £100,000, but averages are closer to £45,000 to £50,000.

Influencer

Influencers market and promote lifestyles and products on social media platforms, such as Instagram, YouTube and Facebook through the mediums of photos and videos (vlogs). This often begins as a hobby, but increasingly has become a career for those who have a substantial loyal following and have attracted payment to promote products. This is a relatively new profession, which can be lucrative. Influencers tend to be ordinary people (in contrast to celebrity endorsers) whose followers trust them and value their expertise. Money can also be made through YouTube and Instagram from advertising revenue on posts that have thousands of followers.

Entry, qualifications and training

No qualifications are required to become an influencer although good literacy and communication skills are needed to effectively articulate and inspire the audience. An understanding of human behaviour, motivation and drivers will be useful in effectively marketing and promoting products. A qualification in marketing or an understanding of marketing principles will also be useful.

Personal attributes

Excellent communication skills, both written and verbal, are essential along with a calm, friendly and engaging manner to inspire confidence in products and drive a following and increase audience size. Dedication to consistent, regular posts is needed, especially in the early days when a following is small. You should also be able to creatively think of new ideas to promote products. The key difference between the influencers who "make it" and those that don't often comes down to having a unique voice.

Earnings

Payments to advertise and promote products via social media platforms vary enormously, and depend on the popularity of the platforms used to advertise products, type of audience, number of followers and the products or areas the influencer specialises in. What is popular is susceptible to trends, and losing audience is easier than gaining audience.

Info

Account Planning Group
0208 858 0707
www.apg.org.uk

British Interactive Media Association (BIMA)
020 3538 6607
www.bima.co.uk

Chartered Institute of Marketing (CIM)
01628 427500
www.cim.co.uk

Communication, Advertising and Marketing Education Foundation (CAM)
01628 427 120
www.camfoundation.com

Screen Skills
020 7713 9800
www.screenskills.com

AGRICULTURE

(see Farming and Gardening)

AMBULANCE SERVICE

Ambulance work involves transferring people to hospital. This could be responding to emergency calls, e.g. road traffic accidents, or people taken seriously ill in their own homes. Ambulance staff also take patients who are too ill or frail to reach hospital themselves to and from hospital for planned appointments or treatments.

Ambulance care assistant

Ambulance care assistants usually work in the patient transport service of an ambulance trust, where they drive disabled, elderly and vulnerable people to and from outpatient clinics, day-care centres and to routine hospital admissions. They are sometimes called PTS drivers. They may have to lift or assist patients in and out of vehicles and they have to ensure that their patients are comfortable and safe.

Emergency care assistant

Emergency care assistants normally work alongside a paramedic, attending scenes of accidents and other emergencies. An emergency care assistant carries out a wide range of emergency treatments, treating burns, wounds, fractures and heart attacks. As well as treating patients, emergency care assistants have to liaise with patients' relatives, with members of the public and with staff from other emergency services.

Emergency call handler/medical dispatcher

Emergency medical dispatchers handle emergency 999 calls from the public and from GPs. Some ambulance services split this role into call handlers and dispatchers. Where this is the case, call handlers take down details accurately, quickly and calmly. Dispatchers then decide how best to deal with this situation – how many vehicles to send, for example. In some ambulance services, the same person is responsible for taking down details, logging them onto a computer and sending out the ambulances.

Paramedic

Paramedics (emergency care practitioners) are the senior ambulance service healthcare professionals at an accident or a medical emergency. They assess a patient's condition and give essential and often lifesaving treatment. They use a range of sophisticated equipment and can administer drugs, drips and oxygen. They are trained to resuscitate and stabilise patients and they may also drive ambulances, since they usually work in teams of two to a vehicle.

PTS call handler

PTS (Patient Transport Service) call handlers work in the non-emergency part of ambulance services, organising routine transport to take patients to and from hospital appointments and home after discharge. They deal with requests for appointments and ensure the most efficient use of the available vehicles.

Entry, qualifications and training

Many roles require you to have a full, clean, manual driving licence, then additional training will be provided to use particular types of ambulance.

General entry qualifications for ambulance care assistants and for emergency medical dispatchers vary between ambulance trusts – many require GCSEs, NVQs and/or relevant work experience. PTS call handlers don't need academic qualifications, though each ambulance service sets its own entry requirements. Training is on the job and covers how to use communications equipment and customer care skills.

Emergency care assistants have often worked as ambulance care assistants first. Academic requirements for this vary between different ambulance services, but GCSEs grades 9–4 are often required. You can become a paramedic by completing a university course, a trainee scheme, an apprenticeship, or working towards the role. The NHS Health Careers website will give you more information on what is required. Broadly, paramedics qualify either by training first as an ambulance technician or by doing a diploma, foundation degree or degree course in paramedic science. Appropriate courses are approved by the Health and Care Professions Council (HCPC).

Training relevant to particular roles is given on the job and through special training courses on lifting and handling patients, advanced driving, etc. Ambulance technicians and paramedics need regular training to keep them up to date with new equipment and drugs.

Personal attributes

For every role in the ambulance service it is essential that you have very good communication skills and a calm and reassuring manner. All those roles where you are dealing with emergency situations require you to act quickly but carefully. Paramedics and technicians dealing with emergencies have to be able to cope with distressing and sometimes frightening situations. They have to have good practical skills for handling complex and sensitive equipment and they have to be able to think quickly and take appropriate decisions.

Earnings

There is a structured NHS pay scale for all ambulance staff. The NHS website lists pay rates for each job title.

An ambulance care assistant earns between £17,600 and £20,795. A paramedic earns between £24,200 and £37,200. A fully qualified ambulance technician earns around £22,000. Many ambulance jobs also attract 'antisocial working hours' payments. All staff earn an extra 25 per cent working in central London and an extra 10 per cent if working in outer London.

Info

NHS Careers
0345 60 60 655
www.healthcareers.nhs.uk

British Ambulance Association
www.baa999.com

College of Paramedics
01278 420014
www.collegeofparamedics.co.uk

Health and Care Professions Council (HCPC)
0300 500 6184
www.hcpc-uk.org

Skills for Health
020 7388 8800
www.skillsforhealth.org.uk

ANIMALS

(see also Veterinary Science)

Working with animals is always a popular career choice. The number of openings in each occupation may be small, but the range of occupations is broad.

Animal care worker

Animals in rescue centres, kennels, catteries, animal sanctuaries and animal hospitals all need looking after seven days a week. It would be your job, as an animal care worker, to provide this care. You could be looking after dogs, cats, rabbits, rodents, birds or even more exotic animals. You would have to feed and perhaps exercise animals. You would have to ensure that bedding, cages and exercise areas were kept clean and that animals felt reassured and cared for. In some posts you might have to do some administrative work and also advise people on the care of their animals or animals they are about to adopt. Some animal care workers become auxiliaries in animal hospitals or collection officers for the Royal Society for the Prevention of Cruelty to Animals (RSPCA).

Entry, qualifications and training

The right attitude and some relevant experience – either paid or voluntary – are more important than qualifications. Some organisations may require you to have passed GCSEs, especially if you want to go on to part-time study. Work with animals is popular; a good way to improve your chances of success is to do some relevant voluntary work (see the Info panel to find out where to volunteer). A college course may enable you to build some of the knowledge and skills, which might include a Level 1 Certificate in Introduction to Animal Care or Level 2 Diploma in Animal Care, for example. You may be able to find an intermediate level apprenticeship in animal care or animal boarding care and many colleges offer part-time animal care certificates and diplomas.

Personal attributes

You must be kind, gentle, calm and confident when handling animals. You need to be patient and you can't be squeamish. While being caring is essential, you must be resilient enough not to get too easily upset when dealing with badly treated or neglected animals. You need to be practical, you might need record-keeping skills and you should be good at dealing with humans as well as animals.

Earnings

Pay is often on the low side, starting at the minimum wage, and workers are often employed on a casual basis – many employers are charities on tight budgets. Senior workers may earn up to £15,000.

Info

Lantra
02476 696996
www.lantra.co.uk

People's Dispensary for Sick Animals (PDSA)
0800 917 2509
www.pdsa.org.uk

Royal Society for the Prevention of Cruelty to Animals (RSPCA)
www.rspca.org.uk

College of Animal Welfare
01480 422060
www.caw.ac.uk

Animal Care College
01344 636 436
www.animalcarecollege.co.uk

Association of Dogs and Cats Homes
www.adch.org.uk

Blue Cross
0300 790 9903
www.bluecross.org.uk

Animal groomer

Working as an animal groomer you are most likely to be working with dogs, though occasionally you may find yourself grooming other animals. Grooming involves shampooing, drying, brushing, combing, fur clipping and claw trimming. Many breeds of dog have to have their hair or fur cut in a very particular way, for either health or appearance reasons. As an animal groomer you must become familiar with all these requirements. Most businesses are small, private establishments, though some are part of other establishments, including pet shops, garden centres and kennels. Some mobile groomers visit animals in their own home.

Entry, qualifications and training

You don't need formal qualifications, though good GCSE results are a plus. There are three ways to train: you can work with an experienced, qualified groomer and learn your skills from them, you can do a college course or you can take an apprenticeship. There are specific courses for dog grooming offered by colleges and some private training centres, for example. These include a Level 2 Certificate for Dog Grooming Assistants, and Level 3 Diploma for Dog Grooming. Apprenticeships in this field are rather few and far between, so you may end up paying to qualify through a private college. A BTEC certificate or diploma may help you get a training place with a salon.

Personal attributes

You must be calm, kind and confident when handling animals – they don't always share their owners' enthusiasm for grooming. You must have good practical skills and take a pride in your work. You need to be able to communicate with pet owners and you may need business skills if you decide to run your own independent grooming salon or mobile grooming parlour.

Earnings

Dog groomers earn between £13,000 and £19,000 if working in a salon. Self-employed groomers charge varied rates for their service, however this usually ranges from £25 to £90, depending on the breed of dog and what the grooming entails.

Info

Pet Care Trade Association
www.petcare.org.uk

Lantra
02476 696996
www.lantra.co.uk

Animal technician

(see Laboratory technician)

RSPCA/SSPCA inspector

If you work as an inspector for the Royal Society for the Prevention of Cruelty to Animals (RSPCA) or the Scottish Society for the Prevention of Cruelty to Animals (SSPCA) you would work to check and improve the welfare of animals in many different situations. Part of the job is to respond to complaints from members of the public about alleged cases of cruelty or neglect, to follow up these cases and, if necessary, to remove the animals. Another part of your role would be to check the welfare of animals in kennels, stables, zoos and pet shops. You would also check on the welfare of animals at events such as horse races, dog and cat shows. You would also have to inspect animals on farms to ensure that all the relevant legal welfare standards are being adhered to. Your role would not simply be one of checking, you would often advise animal keepers and pet owners on how to care better for their animals. In some situations you would have to work with the police if animals had to be removed from a premises. You could also be involved in the rescue of wild animals who have been injured.

Entry, qualifications and training

Anyone wishing to become an inspector must apply to join as an animal welfare officer. For this you need five GCSEs grades 9–4, a full and current UK driving licence, to be physically fit and able to swim 50 metres. Training is on the job and covers all aspects of the work – legal, practical and emotional. In Scotland, training starts at the headquarters in Edinburgh; in the rest of the UK it is at local offices. Animal welfare officers can also work towards NVQ level 3 qualifications in many aspects of animal care while undergoing training. There is great competition for jobs with the RSPCA and the Scottish Society for the Prevention of Cruelty to Animals (SSPCA) and working as a volunteer before you apply is one way to strengthen your application. You can find more information about entry criteria on the RSPCA and SSPCA websites.

Personal attributes

Inspectors have to be very good at handling animals of all kinds. They must be calm, kind and authoritative. They need excellent interpersonal skills, must be able to be assertive, to deal with both sensitive and potentially confrontational situations. They must be able to speak in public, whether it is in court or in a classroom.

Earnings

Trainee inspectors earn £19,000 to £23,000. Fully trained inspectors earn from £24,000 to £28,000. An accommodation allowance is included in the salary and there are additional allowances for officers working in or close to London.

Info

Volunteering UK
020 7713 6161
www.ncvo.org.uk

Volunteering Scotland
www.volunteerscotland.info

Royal Society for the Prevention of Cruelty to Animals (RSPCA)
www.rspca.org.uk

Scottish Society for the Prevention of Cruelty to Animals (SSPCA)
www.scottishspca.org

Zookeeper

Snakes, elephants, penguins, birds, fish, insects and many more animals in zoos and safari parks are all under the care of zookeepers. As a zookeeper you will have to feed and water animals, clean out their pens and cages and put in fresh bedding. You will have to monitor them to see that they are healthy, and keep records of their weight, health, their food preferences, etc. You may have to work closely with vets either to care for a sick animal, or to work on breeding and conservation programmes. You will also have to answer questions from visitors to your zoo or park. This PR role is very important with concerns about animal welfare and the roles of zoos in captive breeding or return-to-the-wild programmes being very important. Many keepers develop highly specialised knowledge of the care of a particular species or group of species.

Entry, qualifications and training

You can become a zookeeper by completing a university course, a college course, or an apprenticeship. You don't usually need academic qualifications, though some employers may ask for GCSEs grades 9–4 including English and one science. Most zoos expect you to have experience of working with animals and the main way to acquire this is through volunteering. Most zoos have volunteer schemes, though these are popular and competitive. The British and Irish Association of Zoos and Aquariums website gives contact details for all zoos and wildlife parks. If you want to work in a safari or wildlife park you will need a driving licence. Your application may be strengthened by acquiring one of the following: a BTEC First Diploma and National Certificate/Diploma in Animal Care or Animal Management, a City & Guilds qualification in Animal Care, or NVQ levels 1 and 2 in Animal Care. Check individual colleges for entry requirements.

Some zoos may run apprenticeship schemes from time to time. Training is on the job and you may be able to work for some of the qualifications just listed on a day-release basis. Once you have worked as a zookeeper for at least a year, you can do a two-year part-time block-release foundation degree in zoo resource management at Sparsholt College in Hampshire. You can do foundation degrees and degrees in animal management at some other colleges and universities.

Personal attributes

You must love animals and be good at assessing their condition and monitoring behaviour. You have to be practical, calm, confident, happy working in the open air and not squeamish about smells. You must be very alert and safety conscious, especially when working with dangerous animals, and remain calm in stressful situations. You should be able to work as part of a team, be interested in science and the environment, and be able to communicate with members of the public in a friendly and informative way.

Earnings

Salaries start from around £12,000 to £16,500. Experienced zookeepers can earn from £17,000 to over £21,000.

Info

British and Irish Association of Zoos and Aquariums (BIAZA)
020 7449 6599
www.biaza.org.uk

Sparsholt College
01962 776441
www.sparsholt.ac.uk

Lantra
02476 696996
www.lantra.co.uk

Dogs

Assistance dog trainer

Assistance dog trainers and instructors train dogs to help people with physical disabilities, hearing or sight impairments, or who are prone to seizures, to live independently. There are four types of assistance dogs. Guide Dogs for the Blind help people to avoid obstacles, find entrances, stairs, etc. Disability assistance dogs do such things as pick up a telephone, press an emergency button or load a washing machine. Hearing dogs alert people to sounds such as a doorbell or a telephone. Seizure alert dogs watch for telltale signs of an impending seizure, warn their owners and care for them if a seizure does occur. Most trainers are employed by the four relevant charities; they are listed in the Info panel. Trainers work closely with dogs to teach them the skills they need and then they work with the dog and the human with whom it is going to live to teach that person how to use the dog and also how to care for it properly.

Entry, qualifications and training

You must be at least 18 years old and have a full, clean driving licence. Academic and other requirements vary between the different employer organisations, so you should contact them for details. In general, you will need qualifications that are relevant to your client group, e.g. know British Sign Language if you are working with hearing-impaired people and their assistance dogs. You will also need to pass enhanced background checks. GCSEs grades 9–4 may be required and some employers prefer one of your subjects to be a science. You will also be able to complete an apprenticeship. Different apprenticeships have different academic requirements. For example, you will need four or five GCSEs grades 9–4 and A levels, or equivalent, for a higher or degree apprenticeship.

Personal attributes

You must have great patience and a real understanding of, and interest in, animal behaviour. You should also get on really well with people, who often need a lot of encouragement and support when they first acquire an assistance dog. You should be practical, well organised and good at thinking up solutions to problems.

Earnings

Starting salaries are around the minimum wage a year, rising to £20,000 with experience. Salaries for trainers working with hearing dogs are a little bit higher. An experienced assistance dog trainer might earn up to £27,000.

Info

Guide Dogs for the Blind
0118 983 5555
www.guidedogs.org.uk

Hearing Dogs for Deaf People
01844 348100
www.hearingdogs.org.uk

Support Dogs
0114 261 7800
www.supportdogs.org.uk

Canine Partners
08456 580 480
www.caninepartners.org.uk

Dogs for Good
01295 252600
www.dogsforgood.org

Dog handler

Dog handlers work for the police, the armed services, HM Revenue & Customs, fire and rescue services and private security firms.

As a dog handler you would always work very closely with your dog, although the work would depend on who employed you. Your work could entail trying to find missing persons, chasing criminals, working closely with armed officers, checking for explosives, drugs or stolen goods or trying to find human remains. You and your dog would work as a team and you would be responsible for the care and supervision of your dog. With more experience, you might also train your own dog or train dogs for other handlers to use.

Entry, qualifications and training

You can become a dog handler by completing an apprenticeship, working towards this role, or applying directly. However, in most organisations you are not taken on as a dog handler. You start like any other recruit and dog handling is a specialist area for which you may then get the opportunity to train. You need to check the entry requirements of the other different career paths, but many will require you to have at least four GCSEs grades 9–4. Private security firms often want you to have experience of dog handling before you work for them as a dog handler. You'll also need a Security Industry Authority licence.

Gaining experience by volunteering with the Rescue Dog Association may also help with your application.

Personal attributes

It is essential that you love working with dogs and that you are confident and sure of yourself when handling them. The bond that builds up between handler and dog is often very strong and you may have to spend a lot of time working on your own, just with your dog. Depending on the organisation you are working for, you may have to work in stressful or dangerous situations, or in uncomfortable and unpleasant conditions. You also need to be good at communicating with people.

Earnings

Salaries vary according to who employs you, but are around £16,000 for new dog handlers and up to £36,000 or more for handlers with experience and other management responsibilities.

Info

Police Recruitment
https://recruit.college.police.uk
0800 496 3322

Security Industry Authority (SIA)
www.sia.homeoffice.gov.uk

RAF Careers
www.raf.mod.uk

National Search and Rescue Dog Association
www.nsarda.org.uk

Army Careers
020 7218 9000
www.army.mod.uk

UK Visas and Immigration
www.gov.uk/government/organisations/
uk-visas-and-immigration

National Association of Security Dog Users
01483 224 320
www.nasdu.co.uk

Kennel worker

Kennel staff care for dogs in kennels: feeding, grooming and exercising the dogs and keeping their kennels and exercise areas clean. Where animals are sick or recovering from an operation, the kennel staff must also be able to provide adequate nursing care.

The balance of your work depends on what type of kennel you work in. If you are working in a greyhound training kennel you will spend a lot of time training and exercising your dogs. If you work at a boarding kennel you may spend more time reassuring your dogs. There are also quarantine kennels and breeding kennels where duties include weaning and training puppies, preparing dogs for shows and possibly handling them.

Entry, qualifications and training

No formal qualifications are needed to work in kennels and most employers prefer school leavers to train on the job. Some employers may ask you for GCSEs grades 9–4, including maths and English. You could also complete a course at college such as the Level 2 Diploma in Animal Management for which you may need two GCSEs grades 3–1 for a level 1 course, or two or more GCSEs grades 9–3 for a level 2 course. The NVQ level 2 in Animal Care and the National Small Animal Care Certificate are nationally recognised by the industry and provide a good base for further study. There are some intermediate level apprenticeships available in kennel work – check your local information. You can also gain experience through volunteering to show your commitment and enthusiasm to employers, which you may be able to gain through the Blue Cross or RSPCA, for example.

Personal attributes

Good health, general fitness and stamina are required for this manual, physically demanding, outdoor work. Kennel staff must be unsentimental about animals but at the same time have a genuine concern for their well-being; they require patience and a placid but firm nature. A willingness to work long days, weekends and public holidays is also required.

Earnings

Kennel workers earn around £12,000 to start with. Experienced kennel workers earn between £14,000 and £17,000.

Info

Lantra
02476 696996
www.lantra.co.uk

College of Animal Welfare
01480 422060
www.caw.ac.uk

Animal Care College
01344 636436
www.animalcarecollege.co.uk

Horses

The main job roles in working with horses are outlined below. There are other possibilities such as heavy horse work in forestry or equine dentistry, but these opportunities are fewer in number.

Farrier

If a horse needs new shoes it is a farrier who makes and fits these shoes. Working mainly with metal, but sometimes plastic and other modern materials, farriers measure, shape and fit shoes for every kind of horse and pony.

While horse riding is a very popular leisure activity there are still only a few training opportunities each year to learn this highly specialised skill.

Entry, qualifications and training

To work as a farrier you have to register with the Farriers Registration Council and the only training route is an advanced apprenticeship available at three colleges – Hereford and Ludlow, Myerscough in Lancashire and Warwickshire College. The apprenticeship includes periods of work placement with a qualified farrier and college based learning. To qualify for this advanced apprenticeship you need four or five GCSEs grades 9–4, including English, maths and science. You may also require the City & Guilds Forging Certificate. Colleges also offer access courses if you don't meet these requirements. The final two months of training is a probationary period with a farrier and if you pass this you can register as a farrier.

Personal attributes

You have to be confident handling and enjoy working closely with horses of all sizes and temperaments. You have to have good practical skills and be able to work quickly and accurately. You have to have good people skills too. You may have to point out a health problem with a horse's leg or foot that the owner has not noticed. Since almost all farriers are self-employed you also have to be able to run your own business.

Earnings

First-year apprentices earn the minimum wage (see page x for information on the current minimum wage rates), regardless of their age. Apprentices aged over 19 who have completed their first year are entitled to the minimum wage for their age; those under 19 continue to earn the minimum wage an hour. There are also differences according to how old you are when you start your apprenticeship. The average salary starts at around £16,000. Qualified farriers are self-employed – average earnings are £30,000, but many farriers earn more than this.

Info

Farriers Registration Council
01733 319911
www.farrier-reg.gov.uk

Forge & Farrier
07747 602978
www.forgeandfarrier.co.uk

Lantra
02476 696996
www.lantra.co.uk

Horse groom

Grooms work in racing stables, private stables, studs and breeding concerns, riding schools, occasionally (seasonally) with polo ponies and at trekking centres.

Grooms look after all aspects of a horse's welfare. As a groom you would brush and wash horses; clean out stables; feed and water; and prepare bedding. You would also clean tack, saddle-up horses and exercise them. You may ride or lead them depending on what kind of exercise they need. If your horses travel for racing or breeding purposes, you would travel with them ensuring that they are properly cared for whether you are travelling by road, sea or air.

Entry, qualifications and training

You can become a horse groom by completing a college course, an apprenticeship, or specialist courses run by professional bodies. However, no formal qualifications are necessary but it is recommended that grooms take the British Horse Society (BHS) examinations stages 1, 2 and 3 in Horse Knowledge and Care, which comprise the Grooms Certificate. Alternative options are NVQs in Horse Care, levels 1, 2 and 3.

Training is usually on the job and should be sufficient to prepare students for exams. There are also courses of varying lengths to prepare students for particular exams; however, the fees are often high. Funding may be available for the achievement of BHS qualifications provided the applicant is not eligible for any other type of funding.

Personal attributes

A love of horses is essential, plus patience and the willingness to work long hours and perform many routine tasks. A heavy goods vehicle driving licence may be an advantage.

Earnings

Stable staff generally earn the minimum wage. In some cases food and accommodation may be free, in others they may be deducted from the wage. The hours may be long. The BHS issues guidelines on salaries for those with BHS qualifications; details are on its website.

Info

Lantra
02476 696996
www.lantra.co.uk

British Racing School (BRS)
01638 665103
www.brs.org.uk

Thoroughbred Breeding Association
01638 661321
www.tba.co.uk

Association of British Riding Schools (ABRS)
01403 790294
www.abrs-info.org

British Horseracing Authority
020 7152 0000
www.careersinracing.com

Horse riding instructor

Riding instructors teach people – individuals or groups – how to ride horses. They may also accompany riders who hire horses by the hour, and be required to help train horses and look after them, cleaning tack and stables. The work includes teaching in riding schools and clubs and in summer camps, training competition riders and occasionally sitting as a judge or examiner.

Entry, qualifications and training

You can become a horse riding instructor by completing an apprenticeship (which have their own entry requirements) or specialist courses run by professional bodies. While you may not need formal qualifications to train you do need to work towards a series of certificated examinations offered by either the British Horse Society (BHS) or the Association of British Riding Schools (ABRS). Both offer several levels of qualification from preliminary to assistant instructor and instructor. There are three routes to working for these examinations: you may be able to get an apprenticeship; you could train as a private fee-paying student at riding stables; or you could attend a college course that includes BHS or ABRS qualifications. If you do opt for a college course or manage to obtain an apprenticeship you may need three or four GCSEs. However you choose to train and qualify, you will need to have a strong background in riding and in handling and caring for horses.

Personal attributes

A love for and understanding of horses and good confident riding ability are essential. You also need to be good at communicating with people of all ages and different levels of ability. You should be observant, encouraging and sensitive. You must have a good awareness of safety issues.

Earnings

Trainees and assistant instructors earn between £12,000 and £17,000 and qualified instructors earn up to £25,000. Earnings vary according to whether accommodation and meals are provided. Some experienced instructors are self-employed and with experience and a good reputation can earn more than £35,000.

Info

Lantra
024 7669 6996
www.lantra.co.uk

British Equestrian Federation (BEF)
024 7669 8871
www.bef.co.uk

Riding for the Disabled Association (RDA)
01926 492915
www.rda.org.uk

Association of British Riding Schools (ABRS)
01403 790294
www.abrs-info.org

British Horse Society (BHS)
024 7684 0500
www.bhs.org.uk

Jockey

Jockeys ride racehorses in competitions on flat ground or over jumps (National Hunt). They may ride for one racehorse trainer or for several, and owners and trainers are interested in getting the best jockeys for their horses. Jockeys are also involved in preparing the horses for races, exercising them to bring them to best possible racing condition. Jockeys have to build up knowledge of individual horses, understand racing conditions, how the ground will affect performance, and work out the most effective racing strategy.

Entry, qualifications and training

Most jockeys start as stable hands working for trainers in racing yards. You can become a jockey by completing an apprenticeship (which have their own entry requirements), working towards this role, or moving from amateur to professional racing. There are no specific academic requirements to become a stable hand; if you want to become a jockey there are strict weight limits, about 9 stone 7lb for a jump jockey and 8 stone for flat racing. You then have to persuade a trainer to take you on as either an apprentice jockey for flat racing, or a conditional jockey if you plan to become a jump jockey. You can prepare for work in a racing yard by doing the NVQ level 1 and 2 Racehorse Care Residential Course. This course is free if you are aged between 16 and 22. There are NVQs levels 1 and 2 available in Racehorse Care. You can do these at a residential course at the British Racing School or the Northern Racing College. Places on these courses are highly sought after and are free if you are aged between 16 and 25. Day-release courses in racehorse care are also available at some local colleges. Details of these are given on the British Horseracing Authority website.

The key to being taken on to train as a jockey is that you must have exceptional riding skills in order to get yourself noticed by a trainer. As an apprentice or conditional jockey, you train on the job. The trainer takes responsibility for where and what horses you ride and decides when you are competent and ready to race-ride (usually after about two years). You can then apply to the Horseracing Regulatory Authority for a licence to ride.

Personal attributes

You must have a love of horses as well as of riding, since in your early days you will be involved in a lot of horse care, and for good riding you need to be able to build up a real bond with your animals. You must be confident, physically brave, determined and able to handle disappointment. Your people skills need to be nearly as good as your horse skills.

Earnings

Earnings are varied. As a stable hand you earn around £10,000 and if you decide to become a groom rather than a jockey your earnings rise to between £11,000 and £16,000. Jockeys' earnings include a percentage of prize money and a fee for each ride. Every jockey is paid the same fees, regardless of experience and reputation, but higher earnings come from being offered a greater number of rides. Experienced and successful jockeys can also earn money through sponsorship. Many jobs in racing yards provide free or subsidised accommodation.

Info

Lantra
024 7669 6996
www.lantra.co.uk

Jockeys Employment and Training Scheme (JETS)
01635 230410
www.jets-uk.org

Northern Racing College (NRC)
01302 861000
www.northernracingcollege.co.uk

British Horseracing Authority
020 7152 0000
www.careersinracing.com

British Racing School (BRS)
01638 665103
www.brs.org.uk

Stable hand

Stable hands (formerly known as stable lads or stable lasses) do a lot of labouring work; mucking out, fetching straw, filling haynets and sweeping. They must also learn to groom and exercise the horses, and usually become responsible for a certain number of their 'own'. On race days, a stable hand will accompany a horse, groom it, walk it round before the race and lead it into the winner's enclosure if it wins.

Entry, qualifications and training

There are no formal qualifications required to start work as a stable hand, but the ultimate goal for many stable hands is to become a jockey. If this is the case, you will need to fulfil weight requirements (*see Jockey*). You can prepare for work in a racing yard by doing the NVQ levels 1 and 2 Racehorse Care Residential Course. You can do these at the British Racing School or the Northern Racing College. Places on these courses are highly sought after and are free if you are aged between 16 and 25. Day-release courses in racehorse care are also available at some local colleges. Details of these are given on the British Horseracing Authority website. You will usually have to complete a traineeship to become a stable hand.

Personal attributes

You must be really passionate about horses. You need to feel confident and calm when handling them. You should not mind hard physical work in all weathers. You should be practical and observant. As your work progresses from feeding, grooming and cleaning to helping exercise horses you will have to become a confident and ultimately courageous rider if your aim is to ride as a jockey.

Earnings

As a stable hand you earn around £10,000 and if you decide to become a groom rather than a jockey your earnings rise to between £10,000 and £16,000. Many jobs include free or subsidised accommodation.

Info

Lantra
024 7669 6996
www.lantra.co.uk

Northern Racing College (NRC)
01302 861000
www.northernracingcollege.co.uk

British Horseracing Authority
020 7152 0000
www.careersinracing.com

British Racing School (BRS)
01638 665103
www.brs.org.uk

ANTHROPOLOGY

Anthropologist

(see also Social researcher/Social scientist)

Anthropology is an academic discipline linked to social science and evolutionary biology. It is concerned with the development of human societies, making comparisons between different communities and cultures. Much of the work still concerns non-industrial, 'primitive' or rural cultures, but changes brought about by contact with more sophisticated outside influences and pressures from 'modern' societies are an important aspect of study, and many anthropologists now undertake research in urban or industrial societies. The career involves a combination of research, teaching and finding out more about the people being studied by going to live with them over a period of time.

Increasingly, anthropologists are finding employment as consultants, for instance in the development, health and humanitarian fields and in such professions as journalism, human resource management, planning, tourism and heritage, museum curatorship and medicine.

Entry, qualifications and training

A good degree in anthropology. Postgraduate study is usually required.

Personal attributes

Those wishing to embark on this career must normally be committed to an academic way of life, although there is growing demand outside universities. Field researchers must be prepared to spend long spells abroad, often in basic conditions. Physical and mental stamina is required, as well as independence and resourcefulness. Anthropologists must be prepared to work on their own. However, as anthropology has diversified, so the ways of working have become more varied too and anthropologists now work in every imaginable setting, from offices and day-care centres to out in the field. Linguistic ability is useful.

Earnings

There is little salary data available, but many anthropologists would earn similar rates to research workers in universities – around £23,000 to £30,000 for junior staff and up to £32,000 with experience. Salaries vary and can even be higher than £32,000. On fieldwork overseas, earnings may include living and many other allowances.

Info

The Royal Anthropological Institute
020 7387 0455
www.therai.org.uk

ANTIQUE DEALER

To become a successful antique dealer, buying and selling old and valuable objects of many kinds, you need expert knowledge of the field combined with astute business sense. Many dealers specialise in particular types of antiques, such as paintings, ceramics, jewellery or furniture. One of the most specialised areas of the work is art valuing – where a highly detailed knowledge of painting or other art forms is essential. Dealers may sell from shops, antique markets, antique fairs via the internet and using auction sites.

Entry, qualifications and training

While there are no formal entry qualifications, experience in a saleroom or an antique shop is extremely useful. Some antique dealers have degrees in fine arts or applied arts and there are one or two specific postgraduate courses in understanding the arts and antiques market. Large dealers such as Christie's and Sotheby's offer a few training places to graduates. Training is on the job if you are employed by a large auction house, but otherwise it is mainly through your own study, persistence and research. You can start to learn by visiting antique fairs and markets. To build your knowledge, you could also take a part-time or short residential course, including those in antiques or history of art, for example.

Personal attributes

A real interest in antiques in general or a particular category – books, ceramics, toys, etc – is essential. Many dealers are also collectors. You have to have a keen eye for detail, which can help distinguish genuine articles from fraudulent ones, a professional, confident manner with people, and sound business sense. You need to enjoy travel and be happy to work at weekends, searching for items at antiques fares and markets.

Earnings

Earnings vary widely because so many antique dealers are self-employed and have to make earnings through commissions on what they sell. Starting in an antique shop or an auction house sales room, staff earn around the minimum wage to £21,000. As a manager in a large dealership, you could earn up to £28,000. Successful dealers in good economic times may earn far more, but this sector depends on a good economic climate. The average UK salary in 2018 for an art dealer was £29,600.

Info

The British Antique Dealers' Association
020 7589 4128
www.bada.org

Sotheby's Institute of Art
020 7462 3232
www.sothebysinstitute.com

Christie's Education
020 7389 2004
www.christieseducation.com

ARCHAEOLOGY

Archaeologist

Archaeologists learn about the past through examining ancient sites. They carefully unearth remains, such as bones, coins, pottery, tools and other artefacts to discover as much as they can about our human past.

The archaeological 'dig', which refers to excavating a site, is only one part of the job. Bones and other objects have to be identified, studied using various scientific methods to find out how old they are, whether they are genuine, even what they are. Archaeologists have to identify suitable sites to excavate in the first place, through studying historical documents, maps, etc; or building up a picture that starts with an accidental find. Their work can also include looking at planning applications to see whether they have any implications for ancient sites, advising on the conservation of objects and building up computer models of how life used to be, based on the objects unearthed. Archaeologists also work in education, both academic and popular interest.

Entry, qualifications and training

There are several degree courses in archaeology and most people who work as archaeologists will also have a postgraduate qualification and some work experience of volunteering on archaeological digs. There are also postgraduate courses in archaeological conservation.

Personal attributes

Archaeologists need to be practical, thorough and very careful and observant. They should be able to work well as part of a team, or as a team leader. They need to have a real passion for and commitment to their work.

Earnings

Salaries for archaeologists range between £17,000 and £40,000. Salaries for excavators and site assistants start at £17,650, but contracts are often short-term only. Supervisors earn from £18,000 to £21,000. Senior archaeologists managing site projects earn £27,000 to £30,000, and above. Archaeologists working in museums or in universities are paid according to local authority or lecturer pay scales.

Info

Council for British Archaeology
01904 671417
www.archaeologyuk.org

**Training Online Resource
Centre for Archaeology (TORC)**
www.torc.org.uk

British Archaeological Jobs Resource
01368 840847
www.bajr.org

English Heritage
0370 333 1181
www.english-heritage.org.uk

Archeology in Northern Ireland
028 9082 9000
www.communities-ni.gov.uk

Creative & Cultural Skills
020 7015 1800
www.ccskills.org.uk

ARCHITECTURE

Architecture is the profession that produces designs for new buildings and for conversions of or extensions to existing buildings. It demands a combination of artistic imagination with scientific and technical knowledge.

Architect

Architects are experts in building design and construction. They advise individuals, developers, local authorities and commercial organisations on the design and construction of new buildings and the area around them. They have to take account of the environmental impact of construction and consider issues such as how energy efficient they can design a building to be. Architects are also involved in the restoration and conservation of historic and existing buildings.

Architects create designs through drawings, usually produced with computer-aided design (CAD). Drawings are based on information supplied by the client on the function of the building, the proposed budget and the site. An architect needs to have an understanding of structure, building materials, finance, planning law and creative design, and in many building projects acts as the coordinator in a team of specialist consultants such as engineers, builders and interior designers.

Opportunities exist for employment in private practice, with local authorities, in research, teaching, central government and some industrial organisations. Increasingly, interior design companies and companies working in associated fields employ architects as part of their team. Specialist areas can include domestic, public building and retail architecture. The use of CAD packages plays a significant part in the work of architects.

Entry, qualifications and training

Architecture is a graduate-level profession, unless you have considerable experience as a building surveyor, architectural technician or architectural technologist. The usual route to qualifying consists of four stages, a three-year degree approved by the course is registered with the Architects Registration Board (ARB). This is referred to as part 1. This is followed by stage 1, a 12-month period in supervised training with an architectural practice. Next you have to take a two-year postgraduate degree or diploma, this is part 2. Finally you need to complete at least one year's experience with a firm of architects, this is stage 2 (there may also be a final qualifying exam), and at this point, if you have passed everything, you are fully qualified. An apprenticeship is another route you can take, which has its own entry requirements. Also, remember that you may need to show course providers a portfolio of your drawings and sketches.

Personal attributes

You need a broad range of skills as an architect: you must have good scientific and mathematical ability, but you also need imagination, creativity and a flair for design. You need good IT skills, sound business awareness and an ability to communicate technical information and ideas to people without a technical background.

Earnings

Generally salaries for architects range between £27,500 and £90,000. Salaries vary depending on the size of practice you work for. The Royal Institute of British Architects (RIBA) provides a rough guide to what you can expect to earn during the various stages of training: the rates for first-year trainees are £16,000 to £21,000; after completing your diploma you can earn £26,000 to £50,000. Salaries in this sector can suffer when the financial and property markets are not doing very well and vary significantly from one part of the UK to another.

Info

Royal Institute of British Architects (RIBA)
020 7580 5533
www.architecture.com

Architectural Registration Board (ARB)
020 7580 5861
www.arb.org.uk

Architectural technologist

Architectural technologists work alongside architects and other professionals as part of the building design and construction team. Technologists can negotiate the construction project from inception to completion. Specific specialist skills could include surveying land and buildings, preparing and undertaking feasibility studies, presenting design solutions, analysing and detailing drawings, and managing and applying computer-aided design (CAD) techniques.

Entry, qualifications and training

You can qualify to become an architectural technologist by completing a university course, an apprenticeship, or working towards becoming one. A degree in architectural technology, an HNC/HND in Building Studies (with specific additional units) or an NVQ level 4 in Architectural Technology leads to Associate Membership of the British Institute of Architectural Technologists (BIAT) and the designation ABIAT.

Personal attributes

Architectural technologists should be able to work both as part of a team and on their own initiative. Attention to detail is necessary, as is the ability to take account of other professionals' needs. Effective communication skills are necessary when working as part of the team, liaising with clients or tendering for contracts, and architectural technologists should feel comfortable with new technology and innovative concepts.

Earnings

Salaries start at between £20,000 to £25,000, possibly more in London. With experience, salaries rise to between £30,000 and £45,000. This sector is always sensitive to any downturn in the economy.

Info

Chartered Institute of Architectural Technologists
020 7278 2206
www.ciat.org.uk

ARCHIVIST

(see Information Science)

ARMED FORCES

The UK armed forces are comprised of the Army, the Royal Air Force and the Royal Navy. The Royal Marines are part of the Royal Navy. While their main roles are warfare and defence, the armed services take on many other roles. They can be involved in peacekeeping, holding a line in areas of conflict. They may be involved in search and rescue after natural disasters such as earthquakes overseas. In the United Kingdom they may provide help after a natural disaster such as a flood.

While the three armed services employ many civilian staff, most of their work is done by serving forces members, whether this work is catering, support, mechanical repairs to equipment, medical treatment or training and educating their own members.

Army careers

While there are many Army careers, opportunities can be split into these main areas: combat, engineering logistics and support, intelligence, IT and communications, music and ceremony, medicine, human resources and finance.

There are two basic levels at which you can join the British Army – either as a private or as an officer. As a private you may be called a gunner or a signaller according to the regiment you belong to and the work you do. As an officer you start as an officer cadet. In either case there is a clear career structure through which you can climb, to regimental sergeant major as a private, and to lieutenant colonel as an officer.

Rank is the backbone of Army structure and defines your role and degree of responsibility. Soldiers and officers have different terms of rank. Many officers are drawn from the ranks – if you show potential in the Army, your efforts will not go unrewarded.

Entry, qualifications and training

To join as a soldier you must be aged at least 16 and be enlisted before your 36th birthday, pass a medical and meet nationality requirements. You don't normally need formal qualifications, though in some technical and engineering jobs you may. Your local Armed Forces Careers Office (AFCO) will be happy to talk to you in detail. They can also give you a multiple-choice test, sometimes referred to as the BARB test, which can indicate which particular roles you might be most suited to and find most satisfactory. If you are interested in joining, you have to attend a two-day series of selection tests and if you pass these you can then join up. Initial training, referred to as basic training, takes 12 to 14 weeks. After this you will receive further training connected with your specific role and duties and the kinds of activities in which your unit is engaged.

If you are applying to join as an officer, you must be aged 17 to 28 years, 11 months and must also pass a medical and meet nationality criteria. You need seven GCSEs grades 9–4 including English Language, maths and either a science or a foreign language. This requirement is sometimes referred to as needing 35 ALIS points. You also need two A levels or equivalent equal to 72 UCAS points. The Army also runs graduate-entry training for officers. You then have to pass a three-day Army Officer Selection Board. If you are successful, you begin training as an Officer Cadet on the 44-week Commissioning Course (CC) at the Royal Military Academy, Sandhurst (RMAS). The course includes training in leadership and management, tactics, weapons and physical fitness. If you join as a professional officer already qualified as a nurse, doctor, vet, engineer, etc, you take a shortened course. You should check the army careers website for the most up-to-date information on entry requirements.

Personal attributes

For soldiers and officers self-discipline, confidence and initiative are important. You have to be physically fit, quick at reacting to situations and willing to work in highly dangerous or frightening situations. It is essential that you can work as part of a team. Officers and other ranks with leadership roles have to be able to motivate, lead and organise, encourage and discipline colleagues.

Earnings

Pay is linked to rank, length of service and responsibilities. A soldier in training earns around £15,000. Once training is complete earnings are between £18,000 and £28,000. An experienced soldier can earn up to around £35,000. Some higher ranks earn up to £47,000. Non-graduate officer cadets start on £15,000, graduate officer cadets on £25,000. After training, salaries rise to £28,000 to £40,000. The highest ranks earn up to £100,000. There are also additional allowances for working overseas and subsidised accommodation may be provided.

Royal Air Force careers

The Royal Air Force (RAF) is engaged in many different operations, with one of its main tasks flying fixed-wing aircraft and helicopters over UK airspace and in actions all around the world, whether these are under the auspices of NATO, the UN or other situations. Much of the work involves flying and maintaining combat, reconnaissance and transport aircraft. As well as roles associated directly with flying the RAF employs catering staff, engineers, IT specialists, medical staff and administrators. While there are many different opportunities, the two basic levels of recruitment are RAF airman or airwoman (aircrew) and RAF officer. As an RAF airman or airwoman, you would provide specialist support in one of the following areas: aircrew; catering and hospitality; security and defence; medical and medical support; air operations support. RAF officers work in more than 20 roles, but some of the main ones are pilots, air traffic controllers and engineers. The RAF also employs non-commissioned officers in many flight and technical roles and as linguists.

Entry, qualifications and training

To join as an airman or airwoman you do not need formal qualifications. You must be over the age of 16. Upper age limits for joining vary according to the role in which you will be working. You also have to be a UK citizen and you have to pass a medical. Your local Armed Forces Careers Office will be able to provide you with more detailed information. The requirements to join as an officer vary and many applicants are graduates. You will have to pass a series of rigorous selection tests including medical, psychological and intelligence tests. For some roles, e.g. linguists, you will need relevant qualifications. Initial training for airmen and airwomen is 14 weeks, 33 weeks for officers. There is continuing training depending on your role and the operations and activities in which you are involved. There are very often opportunities to gain professional and technical qualifications once you have joined up. Check the RAF careers website for the most up-to-date information on entry requirements.

Personal attributes

A real interest in the RAF is a good starting point. All RAF personnel have to be physically fit, well disciplined, be able to follow or give orders and be good at working as part of a team. Many posts will demand technical or practical skills. Officers will need good leadership skills, be able to motivate and keep other people working together. They will also have to be good at taking responsibility and making quick decisions. All RAF personnel will have to be prepared to work in difficult and dangerous situations.

Earnings

Airmen and airwomen start training on a little over £14,500; £18,000 when training is complete. Senior airmen and women at warrant officer level, the highest non-commissioned rank, can earn up to £48,000. New pilot officers earn £23,500, flying officers earn between £30,000 and £34,000, and squadron leaders earn up to £59,000.

Royal Marines careers

Royal Marines are part of the Royal Navy. They take part in front-line combat (on land and at sea) and are sent at short notice to deal with emergency situations, which may include military operations or natural disasters. The basic entry level is as a commando. As a newly trained recruit, you would usually start as a rifleman. You might be based in a unit responding to emergencies around the world as part of the Joint Rapid Reaction Force, the Fleet Protection Group, guarding UK nuclear weapons or a Fleet Standby Rifle Troop, trained to board ships at sea. The Royal Marines recruit officers as well as commandos. Officers are responsible for leading units in all the activities mentioned above. They are also responsible for training and discipline. Many officers will be qualified professionals – engineers or doctors, for example.

Entry, qualifications and training

To join as a commando you must be aged 16 to 32, male and a British citizen. You do not need any formal qualifications, but you do have to pass a series of selection tests, including a medical and a rigorous physical fitness test. Your initial training lasts 32 weeks and covers teamwork, survival, assault course and weapons training. To apply to become a Royal Marines officer you must pass the rigorous three-day selection process, you must be aged at least 17, a British citizen and at least 1.51 metres tall. You also need three GCSEs grades 9–4. There is also a graduate officer training programme operating in the Royal Marines. Training for officers consists of five stages, from basic training to amphibious craft training. At the end of your training period you will command a troop or unit. Check the Royal Marines careers website for the most up-to-date information on entry requirements.

Personal attributes

All Royal Marines personnel must be resilient, resourceful and determined. You need to be very good at working as part of a team, following or giving orders as appropriate. You must be physically very fit and able to cope with tough conditions. You need to be practical, quick to think and quick to react. Officers must be good leaders, able to keep a team working well together and able to motivate colleagues in challenging situations.

Earnings

After training, commandos earn £20,000 a year, and can earn up to £51,000.

The starting salary for a Royal Marine Officer when joining the Commando Training Centre Royal Marines (CTCRM) is £25,700 a year. After training and experience you could go on to earn £31,000. After 26 months, there is potential to be earning £39,600. Captains earn a salary of over £39,600.

Royal Navy careers

The Royal Navy has operations on the sea (the surface fleet), in the air (the air corps) and in submarines under the water. There are two basic entry levels, either as a rating or as an officer.

Like the other armed services the Royal Navy employs personnel in catering, medicine, dentistry, engineering, logistics, finance and information technology.

Entry, qualifications and training

You don't need formal qualifications to join as a rating, but good GCSEs may increase the variety of roles you can take on. For most ratings you have to be aged 16, but to train as a diver you must be 18. Some other posts have higher age limits. All new naval ratings undergo nine weeks of introductory training at HMS Raleigh in Cornwall. Officers need five GCSEs and 72 UCAS points or their equivalent. Some posts have a height requirement. Ratings have to be aged 16 to join and officers must be 17. For some officer posts you need to be older. Check the Royal Navy careers website for the most up-to-date information on entry requirements.

Personal attributes

All Royal Navy personnel must be good at working as part of a team. They must be physically fit and emotionally resilient – capable of living in fairly confined conditions close to other people. They must be good at taking orders and giving instructions, quick to react and have good practical skills. They must be capable of working in difficult and dangerous situations. Officers have to have all of these qualities combined with the ability to lead, encourage, motivate and organise others.

Earnings

Starting salaries are £15,671 a year for ratings. Leading Ratings (the next rank) earn £33,038 a year. Officers start on a wage of £27,272 and can rise up to in excess of £100,000 for the top-ranked officers.

ART AND DESIGN

The influences of art and design are all around us, in the clothes we wear, the on-screen graphics on our digital devices, the furniture and decorative objects we choose for our homes, the jewellery we buy, the cars we drive, the covers of our favourite magazines and books and all those objects that we are more consciously aware of as art, such as pottery, paintings and sculptures.

Art therapist

(see Therapy Specialisms (arts-based))

Artist

Artists communicate ideas, emotions and thoughts through visual media such as painting, print making, digital fine art or sculpture. They work with a wide range of materials, though most artists develop a preference for working with particular materials and in particular styles. They earn money by selling work that they produce either independently or by undertaking commissioned work. A few artists may be employed as artist-in-residence at a gallery or for some other organisation. Some work on community arts projects or as art teachers. As an artist, your work may also involve liaising with galleries, sourcing materials, coming up with new ideas, managing, marketing your work and building up a business.

Entry, qualifications and training

While some artists have no formal qualifications and may simply be self-taught and have a rare talent, the majority of artists will have a degree in an arts-related subject. There are many fine arts degrees in subjects including painting, digital fine art, print making, sculpture and photography. There are also degrees in art criticism and contextual art. To get onto an arts degree course you normally have to have completed a foundation year and prepare a portfolio of your work to demonstrate your artistic ability.

Personal attributes

You must have flair and imagination and a really strong desire to work with your chosen subjects and media. You have to be resilient, good at building up relationships with people, flexible and able to handle disappointment. You also need to be able to work on your own and sometimes to work long hours.

Earnings

As an artist trying to make your way into the creative world it is very difficult to make a living entirely from your art. You can get advice on how to price your work, but many new artists assist more experienced artists and this work pays between £8 and £10 per hour. Salaries in teaching are between £22,000 and £35,000 depending on your level of experience and geographical location.

Info

Creative & Cultural Skills 020 7015 1800 www.ccskills.org.uk	**The Artists' Information Company** www.a-n.co.uk

Arts administration

Arts administration describes many roles with a variety of organisations, including national or regional arts bodies, local authorities, theatres, orchestras, ballet companies, art galleries, arts centres and community arts projects.

Art gallery curator

What your day-to-day work involves as an art gallery manager depends very much on the size of the gallery you manage. Your work could include choosing artwork to be displayed, arranging for conservation of existing items, ensuring that items remain secure, and commissioning work. The gallery may sell work, in which case you will need to work with artists and help to bring likely buyers into the gallery. In a small gallery you may be involved in some of the basic daily administration as well, hiring staff, talking to visitors and producing publicity materials.

Arts administrator

Your work could include any combination of the following: choosing venues, managing venues, arranging sponsorship, managing budgets, hiring staff, developing future strategies, putting on cultural events, building links with local communities, organising marketing and publicity and sorting out appropriate security arrangements for events. Working in a small arts centre, you are likely to be involved in all the daily administrative tasks. Working for a large organisation, you may specialise in aspects such as marketing, finance or planning.

Community arts worker

Through projects and support, community arts workers help local communities to participate in and develop arts activities of all kinds, including music, dance, drama, film-making, creative writing, photography and mural painting. As a community arts worker you help people to develop not just their artistic, but also their organisational skills. You may have to attend meetings, argue your case for funding and help find sponsorship.

You could, for example, be working with a local youth group encouraging them to do mural painting rather than spray graffiti. You might work with local care home residents to encourage creative writing about local history. The range is very wide.

Entry, qualifications and training

There are two main ways to get into gallery management or arts administration. You can get into arts administration by completing a university course, an apprenticeship, and volunteering to gain experience. It is possible to work your way up from a junior administrative position, but many arts administrators are graduates with a relevant degree in arts, arts administration, business or marketing. Even more important than any formal qualification is relevant experience. You can become a community arts worker by completing a university course, a college course, an apprenticeship, and volunteering to gain experience. Community arts workers usually have a background of experience and qualifications in one of the performing or creative arts and may also have a background in arts administration, community work or teaching. For both arts administration and community arts work, voluntary or temporary experience is of enormous value.

Personal attributes

Whatever aspects of arts administration appeal to you, you need to be passionately committed, enthusiastic and really interested in your chosen field. For some of the more senior jobs a great deal of self-confidence is needed if you are to negotiate sponsorship deals or organise major cultural events. Many roles also require you to work closely with members of the public, so you need to be an excellent communicator. Many roles also require good financial acumen.

Earnings

Trainee administrators earn between £15,000 and £21,000. Gallery curators earn from £18,000 to £28,000. Curators of well-known city-centre galleries can earn up to £40,000. Community arts workers earn £16,000 to £26,000. This particular sector is under extreme financial pressure at present.

Info

Arts Council England
0161 934 4317
www.artscouncil.org.uk

Arts Marketing Association (AMA)
01223 578 078
www.a-m-a.co.uk

Voluntary Arts Network
029 2039 5395
www.voluntaryarts.org

Creative & Cultural Skills
020 7015 1800
www.ccskills.org.uk

National Campaign for the Arts
www.forthearts.org.uk

Museums Association
020 7566 7800
www.museumsassociation.org

Graphic designer

Graphic designers produce visual images for all kinds of media including magazines, books, advertisements, posters, corporate information, websites, computer games, packaging, displays and exhibitions.

As a graphic designer you would work to a brief from your client, developing and interpreting their idea to produce something that gets the message across with maximum visual impact. You could use skills from many different disciplines including illustration, fine art, printing, photography and computer-aided design. The work is so varied that most graphic designers specialise in a particular type of work, e.g. magazines, computer games, packaging, etc. Many graphic designers now work exclusively in digital design, creating images for use across all platforms (mobile, tablet, PC) and channels (email, websites, Twitter etc). Senior graphic designers will also commission work from other specialists such as photographers or illustrators to incorporate into their final designs.

Entry, qualifications and training

You can become a graphic designer by completing a university course, a college course, or an apprenticeship, such as an advanced apprenticeship in design, and specialise in graphics. Most graphic artists have a foundation degree, HND or degree in a relevant subject. These include graphic design, fine art, 3D design, photography, printing, and illustration. In most cases to get onto a degree or HND in art you need to complete a foundation degree first. You will also need to be familiar with current design software, e.g. Illustrator, InDesign, Photoshop. You can do courses in these at college or through self study. Some graphic artists are able to find work without academic qualifications if they have a really good portfolio of work to show prospective employers.

Personal attributes

You must be creative and imaginative with hand drawing as well as computer-based design skills. You should have some knowledge of printing technology, be able to work to a budget and to deadlines, and be an excellent communicator.

Earnings

Junior designers earn between £16,000 and £24,000. Experienced designers earn between £25,000 and £50,000. Someone with exceptional talent and a good reputation can earn more than this and many graphic designers are self-employed, working freelance.

Info

Chartered Society of Designers (CSD)
020 7357 8088
www.csd.org.uk

Creative & Cultural Skills
020 7015 1800
www.ccskills.org.uk

D&AD (Global Association for Creative Advertising and Design)
020 7840 1111
www.dandad.org

Illustrator

Illustrators use painting, drawing and multimedia technology to provide illustrations in a whole variety of media and for a wide range of clients. They might illustrate children's books, work for magazines, or create artwork for posters and storyboards for advertising clients. They may design greetings cards or designs to appear on ceramics. They may work on corporate brochures and increasingly they work on multimedia materials. The aim of an illustration can be to entertain, inform or persuade. Many illustrators become specialists in a particular area such as scientific or technical illustrating.

Entry, qualifications and training

To be successful as an illustrator, your portfolio of work is more important than formal qualifications. Many entrants have degrees in graphic design, fine art, fashion or similar, but this is not essential. Your portfolio and your ability to promote yourself and your work are very important. Illustrations don't just have to be creatively good: you have to be clear about the message or idea that they are conveying. This ability to translate an idea or a thought into a design is what clients look for.

Personal attributes

Working with authors and publishers you have to have excellent communication skills. You need the imagination to come up with exciting illustrations and then the skill to create these. On other occasions you might need to be very accurate – producing scientific illustrations for textbooks for example. You have to be good at promoting and marketing yourself.

Earnings

Since illustrators work freelance it is hard to give typical salary details, but the Association of Illustrators can give help and advice on how to charge and how to price your work.

Info

The Artists' Information Company
www.a-n.co.uk

The Association of Illustrators
020 7759 1010
www.theaoi.com

Creative & Cultural Skills
020 7015 1800
www.ccskills.org.uk

Interior designer

Interior designers work for commercial companies and private clients advising and planning the internal decor of buildings from private houses to hotels, restaurants, schools, hospitals, offices, shops, theatres and other public and commercial buildings.

As an interior designer you would help a client choose appropriate materials, colour schemes for all aspects of internal decor from flooring to lighting, furniture, wall coverings and other decorations. You would have to work to a client's brief and consider not just the look of your ideas, but their practicality, environmental impact, durability and the budget within which your client wishes to work. There is a lot of project management involved in this work. You would discuss initial ideas with a client, produce drawings, work out costings, source appropriate materials and often supervise the work to make sure that your design ideas are carried out.

Entry, qualifications and training

Entry to art school and college via a foundation course is the same as for a product designer (see entry below). You can also gain the knowledge and skills you need by completing a university course, a college course, or an apprenticeship. Once at art college, the student may specialise in interior design.

Personal attributes

A natural aptitude for art and the ability to work as part of a design team and to present work to customers are necessary.

Earnings

Junior designers earn from £16,000 to £25,000. With experience this range is £25,000 to £45,000, though few achieve the top of the range. Interior designers working freelance set their own hourly rates or fees per job.

Info

Chartered Society of Designers (CSD)
020 7357 8088
www.csd.org

The British Institute of Interior Design
020 7628 0255
www.biid.org.uk

The Interior Design Institute
www.theinteriordesigninstitute.co.uk

Creative & Cultural Skills
020 7015 1800
www.ccskills.org.uk

Product designer

Every object we use, from a mobile phone to a car, from a hairbrush to a washing machine, has been created to look or feel right as well as do its job. Product designers work in manufacturing of every imaginable product – household goods and furniture to specialised equipment for science, industry and commerce.

As a designer you would work closely with engineers, manufacturers, colour scientists and psychologists to help design items that would appeal to consumers in highly competitive markets. Your work would be varied, from being involved in the initial discussion of an idea, through producing drawings (probably using CAD), testing suitable materials, constructing models or prototypes and perhaps being involved in market testing.

Entry, qualifications and training

Employers recruit from those with an HND or degree in a design-related subject; some courses offer specialist modules in industrial design. Entry to such courses is normally via a National Diploma course after GCSEs or a foundation course at an art college after A levels. Applicants for art and design courses are expected to have a portfolio of their artwork when interviewed.

Personal attributes

As well as artistic ability, an understanding of mass-production processes is necessary; the industrial designer should also be able to work as part of a team, to schedule and recognise the needs of the consumer.

Earnings

Trainees initially earn around £25,000, rising to around £30,000 with a few years' experience. Senior product designers can earn around £65,000 and higher.

Info

Chartered Society of Designers (CSD) 020 7357 8088 www.csd.org.uk	**SEMTA (Science, Engineering, Manufacturing and Technologies Alliance)** 0845 643 9001 www.semta.org.uk

Signwriter

Signwriters design and paint company names and logos on to shop fronts and the sides of vans and lorries; they may also paint estate agents' signboards and a wide variety of other temporary signs and notices. Signwriters increasingly use a range of materials and techniques, including computer technology, to create signs. The letters are often formed from plastics, metal or wood and stuck on to the background.

Some signwriters are in business on their own; others work for companies.

Entry, qualifications and training

There are no formal academic entry requirements for this type of work, but artistic talent combined with an interest in lettering is important. Some graphic design courses include typography and signwriting and provide wider training. Some commercial signwriting firms take on trainees, and NVQs in Assembly, Fabrication and Manufacturing Processes and Sign Making are available at level 2.

Personal attributes

You have to be practical, creative and imaginative. As well as having artistic flair you must be a good speller and an accurate worker. You need excellent communication skills and a good grasp of running your own business.

Earnings

Earnings vary and you are likely to earn no more than the minimum wage at the start of your career. The highest salaries are around £21,000 to £25,000.

Info

British Sign and Graphics Association 0845 338 3016 www.bsga.co.uk	**Creative & Cultural Skills** 020 7015 1800 www.ccskills.org.uk

Web designer

(see Journalism for Web content editor)

Web designers design and plan websites either for their own company or for clients. They focus on the look and feel of a website. (This is in contrast to a web *developer*, who writes code to make it work – *see Information and Communication Technology for Software developer*). Web designers meet with clients to discuss what they want the site to do and who will use it. They draw up a plan, showing the site's structure and how the different sections work together. They decide on layout, branding, colours and text, liaising with the clients' own designers and copywriters, where appropriate. They add multimedia features like sound, video and animation. They then test the website to ensure everything works before uploading it to the client's server and publishing it online. Many designers work on a freelance basis. The availability of jobs in this area is decreasing as increasingly sophisticated software packages are making web design less of a specialist area.

Entry, qualifications and training

You could become a web designer by completing a course at university in web design and development or multimedia design, for example; a course in Web Design and Development at college; or an apprenticeship in creative and digital media. Web designers usually have a background in design rather than IT. Many have trained initially as graphic designers, but have then done some web-specific IT training. Your portfolio will be more important than your qualifications when it comes to providing evidence of both your creative and technical skills.

Personal attributes

You will need strong creative skills together with a sound understanding of current web design tools. You will need to be able to communicate successfully with clients, both in listening to what they want and in explaining how you can make this possible. You will need to be happy to work to deadlines. If working freelance you will also need the confidence to negotiate your own fees.

Earnings

Web designer pay starts within a range of £20,000 to £25,000. Once you become more experienced, you can expect to earn between £30,000 and £40,000 a year. Freelance web designers set their own rates, from £200 a day.

Info

Creative & Cultural Skills
020 7015 1800
www.ccskills.org.uk

World Wide Web Consortium (W3C)
www.w3.org

ASTRONOMY

Astronomer

Astronomers study the sun, moon, planets, stars, comets, asteroids and other objects in the sky. They study many aspects of the universe including its origin. Gathering data on the ground and via satellites they analyse radio, infrared, optical, ultraviolet, X and gamma radiations emitted from these objects, to learn what they can about the structure, history and likely future behaviour of such objects. The work might also involve designing and developing new instruments for measuring data from the skies, or developing software for modelling. Astronomy is a highly academic discipline and many astronomers will specialise in one small area of study such as sun spots, decaying stars or planets in the outer solar system.

Entry, qualifications and training

To become a research astronomer, a good degree in physics or maths is necessary and it is possible to do degrees in astronomy or astrophysics. This is normally followed by postgraduate study and research. Various grants are available to support students undertaking such courses.

Astronomy-related careers at an engineering or technical level are open to those with skills in applied physics, electronics, computing, optics and mechanical engineering.

Personal attributes

Astronomers need curiosity and imagination; they must be able to make logical deductions from the available observations. Working long and unusual hours and travelling to remote observatories may also be involved.

Earnings

A junior researcher in astronomy earns between £29,000 and £36,000. Senior researchers earn more than £35,000. Senior lecturers and astronomers associated with prestigious research projects or working with technical organisations may earn far more than this.

Info

Science and Technology Facilities Council
01793 442000
www.stfc.ukri.org

Royal Astronomical Society
020 7734 4582
www.ras.org.uk

AUCTION

Auctioneer

The auctioneer's work involves the sale by auction of property of all kinds, including buildings (houses, farms and estates), livestock, and goods such as furniture, antiques, paintings, glass, toys, carpets and china. The work also entails valuations for various purposes, including investment and insurance.

Entry, qualifications and training

An auctioneer's work involves the valuation of land and property, so surveying or valuation qualifications are necessary. There are two components to qualifying as a chartered surveyor or valuer. First is successful completion of a Royal Institution of Chartered Surveyors (RICS) accredited degree or diploma, followed by enrolment onto the Assessment of Professional Competence (APC). The latter is two years' practical training while in employment, finishing with an RICS professional assessment interview. One-year full-time and two-year part-time postgraduate conversion courses are also available.

Personal attributes

Attention to detail is important for this job, together with a practical attitude and an aptitude for figures. In fine art auctioneering, a certain flair and the ability to distinguish a fake from the genuine article are essential.

Earnings

Newly qualified valuers earn around £20,000. Experienced valuers and auctioneers earn from £25,000 to £40,000. Any earnings linked to the property market and where commission is part of the package will be affected by the current state of the property market.

Info

Arts Marketing Association (AMA)
01223 578 078
www.a-m-a.co.uk

Creative & Cultural Skills
020 7015 1800
www.ccskills.org.uk

Royal Institute of Chartered Surveyors
024 7686 8555
www.rics.org

Institute of Revenues, Rating and Valuation
020 7831 3505
www.irrv.net

AUDIOLOGICAL SCIENTIST

Audiological scientists work with patients experiencing problems with either hearing or balance. They identify, assess and treat disorders, recommending and providing appropriate rehabilitation and management. Most audiologists work in hospitals. Many choose to specialise in particular client groups such as babies, young children or older people. They may choose to specialise in particular conditions such as tinnitus or balance problems.

Entry, qualifications and training

There are two training routes to qualification. In either case you need a good honours degree, usually a 2.1 in a relevant subject such as physiology, applied physics, engineering or biology. Other subjects such as psychology or biochemistry may also be accepted. You can then apply to the NHS Science Training Programme (STP) or you can apply for a university based MSc in audiology or audiological science. In either case you can then register to practise. There is currently a high demand for suitable applicants to train in this field. The British Academy of Audiology provides a list of all relevant MSc courses. The NHS Health Careers website provides more information on different points of entry into a career as an audiologist.

Clinical scientists in audiology who have successfully completed their training must register with the Health and Care Professions Council (HCPC) in order to practise.

Personal attributes

Audiologists need to be able to communicate with people of all ages. They need to be able to think logically and adopt a scientific approach combined with caring and patience.

Earnings

Newly qualified audiologists earn between £21,000 and £28,000. With experience and responsibility this rises to £35,000 to £43,000. Salaries in the private sector may be higher.

Info

The British Academy of Audiology
01625 664545
www.baaudiology.org

British Society of Audiology
0118 9660622
www.thebsa.org.uk

Health and Care Professions Council (HCPC)
0300 500 6184
www.hcpc-uk.org

NHS Careers
0345 60 60 655
www.healthcareers.nhs.uk

Skills for Health
020 7388 8800
www.skillsforhealth.org.uk/nsahealth

Association of Clinical Scientists
020 7940 8960
www.assclinsci.org

B

BAKERY

Baker

All the bread, cakes, pastries, biscuits and pies we eat are made by bakers who work in three types of bakery – plant, in-store or craft. Plant bakeries are large food manufacturers, where most of the work is automated processes; it is the baker's job to oversee these processes. In-store bakers working in the bakery departments of supermarkets use some automated processes, but do more hand preparation and finishing of some products. Craft bakers make products for local bakers' shops, delicatessens and farmers' markets. Craft bakers do more work by hand, and they may be closely involved in developing new products and trying out new recipes.

Entry, qualifications and training

You may not need formal qualifications to train as a baker. If you train through an apprenticeship, individual employers may ask for three or four GCSEs. Training is on the job, and typical training time for a baker is one to three years. You can also work towards levels 1, 2 and 3 qualifications in baking skills, including specialist areas such as pastry techniques and cake decoration. You may also be able to work through an apprenticeship to qualify as a baker.

Personal attributes

In all areas of baking you must have a good appreciation of food hygiene and public health. You need good practical skills and good manual dexterity for some of the more fiddly processes in craft baking. In plant bakeries you need to be able to cope with hot, noisy conditions. In all cases you are likely to have to work as part of a team and you may sell products to customers if you work in a supermarket or a local shop.

Earnings

Trainees' earnings start at around £13,000. Craft bakers or supervisors in plant bakery production can earn £20,000 to £25,000 (more in London). A bakery manager can earn around £30,000. Experienced bakers may be able to earn up to £40,000.

Info

National Skills Academy for Food & Drink
0845 644 0558
www.nsafd.co.uk

People 1st (for retail aspects of baking)
020 3074 1222
www.people1st.co.uk

Federation of Bakers
020 7420 7190
www.fob.uk.com

BANKING AND FINANCE

Banking covers a range of financial activities. Retail banks and building societies provide services to private individuals and businesses throughout the country. They operate from high street branches, call centres and provide online banking facilities for their customers. Retail banks serve individual customers, helping with all their personal banking needs. Corporate investment banks provide financial services to large companies and other organisations.

Bank customer service adviser

Bank and building society customer service advisers deal with all the daily enquiries made by customers in person, by telephone or via the internet. They work either in high street branches or at call centres. They are responsible for processing cash and cheques, entering account details onto computer systems and issuing foreign currency. They also book appointments for customers who need more specialised advice. Senior cashiers handle more complex enquiries and also supervise small teams of cashiers.

Entry, qualifications and training

Each bank sets its own entry requirements. Some do not ask for specific qualifications, but they set entry tests that assess maths, English and computer skills. Many banks require four or five GCSEs grades 9–4 including English and maths. Training is on the job and often includes options to study for NVQ levels 2 and 3 in Retail Financial Services, NVQ levels 1 and 2 in Contact Centre Operations, levels 3, 4 and 5 for contact centre professionals (if you work in a call centre) or NVQ levels 2 and 3 in Customer Service. Anyone interested in management may be able to study for one of the diploma courses listed in the 'Bank manager' entry below.

Bank manager

Bank managers plan and deliver effective sales strategies and monitor the performance of new and existing financial products. Bank managers work either in high street branches, taking responsibility for day-to-day management, or in more specialised posts in corporate or commercial departments at regional or head office level. Their work involves talking to customers, offering advice and planning the workload of other staff in their branch or department. The financial services sector is now extremely competitive, so product sales are a key part of the manager's role.

Entry, qualifications and training

There are two routes to management – either joining a training scheme run by a bank, or gaining promotion after joining the bank as a cashier/customer services adviser. Most banks expect management trainees to have a good honours degree in a business- or finance-related subject, but it is worth checking individual requirements. Some banks will accept A-level entrants or applicants with HNDs. For anyone already working for a bank and wishing to get into management, being good at dealing with customers and having some supervisory experience are important.

There are several professional qualifications you can work towards on a part-time basis. These include the Professional Diploma in Financial Services Management (Professional DFSM), and the Applied Diploma in Retailing Financial Services. Management training programmes in banks are normally quite structured and often include the requirement to study for one of the above qualifications.

Personal attributes

All bank staff need very good communication skills. You must be able to explain complex information and be assertive enough to disappoint people sometimes. You must have good IT skills and the ability to interpret figures and other financial information. In management you have to be able to take responsibility for motivating other staff and for implementing sales policies. As a cashier, you may well want to develop some supervisory and management skills by working towards becoming a senior cashier or a customer services adviser in a specialised area such as mortgages or personal investment.

Earnings

Customer service advisers start on £15,000 to £18,000, rising to between £18,000 and £28,000 with experience. Earnings often include bonuses or commission for selling financial products to customers. Management trainees earn between £25,000 and £30,000. Some banks pay a joining bonus of between £3,000 and £5,000 to their graduate trainees. Experienced managers earn between £28,000 and £40,000. Bank staff in senior positions can earn up to £100,000. Many roles include the payment of bonuses.

Corporate investment banker

Corporate investment bankers provide many financial services to companies, institutions and governments. They advise on such matters as mergers and acquisitions, buy-outs, share issues, flotations and raising capital. They advise their clients on strategic financial planning. Corporate investment bankers work in dedicated teams, focusing on specific transactions or market sectors. They also work alongside other related professionals such as lawyers and accountants. The work includes researching financial markets.

Entry, qualifications and training

This is a degree level profession, but a good 2.1 in any subject is acceptable. You also need to have a record of a strong academic performance and many employers set UCAS point requirements as well as the degree. A second language can be an advantage and knowledge of and interest in the financial markets is very important. The selection process is based very much on having the right skills for the job, including numerical and analytical skills.

Personal attributes

You must be self confident and good at working as part of a team. You need to be motivated and committed and have a lot of energy. You need to be able to manage projects and to work under pressure.

Earnings

Starting salaries are between £30,000 and £40,000. After three or four years this rises to £50,000 to £75,000. Successful investment bankers earn a basic salary of £150,000 plus bonuses.

Info

Building Societies Association
020 7520 5900
www.bsa.org.uk

London Institute of Banking & Finance
01227 818609
www.libf.ac.uk

UK Finance
www.ukfinance.org.uk

Commodity broker

Commodity brokers buy and sell commodities, including tea, coffee, grain, oil, gas and metals. They work either for companies that specialise in dealing in commodities trading or for companies that produce and/or grow the commodities. As well as trading in the actual products, they trade in futures (commodities that will be produced or grown in the future). They have to monitor world markets, possibly visiting sites and countries where commodities are produced. They have to advise clients when to buy, when to sell and where to place themselves in the market. They also have to work closely with shipping, transport and insurance organisations. When much of the financial services sector faces difficulties, commodities trading becomes very busy as commodities are seen as (though they are not necessarily) more reliable.

Entry, qualifications and training

While there are no specific entry qualifications, most successful applicants have a 2.1 degree in a relevant subject such as economics, maths, science, business or finance. The recruitment process can be very demanding, including several interviews and psychometric tests.

Personal attributes

You must be highly numerate and an excellent communicator. You have to be able to take decisions under pressure, accept responsibility and work as part of a team. Being able to live with job insecurity is also important; opportunities in this work fluctuate widely.

Earnings

New entrants earn between £25,000 and £50,000 and experienced brokers with a successful trading record can earn extremely high salaries. It is a volatile market, though, with considerable associated risk.

Info

eFinancial Careers Ltd
020 7997 7900
www.efinancialcareers.co.uk

Intercontinental Exchange (ICE)
www.theice.com

The London Metal Exchange
020 7113 8888
www.lme.com

Corporate treasurer

Treasury in a company is key in determining the firm's financial strategy and financial policy – advising on what businesses to invest in, organising the appropriate funding for this, and controlling the risk in the organisation. A treasurer works in a team to protect a company's financial assets and to ensure the company has the necessary cash available to run its business. The treasury team will deal with banking requirements and funding for the business and manage financial risk. Treasury therefore incorporates raising and managing money; currency; commodity and interest rate risk management and dealing; and, in some organisations, the related areas of insurance, pensions, property and taxation. The size of a treasury team is dependent on an organisation's size and capabilities.

Entry, qualifications and training

Any degree is acceptable, although accountancy, finance, economics or mathematics are favourite. As with many roles, training will be largely on the job. Some large companies offer training programmes for finance/accounting graduates from which it may be possible to request a secondment within the treasury function. You can also enter through the tax, corporate, finance, legal or accounting functions. The professional body for corporate treasury is the Association of Corporate Treasurers (ACT). It provides a range of well-respected industry qualifications and training courses.

Personal attributes

A career in treasury requires you to work in a fast-paced environment. A key part of the role involves handling relationships with shareholders, banks and other lenders, so strong communication skills are essential. An effective treasurer needs to be able to analyse and absorb information quickly, be numerate, accurate and pay close attention to detail, but you need to be innovative too. You will almost certainly be dealing with sums of money running into the millions, even billions, which requires a strong nerve. It is a demanding but extremely rewarding career.

Earnings

Junior or assistant corporate treasurers start on £25,000 to £35,000. Qualified treasurers with experience earn £50,000 to £75,000. It is possible to earn more than £100,000 in this profession.

Info

Association of Corporate Treasurers (ACT)
020 7847 2529
www.treasurers.org

Economist

(see Economist)

Financial adviser

Financial advisers provide advice on all aspects of financial planning to a wide range of clients. They provide advice to individuals, corporate clients and other groups of people such as societies or charities. They offer advice on such diverse matters as loans, mortgages, pensions, investments and other financial products and services.

Their work involves meeting clients and explaining financial products and services to them clearly and carefully. They have to assess people's different financial circumstances in order to advise on the most suitable products. They conduct in-depth research into different products and liaise closely with banks, building societies, insurance companies, etc – the financial product suppliers. They are often self-employed, so they also have to be good at marketing and promoting themselves and seeking out new clients.

Half the financial advisers working in the United Kingdom class themselves as independent rather than tied advisers. Being independent does not necessarily mean being self-employed. Both tied and independent financial advisers may work for an organisation or may be self-employed. Many independent advisers work for firms which themselves are known as independent financial advisers.

Tied advisers work for financial services companies, insurance companies, investment firms, banks and building societies. Some are employed by estate agencies, law firms and by retailers that have developed financial services as a part of their business.

Entry, qualifications and training

You don't have to be a graduate, although a degree in business studies, accountancy or financial services can give you an advantage. Many employers are happy to take people from a wide range of working backgrounds and do not require academic qualifications. You nearly always need a driving licence, and some employers set a lower age limit of 21 or older for trainees.

All entrants to the profession have to pass the Financial Planning Certificate examinations parts 1, 2 and 3 or the Certificate for Financial Advisers in order to be licensed by the Financial Conduct Authority. A lot of the training is provided on the job and when you start you often learn by shadowing a more experienced adviser. Advisers who work for financial organisations, rather than independently, can progress to management posts in the financial services sector.

Personal attributes

You need excellent communication skills, to be able to talk convincingly to corporate clients and sensitively to private individuals. You must be smart, well organised and highly motivated – this is a competitive sector. You need good numeracy and IT skills and the ability to deal with highly complex information.

Earnings

If you are employed by financial services companies your earnings are made up of a combination of a basic salary plus commission on products sold. Basic salaries are between £22,000 and £30,000. Achieving sales targets can boost earnings to between £30,000 and £60,000. In a difficult marketplace these commissions and target-related earnings are much harder to achieve. Some independent financial advisers charge a fee to clients rather than earning commission on products sold.

Info

Chartered Insurance Institute
020 8989 8464
www.cii.co.uk

London Institute of Banking & Finance
01227 818609
www.libf.ac.uk

Personal Finance Society
020 8530 0852
www.thepfs.org

Fund manager

Investment fund managers invest the funds of other people – private clients and institutions, such as insurance companies, charities, independent schools and specialised research institutions. Managers must keep their clients' interests continually under review, offering advice on how to retain their clients' income and when to change investments. Investment fund managers may be employed by the larger institutions or work in specialist firms that tend to serve smaller clients.

Entry, qualifications and training

Investment banks and stockbroking firms prefer to recruit graduates. A good honours degree in any subject is acceptable, but degrees in accountancy, business, economics or maths are especially relevant. Some investment analysts need in-depth knowledge of particular industry markets, so it may be useful to have experience in areas such as energy, engineering, mining or life sciences. Training is on the job and graduates are usually placed with a more experienced analyst and given other structured training. Initial training takes around three years.

Trainees are usually required or encouraged to study for relevant professional qualifications. Two of the most widely offered are the United Kingdom Society of Investment Professionals (UKSIP) Investment Management Certificate (IMC) and the Chartered Institute for Securities and Investment (CISI) Certificate in Securities and Financial Derivatives. Many analysts then carry on to study for more advanced diplomas.

Personal attributes

You must have an enquiring mind and be persistent and thorough in your research. A broad range of interests, including politics and economics as well as finance, is important. You have to be confident dealing with people, one-to-one or at meetings with senior representatives of companies. You should be able to write clear, concise summaries of statistical data and other research findings.

Earnings

Typical starting salaries are £30,000 to £40,000 in London, with bonuses of 20–100 per cent possible in the first three years, salaries are lower in other parts of the UK. After five to eight years, salaries rise to between £70,000 and £100,000, with bonuses of 40–100 per cent possible. Salaries vary according to the nature and size of the company and geographical location. Salaries are higher with investment banks.

Info

Chartered Institute for Securities & Investment (CISI)
020 7645 0777
www.cisi.org.uk

CFA Institute
www.cfainstitute.org

CFA Society of the UK
020 7648 6200
www.cfauk.org

Investment analyst

Investment analysts analyse the financial markets to advise on the best investments for clients. Investment managers rely on their information. There are two main types of investment analyst. First are those who work for stockbrokers and undertake their own analysis to provide information for fund manager clients. The aim is to generate 'buy and sell' orders for the stockbrokers for whom they work. This is known as the 'sell side'. Second, there are those who work for investment management institutions. They provide ideas and information to enable their in-house fund managers to make the best decisions for their clients. This is known as the 'buy side'. The majority of investment analysts work on the 'sell side'.

Entry, qualifications and training

While there are no formal entry requirements, most investment banks will only consider you if you have a 2.1 degree and some employers require an MSc or an MBA. Relevant subjects such as economics or business are preferred and the selection procedure is tough. If you do not have a relevant degree, it is really important that you are able to demonstrate your understanding of how financial markets work. Some people move from investment analysis or investment administration into stockbroking. To practise as a stockbroker you must register with the Financial Conduct Authority (FCA). The Financial Services Skills Council can provide you with a full list of all the qualifications that allow you to register. Investment banks and other firms that take on trainee brokers offer in-house training.

Personal attributes

A great aptitude with numbers and excellent communication skills are essential. You must be calm under pressure, able to take decisions and happy working on your own or as part of a team.

Earnings

Trainees start on £28,000 to £35,000 rising to £50,000 to £80,000 (lower outside London). Experienced and successful brokers can earn £150,000. When the economy is in trouble, job insecurity may balance out the high salaries.

Info

CFA Society of the UK
020 7648 6200
www.cfauk.org

Chartered Institute for Securities & Investment (CISI)
020 7645 0777
www.cisi.org.uk

Pensions management

Clear advice to people purchasing pensions and effective management of funds invested in pensions are very important. Changes in legislation are likely to lead to an even greater focus on this financial sector.

Pensions are either in-company, where schemes are provided for that company's own employees, or private and available for purchase by individuals. Companies offering private pension schemes for purchase employ advisers to potential customers. In-house and private pension schemes employ administrators and managers.

Pensions manager

Your key responsibility as a pensions manager is to ensure that the funds invested in that pension perform well – so that organisations and private individuals who have paid into pension schemes get a good return on their money and there are always funds available to pay out in the form of pensions. Your work could also include managing teams of pensions administrators and advisers and developing and marketing new pensions products. You could be involved in resolving disputes or more complex claims and liaising with actuaries, auditors, lawyers and investment consultants. You may also have to prepare and present annual reports on the performance of the pension scheme(s) you manage.

Entry, qualifications and training

This is a mostly graduate profession and degrees in economics, business, finance or law are the preferred subjects. It may often be a second career for someone who has already worked in other areas of finance such as insurance. There are relevant professional qualifications run through the Pensions Management Institute and you can work towards these while employed. It is possible to work your way up through starting in pensions administration if you do not have appropriate academic qualifications.

Personal attributes

You need a wide range of interpersonal skills – good at talking to people, influencing and negotiating and writing clear reports and summaries. You must have good numeracy skills and be able to analyse complex information. You have to be good at taking decisions and have common sense, confidence and integrity.

Earnings

In pensions administration salaries start at around £20,000. Pensions managers earn from £25,000 to £30,000 plus bonuses, but with experience this rises to £50,000 to £80,000.

Info

Pensions Management Institute
020 7247 1452
www.pensions-pmi.org.uk

Stockbroker

Stockbrokers buy and sell securities on the Stock Exchange on behalf of investors, who may be individuals but are increasingly institutions such as banks, insurance companies, pension funds or unit trusts. They also advise clients on shares they hold and suggest good times to sell or buy. Stockbrokers work from their offices using the phone and internet to keep in touch with financial markets and news.

Entry, qualifications and training

This is normally a graduate profession and you have to have at least a 2.1. Stockbroking is a profession regulated by the Financial Conduct Authority (FCA) and they can provide a list of accepted qualifications. Some of the approved qualifications include Master's degrees in financial services or actuarial qualifications. A foreign language, especially French, German, Japanese or Russian, can be very useful.

Personal attributes

Excellent communication skills and good numeracy and IT skills are essential. You have to be able to keep calm under pressure, work as part of a team and be of a trustworthy disposition.

Earnings

Salaries start at around £25,000 to £35,000 plus commission, but with some experience £50,000 to £79,000 is more typical. Some stock brokers earn more than £100,000.

Trader/dealer

Traders or dealers fall into three categories, each working in different ways and/or for different client groups. Flow traders buy and sell such products as shares, bonds, commodities and foreign exchange on the financial markets. They buy and sell on behalf of banks or other financial institutions' clients. They try to minimise risk and maximise profits for their clients. Proprietary traders trade on behalf of a bank or financial institution rather than its clients. They try to buy at low prices and sell high. Flow and proprietary traders work mainly in dealing rooms, constantly tracking market performance and making decisions about when and what to buy and sell. Sales traders deal directly with clients, providing market information and promoting new financial ideas to clients. Their role includes preparing detailed reports based on market information.

Entry, qualifications and training

This is now very much a graduate profession – you normally need a good degree, and while any subject is acceptable, business studies, economics, maths and politics are particularly useful. You may also get in if you have an HND or foundation degree in one of these subjects. This has been a highly competitive area and you are likely to face a rigorous selection process. If you have not gone on to higher education, it may be possible to work your way in from an administrative job for a bank or other financial organisation, especially if you are able to build up a good network of contacts. Most training is on the job, combined with work towards financial sector qualifications.

Personal attributes

All traders have to be able to develop a really good knowledge of financial markets and to apply that knowledge. In work other than sales, a good trader should be able to take risks, but in a balanced way – weighing up benefits and dangers realistically. Traders working in dealing rooms have to be resilient and able to think quickly and take decisions under pressure. Traders working in sales have to build up excellent relationships with their clients.

Earnings

Initial earnings are between £20,000 and £50,000 and with a few years' experience and a successful record some salaries are very high – £150,000 plus with large bonuses and other benefits.

Info

Chartered Institute for Securities & Investment (CISI)
020 7645 0777
www.cisi.org.uk

BEAUTY

(see also Hairdresser)

There are many occupations in this sector – a sector which has grown over recent years. There are therapists who provide body and facial treatments, undertake body piercing, nail treatments or give advice on what colour to wear. There are make-up artists who work in film and television. The sector has expanded in recent years, with more salons, spa hotels and private practitioners.

Beauty sales consultant

Beauty sales consultants work on cosmetics counters in large department stores, or in individual stores owned by a particular brand of make-up and beauty products. Consultants advise customers on what products, colours or fragrances might suit them best. They may apply make-up on customers, so that the customer can see the results before making a purchase, and they also demonstrate new products or gadgets.

Entry, qualifications and training

You don't need formal qualifications to train – your employer normally provides an introductory course. There are several NVQ level 2 courses available in beauty consultancy for which you can study on a part-time basis, for example. Previous experience in either retail or beauty therapy can also be very useful.

Personal attributes

You need to have excellent communication skills, to be able to talk to people, make them feel comfortable and encourage them to purchase products. You need to be practical and sensitive when applying make-up and other beauty products. You often have to organise your own product displays, so you must be imaginative and have good visual awareness. You need to be highly presentable yourself – a good advert for what you are selling.

Earnings

Trainees earn around the minimum wage, rising to £19,000 with experience – though positions are often not full time. Consultants are often expected to meet sales targets and earn part of their salaries through sales commission on products sold.

Info

People 1st
020 3074 1222
www.people1st.co.uk

Hairdressing and Beauty Industry Authority
(HABIA)
08452 306080
www.habia.org

Beauty therapist or beautician

Beauty therapists work in salons, health spas, hotels and private homes and, at the glamorous end of the market, for film, television and fashion magazines. Beauty therapists offer all kinds of treatments to their clients, such as facials, massage, make-up, manicures, eyelash and eyebrow treatments, waxing and body toning and tanning treatments. Beauty therapists who visit clients in their own homes have to be good business people, keeping accounts, ordering stock and keeping up to date with the latest developments. The top end of the market is highly competitive, but it is a profession that gives you a lot of flexibility.

Entry, qualifications and training

You normally need three or four GCSEs grades 9–4 and then there are several relevant qualifications, including the City & Guilds diploma in beauty therapy, Edexcel national certificate and diploma in beauty therapy sciences, Vocational Training Charities Trust (VTCT) advanced diploma in beauty therapy and NVQ level 3 in beauty therapy. You can either go to a further education or private college full time, or work as an assistant in a beauty salon and attend college part time. Private college courses may be shorter and more intensive, but they are also expensive. There may be opportunities to train for this work through an apprenticeship.

Personal attributes

As a beauty therapist you have to look neat, presentable and well groomed. You must be friendly, welcoming and able to put clients at ease; you also need to be tactful and sensitive. You must be comfortable working in close physical proximity with your clients and you need reasonable stamina as you will be on your feet for most of the time. If you run your own business you need all the appropriate business skills too.

Earnings

Beauty therapists earn between £14,000 and £18,000 while salon managers earn between £20,000 and £25,000. Beauty therapists often receive tips and they may also make commission from selling cosmetics and beauty products. Some beauty therapists are self-employed, in which case earnings vary according to how much work they undertake.

Info

Vocational Training Charitable Trust (VTCT)
023 8068 4500
www.vtct.org.uk

Hairdressing and Beauty Industry Authority (HABIA)
08452 306080
www.habia.org

International Therapy Examination Centre (ITEC)
www.itecworld.co.uk

Freelance Hairdressers Association
01582 431783
www.thefha.org.uk

City & Guilds
0844 543 0000
www.cityandguilds.com

SkillsActive
0330 004 0005
www.skillsactive.com

Body artist/tattooist

Body artists/tattooists working in studios or parlours draw designs of words, patterns and pictures on the bodies of customers. This form of body adornment is currently very popular. The body artist either draws the design freehand or works from a transfer placed on the customer's skin. He or she then follows the outline with an electrically operated needle that delivers permanent ink dyes just under the skin. An important part of the work involves explaining clearly to potential clients what is involved and ensuring that they do understand the permanent nature of a tattoo. Many body artists also have to work on clients to correct tattoos, or cover them up.

Entry, qualifications and training

No formal qualifications are required, but you will have to persuade a registered tattooist to take you on as an apprentice. It is illegal to tattoo if you are not registered with your local Environmental Health Department. This department should be able to provide you with names of local registered artists and the Tattoo Club of Great Britain can also help you with this. Training takes from one to three years, but it takes at least five years to become really competent.

Personal attributes

Body artists/tattooists must have a flair for design and also be very good at working with people. Customers may want a tattoo, but they are often a bit nervous about it. Body artists must be extremely careful about their artwork, since the designs are permanent. They must also have scrupulous hygiene and health and safety awareness.

Earnings

Trainees earn around £12,000 rising to £17,000 with considerable experience. It is possible to earn significantly more if you develop a really good reputation and have obvious talent, or if you work in a highly fashionable studio.

Info

The Tattoo Club of Great Britain
01865 716877
www.tattoo.co.uk

Body piercer

Body and facial piercings from simple earrings to a whole range of other jewellery and metal decorations have become very popular. As a body piercer you would first discuss with your client what they had in mind and show them appropriate examples of the kinds of jewellery or decorations they were considering. You would explain the piercing procedure to them and if they wished to go ahead you would clean and prepare the area of skin to be pierced, carry out the piercing with either a needle or a piercing gun and then fit the ornamentation they had chosen. You would explain any aftercare procedures they needed to follow to ensure that the piercing remained clean and healthy.

Entry, qualifications and training

You do not need formal qualifications to train as a body piercer. Most people train through an apprenticeship at a piercing studio working with experienced body piercers. Studios must be registered with local environmental health departments. The apprenticeship lasts from one to three years and covers health and safety, hygiene, disinfection, sterilisation and customer care as well as the practical skills of carrying out piercings and fitting jewellery and ornaments. If you only wish to do ear piercing you can do a short course with the Vocational Training Charitable Trust (VTCT).

Personal attributes

You must have very good hand–eye coordination and a steady hand. You must be good at putting people at ease and also comfortable yourself with people's bodies and the kinds of piercings they may wish to choose. Attention to health and safety and hygiene procedures is essential. If you become self-employed or wish to run your own studio you will need good business and marketing skills.

Earnings

Earnings are varied for this profession. During training you may only be paid travelling expenses, although some studios pay up to £10,000. With experience and working in a busy, popular studio, you could earn up to £18,000.

Info

Vocational Training Charitable Trust (VTCT)
02380 684 500
www.vtct.org.uk

Make-up artist

Make-up artists prepare and work on make-up and hair styling for clients, including artists' models, singers, dancers, actors and others appearing on television and in films. Make-up artists also work in other settings – on cruise liners, in beauty salons in large hotels, stage shows, fashion shows or in the medical profession, where they provide make-up to camouflage clients' injuries following an accident or surgery.

An experienced make-up artist works on more versatile projects using elaborate make-up, wigs, prosthetics and other materials for television and film productions.

Entry, qualifications and training

While there are no set entry qualifications, many applicants have degrees or HNDs in art and design-related subjects and/or beauty therapy and hairdressing qualifications. There is a wide range of training courses available and Creative Skillset gives useful advice on these. Examples of some relevant qualifications include the BTEC/SQA National Certificate/Diploma in Performing Arts (Make-up), Vocational Training Charitable Trust (VTCT) Level 3 Diploma in Theatre and Media Make-up, and International Therapy Examinations Council (ITEC) Level 3 Diploma in Fashion, Theatre and Media Make-up. The London College of Fashion offers a foundation degree in make-up artistry. Most people start as a make-up assistant while doing one of the courses mentioned above.

Personal attributes

You need to have artistic flair and imagination. You must be practical, methodical and patient, but you must also be able to work quickly under pressure. You should be able to get on well with all sorts of people, and be confident and tactful, able to make suggestions and put people at ease. You may need good research skills if, for example, you are trying to create the look of a particular historical period.

Earnings

Earnings are varied for this profession. Many new entrants to the profession work for free to gain experience. After this there are recommended industry minimum pay rates for film and television work. Current rates are £250 per day for junior make-up/hair assistant and £350 for make-up designer prosthetics. Experienced artists working on major productions can earn as much as £3,000 per day – but it is only the rare few who achieve these incomes.

Info

Screen Skills
020 7713 9800
www.screenskills.com

National Association of Screen Makeup and Hair Artists (NASMAH)
01932 660935
www.nasmah.co.uk

Vocational Training Charitable Trust (VTCT)
023 8068 4500
www.vtct.org.uk

Hairdressing and Beauty Industry Authority (HABIA)
0845 230 6080
www.habia.org

Nail technician

As greater numbers of people are going to salons to have either regular manicures or false nails or nail extensions applied, so there has been a growth in this specialist area of beauty therapy. There are now many salons that specialise purely in nail care, treatment and decoration. Nail technicians do manicures, apply, maintain and repair false nails and extensions, and decorate both natural and gel nails with polish or with painted artistic designs.

Entry, qualifications and training

There are usually no formal qualifications required to get into this work, but some large salons may require you to have GCSEs in English, maths and a science. Many nail technicians are qualified beauty therapists who choose to specialise in nail technology. If this is not the case, then a good way to start is by working towards an NVQ level 1 in Beauty Therapy and then trying to gain work as an assistant in a salon. Once you have learnt the basics about nail care and nail treatments and decoration, there are further NVQs levels 2 and 3 in Nail Care and Nail Technology towards which you can work while employed.

Personal attributes

You have to be smart and presentable and have a friendly and pleasant manner. You should have good manual dexterity and an interest in colour and design. You should have a careful and patient approach to your work, and a good awareness of health and safety and hygiene issues.

Earnings

Earnings are usually £12,500 to £16,000. With experience, nail technicians can earn up to £25,000. In some city-centre salons with a really good reputation earnings can be up to £25,000. Many nail technicians are self-employed, as this is work that can be done from home or by visiting clients in their homes.

Info

Vocational Training Charities Trust (VTCT)
023 8068 4500
www.vtct.org.uk

Skills Active
0330 004 0005
www.skillsactive.com

Hairdressing and Beauty Industry Authority (HABIA)
0845 230 6080
www.habia.org

BIOLOGY

Biology is the study of living organisms, plants and animals in their natural habitats and in laboratory conditions.

Biochemist

Biochemistry is the study of chemical substances and processes in living cells and tissues. Most biochemists work in laboratories, although some make their careers in education or industry, in brewing, food technology, forestry, agriculture, dietetics, pharmaceuticals, management and planning.

Many biochemists are employed in hospitals; they are referred to as clinical biochemists. They manage and develop the service and carry out research into diseases. Pharmaceutical firms also employ biochemists to develop new drugs and study their effects on diseases and patients. Qualified biochemists are also employed in research institutions funded by the Medical Research Council, the National Institute for Medical Research and Biotechnology, and the Biological Sciences Research Council, as well as some funded by charities.

Entry, qualifications and training

Most biochemists are graduates with a degree in biochemistry or chemistry. Increasingly, many applicants also have postgraduate qualifications in biochemistry or clinical chemistry. Work experience in a laboratory while studying for your degree is really useful. It is possible to work your way up by starting as a laboratory technician and doing a degree in biochemistry part time.

If you choose to work for the NHS as a biochemist, you normally start training as a clinical biochemist and work for professional qualifications as a clinical scientist. In industry and research, once you are working as a trainee biochemist your employer may encourage or require you to take further postgraduate qualifications.

Personal attributes

You need all the skills of a good scientist. You must be a good problem solver and be able to think creatively. You need to pay great attention to detail, follow procedures carefully and be highly observant. You should be practical, with reasonable IT skills. You must be able to work as part of a team, or capable of working on your own. At senior level your work may involve management of other staff and various projects.

Earnings

Starting salaries range from £26,500 to £29,000. Experienced biochemists can earn £35,000 to £60,000. In the NHS, biochemists' salaries are linked to a clear graded structure. Research jobs in industry may offer higher salaries than those in the NHS and the public sector.

Info

NHS Careers
0345 60 60 655
www.healthcareers.nhs.uk

Skills for Health
020 7388 8800
www.skillsforhealth.org.uk/nsahealth

Royal Society of Biology
020 3925 3440
www.rsb.org.uk

Institute of Biomedical Science
020 7713 0214
www.ibms.org

Association for Clinical Biochemistry
020 7403 8001
www.acb.org.uk

Biochemical Society
020 3880 2793
www.biochemistry.org

Biologist

Biologists work in many fields, including medicine, food manufacture and the natural environment. As a biologist you would specialise in one of these areas and perhaps in a very specific aspect of that area. Biologists might study the marine environment, or work in the food industry to ensure that food is free of contamination and has a maximum shelf life. They might work in medicine studying the human immune system or for an environmental protection organisation studying habitats and ascertaining how best to preserve them. Many people who graduate in biology also choose to teach the subject in school or university. The working day of a biologist will vary enormously depending upon the field in which he or she works. Scientific study, observation of results, solving problems and working as part of a team are likely to be key aspects of the work.

Entry, qualifications and training

Most biologists have a degree in biology, biological science, marine biology, microbiology or conservation biology. It may be possible to start at technician level with four GCSEs, including maths, English, and a science in grades 9–4, but many employers ask for A levels or a degree even for technician-level entry. For research work many applicants offer postgraduate qualifications too.

Personal attributes

You need an enquiring mind, a systematic approach and a rigorous attention to recording detail regardless of the field of biology in which you work. You must be able to solve problems, but also pose the questions to which it is worth finding an answer. Being able to work on your own, but also as part of a team sharing results and exchanging ideas, is very important.

Earnings

Salaries depend on who employs you as well as how much experience you have. A junior research biologist starts on £20,000 to £23,000 a year. In industry senior research biologists can earn £35,000 to £50,000, and even up to £70,000 depending on experience.

Info

Royal Society of Biology
020 3925 3440
www.rsb.org.uk

Biomedical scientist

(see Medical and Healthcare Science)

Biotechnologist

Biotechnologists work in agriculture, the food industry, medicine and the environment. They apply their knowledge of biological systems and structure in plants and animals to solve problems and develop products and processes in all these sectors. Applications of biotechnology are wide, but examples include developing vaccines and hormones to help treat inherited diseases; the study of human genetics, plants, animals and other organisms to understand the nature of inherited disease; and the development of genetic modification to alter certain properties of plants and seeds. Other examples include manufacturing enzymes that can preserve food, developing dyes and detergents for the textiles industry.

Entry, qualifications and training

To work as a biotechnologist you need a degree in a subject such as biotechnology, bioscience, microbiology, biochemistry, chemical engineering or a related biological science. You should also consider which specific area of biotechnology interests you – e.g. food, agriculture or medicine – as some degree courses offer work placements in industry and having experience in the field that particularly interests you will be helpful when you come to apply for jobs. Since so much of the work is research-based, you may also need an MSc or a PhD plus several years working as a laboratory assistant or a research assistant before you can progress to becoming a biotechnologist.

Pharmaceutical companies often have in-house training schemes. Your training covers working with advanced technical equipment, computing skills and project management. If you don't join this sector with a postgraduate qualification, it is often possible to study for this on a part-time basis. Many postgraduate biotechnology courses allow you to develop specialised expertise.

Personal attributes

An enquiring mind and an interest in biology and chemistry are essential. You need to be a good, imaginative problem solver, but also highly meticulous and accurate in the way you work. Good

IT and writing skills are also important. You have to be able to work well as part of a team, but also be good at working on your own without supervision.

Earnings

Salaries for biotechnologists start at £19,000, but more experienced biotechnologists can earn up to £60,000. Trainees earn between £21,000 and £27,000. You may start on less as a junior research assistant or laboratory assistant. Senior biotechnologists earn £30,000 to £45,000.

Info

Association of the British Pharmaceutical Industry (ABPI)
020 7930 3477
www.abpi.org.uk

Biotechnology and Biological Sciences Research Council
01793 413200
www.bbsrc.ac.uk

SEMTA
0845 643 9001
www.semta.org.uk

Royal Academy of Engineering
020 7766 0600
www.raeng.org.uk

Botanist

Botany is the study of plants of every kind – flowers, food crops, trees, fungi, algae, mosses and lichens. While this is not a large field of employment, there are opportunities in agriculture, horticulture, government departments, the food industry and environmental conservation. Botanists study all aspects of plant life, including anatomy, chemistry, molecular biology and habitat. Job roles vary, but can include monitoring the prevalence or decline of particular plant species, classifying plants (taxonomy), searching for and identifying new species, working out how to extract chemicals from plants and looking at the effects of pollution, urban development or leisure activities on plant species. Botanists work in laboratories but also out in the field collecting and recording specimens. Their work can also include presenting research information and teaching.

Entry, qualifications and training

Botanists are normally expected to have a degree in either botany (often referred to as plant biology) or a closely related science. The Field Studies Society and the Botanical Society of the British Isles run some training courses in species recording and monitoring.

Personal attributes

Your interest in plants, or a specific group of plants, such as trees, seaweed, roses, toadstools, etc, needs to be backed up with excellent observational skills, the ability to record information very carefully and to be able to draw logical conclusions and explain these to others. You also need good communication skills: working as part of a team, supervising other field workers or arguing a case for environmental protection of a specific piece of land, for example.

Earnings

Junior research botanists earn between £20,000 and £23,000. Senior researchers earn up to £30,000 and senior lecturers in a university are paid up to £55,000. Posts in industry may pay more, while some posts in environmental conservation may be on the low side.

Info

Field Studies Society
01743 852100
www.field-studies-council.org

Royal Society of Biology
020 3925 3440
www.rsb.org.uk

Botanical Society of the British Isles
07725 862957
www.bsbi.org.uk

BOOKMAKER

As a bookmaker or in betting shop management, you work with people who are placing bets on everything from horse and greyhound racing results to whether or not there will be a white Christmas. The majority of betting shops are part of large chains, but there are a few small, independent operators. Part of the role of shop managers and cashiers is to improve its image and make outlets more appealing to customers. Betting shops face competition from online gambling services. The day-to-day work includes greeting customers, explaining and promoting products, taking bets, paying out winnings and dealing with complaints. Managers also organise staff rotas, recruit and train staff and monitor sales to see that targets are met.

Entry, qualifications and training

Many entrants start as cashiers in betting shops and don't need formal qualifications other than a good general education. You might then be able to work towards an NVQ Level 3 in gambling operations. However, many off-course bookmakers do take on management trainees who have HNDs, degrees or other qualifications. Business-related subjects are the most sought after. At any level, you are likely to have to take a maths test to check how well you deal with percentages and calculating odds. A background in retail or other customer service roles is useful.

Personal attributes

You need excellent customer service skills, a lot of common sense, good numerical skills and the ability to manage other people.

Earnings

Salaries for bookmakers start at £14,000, with experienced bookmakers earning up to £45,000. Cashiers often start on the minimum wage but can earn up to £15,000. Trainee managers earn between £14,000 and £19,000, while branch managers earn between £20,000 and £40,000.

Info

People 1st
020 3074 1222
www.people1st.co.uk

National Association of Bookmakers Ltd
01625 422884
www.nab-bookmakers.co.uk

BOOKSELLER

Facing competition from online and e-book sales, book selling may be going through testing times, but it does still offer opportunities in independent book shops, book store chains, and specialist bookshops dealing in such areas as legal books, para-psychology or antique books. As a bookseller you may have to choose what titles to buy from publishers and wholesalers, manage stock, have a good knowledge of the books you sell and be able to promote and market particular books or authors. Most importantly, you would have to be able to talk knowledgeably and helpfully to your customers. This level of customer service may be what a bookshop can offer which online purchasing cannot.

Entry, qualifications and training

No formal qualifications are necessary, but in practice many staff working in bookshops have either a degree or a diploma; business-related disciplines are very popular with employers. Bookshop chains offering management training set their own entry requirements – normally five GCSEs grades 9–4, A levels, or other academic qualifications. Most training is on the job, with an induction course to get you started.

Personal attributes

It helps to be interested in books and widely read. You must enjoy dealing with people and be happy to answer questions and offer advice. You need good IT skills both for ordering stock and for researching product queries for customers. A flair for organising window and counter displays and a talent for marketing are also very useful.

Earnings

Earnings are from £14,000 to £18,000 for trainees while store managers and senior staff working for large chains earn between £20,000 and £45,000. Some companies run bonus schemes for achieving high sales.

Info

People 1st
020 3074 1222
www.people1st.co.uk

The Booksellers Association (BA)
020 7421 4640
www.booksellers.org.uk

BREWING

Brewing and brewery work are the manufacture and production of beer and lager for the hospitality and retail sectors. Breweries can be large, supporting their own pub and hotel chains, or they can be small, independent local breweries that sell to free houses and retail customers. They can also be micro breweries where members of the public brew their own batches of beer under supervision and guidance from brewing professionals. While breweries employ a range of staff, including marketing, finance and human resource professionals, the two groups of brewing specialists they employ are brewery workers and technical brewers.

Brewery worker

Brewery workers or brewery operatives work under the supervision of technical brewers helping with the manufacture and production of beer or lager. In small breweries they are often involved in all the different processes of manufacture. Working for larger companies, they may specialise in one process. The work could include weighing and mixing ingredients, monitoring quality, packing products, cleaning equipment, and loading and storing the beer.

Entry, qualifications and training

You do not need formal qualifications, but GCSEs including science or another technical subject could be useful, especially if you would like to progress to more technical and supervisory work. Training is on the job.

Personal attributes

You have to be good at following instructions, observant and careful in your work. You need to be able to cope with routine work while being prepared to be flexible as well. You are often working as part of a team and you may need to develop the skills of supervising others.

Technical brewer

Technical brewers or brewing technologists are responsible for developing and overseeing the production of beers and lagers. They have to decide on the right mix of ingredients, the temperatures at which processes should take place and the length of time that each part of the brewing process should take. It is their responsibility to ensure the quality and consistency of the product and to analyse and correct problems when they arise. They also have to source the right quality of raw materials and work within set budgets.

Entry, qualifications and training

Most trainee technical brewers have degrees in relevant subjects. Useful subjects include biological science, chemistry, chemical engineering and food technology. There are a few degrees available in brewing and distilling technology. You may get into this work with a BTEC or HND.

Personal attributes

You need a combination of good technical skills, being methodical, careful and good at problem solving, along with excellent management skills.

Earnings

Brewery workers start on the minimum wage to £13,500, with experienced brewery workers earning up to £25,000, and technical brewers on £18,000 to £22,000. Senior technical brewers with management responsibility working for large breweries may earn £45,000 plus.

Info

Institute of Brewing and Distilling
www.ibd.org.uk

British Beer and Pub Association
020 7627 9191
www.beerandpub.com

National Skills Academy for Food & Drink
0845 644 0558
www.nsafd.co.uk

BROADCASTING

(see also Film and Television Production and Performing Arts)

Broadcasting encompasses many different career opportunities in radio. You should also look at the section on film and television production as there are many similar roles in both sectors, e.g. sound recording, research and editing.

Radio, even with all the competition from new media, is still very popular in the United Kingdom, employing around 5 per cent of those working in the creative sector. It covers a diverse mix of broadcasting outlets. The BBC is the largest and broadcasts national and local stations. There are several commercial radio stations, national and local, and there is also community radio: hospital radio, for example. There are also many independent production companies developing drama, documentaries and other programmes and they may produce work for public and commercial radio outlets. Broadcasts are many and varied, designed to inform, educate, update or entertain listeners, and the remit of each programme will be different. As well as the specific careers outlined below, you may also find openings in finance, administration, IT support and marketing – just as with any other organisation, large or small.

Broadcast editor

Editors work to ensure that the finished programme is of the highest quality. For anything that is pre-recorded, editors go through the material, making sure that the quality of sound is correct, that the programme fits exactly to time and that anything inappropriate is removed. If editing live programmes, they work with producers to ensure that everything runs smoothly and to time. Increasingly, even though radio is not a visual medium, editors work with other staff to put appropriate pictures, recordings and other material on a website associated with the radio broadcast.

Broadcast engineer

Broadcast engineers or transmission engineers work to ensure that programmes go out at the right time and are of the best possible quality. You might be based in a studio or with an outside broadcasting unit. Your role could include testing equipment, setting up links between different studios or between studios and outside broadcasts. You may be developing links between programmes and associated multimedia facilities. You would certainly have to solve any problems, such as breaks in transmission, as quickly as you can.

Broadcast journalist

(see Journalism)

Broadcast presenter

Presenters work at the front line of radio and television, entertaining or informing the audience. They work on many different types of programme, including current affairs, documentaries, special interest and game shows. They work in all areas of broadcasting – national and regional television and radio, satellite and cable channels. Another version of presenting is the role of continuity announcer. They are the people who make announcements between scheduled broadcasts. Presenters and announcers have to do a great deal of preparatory work and liaise closely with their production staff, so it is not simply a matter of presenting a programme.

Broadcast researcher

Researchers work for producers, programme commissioners and presenters gathering all kinds of background information required for a broadcast to be interesting, accurate or entertaining. This research may involve finding out more about potential interviewees, ascertaining who might be an ideal interviewee, and researching facts – historical, cultural or current affairs related.

Broadcast sound engineer

Sound engineers are responsible for recording any radio station's output. This may be in a studio or on location, eg the seashore for a nature documentary or a concert hall for a live recording of an orchestral work. Engineers work to ensure that maximum quality of sound is produced and that there are no breaks in transmission. The work involves ensuring that all the technical equipment is functioning properly, solving problems the second they arise and working very closely with producers, presenters and other studio staff.

Broadcast sound technician

Sound technicians are part of the team that supports sound engineers. They help set up equipment and check and test that it is working properly. They may also work with the finished recording, cutting out unnecessary background noise, getting the levels right, or adding sound effects.

Producer and assistant producer

Radio producers are responsible for the content of audio broadcasts on radio, and increasingly through internet versions of radio broadcasts. The producer takes responsibility for the whole process. This starts with generating ideas and entails liaising with presenters, DJs, engineers and broadcasting assistants throughout the planning and the actual output of the programme. They are also responsible for ensuring that audience feedback and responses to a particular programme are gathered and used to inform the planning of future programmes. Assistant producers help producers with all aspects of the work, but often carry out more of the basic administration and organisation. It is usual to start as an assistant producer.

Radio broadcast assistant

Broadcast assistants are referred to in the business as 'BAs'. Your work as a broadcast assistant would involve supporting all aspects of programme making and transmission. You would help presenters and producers with administration, technical support in the studio and generally help out wherever you can. You would often meet and greet guests and explain to them what to expect – especially if they are not familiar with studios and how they work.

Entry, qualifications and training

In this popular, competitive sector any experience you can gain in student broadcasting, volunteering to help on a hospital or other community station or any other relevant experience is tremendously helpful and undoubtedly strengthens your application. You also have to be able to convince potential employers that it really is radio that interests you, above TV or any other platform. Many people are prepared to work for free for a while to gain experience.

Broadcast engineer

Broadcast engineers are normally graduates with degrees in electronics, electronic engineering or broadcast engineering. It may be possible to get a traineeship with an HND or foundation IT degree. It is sometimes possible for graduates of other disciplines to get into this work, but they need good A level maths and demonstrable technical/IT skills. Technician-level training or entry is sometimes possible with five GCSEs grades 9–4 including maths, English and a science.

Broadcast journalist

You need either a relevant degree or postgraduate qualification, or a background in magazine or newspaper journalism. Some companies offer a very limited number of training schemes, and competition for these is fierce.

Broadcast researcher

Broadcast researchers usually have a degree, though the subject does not particularly matter. It is more important that you can demonstrate that you have good research and communication skills. Like all broadcasting jobs, competition for this work is fierce, so some researchers start work in other administrative roles and move into research.

Producer and editor

Producers, assistant producers and editors come from a variety of backgrounds. Many are graduate entrants, with degrees or postgraduate qualifications in broadcast journalism or broadcast production, simply because there is such great competition for this work. Good technical qualifications, A levels or an HND can be an advantage if you don't have a degree.

Radio broadcast assistant

While radio broadcast assistants don't necessarily need formal qualifications, this is such a competitive industry that many applicants do have A levels or degrees. Getting a job as a BA is a very useful first step on the ladder to working as an assistant producer and then producer.

Personal attributes

You must be truly passionate about the medium. Listen to radio, learn about it and think about it. While there are some skills particular to specific roles, there are many skills and qualities essential to anyone working in radio. You have to have excellent communication skills and an ability to work well as part of a team. If you are in a front role such as announcer or presenter, you need self-confidence and an ability to think on your feet. If you are more behind the scenes, you need equally quick reactions – dealing with equipment failure or a guest who fails to arrive, for example. In all roles you have to be happy to cope with constant change and embrace changes in technology.

Earnings

Earnings vary widely depending on the job you do, your level of experience and the qualifications you have. Generally, at the start of your career, earnings may be relatively low. Salaries for assistant-level jobs are around £15,000 to £20,000 in London, £12,000 to £18,000 in other areas. Senior producers can earn £30,000 to £40,000. Presenters work on individually negotiated contracts.

Info

BBC
www.bbc.co.uk

Broadcasting Entertainment Cinematograph and Theatre Union (BECTU)
020 7346 0900
www.bectu.org.uk

Radio Centre
020 7010 0600
www.radiocentre.org

Community Media Association
0114 279 5219
www.commedia.org.uk

Hospital Broadcasting Association
0300 121 0500
www.hbauk.com

National Council for the Training of Journalists
01799 544014
www.nctj.com

The Radio Academy
www.radioacademy.org

Screen Skills
020 7713 9800
www.screenskills.com

BUSINESS

Business administration covers those many roles required to ensure the smooth day-to-day running of a business. 'Business' being any organisation in the public, private or not-for-profit sectors providing every kind of product and service. There are too many job titles to cover them all and job titles may vary yet describe a similar role. Below, however, are some of the most commonly found job titles, ranging from company secretary at director level to the day-to-day role of a receptionist.

Administrative assistant

Administrative assistants undertake a wide variety of routine and clerical tasks in every kind of office and organisation. The same job shares many different job titles, including clerical assistant, clerical worker, office assistant, office junior and administrative support worker. It is hard to describe a typical job because you may be working in such different settings and dealing with such different office procedures. You may be the only administrative worker in a very small company, or you could be working in a hospital, a local authority department, a charity or a multinational company. There are some common threads to the work. These include processing paperwork, entering data into computer or digital files, dealing with telephone queries, arranging filing systems (electronic and paper), dealing with incoming post and sending out correspondence, checking and updating records, photocopying and gathering and disseminating information. Some jobs involve considerable responsibility, with the opportunity to manage other members of staff.

Entry, qualifications and training

Employers usually expect a good standard of general education including four or five GCSEs grades 9–4 including English and maths. A lot of the training is on the job because you will need to learn about an organisation's particular systems, procedures and structures. Administrative and clerical work can be a very good starting point for other careers in finance, human resources and many other fields. It is common to find people with A levels and degrees starting their careers in administration and clerical support, but this is by no means essential. College courses in administration leading to NVQ levels 1 and 2 awards may improve your chances. You may also be able to train through an apprenticeship in business administration.

Personal attributes

You need good written English skills, including good spelling and grammar. You may need to have good numeracy skills and you should have good basic IT skills. You need to be able to deal with people and cope with problems, but also concentrate on repetitive tasks.

Earnings

Reflecting the wide range of jobs with many different types of employer, salaries vary considerably. A typical range of starting salaries is £14,000 to £18,000 – more in London and other large cities. Experienced staff earn between £16,000 and £30,000.

Info

Instructus Skills (formerly Skills CFA)
01536 738631
www.instructus-skills.org

Company secretary

All public limited companies must employ a qualified company secretary and many private companies and other organisations choose to do so. Company secretaries work for banks, insurance companies, trade unions, employer organisations, housing associations, charities and businesses of many kinds. The company secretary's duties include ensuring that the company complies with relevant legal and regulatory matters, administration of mergers and acquisitions, drafting contracts, advising the board of directors on company law and procedures and maintaining company records. Other duties can include pensions administration, personnel matters, shareholder issues, property management and finance.

Entry, qualifications and training

Most company secretaries have substantial business experience. Many have degrees or professional qualifications in business, law, accountancy or public administration. To be the secretary of a public limited company you must by law either qualify with the Institute of Chartered Secretaries and Administrators (ICSA) or be an accountant, solicitor or barrister. To qualify as a company secretary you must complete the ICSA International Qualifying Scheme (IQS). How much you will have to study depends on your previous qualifications, since law or accountancy qualifications will give you exemption from some papers. There are also some university postgraduate courses that meet the IQS requirements. The ICSA website lists these.

Personal attributes

You need excellent written and spoken English and very good presentation skills. You should be able to deal with highly complex information and be very well organised. You need to be a good problem solver who can employ sound judgement.

Earnings

Salaries start at around £30,000–£35,000 – remember that this is normally a second career for most people. Salaries rise from £40,000 to £90,000 according to responsibilities and size and type of employer. A few company secretaries earn £130,000 plus.

Info

Institute of Chartered Secretaries and
Administrators (ICSA)
020 7580 4741
www.icsa.org.uk

Instructus Skills (formerly Skills CFA)
01536 738631
www.instructus-skills.org

Personal assistant

(see also Secretary)

Personal assistants, also referred to as PAs, executive secretaries or executive assistants, work for every kind of commercial business, government, professional and charity organisation. As a personal assistant your role is to help ease your manager's workload by providing secretarial support and dealing with a range of administrative tasks.

Your duties are likely to be varied, but typical tasks include managing your manager's diary, booking appointments, screening and dealing with telephone calls, dealing with e-mails and paper correspondence, keeping records, collecting information for meetings or reports, writing letters and e-mails, taking minutes of meetings, making travel arrangements and arranging meetings. At a senior level you may stand in for your manager when he or she is away, handle accounts problems and act as office manager.

Entry, qualifications and training

A minimum of GCSEs in maths and English is usually required, but it is not uncommon for people with A levels or degrees to go into this work. There are some advanced level apprenticeships available to train as personal assistants. Any relevant IT training courses on software packages for managing data or accounts are also useful. Some colleges run full- and part-time secretarial and administrative courses to GNVQ levels 2 and 3. Courses can also be taken through part-time study while working, through the London Chamber of Commerce and Industry Examination Board (LCCIEB), Oxford, Cambridge and RSA Examination Board (OCR) and Pitman Qualifications (City & Guilds), which offer relevant qualifications that take one to two years to complete. Personal assistant work spans everything from fairly junior jobs in small companies to extremely responsible roles working with directors of large organisations. The training courses available reflect this, and courses are offered at several different levels.

Personal attributes

You must be friendly but discreet and diplomatic. You need to be extremely well organised and calm when you are under pressure or working to deadlines. Knowing when to use your own initiative is also important.

Earnings

Salaries for a personal assistant, executive secretary, and executive assistant start around £18,000, a little less outside London and the M25. Salaries vary depending on the size, type and location of the organisation for which you work and the seniority of the person to whom you are personal assistant. An experienced personal assistant to a senior manager can earn up to £50,000.

Info

Instructus Skills (formerly Skills CFA)
01536 738631
www.instructus-skills.org

Receptionist

As a receptionist, you are the one who welcomes visitors to an organisation. It is your job to direct them to the person or department they need to see, to confirm appointments and to provide information. You may also deal with telephone enquiries. Receptionists work in many settings: hotels, health centres, government offices and private businesses of many kinds. Where you work determines what your day-to-day tasks are likely to be. In a hotel you welcome guests, make bookings and prepare the final accounts. In a small company you may combine your reception role with other administrative work such as filing and photocopying.

Entry, qualifications and training

While formal qualifications are not essential, many employers do require you to have GCSEs grades 9–4 in English and maths; knowledge of other languages is important. Many further education colleges offer one-year full-time courses and a range of part-time courses in reception skills. A range of qualifications is available, including NVQs at levels 1, 2 and 3.

Personal attributes

Receptionists should be friendly and pleasant, with a good phone manner and neat appearance. They also need stamina as they are often expected to work shifts that include evenings and weekends. They should have a real liking for people and a good memory for faces. Computer literacy is also important.

Earnings

Receptionists earn between £12,000 and £21,000, more than this in London or if the work involves other duties and responsibilities. Hotel receptionists earn between £12,500 and £24,000.

Info

Instructus Skills (formerly Skills CFA)
01536 738631
www.instructus-skills.org

Secretary

Secretaries work in all types of organisation. Sometimes they are assigned to one person, sometimes they provide support services for several people. Most secretaries need to have well-developed IT skills but there is still a demand for those with shorthand and audio typing. As well as producing documents, secretaries undertake a range of organisational tasks such as arranging travel and meetings. They may also work as receptionists and deal with callers and queries by phone or e-mail. Those in senior positions may make decisions on behalf of managers.

Bilingual secretary

Bilingual secretaries are fluent in a second (even a third) language and may work in commerce, overseas or as an employee of an international organisation. The work will include composing, reading and translating documents in the foreign language. They may use speaking/listening skills in their languages for telephone work, receiving visitors and interpreting at meetings.

Legal secretary

Accurate skills have always been paramount for legal paperwork, but word processors have made the job easier. Legal secretaries are employed by barristers and solicitors in professional practice and in large commercial organisations.

Medical secretary

Medical secretaries are good administrators, keep records, and handle correspondence and filing. They work in hospitals, for individual doctors/consultants and in health centres. Accuracy and confidentiality are essential, as is a thorough knowledge of medical terminology.

Entry, qualifications and training

There is a range of full- and part-time courses available. Courses usually include word processing, audio, shorthand and office procedures. There are training opportunities for young people leading to NVQ levels 1, 2 and 3 in Administration.

GCSEs are usually required to obtain a place on a full-time secretarial course. A good working knowledge of the English language is essential. Additional qualifications are needed to specialise as a legal, medical or farm secretary. There are a number of postgraduate diploma courses for graduates wishing to train as bilingual secretaries. There are also some advanced level apprenticeships available in both legal and medical secretarial work.

Personal attributes

Above all, secretaries have to be well organised, calm and pleasant. They have to be able to cope with working under pressure and producing work for deadlines. People skills are very important, especially when working in healthcare or other sensitive areas. Discretion and tact are also important.

Earnings

Outside London pay starts at £14,000 to £18,000, and in London entry-level is higher at £19,000 to £25,000. Jobs in not-for-profit organisations tend to be at the lower end of the pay scale; employment in banking, finance and law firms is at the upper end. With 10 to 15 years' experience, salaries can rise to £30,000–40,000.

Info

Instructus Skills (formerly Skills CFA)
01536 738 631
www.instructus-skills.org

The Institute of Legal Secretaries and PAs
020 7100 9210
www.institutelegalsecretaries.com

CABINET MAKER

Cabinet makers build individually designed and produced pieces of wooden furniture such as chairs, tables, bookcases, chests of drawers and storage or display cabinets. They may also restore antiques or repair damaged furniture. Cabinet makers start by making a drawing, either by hand or on computer. They then choose the appropriate quantity and quality of wood to employ and, using a range of tools, they construct the item from scratch. If they are employed by a company, they may not be so involved in the drawing and planning stage. Many cabinet makers, however, are self-employed and their work would include discussing every aspect of the design and the cost with their customers.

Entry, qualifications and training

You don't need specific qualifications, but some employers may require GCSEs, particularly in maths or a technical subject. If you are aged between 16 and 24, you could train through an apprenticeship. If you are over 24, you need to have some relevant skills, experience or qualifications.

There are several college-based City & Guilds courses in furniture production – these are aimed at newcomers and current employees in the industry. You could opt for a higher level qualification in a course that combines furniture design and practical skills – there are degree, foundation and HND courses available in furniture design and furniture making.

Personal attributes

You must be very practical and confident using machines and hand tools. You should be able to follow a technical drawing, adapt designs and do drawings of your own. You need good numeracy skills and if you become self-employed you also need some business awareness.

Earnings

Earnings start at around £14,000, rising to £18,000 with three or four years' experience. Cabinet makers who become really skilled and get a good reputation can earn £30,000 plus.

Info

British Woodworking Federation
020 7637 2646
www.bwf.org.uk

The Guild of Master Craftsmen
01273 478449
www.guildmc.com

CALL CENTRE OPERATOR

Call or contact centre operators work for many different business and service providers, dealing with customer queries on the telephone, by e-mail, text, fax or letter. Telephone work is the most likely and is what most people think of as call centre work. You might work for a mail order catalogue, a financial services advice line, a utilities provider, an IT support company or an organisation offering welfare, health or counselling advice of some kind. The type of employer you work for will determine the range of duties you undertake, but you are always likely to be involved in many of the following: answering queries, providing further information, referring callers to other agencies, updating computer records or selling products and services. As you gain experience, your work is likely to include supervising other staff and training new members of the team.

Many call/contact centres operate 24-hour services, so there are often opportunities to work as a shift supervisor and then to progress to a position with more management responsibility.

Call centre manager

Call centre managers ensure the smooth running of the centre. The work involves drawing up work rosters, training new recruits and dealing with those customers who have a more complicated query or who wish to complain.

Entry, qualifications and training

You don't always need formal qualifications – employers set their own entry requirements, which can include GCSEs grades 9–4 in maths and English. Job interviews often include practical tests to assess your telephone manner and your IT skills. Most employers offer training in call centre techniques and in any specialist knowledge that applies to its particular products or services. There are some college courses in call centre techniques; these include City & Guilds in Contact Centre Operations and a BTEC introduction to Contact Centre Operations. Courses such as these cover telephone manner, confidentiality, data management and other communication skills. In some areas you may be able to take an apprenticeship in call/contact centre skills. Having built up some experience in this work, and if you gain promotion to supervisory or management level, there are several further qualifications you could work towards. These include Telesales levels 2 and 3, Contact Centre Operations levels 1 and 2, and Contact Centre Professionals levels 3, 4 and 5. These NVQs cover areas such as developing customer relationships, IT skills, sales techniques, managing staff and resources, quality control and performance management.

There are sometimes openings for graduates to join call centres at management level.

Personal attributes

On the telephone, you may need to be persuasive, patient, sympathetic, thick-skinned, sensitive or calm. Clearly you need a different mix of skills to deal with someone who is placing a catalogue order compared to someone who is anxious that they cannot pay a utility bill, for example. You need good IT skills, the ability to work under pressure and to take responsibility if you want to progress to supervisory and management levels.

Earnings

New call centre staff earn between slightly above the minimum wage and £16,500, rising to £17,500 to £19,000 with experience. Managers earn £20,000 to £25,000 but in a large company can earn considerably more. There may be opportunities to earn bonuses or commissions on sales made or customers signed up.

Info

Institute of Customer Service
020 7260 2620
www.instituteofcustomerservice.com

Tech Partnership Degrees
https://www.tpdegrees.com

Customer Contact Association (CCA)
0141 564 9010
www.cca.org.uk

CAREERS ADVISER

Careers advisers help school and college students and adult jobseekers of all ages. They help their clients choose career options, write CVs, prepare for interviews, consider training or education opportunities, move from unemployment into work or training, or change career direction. The National Careers Service is a major employer, but it contracts this work out to many different organisations. Careers advisers can work in schools, job centres, colleges, community centres, probation offices, youth centres, libraries, health centres, for private employers or for training providers.

Careers advisers may work one-to-one with their clients face to face, on the telephone or by e-mail. They provide training sessions, workshops or discussions for groups of jobseekers or school students. They also have to work closely with employers, training providers and educational establishments, keeping themselves well informed on current opportunities.

Entry, qualifications and training

Most employers look for candidates who have, or who are willing to work towards, a Qualification in Careers Guidance (QCG). You can do this as a one year's full-time course or two years' part time. These courses combine academic study with practical experience, training in interview techniques, etc. The normal entry requirement for a QCG is a degree in any subject. However, subjects such as psychology or education may give you the edge. Experience of working with young people in any setting will also strengthen your application.

Personal attributes

Excellent communication skills are essential. You are dealing with young people, their parents, teachers, employers and other professionals. You have to be well organised, good at disseminating information, able to present material to individuals and groups, and have reasonable IT skills. You should be confident, persuasive, assertive and tactful, and you must be a good listener.

Earnings

Pay for trainees ranges from £18,000 to £23,000. Part-qualified advisers earn between £21,000 and £27,000. There is no national agreed pay scale for careers or personal advisers but pay can go up to £50,000. Pay is higher in the higher education sector than for work with school leavers.

Info

National Careers Service
0800 100 900
www.nationalcareers.service.gov.uk

Inspiring Futures
https://inspiringfutures.org.uk/about

Career Development Institute (CDI)
01384 376 464
www.thecdi.net

Association of Graduate Careers Advisors
0114 251 5750
www.agcas.org.uk

CARPENTRY

(see Cabinet maker and Construction trades)

CARPET FITTER/FLOOR LAYER

Carpet and flooring retailers, furniture stores and department stores all employ their own trained personnel who deliver and fit carpets and other floor coverings to customers' homes, shops, offices or hotels. Some fitters are also self-employed. The work can include measuring up and providing quotes for what the work will cost and advising customers on suitable types of flooring or carpet products.

Entry, qualifications and training

GCSE English and maths or equivalents are usually required, especially if you train through an apprenticeship. Training is mainly given on the job, working with an experienced fitter, although in some firms there are possible opportunities for day-release courses leading to the examinations of the National Institute of Carpet and Floorlayers. Short one- to five-day and tailored courses are available through the Flooring Industry Training Association.

Personal attributes

Strength and fitness are important in order to handle heavy rolls of carpet. A good head for calculations and an eye for detail (such as matching patterns) are also essential. Generally, too, it is necessary to be able to drive.

Earnings

Trainees earn between £12,000 and £15,000. Experienced carpet fitters earn up to £30,000. Some employers provide a vehicle as part of their salary package. Some carpet fitters become self-employed.

Info

CITB (Construction Industry Training Board)
0344 994 4400
www.citb.co.uk

Flooring Industries Training Association
0115 950 6836
www.fita.co.uk

National Institute of Carpet and Floorlayers
0115 958 3077
www.nicfltd.org.uk

UK Flooring Academy
01283 711428
www.carpet-fitting-courses.co.uk

CARTOGRAPHER

Cartographers make maps of every kind, from the map you might take on a walk to the maps that supply your satellite navigation system. They make highly specialised maps for industry, eg mining or shipping. Some also make globes or other 3D models.

Cartographers are employed by several government departments – the Ordnance Survey, the Ministry of Defence, the Met Office and the Department for Transport, for example. Local authority planning departments may employ cartographers and in industry they may work for utilities companies, oil companies or the leisure industry.

Work varies and most cartographers become specialists in one type of mapping. Tasks could include updating current maps, checking maps and charts for accuracy or making maps for as yet uncharted regions (not so many of these now). Work could involve carrying out land surveys and liaising closely with surveyors. Cartographers use desktop publishing, digital photography and sophisticated software to model and produce data and to collect information from remote sensors and satellites. They also work on geographical information systems (GIS), which link all kinds of data such as population statistics with maps.

Entry, qualifications and training

Most trainee cartographers are graduates, though it may be possible to get into this work if you have an HND. The British Cartographic Society website gives a list of degrees which include cartography subjects. One of these could give you the edge as an applicant. Other useful degree subjects include geology, earth science, geography, physical science, computing or geographical information systems (GIS) and mathematics. Another way into this career area is as a geospatial survey technician, through a geospatial survey technician advanced apprenticeship, geospatial mapping degree apprenticeship or becoming a trainee cartographic technician.

Personal attributes

You must be interested in geography and the environment. You need to be able to work accurately, paying attention to detail, and you should have good spatial awareness and a good sense of design. Excellent computer skills are very important. As you progress to more senior roles, you also need to be able to take responsibility for managing projects and staff.

Earnings

Cartographers earn between £18,000 and £23,000; with experience salaries rise to around £45,000, and more if you are a project leader or have other management responsibilities.

Info

The British Cartographic Society
www.cartography.org.uk

Society of Cartographers
www.soc.org.uk

Ordnance Survey (OS)
03456 05 05 05
www.ordnancesurvey.co.uk

Association for Geographic Information
www.agi.org.uk

Remote Sensing and Photogrammetry Society
www.rspsoc.org.uk

CATERING

(see Hospitality and catering)

CHARITY WORK

An increasing number of young people leaving school, college or university want to contribute to and improve society as well as earn a living. Experienced workers who no longer have as much pressure to earn a high income may also move to the charitable sector, perhaps working part time. The charitable sector (also known as the third sector) is quite large, with many job roles similar to other organisations, and looking for work in the charitable sector rather than for-profit business is realistic, although salaries may not be as high. Charities are vulnerable to changes in funding levels, and many roles are on temporary contracts. The culture and values of a charity's workplace may well be shaped by the good cause it aims to support, but although profit is not the aim, charities need to take a similar approach to other businesses to maximise their income. Roles may be stressful, but also rewarding. Key roles are in marketing and communication, finance, IT and administration, and details can be found under these specific entries. Roles more specific to charities include fundraising, lobbying, policy and research, aid work and managing volunteers.

Charity Officer

Charity officers, also known as charity administrator or project development officer, will carry out many general roles in smaller charities, to ensure the charity as a whole functions well. In larger charitable organisations the focus may be on a specific area of the charity's work, such as project management, volunteer or donor management.

Entry, qualifications and training

A degree is not needed for the role of charity officer, but new entrants often have a degree in business studies or other social science. Other ways into an organisation is by having experience or qualifications in an area that aligns with the charity's purpose, or experience of a similar role in the private or public sector.

Personal attributes

Commitment to the aims of the charity is key. Smaller charities will call for multi-tasking across a range of tasks, and the ability to prioritise. Good communication and interpersonal skills is important when working with volunteers.

Earnings

Charity officer salaries start around £15,000 to £20,000 per year. Salaries for specialist and professional posts range from £20,000 to £35,000, and are above £30,000 at senior level and up to £60,000 in the largest charities.

Fundraiser

Fundraising managers work mainly for charities, but also for pressure groups, community projects and other organisations. They are responsible for overseeing all those activities that help their organisations to generate income. Their varied activities include working with advertisers and marketing specialists to decide how to target a particular audience; working with businesses to obtain corporate funding such as the sponsoring of a project; and organising special fundraising events. They are also responsible for managing trading through charity shops or mail order catalogues; keeping in touch with donors; and organising and supervising the work of volunteers. The particular mix of tasks varies greatly. Large charities may employ fundraising managers who specialise in just one of the above areas. Working for a small charity, you may have to turn your hand to anything and everything.

Entry, qualifications and training

While there may be no specific entry qualifications, many fundraisers are graduates with a degree in business studies or marketing. This work is now highly competitive and organisations have to consider who will really be able to help them generate income. A background in advertising, public relations, finance or marketing is ideal. Having done some voluntary work for your chosen charity, or for something similar, can also strengthen your application.

The Institute of Fundraising offers a part-time foundation course in the basics of fundraising, for people who have just embarked on this career. It also offers a certificate in fundraising management, which is equivalent to NVQ level 4. A great deal of training is informal and on the job. A social media and digital marketing higher apprenticeship could also help you to get into online fundraising.

Personal attributes

A full range of excellent interpersonal skills is essential. You must be persuasive, good at negotiating and able to speak confidently to groups of people. You need good business sense, IT skills and numeracy, and the knack of spotting an imaginative solution or coming up with an appealing idea.

Earnings

Fundraising managers earn between £20,000 and £25,000. With experience and working for a large organisation it is possible to earn up to £60,000. Some vacancies with small organisations or community groups will be less well paid and many may be part time with pro rata pay for hours worked.

Info

Institute of Fundraising
020 7840 1000
www.institute-of-fundraising.org.uk

NCVO
020 7713 6161
www.ncvo.org.uk

Volunteer Now
028 9023 2020
www.volunteernow.co.uk

Volunteering Wales
0300 111 0124
www.volunteering-wales.net

Volunteer Scotland
01786 479593
www.volunteerscotlan.net

Association of Charitable Organisations
www.aco.uk.net

CHEMISTRY

Chemistry is the branch of science concerned with the substances of which matter is composed, the investigation of their properties and reactions, and the use of such reactions to form new substances.

Analyst

Analytical chemists (analysts) study the chemical properties of substances to determine how these properties will affect the performance and behaviour of that chemical in the production process, or in a finished product. They work in a variety of scientific and technical fields from pharmaceuticals, toxicology and forensic analysis to product and process development, testing and quality control in many manufacturing processes.

Public analysts are employed by local authorities to examine, for example, the state of the water supply; the adequacy of the sewage treatment system; toxic and suspect materials; and leaching from landfill sites. They may also be asked to examine food from a suspect restaurant. Public analysts are frequently required to give witness on their findings in courts of law, and should be familiar with the law relating to goods and services.

Chemist

Chemists study the structure and make-up of chemicals and other substances. They interpret the way substances interact and react under different physical conditions. They apply their knowledge in a variety of ways, eg to create new food products or materials such as plastics and artificial fibres. They work in many industries, developing new drugs for the pharmaceutical sector, analysing the impact of climate change on oceans, keeping water supplies safe and clean or developing products to improve the shelf life of food and drink. They may also work in forensics, examining the substances at the scene of a crime.

Some professional chemists are referred to as analytical chemists and their work focuses specifically on analysing chemicals and other materials, but they can still work across several different industries and sectors. Some chemists also work in academic research.

The chemist's work involves planning and conducting experiments, analysing results and writing up and/or presenting the results he or she produces. The work often involves the management and supervision of other laboratory staff.

Entry, qualifications and training

To work as a chemist or analyst you need a degree in either chemistry or chemical science. Many employers prefer you to have a postgraduate qualification as well, or to have done a course that includes a placement in industry. Many graduate chemists may have to start work as a laboratory technician in a laboratory involved in the aspects of chemistry that interest them. Training is on the job, covering the use of technical equipment, computer packages, and health and safety. If you don't have a postgraduate qualification before you start work, you may be able to work towards this while you are employed.

Personal attributes

You must combine an interest in chemistry with an enquiring mind and a patient, persistent attitude to solving problems. You should be accurate and thorough in all your work, and highly observant. You need to be good at handling delicate equipment and confident with IT. If you are supervising other staff you need good management and the ability to motivate colleagues.

Earnings

New graduate chemists earn between £18,000 and £25,000, higher salaries being paid to entrants with PhDs. Experienced and/or senior analysts can earn £35,000 to £60,000.

Info

Analytical Science Network (ASN) c/o Royal Society of Chemistry
www.rsc.org/Membership/Networking/InterestGroups/Analytical/ASN.asp

Royal Society of Chemistry (RSC)
020 7437 8656
www.rsc.org

Royal Pharmaceutical Society
020 7572 2737
www.rpharms.com

SEMTA
0845 643 9001
www.semta.org.uk

CHILDCARE

Working with and caring for children, especially preschool-aged children, offer several career options. The main ones are described here, but there are others such as school lunchtime supervisors (for part-time work) and childcare inspectors for people who already possess some background in childcare or other relevant experience.

Childminder

Childminders work in their own homes looking after other people's children while those people are out at work or studying.

As a childminder you could care for babies and preschool children during the day, you could also look after older children before and after they attend school. As a childminder you would have to ensure that the children in your care felt safe and secure. You would be responsible for their meals while they were with you. For younger children and babies you would have to look after their physical needs, changing nappies, ensuring that toddlers washed their hands, etc. You would also have to provide a range of play activities both indoors and outside. You might also have to take children on outings, to the shops or to the park. If you are looking after older children you may have to take them to playgroups or after-school activities.

Entry, qualifications and training

You do not need formal qualifications to become a childminder but you must be aged over 18. If you are caring for children under the age of eight in England, you must be registered with the Office for Standards in Education, Children's Services and Skills (Ofsted).

In England your local authority's Families Information Service (FIS) can provide you with information on how to register and send you an application pack. You have to be interviewed, pass a medical, take a paediatric first aid certificate, have a criminal records check administered by the Disclosure and Barring Service of the Home Office and your home is also inspected. If you are approved, you must take a registered training course as part of the Early Years Foundation Stage (EYFS). The Council for Awards in Care, Health and Education (CACHE) and the Professional Association for Childcare and Early Years (PACEY) have developed NVQ level 3 certificate and diploma courses in home-based childcare.

In Scotland you should contact the Care Commission, in Wales the Care Standards Inspectorate and in Northern Ireland your local Health and Social Care Services Trust.

You may be able to start as a childminding assistant. Some childminders employ an assistant so that they can either care for more children or because they are caring for children who have special needs.

Personal attributes

Of course, you have to really enjoy working with children and to be prepared to share your home with them. You should have an open-minded attitude about different ways of bringing up children and you should be quite comfortable with both you and your home being scrutinised. You have to be extremely responsible, sensitive and patient. You need to be practical, with a sense of humour, and keep calm if problems arise. You have to be able to communicate well with parents as well as with their children. You need to be imaginative, sympathetic and sensible. You need to be very alert, especially on matters of health and safety.

Earnings

Earnings vary considerably for childminders. London childminding rates are higher than other areas. What you earn depends on how many children you are caring for and for how long, and childminding tends not to be a full-time role. As a childminder you are responsible for paying your own tax and insurance and you have to provide toys and the right environment for children from your earnings.

Info

Office for Standards in Education, Children's
Services and Skills (Ofsted)
0300 123 1231
www.ofsted.gov.uk

Scottish Childminding Association
01786 445377
www.childminding.org

Professional Association for Childcare and Early
Years
0300 003 0005
www.pacey.org.uk

Council for Awards in Care, Health and Education
(CACHE) (part of NCFE)
0191 239 8000
www.cache.org.uk

Nanny

Nannies work in private houses caring for babies and children of parents who are working or need help with childcare, for whatever reason. Your work depends very much on the ages of the children you care for. If you are looking after young babies you are likely to be bathing, feeding, changing nappies, dressing, etc. For older children, you may be meeting them from school, preparing meals, taking them to activities, helping them get ready for school, playing or just spending time with them. Some nannies live in with the families they work for – others come to work each day. In either case, working hours can be longer than a normal nine-to-five day.

Entry, qualifications and training

While you may not need to have formal qualifications to work as a nanny, many employers will consider you far more favourably if you do. In September 2010 new Children's Workforce Development certificates and diplomas at NVQ levels 2 and 3 were introduced. These are offered at state and private colleges. A college qualification such as the Level 1 Award in Introduction to Health, Social Care and Children's and Young People's Settings, or Level 2 Certificate for the Children and Young People's Workforce may also help you to enter this profession. A first-aid qualification can also help you gain employment as a nanny. Many nannies do have nursery nursing qualifications.

Personal attributes

You have to enjoy working with babies and children of all ages. You have to have a mature, calm and sensible attitude that inspires confidence in parents or other carers. You need to have a lively, enthusiastic personality to help children play, learn and socialise. You have to be practical and may need to be able to cook basic meals for children and to hold a driving licence.

Earnings

Nannies earn from £15,000 to £23,000 – sometimes much more in some geographical locations. Some posts also include board and lodging and other benefits.

Info

Council for Awards in Care, Health and Education
(CACHE) (part of NCFE)
0191 239 8000
www.cache.org.uk

Skills for Care and Development
0113 241 1240
www.skillsforcareanddevelopment.org.uk

Nursery nurse

A nursery nurse works with babies and children under eight in the public, private and voluntary sectors. This can include schools, nurseries and hospitals. In schools, nursery nurses work in nursery, reception and infant classes alongside the teacher, providing and supervising educational and play activities. They may also be involved in providing out-of-school care at after-school clubs and on holiday schemes. Nursery nurses in hospitals can work in maternity and special care units, and on children's wards. Day nurseries, both private and local authority, employ nursery nurses to care for children under five whose parents are unable to care for them during the day. Nursery nurses can also be employed in clinics, residential homes, the community, family centres and private homes as nannies.

Entry, qualifications and training

You don't necessarily need academic qualifications, but many employers and course providers expect you to have three to five GCSEs grades 9–4. You can study for a two-year full-time NVQ level 3 award or you can work as a nursery assistant and study for qualifications part time. There are several different awards towards which you can work, including: CACHE Level 3 Diploma in Child Care and Education; the BTEC National Diploma in Children's Care, Learning and Development; and NVQ level 3 in Children's Care, Learning and Development. The government now expects all professionals to work towards Early Years Professional Status (EYPS). There are several ways to achieve this and how you do it will depend on what qualifications you already have, how much experience you have and which particular pathway your employer supports and encourages. EYPS is an addition to, not an alternative to, the qualifications listed above.

Everyone working with young children has to undergo a Disclosure and Barring Service (DBS) check to ensure that they have no criminal convictions that would make them unsuitable for this work.

Personal attributes

You must really enjoy working with children. You have to be patient, calm, imaginative and practical. You need to be well organised and good at working as part of a team. You should be observant, safety conscious, sensitive and very good at communicating with children. You will also have to be able to build up good relationships with parents and other professionals.

Earnings

Trainees are usually employed as apprentices and paid the standard Government-recommended rates. Qualified nursery nurses' pay starts at the minimum wage and rises to £19,000 with experience; nursery managers can earn £25,000 to £38,000.

Info

National Day Nursery Association
01484 407070
www.ndna.org.uk

Office for Standards in Education Children's Services and Skills (Ofsted)
0300 123 1231
www.ofsted.gov.uk

Council for Awards in Care, Health and Education (CACHE) (part of NCFE)
0191 239 8000
www.cache.org.uk

Skills for Care and Development
0113 241 1240
www.skillsforcareanddevelopment.org.uk

CHIMNEY SWEEP

Chimney sweeps clean and remove soot and other debris from chimneys and flues of open fires, wood-burning stoves and other oil, gas, coal or wood-burning heating and cooking appliances. Cleaning chimneys reduces the risk of chimney fires and the levels of dangerous emissions. This work had gone into decline, but increasing numbers of people are installing wood-burning stoves because they are considered a more environmentally friendly and economical form of heating. The work involves inspecting the job to be done and then removing soot and debris with special vacuum equipment and old-fashioned brushes. As a chimney sweep you remove the soot and dirt you have collected and leave the premises clean and tidy. You also advise customers on how to maintain or operate chimneys, flues and appliances safely.

Entry, qualifications and training

Nearly all chimney sweeps are self-employed, so you have to fund your own training, purchase of equipment and insurance. No formal qualifications are necessary, but a background in practical, physical work is a useful start. The National Association of Chimney Sweeps (NACS) offers training and advice. Other than this, you may be able to find a local chimney sweep who is prepared to offer you some on-the-job training. A driving licence and vehicle are essential, as you will need to transport equipment and travel between customers.

Personal attributes

You have to be reasonably physically fit and be a good practical problem solver, with a systematic and tidy approach to your work. You also need to be good at talking to customers. Being self-employed, you need to know how to market, promote and manage your business.

Earnings

Since most sweeps are self-employed, earnings depend on the number of customers you have and what you charge per job. Prices vary from around £30 to £90 per chimney. The work is also seasonal – most people have their chimneys swept from early spring to late autumn, not midwinter when they are using their fires and stoves.

Info

National Association of Chimney Sweeps (NACS)
www.nacs.org.uk

Guild of Master Chimney Sweeps
www.guildofmasterchimneysweeps.co.uk

CITB (Construction and Industry Training Board)
0344 994 4400
www.citb.co.uk

CHIROPODIST (OR PODIATRIST)

(see Podiatrist)

CIVIL AVIATION

Civil aviation includes those occupations concerned with civil aircraft, including passenger and goods transportation. The key roles associated with civil aviation are outlined below, but there are others – working as a baggage handler, as an information assistant at an airport or in security positions – all part of the world of civil aviation.

Aeronautical engineer

(see also Engineering)

Air traffic engineers are responsible for the efficient operation of the wide range of sophisticated telecommunications, electronic systems and specialist equipment needed in air traffic control centres, airports and other specialist centres. This involves the installation, calibration and maintenance of radar, air-to-ground communication systems, navigational and landing aids, computer data and processing equipment, and visual display units. Opportunities may exist for engineers to look after day-to-day maintenance and, at graduate level, for field management, installation and development work.

Air cabin crew

Flight attendants (air cabin crew) look after the safety, comfort and welfare of passengers. Before a flight they check stocks of equipment, welcome passengers on board and go through safety routines. During the flight they serve food and drink and on budget airlines they also sell these items. They must be ready to respond in a crisis, such as a passenger being taken ill or, more rarely, something going wrong with the flight.

Aircraft maintenance engineer

Aircraft maintenance engineers make sure that aircraft are airworthy. They maintain, service and overhaul the aircraft, their engines and equipment, working to very high standards set by the Civil Aviation Authority (CAA). Every part of every job is checked and certified. Engineers usually specialise in either mechanics or avionics, and work on major overhaul or on 'turnarounds' – the work carried out after each flight. Apart from working with airlines, other opportunities are found with firms that specialise in aircraft maintenance. There are also a few openings for professional engineers in works management, production, planning, and research and development.

Air traffic controller

The safe and efficient movement of all aircraft through British air space and airports is the responsibility of National Air Traffic Service (NATS) air traffic control officers and assistants. With the aid of sophisticated radio, radar and computer systems and with visual checks on visibility and weather conditions made from the control tower, they ensure that aircraft are kept a safe distance apart and that pilots are well advised as to their position and prevailing conditions, given clearance to land and directions to loading bays. Air traffic controllers mainly work for NATS, although there may be limited opportunities with other employers, such as local authorities or aircraft manufacturers. All must hold a CAA licence stipulating the service they are qualified to give and where they can operate. Some of the more routine tasks, such as checking flight plans, updating weather information, logging aircraft movements and keeping runways clear, are carried out by air traffic control assistants. Prospects for promotion to officer level are good; air traffic control staff are employed to work at any location within the country.

Airline customer service agent

Airline customer service agents work for individual airlines, handling companies, and airports and terminals. They deal with passengers from the moment they check in to when they board their flights. They are responsible for checking in luggage as well as customers. Customer service agents have to ensure that unaccompanied children or other passengers with special needs are safely escorted to their flights and they are also expected to calm nervous passengers before they board their planes.

Airline pilot

Commercial pilots in the United Kingdom fly fixed-wing aircraft and helicopters. Before take-off the pilot must prepare a flight plan, study the weather, make sure that the craft is airworthy, check that the cargo and fuel are safely loaded and work out estimated arrival times. Little time is spent actually flying the aeroplane manually. The pilot spends most of the time carefully monitoring sophisticated computer-controlled automatic flying, navigational and communications systems. Pilots keep in touch with air traffic control and must be prepared to deal with sudden changes in weather and other conditions. Pilots work irregular hours but their actual flying time is strictly controlled.

Most UK pilots are employed by one of the major carriers of passengers and goods, and when flying large aircraft they are part of a team. Opportunities for pilots of small aircraft and helicopters are to be found in flying executive jets, in the field of air taxiing, conducting aerial surveys, or as test pilots or flying instructors.

Entry, qualifications and training

Aeronautical engineer/Aircraft maintenance engineer

Entry to aircraft maintenance engineering is via craft, technician or student apprenticeships; entry qualifications depend upon the type of apprenticeship. The apprenticeships take the form of on-the-job training and part-time study at local colleges to prepare for aeronautical engineering/ aircraft maintenance engineering qualifications offered by City & Guilds and Edexcel (BTEC)/SQA or the CAA. Qualified aircraft engineers (including those from the armed forces) have to meet certain practical experience requirements before they can take examinations to become licensed aircraft maintenance engineers. There are some full-time courses in aeronautical engineering and aircraft maintenance, usually lasting two and a half years. You could also do a foundation degree, higher national diploma or degree in aerospace engineering, avionics, or a related subject like electrical or electronic engineering mechanical engineering, for example.

Air cabin crew

Airlines usually train their own cabin crews at special centres on courses lasting four to six weeks. Applicants should be over 18, have a good level of general education to GCSE standard, preferably including English and maths, and have conversational fluency in at least one European language. Experience in a customer care setting can be helpful.

Air traffic controller

All applicants must have five GCSEs grades 9–4 including English and maths, The National Air Traffic Service (NATS) offers three structured development programmes – one for college leavers with an HND or equivalent, a sandwich degree course programme and a third programme for graduates. Any subject that develops a high level of numeracy skills will improve your chances of success. You must be over the age of 18 when you apply and meet the necessary Civil Aviation Authority medical standards. Trainers and employers look for aptitude as much as for academic qualifications.

Airline customer service agent

There are no standard entry requirements, but individual airlines and handling companies set their own requirements. They normally ask for a good standard of education and may require you to have GCSEs grades 9–4 in English. A foreign language qualification can also be useful, as can previous experience in customer service work. You will need to live reasonably near an airport and you may well need your own transport because shift work could make reliance on public transport difficult. You will have to undergo security checks and many companies also ask you to have a medical examination.

Airline pilot

UK pilots are required to hold a licence issued by the Joint Aviation Authorities (JAA), which represent the civil aviation departments of a group of European states that have collaborated to set common safety standards called Joint Aviation Requirements. Licence holders can work as pilots in any of the JAA member states. Full details of licensing requirements and organisations providing approved courses can be obtained from the CAA (see the Info box). Training to be a commercial pilot costs £70,000–£100,000 and may be integrated (*ab initio*) or modular. Helicopter courses tend to be more expensive. Most applicants wishing to undertake integrated courses are sponsored privately or by an airline. Such sponsorship is highly competitive and difficult to obtain. Trainees are generally expected to contribute to training costs either while training or by repaying some of the fees once in employment. An alternative entry route is via a short-service flying commission with either the RAF or the Royal Navy. All pilots are expected to attend retraining and refresher courses throughout their careers.

Entry requirements for sponsored pilot training vary between airlines, but most ask for a minimum of two/three A levels or equivalent, including maths and physics. Many airlines recruit graduates up to the age of 26. Eyesight must be of a very high standard. Normal colour vision and an excellent level of health and fitness and a Class 1 Medical Certificate are essential.

Personal attributes

Aeronautical engineer/aircraft maintenance engineer

Maintenance engineering requires a combination of practical interest, mechanical aptitude, accuracy and manual dexterity. Engineers must be willing to adapt and to retrain. Very high standards and a responsible attitude are also most important.

Air cabin crew

Air cabin crew must be reassuring and approachable, smart, have lots of energy and stamina and have the confidence and the ability to act quickly and decisively in a firm but polite and tactful manner.

Air traffic controller

The work is stressful; officers need to be able to assimilate and interpret a great deal of information and instantly act upon it. They must be able to react quickly if conditions suddenly change, and be healthy, reliable and emotionally well balanced; good eyesight and colour vision are also important.

Airline customer service agent

You need excellent customer service skills. Delays and changes to flights mean customers are often stressed, anxious or angry. You need to keep calm and follow procedures quickly, but without cutting corners. You must be smart, tidy and presentable and reasonably physically fit.

Airline pilot

Pilots must be very well balanced, physically fit, have stamina, be mentally and physically alert and ready to respond quickly to changing conditions. They must be unflappable, confident, self-assured leaders with considerable technical skill.

Earnings

Airlines operate in a competitive and difficult market. This has affected wages. Earnings vary according to your job – air cabin crew or airline pilot, for example. Each airline sets its own rates of pay. As a guide, air cabin crew and customer service staff start on £12,000 to £14,000. Air traffic controllers earn £13,000 during training and £17,000 to £20,000 on being appointed. Once validated, after two years, salaries rise to £46,000 to £51,000. Pilots earn around £75,000 to £80,000 flying jet aircraft, much less for turboprops. They often have to pay a bond of £15,000 to the company that employs them and pay for much of their own training.

Info

Global ATS Ltd
www.global-ats.com

Airlines UK
020 3709 8935
airlinesuk.org

The British Air Line Pilots Association (BALPA)
020 8476 4000
www.balpa.org

British Women Pilots Association (BWPA)
www.bwpa.co.uk

Civil Aviation Authority (CAA)
020 7453 5825
www.caa.co.uk

People 1st (for passenger transport, hospitality, leisure, travel and tourism)
020 3074 1222
www.people1st.co.uk

Guild of Air Traffic Control Officers (GATCO)
www.gatco.org

National Air Traffic Services (NATS)
01489 616001
www.nats.aero

CIVIL SERVICE

The Civil Service is one of the country's largest employers, offering work in its many departments and agencies. Entry to the Civil Service can be through apprenticeship, graduate programmes or applying directly for advertised jobs. Civil servants work in many occupations and professions, carrying out the work of government. Work ranges from advising ministers on policies to dealing with daily enquiries about planning issues, benefits payments or education. While departments do their own recruitment and set entry requirements for specific jobs, there is an overall structure across most departments. This structure means you can decide at which level you would like to enter and what sort of work appeals to you.

Work falls broadly into three groups: corporate services, which are concerned with finance, IT, human resources and communications; operation services, which is the day-to-day delivery of services through government offices, including all the face-to-face dealings with the public; and policy delivery, which is concerned with developing and implementing policies, working very closely with the government.

Administrative officer and administrative assistant

Administrative officers and administrative assistants carry out the daily clerical and customer contact functions in every department and agency. Their work may involve dealing directly with the public, such as answering telephone enquiries, gathering information, processing documents, keeping records and entering data into computer systems.

Executive officer

Executive officer is the next step up the ladder after administrative officer. Executive officers are responsible for running small teams who carry out day-to-day functions for every department and agency. Tasks and responsibilities include motivating and training members of the team, carrying out annual appraisals and preparing and presenting reports on work progress to senior managers. They also have to deal with problems. If, for example, a client is unhappy with the service he or she has received, this will be referred to the junior manager in the first instance. After two years' successful work as a junior manager, it is possible to apply to join the Fast Stream management development programme.

Fast Stream development programme trainee

The Civil Service offers a fast-track accelerated training programme for recruits who want to get into senior management. Fast Stream entrants can be placed within many central government departments, and there is a special training route for anyone who wants to join the Diplomatic Service and a further pathway called the European Fast Stream. This places trainees in departments where there is a strong focus on European issues.

The programme offers a choice of 15 schemes, each within a profession, and the opportunity to work in multiple departments. These include Fast Stream Economists, Fast Stream Statisticians and Fast Stream Digital, Data & Technology pathways. Government Communications Service also has its own Fast Stream training scheme.

Entry, qualifications and training

At whatever level you enter, a great deal of your training will be on the job. All civil servants have to be either UK nationals or from a Commonwealth or EU country. For some posts, only UK nationals are accepted.

The Civil Service offers apprenticeships based in each of the government's 25 ministerial departments. They offer an opportunity to gain qualifications ranging from Level 2 (equivalent to five GCSE pass grades) to Level 7 (equivalent to a Master's degree). Each department or agency sets its own entry requirements, but there are some common guidelines. To become an administrative assistant or an administrative officer you do not need any formal qualifications. In practice, you often need five GCSEs grades 9–4. Many applicants have A levels or are graduates. Many executive officer posts ask that you have two A levels.

All Fast Stream applications must be made online. The schemes open for applicants in September each year and you have the option to express an interest in more than one scheme and department. Fast Stream graduate trainees need a good honours degree, a First or a 2.1, to be considered for the programme. Fast Stream Economists must have a 2.1 in economics. Fast Stream Statisticians must have at least a 2.2 in a numerate discipline. Fast Stream Technology in Business trainees must have a 2.1 in a business, engineering, technical, mathematical or scientific discipline.

Applicants to the Diplomatic Service must have either a degree or several years' work experience. They must pass a medical, undergo rigorous security checks and be prepared to work anywhere in the world. The Diplomatic Service also participates in the graduate Fast Stream programme.

For posts at all levels, departments often set aptitude tests of various kinds, which are designed to measure the kinds of skills that will be needed to do the job effectively. There is strong competition for Fast Stream posts in all areas.

For undergraduates considering a career in the Civil Service, there are a number of work experience and vacation work opportunities available; see the Civil Service Recruitment website.

Because the Civil Service has a structured route to development and promotion, it is possible to move into higher-level jobs through experience and performance if you do not meet the initial selection criteria for those posts.

In addition there are some internships available. Care leavers aged 18 to 30 may have the opportunity to apply for a 12-month paid internship across multiple departments. First-year undergraduates from diverse backgrounds may be eligible for a five-day placement in a government department to get an insight of what it is like to be on the Fast Stream. Second- or third-year undergraduates from diverse backgrounds can apply for a Summer Diversity Internship Programme (SDIP).

Professional occupations

There are also many opportunities in the Civil Service and its agencies for people with a wide range of vocational and professional skills. There are posts for accountants, actuaries, architects, engineers, chemists, physicists, biologists, vets, lawyers, surveyors, IT specialists and many more. For many of these posts applicants need to have relevant professional and vocational qualifications in particular areas such as science, engineering, law or finance. See the Civil Service Recruitment website for more details.

Personal attributes

Of course, there is some variation in these according to the type of work you are involved in and the level of responsibility you have. All civil servants should have an interest in delivering high quality services and information to government, members of the general public and to other organisations. Civil servants need to be flexible, able to cope with change, be good at working under pressure and good at communicating in both written and spoken English. Beyond this, there are specific skills you will need to help you perform your own role effectively.

Earnings

Salaries for administrative assistants range from £15,000 to £17,000. For administrative officers the range is £17,000 to £23,000 and for executive officers £25,000 to £28,000. The higher salaries are in London. The Fast Stream offers starting salaries from £28,000 and earning potential on completion of up to £55,000. There are small variations between different departments and agencies. Some posts attract performance-related pay bonuses.

Info

Civil Service jobs
www.gov.uk/civil-service
www.faststream.gov.uk

CLEANER

Cleaners may also be referred to as cleaning operatives or domestic service assistants. While most of us think of cleaning as cleaning and tidying domestic premises, the work goes far beyond this. As well as being employed by individuals to work in private houses, cleaners are employed by contract cleaning companies. They clean hospitals, restaurants, industrial premises, office blocks, shops, passenger vehicles and public buildings. Some cleaning companies specialise in house clearance or in cleaning up after fires, floods or other disasters. What your daily tasks involve will depend very much on the premises in which you work, but could include cleaning carpets, hard floors, walls, kitchen and bathroom surfaces and appliances, furniture and other fixtures and equipment.

Entry, qualifications and training

There are no formal entry requirements to get into this work, though in some areas you may be able to undertake an apprenticeship – employers set their own individual requirements. If you work for a cleaning contract company, training is provided on the job and there are good opportunities to progress to supervisory level in this sector.

Personal attributes

This is work where personal attributes are far more important than qualifications. You must be reliable and trustworthy. Depending on the size of operation you work for, you may have to have good team skills or be confident working on your own. If you work in private houses you will have to impress clients with your honesty and integrity. In all instances you need a thorough approach to your work and you must be physically fit.

Earnings

Earnings range between £12,000 and £18,000. Cleaners working full-time hours earn around the minimum wage. You can earn £14,000 to £16,000 as a supervisor or working in highly specialised cleaning. Cleaners working in private houses charge by the hour and this can range from the minimum wage to £20 if you work in an expensive location where your services are in demand.

Info

British Institute of Cleaning Science (BISc)
01604 678710
www.bics.org.uk

Jobcentre Plus and local newspapers for job adverts

CLOTHING INDUSTRY

(see also Fashion)

The clothing industry is diverse and complex, with products ranging from off-the-peg garments that are turned out in thousands, to exclusive haute couture designs from top fashion houses. There are job opportunities in large factories, small workrooms, with large wholesaling firms, in small family businesses and on production lines. The largest sections of the industry are men's and boys' outerwear, women's and girls' outerwear, children's clothing, bespoke tailoring (made to measure) and dressmaking. More specialised areas such as millinery and glove making are relatively small. Skilled workers are generally in great demand in most areas.

Pattern cutter

Pattern cutters work with clothing designers and clothing technologists. They produce the pattern templates from working drawings produced by fashion designers. They either cut patterns by draping material over dummies and cutting the pattern or they have standard cardboard patterns that they develop and alter to create different styles. Increasingly, pattern cutters use computers to help create their patterns.

Entry, qualifications and training

Some fashion design companies and clothing manufacturers offer apprenticeships in pattern cutting. You must have four GCSEs grades 9–4 to apply for these. Your GCSEs should include

English, maths and a design subject. Many trainee pattern cutters have a relevant foundation degree, degree or diploma in clothing technology. Some fashion design degree and diploma courses include relevant technical pattern-cutting skills. The London College of Fashion offers part-time and short, intensive pattern-cutting courses. Training is mostly on the job, but there are several NVQ and diploma courses for which you can study while employed. You may also be able to complete an apprenticeship such as a fashion and textiles pattern cutter advanced apprenticeship in order to secure a role as a pattern cutter.

Pattern grader

Pattern graders produce scaled-up and scaled-down versions of an original pattern (made by a pattern cutter), so that manufacturers can make the same garment in different sizes. Technology plays a key role in pattern grading. Graders use scanning technology to produce extremely accurate patterns in different sizes.

Entry, qualifications and training

Most people start as pattern grading assistants and work their way up after a period of about two years. It is also common to do an apprenticeship in pattern grading with a clothing manufacturer or fashion design company. You can also get into pattern grading or a similar technical role after a degree or BTEC HND in clothing technology and production.

Sample machinist

Sample machinists work to produce sample garments for customers and designers. As a sample machinist, you may work on a number of different product lines or concentrate on a particular style, for example sportswear or evening wear. You also work with a variety of materials, including cotton, wool, synthetics and leather. Sample machinists have to follow carefully the instructions on colour and fabric given by the designer. They then stitch and press the garment to give the designer a clear idea of what the finished item will look and feel like and how it will hang. Experienced sample machinists often take on a quality control role for other machinists.

Entry, qualifications and training

Sample machinists usually start as sewing machinists making up garments once the samples and the design have all been completed. There is a wide range of City & Guilds craft and design courses available in textile machining, machine embroidery and pattern cutting. If you have four GCSEs you may also be able to take an apprenticeship with a clothing manufacturer or fashion design company. Training is on the job.

Sewing machinist

Sewing machinists stitch garments together once the design has been finalised, the material cut and the sample garments completed. They normally work for clothing manufacturers and may be responsible for just one part of production, e.g. turning up hems, making buttonholes, stitching seams or fitting sleeves.

Entry, qualifications and training

No formal qualifications are needed, but many companies will set a practical test to ensure you have appropriate manual dexterity skills. If you are interested in progressing to becoming a sample machinist or a pattern cutter, you may wish to take an apprenticeship. In this case you will need some GCSEs, usually including English, maths and a design subject.

Personal attributes

To work in any of these jobs you need an interest in clothing and textiles. For pattern cutting you should have good technical drawing and computer skills and the kind of numerate skills that mean you can take very precise measurements. You should have an eye for detail and design. Sample machinists need an understanding of fabrics, good hand- and machine-sewing skills and an understanding of the production process.

Earnings

Sewing machinists start on the minimum wage, can start on a salary around £12,000, but up to £21,000 or more with more experience. Pattern graders earn between the minimum wage and £16,000. Trainee pattern cutters and sample machinists start on between the minimum wage and £20,000, and can earn up to £40,000 with experience. The range is wide because fashion design companies tend to pay higher starting rates. Experienced pattern cutters and sample machinists can earn more than £25,000.

Info

Screen Skills	**Textile Institute**
020 7713 9800	0161 237 1188
www.screenskills.com	www.textileinstitute.org

COASTGUARD

Whenever a swimmer is dragged out to sea by a dangerous current, a boat is capsized by strong winds, a ferry passenger falls overboard or a ship runs aground on a sandbank, HM Coastguard coordinates the search and rescue. At its centres around the coast of the British Isles it is responsible for approximately 10,500 miles of coastline and a million square miles of sea.

At these centres, a constant watch is kept on international distress frequencies, satellite, radio and telephone communications, all of which are responded to immediately. HM Coastguard works with and can call upon many resources for search and rescue at sea including lifeboats, helicopters, tugs and local rescue organisations. For onshore rescues, such as people or animals being stranded on cliffs or trapped in mud, they call upon teams of auxiliary coastguards.

Entry, qualifications and training

Most entrants start as watch assistants. For this you need good basic literacy, numeracy and IT skills, and a strong interest in maritime affairs. Watch officers need GCSEs grades 9–4 in English and maths, or their equivalent. For applicants without formal qualifications, the Maritime and Coastguard Agency can set competency tests. Watch officers must also have extensive experience of the sea. Many watch officers have been in the Royal Navy or the Merchant Navy, or have had other first-hand experience of the sea. Auxiliary coastguards must be aged 16 or over. Posts are open to UK nationals and to EU and Commonwealth citizens. Applicants must be physically fit, with good hearing and eyesight.

All recruits attend a training course at the Maritime and Coastguard Agency's Training Centre in Dorset, after which training is a combination of classroom and practice-based assignments.

Personal attributes

As a coastguard you will have to take important decisions quickly and calmly. You need a clear speaking voice and the ability to work with modern communications equipment. You should have good leadership skills and work well as part of a team.

Earnings

Trainees earn £14,000 to £15,500. Salaries for coastguards usually start around £19,000 and can increase up to £32,000 with experience, but depend upon where you work. Watch assistants earn £17,000, and watch officers earn £21,000. Coastguards may also earn additional money for working shifts.

Info

Maritime and Coastguard Agency
www.gov.uk/government/organisations/
maritime-and-coastguard-agency

COLOUR SCIENCE AND TECHNOLOGY

Colour technologists are concerned with producing dyes and pigments that have a wide range of applications, including the textile, paint, rubber, plastics, paper, leather and foodstuffs industries. They must ensure that exact colours can be produced at an economic price and in the right quantities whenever they are needed. They are often involved in research and development projects. Technologists are also employed in sales, management, buying, development and research, quality control, customer liaison and technical services departments (depending on the industry involved and the expertise needed).

Textile technologists may work in the design, manufacture and operation of textile machinery, and in the design, production, colouration, finishing and manufacture of fibres, yarns and fabrics of all types.

Entry, qualifications and training

You can start as a technical assistant, a technician or a graduate trainee. Many applicants are graduates, but if you have good A level grades, especially chemistry, you may well get in as a technician. Larger companies often run formal training schemes of a year to 18 months. Preferred degree or HND subjects include analytical chemistry, applied chemistry, chemistry, colour science, maths, business studies and textiles technology. Some entrants are recruited with art degrees or HNDs in art and design. Most training is on the job and usually includes frequent short courses to ensure that you remain up to date with all the latest technical developments. You could also complete an apprenticeship; or a course or training with a professional body such as the Society of Dyers and Colourists.

Personal attributes

You need very good colour vision and technical ability, plus persistence in solving problems. You should be good at working as part of a team and also be able to develop a good sense of business awareness and the ability to work with and listen to customers or clients.

Earnings

New entrants earn £17,000 to £20,000 as technicians and £22,000 to £29,000 as graduate trainees. Salaries at senior level are £30,000 to £35,000.

COMPLEMENTARY OR ALTERNATIVE MEDICINE

The appeal and range of complementary or alternative (a term preferred by many practitioners) medicine and therapies on offer has grown in recent years. The occupations described here are not exhaustive, but give a cross-section of the more established ones. Some not covered here include colonic therapy, colour therapy and crystal healing. Here are some sources of further information common to many of the therapies listed here.

Acupuncturist

Acupuncture is a system of treatment that involves the insertion of fine needles into one or more points of the body to restore the overall health of the person and help alleviate symptoms from which they may be suffering. Acupuncture can also be used for relieving pain, and in China it is used to anaesthetise patients during operations. It has been practised in China and other Far Eastern countries for thousands of years and is a growing profession in the United Kingdom. Many health professionals, for example nurses and physiotherapists, train as acupuncturists. To practise as an acupuncturist you must take an in-depth course (usually around three years).

Alexander technique practitioner

Alexander technique practitioners teach a form of physical and mental well-being. Practitioners, usually working one-to-one with clients, teach them to develop better posture, poise, balance and coordination. They teach through demonstrating certain physical exercises and techniques, through manipulation, referred to as 'recoordinating', and through explaining and teaching relaxation techniques. Practitioners aim to teach a technique that can be applied to all aspects of daily life. Some clients may simply want to improve their sense of poise or well-being; others may wish to try the technique to help with emotional problems or physical aches and pains. Actors, musicians and other performers may employ Alexander technique practitioners to improve posture, presence and comportment.

Training – with one of three recognised training bodies – covers anatomy, physiology, biology and the science of movement. It also includes supervised practical sessions with clients.

Info

Society of Teachers of the Alexander Technique
020 8885 6524
www.stat.org.uk

Professional Association of Alexander Teachers (PAAT)
024 7671 4698
www.paat.org.uk

Aromatherapist

Aromatherapists use the organic essential oils from aromatic plants to treat a whole range of physical and emotional symptoms. Based on discussing a client's symptoms, lifestyle, diet, overall state of health, etc, the aromatherapist prescribes a combination of essential oils to treat the person. This is done either by massage, or by giving a client oils to use in their baths, on their pillows, or to scent their rooms. While aromatherapists may work in beauty salons, they are also employed by healthcare organisations and often work closely with GPs, nurses and other healthcare professionals. Certificate and diploma courses are run at a number of state and private colleges.

Info

Aromatherapy Council
www.aromatherapycouncil.org.uk

Chiropractor

Chiropractic is a healthcare profession concerned with, but not limited to, the diagnosis, treatment and prevention of structural and functional disorders affecting the musculo-skeletal system. Common complaints include low back and leg pain, headaches and neck and arm pain, as well as sports injuries. Working in a primary contact profession, a qualified chiropractor may be approached directly, without a medical referral, by patients seeking help.

Chiropractors are trained to utilise a wide variety of diagnostic techniques, including X-ray. Manual manipulation (adjustment) of spinal and extremity joints as well as soft-tissue structures is the most common treatment method employed. They will also offer advice on nutrition, rehabilitative exercises and modifications to activities of daily living. There is an increasing demand for chiropractic services and employment prospects are good both in the United Kingdom and in Europe.

To practise as a chiropractor, you must be registered with the General Chiropractic Council (GCC). To join the register, you need to complete a GCC accredited degree or Master's qualification – see the GCC website for a list of approved courses.

Info

British Chiropractic Association www.chiropractic-uk.co.uk	**United Chiropractic Association** www.unitedchiropractic.org
General Chiropractic Council (GCC) 020 7713 5155 www.gcc-uk.org	**McTimoney Chiropractic Association** 01491 739120 www.mctimoney-chiropractic.org
Scottish Chiropractic Association www.sca-chiropractic.org	

Homeopath

Homeopathy is a system of healing that assists the natural tendency of the body to heal itself. There are three main principles of homeopathy. First is treating like with like – what produces the symptoms of a disease may also cure it; the patient is treated by a small amount of the substance causing the symptoms and the natural defences are stimulated. Second, the lower the dose the better the result. Third, the remedy should be unique to the particular patient at a particular time. Homeopathic remedies may be used to treat almost any reversible illness in adults, children or animals.

Many newly qualified homeopaths set up in partnership in a clinic with other homeopaths and some now work with GPs in fund-holding practices. Homeopathic patients may come privately or be referred by GPs. Medical homeopaths (doctors who have trained in homeopathy) work as GPs, private practitioners or in one of the NHS homeopathic hospitals.

Info

Society of Homeopaths 01604 817890 www.homeopathy-soh.org	**British Homeopathic Association** 0203 640 5903 www.britishhomeopathic.org
Alliance of Registered Homeopaths 01825 714506 www.a-r-h.org	**Homeopathic Medical Association** 01474 560336 www.the-hma.org

---

Hypnotherapist

Hypnotherapists help people deal with a whole range of problems, from stress and anxiety to giving up smoking, losing weight or increasing self-confidence. They work by putting their clients in a deeply relaxed state where they can then absorb positive ideas that will help them deal with difficulties or to change their behaviour in some way. The three main training bodies, listed below, are working towards regulating the profession.

Info

The General Hypnotherapy Register (GHR)
www.general-hypnotherapy-register.com

National Hypnotherapy Society
01903 236 857
www.nationalhypnotherapysociety.org

National Council for Hypnotherapy (NCH)
0800 980 4419
www.hypnotherapists.org.uk

Skills for Health
020 7388 8800
www.skillsforhealth.org.uk

Massage therapist

Massage therapists use several different techniques, but they all involve using their hands and fingers to manipulate soft tissue. Most massage therapists are self-employed, but they may work in beauty salons, sports centres and private health clinics, or occasionally for the NHS. Massage therapists work with people who are in pain or suffering stress. They work with sports men and women who have suffered injury and they may work with babies and their parents to help calm babies and improve the bond between parent and child. There are many different techniques and schools of massage; Indian head massage, sports massage and body massage are some of the key specialisms. The General Council for Massage Therapies can give guidance on training.

Info

General Council for Massage Therapies
0870 850 4452
www.gcmt.org.uk

Massage Training Institute
www.massagetraining.co.uk

Sports Massage Association (SMA)
www.thesma.org

Naturopath

Naturopaths work in private practice; naturopathy is not offered by the NHS. They believe in treating the whole patient and in encouraging the body to cure itself, so do not generally give drugs, which, they consider, often treat the symptoms without dealing with the actual cause of a problem. A naturopath uses treatments designed to correct total body chemistry; diet is seen as a major factor and patients are encouraged to eat more natural food. Hydrotherapy is often used to stimulate the blood to a specific area of the body or to draw it away from another (by applying cold packs to combat throbbing headaches, for example).

Naturopaths also need to be skilled in psychology since they recognise that physiological complaints may frequently be caused by psychological problems. Any remedies used tend to be nutritional, herbal or homeopathic, and naturopaths may also be trained in acupuncture or other systems of alternative or complementary medicine. In the United Kingdom, naturopathy is closely linked to osteopathy, and many naturopaths are qualified osteopaths, using these skills in treating their patients. Graduate courses in naturopathy are offered by the British College of Osteopathic Medicine. The usual minimum entry requirements are three good A levels, one of which should be chemistry. Mature students may be considered on an individual basis.

Info

The General Council and Register of Naturopaths
01458 840072
www.gcrn.org.uk

British Naturopathic Association
www.the-bna.co.uk

Nutritional therapist

Nutritional therapists use an understanding of diet and nutrition to help their clients feel better. This could include advising in nutrition to encourage the body's own healing processes if someone is suffering from an illness, or it could be working with clients who want to improve their general sense of well-being. As a nutritional therapist you would normally work with clients one-to-one. Some of the conditions most likely to be treated by nutritional therapists are digestive problems, skin conditions, migraine and allergies. You would discuss your client's symptoms and medical history and based on this information suggest ways in which food and food supplements, or cutting out certain foods from the diet could help them to feel better. Training courses vary: ensure that you choose one that is recognised by the Nutritional Therapy Council.

Info

British Association for Nutrition and Lifestyle Medicine
01425 462532
www.bant.org.uk

Nutritional Therapy Education Commission (NTEC)
www.nteducationcommission.org.uk

Naturopathy Nutrition Association
01908 616543
www.nna-uk.com

Osteopath

Osteopathy is a system of diagnosis and treatment where the main emphasis is on conditions affecting the musculo-skeletal system. Osteopaths use predominantly gentle manual and manipulative methods of treatment to restore and maintain proper body function. They work in private practice and are increasingly being asked to work as part of mainstream medicine. All osteopaths are required to register with the General Osteopathic Council (GOsC). To practise as an osteopath, you need to take a degree approved by the General Osteopathy Council – you can find a list on their website.

Info

General Osteopathy Council (GOsC)
020 7357 6655
www.osteopathy.org.uk

Reflexologist

A reflexologist applies pressure to the feet, or to the hands, to stimulate the reflexes, which acts as a treatment to release tensions in the body, improving circulation and stimulating the body's own natural healing processes. A usual session conducted with a client involves applying pressure to the hands and feet, to clear blockages and improve circulation, easing tension and restoring the body's natural balance to all organs and parts of the body. Courses are available at colleges of further or higher education and private centres throughout the United Kingdom.

Info

Association of Reflexologists
01823 351010
www.aor.org.uk

Reiki healer

Reiki healing is a form of energy-based healing founded in Japan. Reiki healers endeavour to guide energies through the bodies of their clients, attempting to activate natural healing processes within the body. There are many systems of Reiki, but they all aim to help physical, emotional, mental or spiritual problems. Reiki is used to treat pain, stress and tiredness and it aims to induce calm and increase clients' energy levels. It is sometimes used in conjunction with traditional and other complementary therapies.

During a Reiki session, the client lies fully clothed on a bed or sits in a chair while the healer places his or her hands in a sequence of positions over the client's body. The whole body is treated rather than specific symptoms or areas. Treatment can take between one and two hours. Reiki is non-diagnostic, non-interventionist and non-manipulative and no pressure is applied.

Training can be through one-to-one sessions with a Reiki master or healer, or through courses offered at college.

Info

UK Reiki Federation
020 3432 6827
www.reikifed.co.uk

Reiki Association
www.reikiassociation.co.uk

Reiki Council
www.reikicouncil.org.uk

Entry, qualifications and training

You will need to check the requirements for the particular therapy you are interested in with the relevant regulatory or parent organisation.

Personal attributes

The balance of skills that are most important varies between some of the above roles, but good interpersonal skills, with an ability to put people at their ease and reassure them are essential. For osteopaths, chiropractors, acupuncturists and massage therapists, manual dexterity and practical skills as well as a sound theoretical knowledge of the body are necessary. As many alternative therapists are self-employed, you may also require administrative and organisational skills to market and run your business.

Earnings

Salaries vary depending on hours worked, numbers of patients and fee scales. Fees range from around £25 to £100 an hour.

CONSERVATION

(see also Environment and environmental conservation)

Conservation falls broadly into two categories: cultural heritage and the environment. They are each concerned with protecting and preserving – the former our cultural history and the latter the natural environment. This section deals with cultural and heritage conservation.

Conservator

Conservators and restorers look after historic buildings, paintings, pieces of sculpture, ancient books, historic tapestries, carvings, pieces of furniture and other objects. Conservators examine items for any signs of damage or deterioration. They do their best to ensure that objects are looked after properly, and protected and preserved in the most effective ways possible. Finally, they may take steps to restore them to something as close as possible to their original condition.

Conservators have to understand the effect of the environment on different materials, and to ensure that objects are not stored or displayed in harmful conditions. They have to be aware of and be able to control light, humidity, temperature and sources of pollution. They employ many different scientific techniques and they make photographic records of their work.

Entry, qualifications and training

Most conservators have a degree. You need either a degree in art followed by a specialist postgraduate qualification in conservation, or a degree in a specific area of art, e.g. ceramics and glass, or textiles. The Institute of Conservation lists relevant courses on its website. Highly skilled and experienced craftsmen and women who do not have a degree may also be able to get into conservation work if they can demonstrate their practical skills and knowledge of working with specific materials. Apprenticeships and internships are also ways that you can enter this career.

Personal attributes

Conservators must have a blend of interests in artistic, scientific and technical matters. They have to pay close attention to detail and be prepared to work patiently and extremely carefully. They also need to be good communicators, being able to explain their requirements and concerns convincingly.

Earnings

A salary of around £24,500 for entry-level conservators is recommended by The Institute of Conservation. This rises to around £27,000 after two or three years' experience. Senior conservators can earn between £30,000 and £35,000. If you develop a really good reputation and are able to work on prestigious pieces, you may earn more than this, up to £60,000. The cultural and arts sector has been hit by cuts, so salaries may remain somewhat static in this sector.

Info

British Antique Furniture Restorers' Association (BAFRA)
01939 210826
www.bafra.org.uk

Creative & Cultural Skills
020 7015 1800
www.ccskills.org.uk

Institute of Conservation
020 3142 6799
www.icon.org.uk

Museums Association
www.museumsassociation.org

International Institute for Conservation of Historic and Artistic Works
020 7799 5500
www.iiconservation.org

CONSTRUCTION

(see also Surveying for Building surveying and Engineering for Civil engineer)

It is estimated that one in fourteen people in the UK workforce works in construction. Construction is a broad sector. Houses, flats, schools, hospitals, shops, factories, theatres, restaurants, garages, sports stadia, hotels, stables, care homes and warehouses are all examples of buildings. The construction industry encompasses a wide range of occupations involved in the construction and fitting out of new buildings and redeveloping and refurbishing existing building stock.

Construction trades

There are many different construction trades: carpenters, painters and decorators, electricians, plasterers, plumbers and roofers. While they each require specific knowledge and technical skills, they share similar patterns of training and professional qualifications. Check the Entry, qualifications and training section at the end of this entry to find out about the different ways to train and qualify.

Carpenter

There are several different jobs covered by the general term 'carpenter' – what they all have in common is that carpenters work with wood. They use wood to make doors, window frames, skirting boards, floorboards, cupboards and all the other woodwork you can think of in any domestic, public or commercial building. Some of the different roles include bench joiners, who prepare doors and window frames in a workshop ready for other workers to install them in properties; carpenters and joiners who work on site or inside or outside buildings, fitting cupboards, doors, window frames, etc; and wood machinists who prepare floorboards and skirting boards in the workshop ready for the carpenter and joiner to fix in place and finish.

Demolition operative

Demolishing a building properly and safely is one of the most highly skilled areas in construction. Demolition operatives use heavy machinery to bring down walls, buildings and other structures. They have to be acutely aware of safety, calculating exactly how a building will collapse. They are also involved in clearance of the site once the building has been razed to the ground.

Roofer

Roofs come in many different shapes and sizes and are made from many different materials. It is the job of roofers to fix roofs onto buildings and to ensure that these roofs are safe and weatherproof. Within roofing there are several different specialist trades: felt roofing, tiling and slating, lead roofing and many more. You may choose to work mainly with one of these materials and become a specialist, or you may decide to work with all the different types of roofing material.

Scaffolder

Scaffolders build scaffolding that might be used in demolition, but more significantly in construction. They build scaffolding from steel tubes and wooden platforms, and it is essential they build scaffolding that is safe for other construction workers to stand on and work from.

Steeplejack

Steeplejacks work not just on steeples, but also on any high structures; chimneys, clock towers, etc. They have to work at a great height, using special safety equipment, but also have to have a good working knowledge of many different trades because they are likely to have to carry out repairs to and with many different materials: glass, wood, paint, plaster, mortar, etc.

Interior and finishing trades

Once a basic structure has been completed by bricklayers, carpenters, roofers, etc, there is still a great deal of work needed to make the building comfortable to live or work in and useful for the purpose for which it has been built. Ceiling fixers, floor layers, glaziers, painters and decorators, plasterers and plumbers are examples of some of the interior and finishing trades on offer.

Ceiling fixer

Ceiling fixers and dry liners install ceilings, especially in large modern buildings with large expanses of high ceiling. They build structures to fit large sheets of plasterboard to, and cover the whole thing with a very thin layer of plaster.

Electrician

(see Electrician)

Glazier

Glaziers work with glass, installing glass windows, doors and glass partitions. They have to be skilled in cutting and fixing glass, from basic double-glazing to more ornate glass effects.

Painter and decorator

No building looks complete until the important finishing touches of painting, wood staining and papering have been applied. Painters and decorators work inside and outside all kinds of buildings, from private houses to large warehouses, shops and offices.

Plasterer

This is a highly skilled occupation, as plasterers have to line walls or ceilings with a layer of even, smooth and attractive plaster to act as a basis for painting, wallpaper or other finishes. They have to work quickly, achieving the desired finish before the plaster dries out. Some plasterers go on to develop skills in ornamental and decorative plasterwork.

Plumber

Plumbers install and maintain all the necessary pipes, valves, tanks, boilers, etc that keep water and heating systems flowing through any building. They install and maintain drainage systems and repair flashing on roofs.

Tiler

Tilers fix tiles to walls and floors. The work might involve tiling a bathroom or kitchen in a private house, or working as part of a team fitting out a restaurant, hotel or hospital. The work involves marking out areas to be tiled, calculating the quantity of tiles required, preparing the surface, fitting the tiles and finishing with grout or other products. Tilers may be self-employed, work for or with other builders, or for specialist tiling supply companies who employ their own tilers.

Trowel trades

If you work with brick or stone you will learn one of these trades. Of the many construction occupations available, these offer you the chance to be creative as well as using practical skills.

Bricklayer

Bricklayers build the external and internal walls of all kinds of buildings, from private houses to large hospitals, hotels and offices. They build garden walls and lay patios. They work mainly with ready-prepared bricks, building them up in layers, working to produce smooth and weatherproof results.

Stonemason

Stonemasons have employed their skills for hundreds of years, using natural stone as their basic building material. Today stonemasons work both restoring historic buildings and building modern structures. This is highly skilled work and a flair for design as well as practical ability is very important.

Supervisory roles

With so many different workers involved in building projects, both large and small, it is very important that there are people to take overall responsibility for employing workers, purchasing materials, health and safety, and day-to-day management.

Construction project manager

Construction project managers have overall responsibility for the planning, management, coordination and financial control of a construction project. It is their responsibility to see that the clients' wishes are adhered to and that the project is completed on time within the agreed budget.

Site manager

Many site technicians become site managers, taking on more responsibility for larger projects and being in charge of everything that happens on the site.

Site technician

Site technicians get involved with the general running and safety of the site. Your role would include hiring and buying materials and machinery, and organising people and equipment. It would be your responsibility to ensure that budgets and plans are followed, and that everything meets technical requirements.

To become a site technician, you will need to have a strong knowledge of building methods and materials, and health and safety requirements, which you will have to teach workers on your site. You will need good communication and organisational skills, a high level of competence in computing, and work well as part of a team.

There are no specific academic entry requirements to train as a site technician, though it is helpful to have GCSE/Standard Grade passes in science, maths and technology for the measurements and planning.

Entry, qualifications and training

While the array of training routes can seem daunting; there are three ways into construction trades at craft and technical levels. These are through having relevant work experience, through an apprenticeship, or through a college course followed by training with an employer. If you already work on a building site as a labourer, your employer may be prepared to support you through training in one of the building trades.

If you would like to serve a traditional apprenticeship (TA) in a construction trade, you need to find an employer who will take you on and provide the work experience while sending you on day-release to college. During your apprenticeship you normally work towards NVQ levels 2 or 3. How many apprenticeships are on offer and in what trades varies throughout the country; Construction Skills has up-to-date information on availability. To do an apprenticeship you normally need three or four GCSEs grades 9–4, including maths, English and a technical subject. These requirements do vary, though, so check with local colleges and employers.

There are many full-time courses in construction available at local colleges. Entry requirements and exact qualifications vary widely.

If you are still at school and are thinking about careers in construction, a few schools have introduced a new diploma course for 14- to 19-year-olds, but these are not available very widely.

Personal attributes

While a variety of trades have been described and each has its special requirements, there are many skills and qualities that are important for all these occupations. You need to have a special interest in and feel for the particular material you are working with – wood, metal, plaster, stone, etc. You must be good at measuring and calculating, working out how much material you will need, and measuring exactly to ensure that something fits.

For all jobs you must be physically fit, though some work, such as bricklaying, is especially demanding. You may have to climb up and down scaffolding, work outside in unpleasant weather, or work in cramped spaces such as somebody's loft. You need to get on with people. You often work as part of a team, and if you progress to supervisory or management roles you have to be organised and be good at motivating other people. If you are working in private houses, you must be polite, pleasant and trustworthy, and good at coming up with solutions to problems. If you become self-employed you must develop good business and financial skills.

Earnings

For construction trades, pay on completion of an apprenticeship is between around £16,500 and £23,000. Labourers earn £15,000 to £18,000. Experienced construction trades workers can earn up to £36,000 if they have supervisory or training responsibilities. The national rate for apprentices under the age of 19 is £3.40 an hour, but employers may pay more as skills are developed.

Salaries for management posts range from £25,000 to £40,000. Salaries for project managers in large construction projects can go up to £85,000. The construction industry is particularly sensitive to downturns in the economy, and job opportunities vary accordingly.

CRAFTS

Crafts include a diverse mix of occupations involving designing and making useful and/or decorative objects. Such objects can be made of glass, wood, porcelain, metal, leather or living flowers and plants. The medium in which you choose to work affects the skills you require and the training you need to follow. Work is at many levels, from working on a fairly routine production process in a factory to designing and making individual pieces. Here are some common sources of information for many craft occupations.

Blacksmith

Some traditional, rural crafts have enjoyed a revival in interest, and blacksmithing is one of these. Blacksmiths are craftspeople who work with metals including iron, steel, copper and bronze. They heat metal in a forge until it is hot enough to bend or cut and then make it into decorative and very useful objects. Blacksmiths can also make horseshoes, but they need to be qualified as farriers if they are to fit shoes to horses. They might make wrought iron gates, railings, garden furniture, tools and ornaments. They might use traditional hand tools such as hammer and tongs, or modern power tools. Some blacksmiths work in industry designing highly specialized metal tools, but many are self-employed.

Entry, qualifications and training

There are two ways to train. You can either work with a qualified and experienced blacksmith who can train you in the relevant skills. To train by this route, you need to approach individual blacksmiths to see whether they are able to take you on. The alternative is to qualify through a full-time college course. Directories of blacksmiths can be obtained from either the Worshipful Company of Blacksmiths or The British Artist Blacksmiths Association. There are several full-time college courses, including a BA available at Herefordshire and Ludlow College. For work on the industrial side, you may be able to train through an apprenticeship with an engineering company.

Personal attributes

You have to be practical, physically fit and have good hand–eye coordination. If you are making artistic objects and ornaments you will also need creative flair. If working for yourself, you will need to be able to manage your business and market your products.

Earnings

When you are training or doing an apprenticeship pay is likely to be around the minimum wage. Once qualified and experienced you can earn £25,000 to £28,000 – sometimes more.

Info

The Worshipful Company of Blacksmiths
www.blacksmithscompany.co.uk

The British Artist Blacksmiths Association
www.baba.org.uk

Florist

Florists design and create flower arrangements and displays such as table decorations, bridal bouquets, sprays and wreaths. They also sell cut flowers and plants. Florists work mostly with fresh flowers and plants, but may also use silk or other artificial and dried flowers, grasses and natural objects. The work can include providing office displays, making arrangements for banquets, functions and receptions, and decorating hotels and public buildings. Other aspects of the job include selecting and buying stock and running the business side of a shop or floristry business.

Entry, qualifications and training

You don't need formal qualifications to train as a florist and most florists train on the job while studying part time for relevant NVQs in floristry at levels 2 and 3. Helping out in a florist's shop or joining a flower arranging group can strengthen your application. An intermediate and advanced apprenticeship in floristry is another route you could take to enter this career.

There are a few foundation degree and degree courses in professional floristry offered at some land-based colleges. For experienced florists, there are some part-time level 4 and level 5 qualifications in floristry and floristry business.

Personal attributes

You must love working with flowers and plants and have an artistic flair for colour and design. You also need good customer skills, helping people plan flowers for weddings and funerals. You need good business skills if you wish to work for yourself or manage a shop. You are often responsible for choosing and purchasing the flowers you use.

Earnings

Trainees earn around the minimum wage. With experience you can earn £17,000 to £20,000. If you manage a shop you could earn £23,000 to £25,000. If you become self-employed earnings vary, but can be £30,000 plus if you are successful.

Info

British Florist Association
www.britishfloristassociation.org

Lantra
02476 696996
www.lantra.co.uk

Jewellery trade

Design

Jewellery designers craft a wide variety of items either by hand or using methods of large-scale production. These may be very expensive, traditionally styled pieces using gold or platinum, cheaper costume jewellery using synthetic stones and base metals, or fashion accessories made from beads, plastic or wood.

Although there are a few openings for designers of expensive jewellery, the more costly costume jewellery and mass-produced jewellery, there is more scope for original designers on either a freelance or artist/craftsperson basis, making fashionable ranges with semi-precious stones.

Manufacture

The jewellery, silverware and allied industries encompass a vast range of specialist skills. Apart from mounting and silversmithing, other skills needed to support these occupations include gem setting, engraving (hand and machine), enamelling, chasing, engine turning, spinning, electroplating and polishing.

Entry, qualifications and training

To work in a jeweller's shop you do not need any formal qualifications, but some employers do expect you to have GCSEs in maths and English. Training is usually with a more experienced jeweller and you can take NVQs levels 2 and 3 in retail sales and retail operations.

You can study for a Professional Jewellers' Diploma with the National Association of Goldsmiths (NAG). This covers introductions to precious metals, gemstones and hallmarks (the marks that certify a precious metal's quality). This is a distance-learning course that lasts about 18 months. NAG also runs a Professional Jewellers' Management Diploma designed for shop managers or people who would like to become shop managers. There are several independent training courses available for jewellers.

In the jewellery manufacturing trades there are a number of apprenticeships available. Most jewellery designers have a degree in three-dimensional design and have specialised in jewellery design within that course.

Personal attributes

For retail jewellery work you have to have good communication and customer care skills and a real interest in the products you are selling. You should have an eye for detail and an awareness of colour and fashion. You need good numeracy skills and you should be highly dextrous, easily able to handle small and expensive items carefully. Anyone working in jewellery manufacture must be practical and careful, with an interest in scientific and technical processes as well as artistic effect.

Jewellery designers have to be artistic and imaginative, with a good understanding of the properties of different metals, gems and other materials. They also need to be good at promoting their products and have a sound understanding of business.

Earnings

Pay for people working in jewellers' shops starts at around the minimum wage and can go up to more than £30,000, depending on the type of shop. Store managers earn between £17,000 and £45,000. Some own their own businesses, including online jewellery stores. In manufacturing, salaries range from around £14,000 to £18,000 depending on your level of skill and experience.

Jewellery designers earn between around £15,000 and £25,000. Some designers with flair and good market instincts can earn far more than this, especially if they are designing jewellery for the rich and famous.

Info

Creative & Cultural Skills
020 7015 8100
www.ccskills.org.uk

Design Council
020 7420 5200
www.designcouncil.org.uk

The Goldsmiths Company
020 7606 7010
www.thegoldsmiths.co.uk

Goldsmiths Company Directory
www.directory.thegoldsmiths.co.uk

National Association of Goldsmiths (NAG)
020 7613 4445
www.jewellers-trainingonline.org

People 1st (for jewellery retail)
020 3074 1222
www.people1st.co.uk

Leather craftworker

Leather craftworkers make and repair leather items. These include clothing, footwear, furnishings and accessories like handbags and wallets. Some leather craftworkers specialise in products such as saddles and bridles for horses, book covers or weapons and armour for historical societies or theatre companies. The work involves cutting various types of leather from patterns, hand or machine stitching pieces of leather together, fitting fastenings such as buckles, adding linings of other materials and applying finishes such as wax or stains.

Leather technologist

Leather technologists prepare the leather used by craft workers. This involves treating raw leather with various chemical processes such as curing, tanning and liming. It may also involve grading the leather and choosing which types of products it is most suitable for. The work also involves dyeing, finishing and smoothing the leather. Leather technologists work for large manufacturers, small businesses and with individual leather craftworkers.

Entry, qualifications and training

It is not straightforward to get into leather craftwork. You may be able to do an apprenticeship in textiles that includes leatherwork. Alternatively you may be able to do a university degree or college course in fashion and textiles that includes leatherwork, particularly all the practical skills you need to work with these materials.

If you are particularly interested in saddlery, the Worshipful Company of Saddlers and the Society of Master Saddlers run the Saddlery Apprenticeship Scheme, which lasts for four years. You may need to relocate to take up training or employment, especially if you are thinking about rural leather crafts. A lot of training is on the job, learning skills from more experienced craftworkers, but there are several NVQs you can work towards. These include Leather Production levels 2 and 3, Leather Goods level 2 and Footwear and Leather Products Manufacture level 3.

Personal attributes

You need good manual dexterity working with a range of highly specialised tools and equipment. You should have a real interest in the field in which you work, whether this is a rural craft like saddlery, or high fashion. You should be able to work accurately, taking measurements and adding fine detail. You may also need good customer skills.

Earnings

New entrants earn around the minimum wage. Experienced craftworkers can earn up to £20,000. Leather technologists earn £15,000 to £19,000. Senior technologists can earn over £30,000 a year.

Info

The Heritage Crafts Association
www.heritagecrafts.org.uk

Society of Master Saddlers
01449 711 642
www.mastersaddlers.co.uk

Screen Skills
020 7713 9800
www.screenskills.com

The Saddlery Training Centre
www.saddlerytraining.com

Society of Leather Technologists and Chemists
www.sltc.org

Picture framer

Picture framers frame pictures and other artworks of all styles, working for galleries, artists or customers who want a picture, photograph or poster professionally framed. They also frame 3D objects such as dried flowers, seashells, medals and 3D artworks. They work with many types of materials, including wood and metal. They often advise their customers on what type of frame would best suit a particular piece of art, on some occasions visiting the location where the art is to be displayed.

Entry, qualifications and training

There are no formal entry qualifications for this work, though there are several short and part-time courses run on how to become a picture framer. The Fine Art Trade Guild is the trade association for the sector. You can attain its Guild Commended Framer award by taking tests that are offered at centres throughout the United Kingdom. The award is internationally recognised as the qualification for the framing industry.

The Guild also awards advanced qualifications in textiles and mount design and cutting. Guild members are listed in the Guild directory. Membership of the Guild also helps you keep current with new ideas and fashions and to be kept informed of any further courses that might prove useful for you.

Personal attributes

You need a flair for design, and a good appreciation of how to use both colour and texture. You need very precise practical skills, able to measure, cut and work with great accuracy. You need to be able to work well with people when giving advice, but you also spend a great deal of time working on your own. Since picture framers are almost always self-employed, you also have to have good business and marketing skills.

Earnings

Earnings range from the minimum wage to £18,000 if you are working the equivalent of full-time hours. Many picture framers do this work part time and combine it with another job or other activities. With experience, picture framers can earn up to £30,000.

Info

Fine Art Trade Guild
020 7381 6616
www.fineart.co.uk

Potter/ceramic designer

Potters make and design objects from clay. They work with basic earthenware and fine porcelain, making everything from basic kitchen- and tableware to ornaments and individual pieces of art. They may design items for the mass market that will be made on a factory production line. At the other extreme they make expensive individual items to be sold through galleries and displayed at exhibitions. Designers working with mass-market producers will have to liaise with buyers, production managers and other staff and will often play a quality control role in the whole process. Designers who are successful enough to work for themselves will work in a studio with their own wheel, kiln, etc.

Entry, qualifications and training

Most pottery/ceramics designers are graduates with a degree in ceramics or 3D design. If you are considering a course, it is worth checking what practical skills the course covers in addition to its artistic and creative content. To be taken on by a company or a design studio you will need to put together a portfolio of photographs of your work. If you are self-employed, there is a wide range of courses available through local adult education institutes and short-course details are also available from the Studio Pottery website. It is important if you are self-employed to keep up to date with new trends in design, new materials, glazes, techniques, etc.

If you wish to work in the more routine work on the manufacturing side, you will not need formal qualifications.

Personal attributes

You must love creating something with your hands and have a flair for design and good awareness of colour. You need to be imaginative, creative and practical. You need good people skills, being able to interpret design briefs given to you or for working with buyers from shops and galleries. If working for yourself, you need good business acumen.

Earnings

If you are employed by a company or studio, starting pay is around £16,000, rising to between £25,000 and £30,000 with more experience. If you are self-employed, income is much more difficult to predict and can be much lower than for employed designers. Like many art and craft careers, potters may have to boost their artistic earnings by taking on other, more routine work. Many potters increase their income by teaching on pottery courses.

Info

Studio Pottery
www.studiopottery.co.uk

Thatcher

Thatchers are self-employed craftspeople who roof, re-roof or repair thatched buildings with long straw, combed wheat straw, reed and other materials. The materials and methods they use have to preserve the building in its original form. A thatched roof gives good insulation against heat and cold and lasts 20 to 50 years. A roof is thatched by taking off the old thatch and then pegging down layers of new straw or reed.

Entry, qualifications and training

Academic qualifications are not essential. Thatching can be learnt on the job as an apprentice to a Master Thatcher. Training takes four to five years. The Construction Industry Training Board (CITB) offers a Level 2 NVQ Diploma in Roofing Occupations with a specific pathway in Thatching.

Personal attributes

Thatchers need to be robust, good with their hands and not mind bad weather or heights. They also need common sense, and the ability to make decisions and to deal with customers.

Earnings

Salaries start at around the minimum wage, rising to £24,000 with two or three years' experience. In some regions it is possible to earn more than this because there is a high demand for thatches.

Info

National Society of Master Thatchers
www.nsmtltd.co.uk

CUSTOMS AND EXCISE

Customs officers or Border Force Officers work for Her Majesty's Revenue & Customs (HMRC) and the UK Visas and Immigration and Border Force. For officers based at ports and airports (detection officers), the work is sometimes high profile – seizures of drugs or the prevention of human trafficking. Much of the work is more routine but vital; checking people, luggage and documents to ensure that nothing illegal is being brought in or removed from the country. Officers are also responsible for the collection of a range of taxes and duties. They visit businesses, ensuring that the correct duty is being paid on petrol, alcohol or tobacco, for example.

Entry, qualifications and training

You can join either as an administrative assistant or assistant officer or as a direct entrant customs officer or detection officer. To join as an assistant you need five GCSEs grades 9–4, including maths and English. For direct officer entry you must also have two A levels. If you do not meet these selection criteria HMRC do set selection tests to assess your suitability. These test your communication and teamwork skills as well as English and maths. The majority of training is on the job.

Personal attributes

You must be able to get on with people, being polite, tactful and able to question and listen carefully. You should be honest and fair and be able to analyse complex information. For much of the work on the excise and VAT side you must have good numeracy skills.

Earnings

Assistant officers earn between £18,000 and £21,000, officers earn £19,000 to £23,000 and higher grade officers earn between £25,000 and £39,000. At all levels you may earn more through extra payments for working unsocial hours and the higher salaries are in London.

Administrative grade salaries are between £15,000 and £21,000. Junior managers earn between £20,000 and £25,000. Senior managers can earn more than £40,000.

Info

HMRC
www.hmrc.gov.uk

Working for HMRC
www.gov.uk/government/organisations/
hm-revenue-customs/about/recruitment

DENTISTRY

There are many roles besides that of dentist – all combining to provide dental care and services in the National Health Service and private dental care services.

Dentist

Dentists work to keep teeth and gums healthy. They try to prevent, detect and treat tooth decay and gum disease. This involves examining, filling, crowning and extracting teeth, scaling, and cleaning teeth and gums. They design and fit dentures and plates and take corrective measures for teeth growing abnormally. Cosmetic dentistry, whitening or fixing veneers to teeth, is also an expanding area of their work. They are also involved with the rectification of fractured jaws and surgery of the mouth. Much of the dentist's work today is highly technical and requires a lot of manual dexterity. There is growing emphasis on preventive work, and the dentist is expected to counsel and educate.

Opportunities exist both in the United Kingdom and abroad. In general, dental practice dentists work on contract to the NHS, but growing numbers work in private clinics. Some work in hospitals, community services, school services or the armed forces. There are also opportunities for dentists to work in university dental teaching and research.

Specialist areas of dentistry include paediatric dentistry, orthodontics and oral and maxillofacial surgery.

Entry, qualifications and training

To practise as a dentist you must have completed a five-year degree in dentistry – either a BDS or a BChD. To gain a place on one of these courses you must have three A levels (grade requirements vary from AAA to ABB), including biology, chemistry and either maths or physics; some courses are specifically designed for graduates. Some dental schools offer a pre-dental foundation year in science for graduates without suitable science qualifications.

All entrants are assessed at interview on a list of criteria. These are: strong academic ability, self-discipline, commitment to completing this long and demanding degree course, manual dexterity and technical dental skills, plus the ability to maintain intense concentration for prolonged periods and to build relationships with patients and colleagues, high-level communication and interpersonal skills for interaction with patients of all ages and backgrounds, an interest in the welfare of others and a sympathetic manner, good administrative and managerial abilities, information technology skills owing to the increasing use of computers for keeping records and accounts, and for digital imaging of and intra-oral photography. After completing your degree you have to do a period of vocational radiographs training with an approved dental practitioner.

After graduating, trainee dentists take a foundation year referred to as DF1. As a qualified dentist you can specialise by doing further postgraduate training in a specific area of interest, for example orthodontics (straightening or moving teeth).

Personal attributes

As is clear from the skills required by dental schools, you have to be strong academically, with excellent manual dexterity and a real ability to work well with people. You have to be very resilient: most patients are stressed and/or uncomfortable when they visit a dentist, so your people skills contribute enormously to your potential success.

Earnings

Dentists' earnings are affected by the type of work they do and the balance of NHS and private work they undertake. During the foundation year dentists earn £32,050. Dental core trainees earn a basic salary between £37,935 and £48,075. Salaried dentists employed by the NHS who have completed their training earn a basic salary of between £40,629 and £87,000. Some work, such as private cosmetic dentistry, can be very lucrative and take earnings to more than £150,000. The most senior consultant dentists in the NHS earn a basic annual salary of £102,465.

Dental hygienist

Dental hygienists clean, polish and scale teeth and in some cases prepare patients for oral operations. Through lectures and practical experience they also endeavour to educate children and adults on the importance of proper dental care. Dental hygienists work to the written prescription of a dentist.

Entry, qualifications and training

To qualify as a dental hygienist you must complete either a two year foundation degree or diploma in oral health science; a two year diploma of higher education in dental hygiene, or dental hygiene and dental therapy; or a three-year degree in oral health science, or dental therapy and dental hygiene. If you have experience as a dental nurse, this may prove useful. A recognised dental nurse qualification can sometimes take the place of an A level for entry. You will usually require one or two A levels, or equivalent, for a foundation degree or higher national diploma; two to three A levels, or equivalent, for a degree. You normally need A levels for the degree course. The General Dental Council (GDC) website gives a full list of all these courses.

Personal attributes

Manual and visual dexterity is required. Candidates should have an ability to communicate in order to educate patients in good dental hygiene practice. The ability to work in a team is important.

Earnings

Starting salary for a dental hygienist is around £24,000 and can increase to around £37,000 with experience. In some fashionable private practices, earnings can be higher than this.

Dental nurse

Dental nurses prepare the surgery and get the appropriate instruments ready. During treatment they assist the dentist by passing instruments, mixing materials, taking notes from the dentist's dictation for records and making sure the patient is comfortable at all times. Once the patient has left, the dental nurse tidies the surgery and sterilises all the instruments. Sometimes, particularly in general practice, dental nurses also help with reception work – making appointments, taking payments, dealing with the paperwork, meeting and reassuring patients.

Entry, qualifications and training

Many dentists like to train their own assistants and expect applicants to have four GCSEs, including English, maths and a science. Dental nurses must obtain NVQ level 3 in Oral Healthcare or pass the National Certificate of the Examining Board for Dental Nurses. Preparation for this exam can be either at evening or day-release courses or via a full-time college course lasting one to two years. Dental nurses also have to complete two years' practical training in a dental practice.

Personal attributes

Candidates should be equable, sympathetic and have an agreeable nature and an ability to communicate. Good administrative and managerial skills and the ability to work in a team are important.

Earnings

Average earnings range between a starting salary of around £18,813 and £30,112 with more experience. In private practice, earnings vary depending on type of practice and its location. In the NHS, dental nurses earn between ££19,400 and £23,000, while team leader nurses in large practices or hospital dental departments can earn up to £28,400.

Dental technician

Dental technicians design and fabricate a wide variety of different materials and equipment to make crowns, dentures, metal plates, bridges, orthodontic braces and other appliances prescribed by a dentist.

Entry, qualifications and training

To work as a dental technician you must be registered with the General Dental Council and to obtain registration you must complete a dental technician course. These are offered at BTEC diploma, foundation degree and degree level. You can either study full time or apply for a traineeship with a private dental laboratory or a hospital and study on a part-time basis. This usually takes four to five years.

Personal attributes

Good technical skills and the ability to work in a team need to be combined with good people skills, being able to put people at ease, listen to questions and address patients' concerns.

Earnings

Earnings for dental technicians vary between £24,000 for a starting salary and up to £44,000 with more experience.

Dental therapist

Dental therapists work in local authority clinics and hospitals, assisting dentists by carrying out simpler forms of treatment such as fillings and the extraction of first teeth. They also give guidance on general dental care. Dental therapists must always work to the written prescription of a dentist.

Entry, qualifications and training

To become a dental therapist you must take either a diploma in dental therapy or a degree in oral health sciences, including modules on dental therapy and hygiene. The British Association of Dental Therapists (BADT) can provide details of relevant dental schools; diploma courses last two years, degree courses three years.

To get onto either course you need five GCSEs grades 9–4, including human biology, plus two A levels. If you are already a qualified and experienced dental nurse you may be able to do a course without meeting the usual academic requirements. You could also consider entering this career via an advanced apprenticeship as a dental nurse.

Personal attributes

You must be very good at working with people, able to reassure, be calm, encourage and teach. You should have an interest in science and healthcare and you should also be practical, with good manual dexterity and good eyesight. You must be physically fit and resilient.

Earnings

Pay varies, but usually starts around £24,000, and can increase up to £37,000 with experience. With more experience, and working in private practice, you may earn more than this.

Info

NHS Careers
0345 60 60 655
www.healthcareers.nhs.uk

British Dental Association
020 7 935 0875
www.bda.org

General Dental Council
020 7167 6000
www.gdc-uk.org

British Society of Dental Hygiene and Therapy
01788 575050
www.bsdht.org.uk

National Examining Body for Dental Nurses
01772 429917
www.nebdn.org

British Association of Dental Nurses (BADN)
www.badn.org.uk

British Association of Dental Therapists (BADT)
0161 665 5878 (11am to 3pm)
www.badt.org.uk

DIETICIAN

Dieticians study the scientific basis of food and nutrition and then apply that knowledge to giving practical advice and support to people about food and health. They work in hospitals and clinics, in care homes in the community and in the food manufacturing industry.

What your work entailed would depend on where you worked. In a hospital you could be working with individual patients with eating disorders, allergies, or conditions such as diabetes. You could also work with catering staff to ensure that food prepared and served was nutritionally balanced and that special diets such as gluten-free or vegan options were on offer. In industry you could work with manufacturers to help develop new products for the general food market or for specialised services such as food for schools or care homes or meals delivered direct to people's own homes. Working in the community, you could be involved in education, or in one-to-one work with people, teaching them about better food and nutrition.

Entry, qualifications and training

To work as a dietician in the NHS you need either a degree in dietetics or human nutrition or a postgraduate qualification in dietetics. If you choose to do a degree, then you must have three A levels, grades 9–4 including chemistry and one other science. If you opt for the postgraduate route, then you need a good honours degree in a life science, medicine or nutrition. You should check with the British Dietetic Association (BDA) to ensure that the course you are considering meets the approved professional standards.

If you do not want to go through higher education, you may be able to start work as a dietetic assistant in the NHS and train to NVQ level 3 in Allied Health Professions (Support) Dietetics. Applicants for assistants' posts need to have four GCSEs grades 9–4 usually including maths, English and a science.

Personal attributes

You have to be extremely good at talking to people, listening to them and explaining complex information in a way that can be easily understood. You also have to be able to tell people things they would rather not hear. You have to have an aptitude for and an interest in scientific and medical concepts. You have to be able to work well as part of a health professionals team. You may also need presentation skills to explain ideas to groups of people rather than always working one-to-one.

Earnings

Newly qualified dieticians earn around £24,000, with experience and responsibility this can rise up to £37,000. Working in London you earn an additional 20 per cent and 15 per cent in outer London.

Info

Health and Care Professions Council (HCPC)
0300 500 6184
www.hcpc-uk.org

NHS Careers
0345 60 60 655
www.healthcareers.nhs.uk

British Dietetic Association (BDA)
0121 200 8080
www.bda.uk.com

DISC JOCKEY

(see Music)

DIVER

Divers work for many different employers. Some work in the oil and gas industry and for companies that construct offshore wind turbines, surveying, checking and building rigs and pipelines. They work for the police, searching and retrieving evidence or attempting rescues, for the media in underwater filming, and for fish farms, checking stock and equipment. They may also work for surveying companies or for archaeological research. Divers work in the sea, in rivers, in lakes, canals and reservoirs. Divers also work as instructors, either training others to become professional divers or working in outdoor education and leisure, teaching people who are interested in recreational diving. They normally specialise in a particular type of diving and this is determined by how deep they have to dive and by what kind of breathing apparatus they use.

Entry, qualifications and training

You must be extremely physically fit to train as a diver. You must pass a strict medical before you can start to train and you have to pass annual medicals throughout your diving career. Both the medical and the diving training course you complete have to be approved by the Health and Safety Executive (HSE) before you can work as a commercial diver. Professional Association of Diving Instructors (PADI), and British Sub-Aqua Club, for example, offer such courses.

Although you don't need academic qualifications for the actual diving, you may well need qualifications relevant to the industry in which you are working. Scientific divers often have a degree in oceanography. Others may have a degree in surveying. For work in the offshore oil and gas industry, you may need welding or other construction qualifications.

The police and the Royal Navy train their own divers, so you will have to pass their selection procedures.

Personal attributes

As well as physical fitness, you must be able to work in hazardous and frightening conditions. You should have a great awareness of safety issues at all times, and you must be very thorough in checking equipment and following procedures.

Earnings

Divers are usually paid by the day and most divers undertake 150 to 200 dives a year. Rates vary enormously, from £150 a day for inshore work for a surveying or civil engineering company, up to £1,000 a day for some offshore work in the oil and gas industry.

Info

The Underwater Centre
01397 703786

Professional Association of Diving Instructors (PADI)
0117 300 7234
www.padi.com

Cogent Skills
01925 515200
www.cogentskills.com

International Marine Contractors Association
020 7824 5520
www.imca-int.com

The Professional Diving Academy
www.professionaldivingacademy.com/
careers-in-diving/

DOMESTIC APPLIANCE SERVICE ENGINEER

(see also Gas service)

Domestic appliance service engineers service and repair all kinds of household goods, including washing machines, fridges, televisions, DVD players – in fact all kinds of electrical and gas appliances. Service engineers work for retailers, for manufacturers and for servicing companies, and some are self-employed. As well as replacing worn or damaged parts in appliances, they may offer routine servicing, checking that everything is running smoothly and removing dust, limescale or other debris from appliances. They also advise customers on the best way to care for their appliances.

Entry, qualifications and training

While no formal qualifications are necessary, most organisations will expect you to have qualifications and background experience in at least two of the following areas: electrics, electronics, gas fitting, mechanics, plumbing and refrigeration. There are several relevant Edexcel BTEC and City & Guilds courses at levels 2 and 3. Look for courses with units in consumer goods or specialist options on TV, DVD and PC repair and maintenance. People aged 16 to 24 who are interested in this work could consider an apprenticeship in electrics, gas fitting or plumbing. Training is usually provided by the employer and consists of new trainees assisting and learning from a more experienced engineer until they are able to take on more complex jobs or work on their own.

Personal attributes

As well as good practical skills and knowledge of a wide range of appliances, you must have good analytical skills, problem-solving ability and you must be good at dealing with people. You must be polite and friendly to customers, good at explaining problems, and able to listen to their concerns.

Earnings

Earnings start at around the minimum wage. With a few years' experience this rises to £17,000 to £28,000. Anyone with highly specialised skills, such as gas servicing, may earn £55,000 or more.

Info

Gas Safe Register
0800 408 5500
www.gassaferegister.co.uk

Tomorrow's Engineers
www.tomorrowsengineers.org.uk

Domestic Appliance Service Association
0330 111 3272
www.dasa.org.uk

DRIVING

Although many jobs require you to drive, the occupations in this section are those which require professional driving skills and where driving is the main work activity. As well as drivers, there are many other jobs involved in driving and passenger transport, including customer services, engineering and maintenance, information technology, logistics and marketing.

Chauffeur

Chauffeurs drive clients to their destinations, doing their best to ensure that their passenger(s) are comfortable on the journey and arrive safely and on time. Politicians, celebrities, senior executives and wealthy private individuals are among the possible clients of a chauffeur. Some chauffeurs work for one family or individual. Others might work for a large business driving various company members around. Some chauffeurs work for limousine hire companies driving wedding or funeral cars. As well as driving, your duties could include helping clients in and out of cars, assisting with luggage, providing information about the journey and being generally helpful.

Entry, qualifications and training

No formal academic qualifications are required, but you must have several years' driving experience and a full, clean UK driving licence. Some employers like you to have an Advanced Driving Certificate from the Institute of Advanced Motorists or to have completed a defensive driving course. For some posts you will need a foreign language and perhaps other skills such as car maintenance or gardening, if your time spent actually chauffeuring is likely to be fairly limited. If you are working for a family, they may require you to take a DBS (Disclosure and Barring Service) check. Many chauffeurs have worked as taxi drivers or have been in the police force or armed services.

Personal attributes

You must have excellent driving skills, and be careful, confident and sensible. You need to be polite, smart and tactful and able to respect people's privacy and use your discretion. You must be flexible, calm and reasonably physically fit.

Earnings

Pay starts at £14,000 to £19,000. With experience, earnings can rise to £50,000. Some posts bring other benefits such as accommodation or a lot of foreign travel.

Info

IAM RoadSmart
020 8996 9777
www.iamroadsmart.com

People 1st
020 3074 1222
www.people1st.co.uk

British Chauffeurs Guild Ltd
020 8641 1740
www.britishchauffeursguild.co.uk

Careers that Move
www.careersthatmove.co.uk

Courier

Couriers deliver and collect parcels, generally in larger towns and cities. Around 10,000 couriers work in central London. Mostly the delivery or collection is in the same city, sometimes in a different one and very occasionally in another country. Most couriers use a bicycle or motorbike, which they may be required to buy. Couriers carrying packages abroad travel by air.

In large and congested cities there is an increasing trend for couriers to travel by pushbike, and some couriers use small vans.

Entry, qualifications and training

Couriers don't need formal qualifications, but good literacy skills are important. You must be aged 17 or over and have a driving licence appropriate to the vehicle you are to drive, e.g. motorcycle, car or van. A basic knowledge of motor vehicle maintenance can be valuable and motorcycle couriers usually have to provide their own vehicle, plus its road tax and insurance. Once you are employed you can work towards NVQs levels 2 and 3 in Carry and Deliver Goods. Units include road safety and customer care.

Personal attributes

Good, safe driving skills and an ability to deal with people are both important. You are often under a great deal of pressure to be quick, so you must be able to cope with this and not compromise safety. Sometimes knowledge of foreign languages can be useful.

Earnings

Couriers start on around the minimum wage and with experience they can earn £17,000 to £22,000. Motorcycle couriers in London can earn £24,000. Remember that out of these earnings you may have to pay for fuel, insurance and the maintenance of your vehicle. Many couriers are self-employed. Some employers pay bonuses for good attendance, reliability and punctuality.

Info

Skills for Logistics
0117 927 8800
www.skillsforlogistics.co.uk

Driving instructor

Driving instructors teach clients how to drive in preparation for all categories of the Driver and Vehicle Standards Agency's theory and practical driving tests. People who have passed their tests may also go for instruction in advanced driving or refresher courses to increase confidence and skill.

Most instructors are self-employed, either having their own business or existing as an independent operation within a franchise agreement.

Entry, qualifications and training

Driving instructors must be registered with the Driver and Vehicle Standards Agency (DVSA). To register to train you must have held a full UK/EU driving licence for four years and you must not have been disqualified from driving at any time in the last four years. You will have to pass criminal record checks and a series of tests. You can get a starter pack containing all the information you need from the DVSA; it also provides information on approved training courses. Driving schools and other specialist training schools run the training courses and the length and cost of training varies.

You take your theory test first and you can attempt this as many times as you like. Once you have passed this, you have to pass a special driving test and a test of your ability to teach. You must do all three tests within a two-year period. When you have passed you can join the Driving Instructors' Association (DIA) register of approved instructors. The DIA offers the chance for continuing professional development and advanced training and you can take an NVQ level 3 in Driving Instruction.

Personal attributes

As well as excellent, safe driving skills you need an ability to work really well with your students. People learning to drive may be nervous, anxious and lacking in confidence, or alternatively they may be careless and over-confident. You have to be able to work flexible hours and if you become self-employed you have to have good organisational and business skills.

Earnings

Earnings come from hourly charges to learner drivers – £15 to £30 per hour. On qualifying you are likely to earn around £16,000 in your first year, and with experience £23,000 to £25,000. Experienced instructors who have built up a reputation could earn £30,000 plus.

Info

People 1st
020 3074 1222
www.people1st.co.uk

Driving Instructors' Association (DIA)
www.driving.org

Large goods vehicle driver

This work ranges from driving conventional flat-bodied lorries that can carry a variety of loads to driving lorries designed for one purpose, such as car and animal transporters and milk tankers. Drivers often take a load from A to B and then carry one back from B to A in the United Kingdom or across Europe. As well as driving, lorry drivers may have to help with the loading and unloading of goods. Drivers of potentially dangerous products must know how to handle them safely and certification is required.

Entry, qualifications and training

To drive a large goods vehicle you must be aged at least 18, have good eyesight, pass a medical and have good general standards in maths and English. You may not need formal qualifications, but some employers may prefer GCSE maths and English.

There are two ways to get your large goods vehicle (LGV) licence. If you are already working for a transport operator, it might train you. If you are not employed by an operator, you could fund yourself through a driver training school before looking for work.

The LGV licence is divided into two categories: Category C1 allows you to drive rigid vehicles up to 7.5 tonnes, while Category C allows you to drive rigid vehicles over 7.5 tonnes. You can then take a further test that allows you to drive vehicles with trailers (category C+E).

Courses take one to three weeks and cover driving skills, basic mechanics, and loading and securing loads. The test includes vehicle safety questions, specific manoeuvres such as reversing into a bay, 25 miles of road driving and a theory test based on the Highway Code and LGV regulations.

Personal attributes

You must be a good driver with a thorough understanding of road safety, and the patience to tolerate long drives and heavy traffic. You must be happy spending many hours on your own, but also be able to work with warehouse employees and customers and remain pleasant and friendly.

Earnings

On qualifying, earnings are between £18,500 and £22,000. Experienced drivers earn £22,000 to £35,000.

Info

Road Haulage Association
01733 261131
www.rhaonline.co.uk/courses

Skills for Logistics
0117 927 8800
www.skillsforlogistics.co.uk

Freight Transport Association (FTA)
0371 711 2222
www.fta.co.uk

Light goods or delivery van driver

Delivery van drivers deliver all kinds of goods, from supermarket shopping orders to parcels or fresh flowers. You may also be driving valuables such as cash from banks or other premises. The work is not just about driving. Delivery van drivers normally load or help load up the van, plan the most efficient route for deliveries, take the goods from the van to the customers and get customers' signatures for receipt of goods. They may also be collecting parcels from customers to take to some central point. Compared to a large goods vehicle driver you are usually working in a smaller geographical area, say the delivery range of a supermarket or a flower shop. This is not always the case: some parcel delivery companies operate across large distances and across many regions. In recent years, as there has been increasing use of online food ordering and delivery services, many have taken on these roles part time but they can be full time.

Entry, qualifications and training

You don't need formal qualifications for this work, though if you join via an apprenticeship your employer may require you to have some GCSEs grades 9–4. In all cases you need a reasonable standard of maths and English, good eyesight and a clean driving licence. Depending on the size and type of vehicle you are driving you may need an additional licence. In all cases you will need to obtain a Certificate of Professional Competence (CPC). Training usually starts with an introductory course about relevant paperwork, local routes, etc. Some employers may then put you through your CPC. If you wish to drive vehicles carrying valuables, you will have to undertake additional training such as defensive driving.

Personal attributes

You need to enjoy and be good at driving. You should be physically fit and not mind bad weather. You need good communication skills and to be friendly and pleasant to customers. You must be able to balance the need to work quickly and efficiently with the necessity of being a calm and safe driver.

Earnings

Drivers earn between around the minimum wage and £20,000 depending on geographical location and the kind of company you work for. With experience you can earn up to £27,000. Pay is higher if you are driving valuables. Some employers pay bonuses for doing a certain number of deliveries, per day, week, etc.

Info

Skills for Logistics
0117 927 8800
www.skillsforlogistics.co.uk

Skills for Security (for transporting valuables)
01905 744000
https://skillsforsecurity.org.uk

Bus/coach driver

Bus and coach drivers transport passengers either on local or long journeys. Bus drivers work mainly on shorter routes in particular towns or cities, or between a small number of these. Their work involves taking fares, checking passes, giving information about timetables and assisting passengers who may have difficulties, such as a disability or bulky luggage. Coach drivers tend to take people on longer journeys, say between cities or even countries. They may also take people on tours to see sites of special interest or to view impressive scenery. While their work is similar to that of bus drivers, they may also have to load luggage, give information about the sites or countryside through which they are driving and check that all passengers who should be on board are on the coach. Some bus and coach drivers may also be involved in community transport; driving school buses, for example.

Entry, qualifications and training

Your essential qualification for this work is a Passenger Carrying Vehicle (PCV) licence. To drive a bus or a coach you must be aged 21, or 18 to drive a minibus. Many bus and coach companies will take you on and train you to gain your PCV, so long as you already have a full, clean EU driving licence. You can train independently through a driving school; you need to check with local driving schools whether they offer this training option. An EU Directive requires PCV drivers to obtain a Certificate of Professional Competence (CPC). You can get this through periodic short training courses and your employer company should be able to help with this. The Transport Office website carries more details about this. Some employers will give you the opportunity to train to NVQ level 2 in Passenger Transport.

Companies set their own entry standards, but many will expect you to have three or four GCSEs and you will have to meet their medical requirements.

Personal attributes

Safety awareness is paramount. It is the responsibility of any driver to be ever conscious of the safety of his or her passengers. You need to be calm and patient in congested traffic, and with difficult passengers. Your people skills are very important: you need to be polite, helpful and good at giving information. You may also need to be firm and assertive in some situations.

Earnings

New drivers earn between £14,000 and £17,000 – with experience drivers earn up to £33,000. Some coach drivers may also earn additional money in tips.

Info

Careers that Move	**Transport Office**
www.careersthatmove.co.uk	www.transportoffice.gov.uk

Taxi driver

A 'taxi' is a traditional hackney carriage (like the black London taxis). Hackney carriage drivers are allowed to 'ply for hire' – drive around the streets looking for passengers – and can be flagged down by a passenger. They may also operate from taxi ranks in the streets. A minicab, on the other hand, has to be booked by telephone, internet, via apps or in person. Minicab drivers can spend much of their time waiting around for passengers. Hours for both types of driver can be long and antisocial – early-morning drops at airports, pick-ups from late-night parties and a lot of evening and weekend work. Drivers may be owner-drivers or work for a company.

Entry, qualifications and training

Taxi drivers must be at least 21 years of age to be granted a licence, although in practice, because of insurance requirements, most are over 25. A valid Group A driving licence and relevant driving experience are also necessary. Hackney carriage drivers are legally bound to take the shortest or quickest route to a passenger's destination. Trainee drivers usually have to pass special tests, known as 'knowledge tests', to prove that they know their way about sufficiently well. These tests are generally oral, the most demanding being the Knowledge of London Test, which is required before drivers may operate in the capital. This usually takes some 18 months to two years to complete. Specialised training schools exist and there are also special training schemes for the disabled and for people who have been in the forces. In London, too, an additional driving test must be passed before a licence is granted.

Personal attributes

Driving in traffic demands a calm, unflappable personality, with lots of patience. Drivers also need to have a good memory. In addition, a taxi driver must be 'of good character', as a licence will not be granted to anyone who has committed certain offences.

Earnings

Almost all taxi drivers are self-employed and have to pay tax and National Insurance out of their earnings. Owner-drivers generally earn more than drivers employed by a company (who are often on a fixed rate), although they must also finance the repairs and servicing costs incurred by their own vehicles. Average earnings are between £14,000 and £30,000.

Info

People 1st
020 3074 1222
www.people1st.co.uk

Transport Office
www.transportoffice.gov.uk

National Private Hire Association
0161 688 7777
www.phtm.co.uk

ECOLOGY

Ecologist

Ecology draws on a combination of biological science, environmental science and geography. Ecologists work in and study ecosystems (whole environments and the living organisms within them). These organisms include people, animals, plants, birds and insects of every kind. An ecologist studies how these different organisms interact and what external influences might help to either maintain the balance or cause the destabilisation of the whole system. Many ecologists study one particular group or organism, e.g. amphibians, some work on particular types of project, e.g. restoring a former industrial landscape to a wildlife conservation area. Ecologists look at the impact of proposed developments such as housing, quarrying, fishing or agriculture on the area proposed for such a development. Day-to-day work could include carrying out field studies, testing samples in the laboratory, organising school or other educational visits to wildlife conservation areas, or presenting results of research to planning committees, businesses and local community groups. Ecologists work for all of those bodies concerned with the natural environment, both statutory and non-statutory organisations.

Entry, qualifications and training

Ecologists are normally graduates or postgraduates in subjects including ecology, biology, botany, zoology and environmental science. The British Ecological Society website lists undergraduate courses. The Chartered Institute of Ecology and Environmental Management offers training courses at student and professional level. Much of the training is on the job. Work associated with the environment is always popular, so doing some voluntary work either before or during your university studies could strengthen your application for paid work.

Personal attributes

A passion for what you do is essential. The mix of skills you need depends a lot on your particular role. You may have to be very patient and happy working on your own if you are out collecting samples. If you are presenting a paper on a planning issue you will need to be a confident communicator. You often need to be able to work as part of a team and you must have a thorough and methodical approach to much of your work.

Earnings

Ecologists earn £22,000 to £28,000. Senior project managers and ecological consultants can earn £30,000 to £47,000. Some ecologists earn considerably more than this.

Info

Chartered Institute of Ecology and Environmental Management
01962 868626
www.ieem.net

Society for the Environment
0345 337 2951
www.socenv.org.uk

Field Studies Society
01743 852100
www.field-studies-council.org

British Ecological Society
020 3994 8282
www.britishecologicalsociety.org

ECONOMY

Economist

Economists, these days often in the news, work in central and local government, higher education, banks, insurance companies, management consultancies, trade unions and international organisations. They apply economic theory and knowledge and give advice on a whole range of topics related to the economy and finance. They study statistical data and trends to try to interpret and predict how the economy will perform. Their work may cover interest rates, taxation, employment policies, trends in consumer behaviour, what we buy and what we spend. Economists devise methods for sampling data, determine how to analyse data and how to translate them into information that can be used to inform policy decisions, solve problems or plan strategies.

Entry, qualifications and training

Economics is a graduate profession. You need a degree either in economics or in economics in combination with business, finance or law. In these cases the majority of your modules should still be in economics, and must cover micro and macro economics. You need a 2.1 or better and many employers look for high A level grades too. If you have a degree in another subject you may get into economics, but only by completing a postgraduate course in economics. Competition for posts is fierce and you can improve your chances by joining your student industrial society or something similar to demonstrate your interest in business and economics. The Civil Service runs an annual recruitment scheme for graduate economists. Most training is on the job, where you might be sent on several short courses as well as being supervised and guided by senior staff.

Personal attributes

Economists need excellent written and spoken communication skills, and to be good at translating technical and mathematical concepts into everyday language. They need good research skills, and to be able to analyse and interpret a wide variety of data. They need good judgement and must be able to work with great accuracy. They have to be able to work under pressure and manage their own workloads effectively. IT skills are also important.

Earnings

New entrants earn between £28,000 and £35,000. After three to five years' experience salaries rise to between £40,000 and £55,000, and up to £80,000 depending on experience. Many salary packages include other benefits such as private health insurance.

Info

Government Economic Service (GES)
www.gov.uk/government/organisations/civil-
service/about/recruitment

Royal Statistical Society (RSS)
020 7638 8998
www.rss.org.uk

The Society of Professional Economists
01264 737552
www.spe.org.uk

ELECTRICIAN

The distribution of electricity to every home and business and the installation, maintenance and repair of every kind of electrical equipment are the daily work of electricians and electricity distribution workers. There are many types of work, including domestic wiring, work on roads and railways, on lifts, laboratory equipment or individual domestic appliances. There is also a growing area of work concerned with installing solar panels, photovoltaic cells and other sustainable technologies.

Auto electrician

(see Motor industry)

Electrician

An electrician might rewire your house, install the complex wiring for a hospital operating theatre, repair the cables that keep traffic lights working, or set up the lighting system in a theatre. He or she might also repair faulty electrical equipment, from a domestic storage heater to the systems that keep the air conditioning running in a large building. Work on domestic wiring could include fitting wiring to sockets or light switches, fitting fuse boxes and circuit breakers and testing all the wiring you have just installed to ensure that it is safe. If you are rewiring, rather than working on a new development, you would also need to discuss with customers where they would like sockets and light fittings to go. On commercial properties you may be laying cables that support computer networks and connecting computers and other equipment to power points. You could also be installing fire alarms and other security systems, testing systems and repairing reported faults.

Entry, qualifications and training

To qualify as an electrician you must achieve an electrotechnical NVQ level 3. There are various routes to achieving this, but the most common, provided you are between the ages of 16 and 24, is to do an apprenticeship. These are mainly employer-based, but include some college work and practical and written assessments. Though it is not always essential, many employers require you to have GCSEs grades 9–4 in English, maths, technology and a science subject. If you are not eligible for an apprenticeship you can do college-based City & Guilds courses at levels 2 and 3.

Electrotechnical level 3 offers several different pathways, including electrical installation, electrical maintenance, electrical instrumentation and associated equipment, installing highway electrical systems, electrical panel building and electrical machine rewind and repair. A great deal of training takes place on the job.

Personal attributes

You must have good practical and technical skills and be able to follow technical drawings and diagrams. You should be reasonably fit, and for some jobs you need to be able to cope with heights or working in confined spaces. You should have good colour vision. You need to be able to work on your own, or as part of a team, and you must have good communication skills and be able to talk to people without using a lot of technical jargon.

Earnings

Apprentices earn around £3.50 an hour to start with but are entitled to the minimum wage for their age once they have completed their first year. Pay rises to around £18,000 at the end of training. Newly qualified electricians earn £19,000 to £24,000, but experienced electricians can earn much more than this. Many electricians are self-employed, which means earnings are related to how much work they can get and what they charge.

Info

TESP (The Electrotechnical Skills Partnership)   ELECSA
www.electricalcareers.co.uk   0333 321 8220
                                                     www.elecsa.co.uk

---

Electricity distribution worker

We probably only think about electricity distribution work when we suffer a power cut. To be of any use to any of us, electricity must be transmitted from power stations to its many destinations. It is electricity distribution workers who look after these electrical networks that supply electricity to every home, commercial property or installation of any kind. It is their job to help maintain and sustain a safe and constant supply of electricity. Distribution workers usually specialise in one of three areas. First is overhead work, which involves building and maintaining the overhead power lines that we can all see. Second, you could be a cable joiner, fixing and joining underground cables and also connecting domestic and commercial customers to the electricity supply. Third, you could work to fit, repair and maintain the equipment at electricity substations. Day-to-day tasks could include keeping equipment in good working order, installing and dismantling equipment such as transmission cables, assembling or removing components, finding and diagnosing faults and inspecting and testing equipment.

Entry, qualifications and training

You could take up a relevant course at college such as the Level 2 Certificate in Electrical and Electronic Engineering Technology, or Level 3 Diploma in Engineering Technology. You don't always need formal qualifications to get into this work, though many employers offering training do ask for a good general education and may require GCSEs grades 9–4 in English, maths and a technical subject. You might get into this via an engineering apprenticeship and employers offering apprenticeships in this work set their own entry requirements. The apprenticeship is likely to lead to relevant NVQ-level qualifications and which of these you work towards will depend on which area of transmission work you are training to work in. If you have other relevant experience in construction trades you may be able to get into this work.

Personal attributes

You must have good manual dexterity, good eyesight and perfect colour vision. You need to be practical and happy to work in uncomfortable positions, up on a pylon or down a hole for example. You have to be able to work as part of a team and your observation of health and safety matters is truly essential.

Earnings

Once your apprenticeship is over you can expect to earn between £16,000 and £23,000, experienced workers can earn £25,000 to £35,000.

Info

Energy & Utility Skills
0121 745 1310
www.euskills.co.uk

National Grid Careers
www.nationalgridcareers.com

ENGINEERING

Every building we enter, vehicle we drive, kitchen appliance we switch on, electronic gadget we have in our pockets, tap we turn on, bridge we cross or aeroplane we board has been conceived, designed and manufactured by engineers. Examples include the tiniest component in the latest mobile phone, to the safety system on the largest aircraft, from a 3D printer able to 'print' in concrete or plastic, to the blades on a wind turbine, or graphene components to build low-cost water desalinisation plants – these are just a few examples of the role of engineers and engineering in the world today.

Acoustics engineer

Acoustics engineers work with the measurement, management, regulation and control of the noises and vibrations that surround us in our homes, workplaces and environments such as restaurants, shopping centres, railway stations or dance venues. Work could involve carrying out noise assessments on buildings to make sure sound insulation methods meet building regulations, conducting environmental noise surveys, or examining how changes to building design can affect noise levels. The work often requires computer modelling as well as actual monitoring. Some acoustics engineers work in the recording industry, contributing to the design of studios. Other highly specialised areas include designing medical equipment such as ultrasound scanners, which use sound to diagnose or treat medical conditions.

Aerospace engineer

Aerospace engineers design and build aircraft. They work on fixed-wing aeroplanes, space vehicles, satellites, flight simulators, missiles, weapons systems and the various components and technologies for all of these. Work includes developing avionic systems like navigation instruments and communications, researching ways to make fuel-efficient parts, such as wings, fuselage and engines, planning and observing ground and flight tests and managing the manufacturing and building of craft and components.

Agricultural engineers

Agricultural engineers design and produce agricultural machinery; plan, design and construct farm buildings and associated equipment such as milking parlours or grain dryers. They are also concerned with field engineering – irrigation, drainage and land resource planning; and service engineering, involving the sale, servicing, repairing and installation of farm machinery. They are also involved in forestry engineering, amenity and ecological engineering, and precision farming using satellite positioning systems.

Automotive engineer

In the vehicle manufacturing industry, engineers may be employed in design, development, production, operations management and maintenance activities. In motor vehicle servicing, the work tends to be at craft level, with some engineers using their technical base to develop into motor vehicle engineering management. At graduate engineer level, designing vehicles to use different technology such as hydrogen or electricity and developing conventional cars to be much more fuel efficient is a growing aspect of the work.

Biochemical engineer

Biochemicals are chemical reactions or substances produced in living organisms such as bacteria, yeasts or fungi. Biochemical engineers work with industrial processes. They are involved in the research, design, construction and operation of plant used for the processing of biochemicals such as those used in waste management, water treatment, brewing or pharmaceuticals.

Biomedical engineer

Biomedical engineers, also referred to as clinical engineers or bioengineers, work on the research, design, development and maintenance of technology and equipment used to meet patients' clinical needs both during and after medical treatment. They work in the fields of instrumentation, rehabilitation and biomaterials. They build and test prototypes, run clinical trials and evaluate the performance of equipment and materials. Examples of their work include new heart valves, replacement joints and new types of hearing device.

Building services engineer

(see also Construction)

Building services engineers are concerned with heating and ventilation, refrigeration, lighting, air conditioning, electrical services, internal water supply, waste disposal, fire protection, lifts, and acoustic and communication systems. The work involves the planning and design of engineering systems, and supervision of contracts, working in collaboration with architects, surveyors, structural engineers and builders.

Chemical engineer

Chemical engineers work with large-scale processes, not always in the chemical industry. The term 'process engineering' is often used to describe their work, as they are more interested in the physical factors involved in a process than in the chemical reaction itself. Chemical engineers are employed in the oil, chemical, pharmaceutical, food, brewing and process industries.

Civil engineer

Civil engineers devise, plan and manage development in vital areas – the design and construction of state-of-the-art roads, dams, harbours, railroad systems, bridges and airports. Civil engineers also play an important part in the provision of utility supplies, and in managing traffic and transport. Every project is unique and involves the expertise of a team of people who plan, design, build and maintain these essential assets.

Design Engineer

Design engineers design products using computer-aided design (CAD) software. This is a technical rather than artistic role, but needs a creative eye. It primarily involves producing detailed designs from a client's requirements that translate into components that function as required.

Electrical and electronic engineer

The technology of electrical engineering deals with heavy current, while electronic engineering deals with light current. Applications of heavy current include electrical machinery of all kinds, generating stations and distribution systems. Light current is used for such products as transistors, microprocessors and telecommunications equipment. The two fields are often interdependent and training is closely related. Electronics is a rapidly developing field and offers excellent opportunities, as do the allied disciplines of computer hardware and software engineering.

Energy engineer

Energy engineers work on the production and distribution of energy from natural resources such as oil and gas, or renewables such as wind or solar power. Energy engineers work to find efficient, clean and innovative ways to supply energy. They work in many roles including designing and testing machinery, developing ways of improving existing processes, and converting, transmitting and supplying useful energy to meet our needs for electricity. They also research and develop ways to generate new energy, improve the efficient use of energy through reducing emissions from fossil fuels, and minimise harm to the environment.

Environmental engineer

Environmental engineering is a developing and increasingly important profession. Environmental engineers work for local authorities and private companies, large and small. Their work is concerned with assessing the impact of human activity on the environment. The three main areas in which they work are waste management, land reclamation and pollution control. Their work involves visiting many different kinds of site, liaising with surveyors, engineers, scientists and other organisations. They may use computer models to simulate the environmental impact of particular activities.

Manufacturing engineer

Similar manufacturing processes apply in many industries including food and drink, pharmaceuticals, oil and plastics, so manufacturing engineers find roles in all of these. Manufacturing engineers have a high level of technical expertise and skill, which they use to plan, design, set up, modify and monitor manufacturing processes. They work to produce high quality goods using the most cost-effective methods and, working to reduce the impact of production on the environment, they have to be creative designers as well as analytical problem solvers.

Marine engineer

This discipline is related to offshore engineering under the general title of 'maritime engineering', which involves engineering systems and equipment in a maritime environment. Both marine and offshore engineers are involved in design, research, consultancy, survey, manufacture, installation and maintenance activities, the former with vessels of all sizes and types, the latter with offshore platforms, sub-sea installations and under-sea vehicles. Employment opportunities exist within firms offering design and research activities, engine- and shipbuilding firms, classification societies, government bodies, the Merchant Navy and the Royal Navy.

Materials engineer

Materials engineers work in a diverse range of industries, working on the research and development of new materials to advance technologies; innovating and modifying materials to improve the performance and efficiency of existing products; and investigating the failure of products or structures. They work with all types of materials, including plastics, metals, alloys, glass, ceramics and composites. Some of the industries they work in include telecommunications, power generation, sport and medicine. Materials engineers have developed materials used in modern tennis rackets, replacement hip joints and internet broadband connections; these are just a few examples. Most materials engineers have a degree in materials engineering or materials science, or a degree in applied physics or chemistry.

Mechanical engineer

Mechanical engineering is the biggest branch of the engineering industry. It involves the skills of designing, developing, producing, installing and operating machinery and mechanical products of many types. The field is enormous in scope, and most engineers specialise in a particular area. Other branches of engineering, such as electrical and civil engineering, overlap with mechanical engineering to a certain extent.

Mechanical engineers are employed in almost every sector of industry. Some of the largest areas of employment are machine tools, railway engineering, aerospace and the automobile industry.

Mining engineer

Mining engineers work all over the world advising on the safe construction of mines, quarries and tunnels. They also oversee the mining process once extraction begins. They can be involved in mining for fossil fuels, minerals, precious metals or rare earths. They may also be concerned with extraction of oil and gas or of rock and stone. There are limited opportunities in the UK, and many mining engineers work in Europe, Africa, South America and Australia – anywhere rich in natural resources in fact.

Nuclear engineer

Nuclear engineers work to design new nuclear reactors and power generation plants and to monitor and maintain the safe running of both existing and new plants. They are also concerned with the management and storage of nuclear waste and the safe decommissioning of old reactors. Training and supervising other technical staff is often a key role in this work and management of risk and compliance with legislation are crucial.

Operations engineer

Operations engineers are concerned with specifying, evaluation, acquisition, commissioning, inspection, maintenance, asset management and disposal of facilities, systems, vehicles and equipment. Career opportunities exist at craft and technician level in the servicing and maintenance of a wide variety of industries, of which transport is the largest (*see Instrument technician*). Chartered and incorporated engineers may be engaged in asset or fleet engineering management, requiring multidisciplinary engineering, commercial and legal knowledge and encompassing health and safety, reliability, environmental and economic factors, or in specialised inspection roles. Many technicians build on their practical skills by further career development to aspire to these more senior positions.

Petroleum engineer

Petroleum engineers are involved in all the stages of oil extraction from exploration of potential sites to drilling and recovery of oil and gas. Their role is to help obtain the greatest quantities of oil and the lowest cost, but also to work to reduce the environmental impact of such processes.

Process engineer

Process engineers work in large and small companies manufacturing all kinds of products. They develop efficient industrial processes to make the huge range of products on which modern society depends, including food and drink, fuel, artificial fibres, pharmaceuticals, chemicals, plastics, cosmetics, cleaning products, energy and clean water. Their role can be similar to that of chemical engineers.

Production engineer

Production engineers develop and improve manufacturing techniques. They are responsible for designing production systems to ensure that products can be manufactured to the specified design, in the right quantities, at the right price and by the required date. Their work overlaps with production management.

Refrigeration and air conditioning engineer

Refrigeration and air conditioning (RAC) engineers design, install and maintain systems to keep buildings at a comfortable temperature or a correct level of humidity and temperature for a specific purpose. RAC engineers are responsible for the refrigeration systems in supermarkets, or food processing centres. They develop systems to ensure that blood is stored at exactly the right temperature. They install and manage air conditioning systems in leisure complexes, offices and hospitals – private homes too in hotter climates. Ensuring that energy is used efficiently in all these systems is a key part of this work.

Structural engineer

Structural engineers play a part in the design of houses, theatres, sports venues, ships, hospitals, aircraft, bridges, shopping arcades, office blocks and warehouses – in short, any man-made structure. Their role is to design structures that will withstand the pressures and stresses put on them by the environment and by human use. Their work might include analysing the quality and strength of materials proposed for use, calculating the pressure or stress that various parts of a structure such as beams or lintels will be put under and liaising with other professionals such as architects, civil engineers and builders.

Water engineer

Water engineers mostly work for water companies and river authorities, ensuring the supply of fresh water, and dealing with the reclamation and disposal of water that has been used.

Entry, qualifications and training

Encompassing many careers, engineering offers many levels of entry. This section shows the main training pathways. The various engineering bodies and the relevant sector skills councils provide more detailed information.

It is difficult to move from one engineering profession to another. You need to decide at an early stage which type of engineering you wish to pursue and should read widely so that you understand the careers available.

Graduate engineers

Most professional engineers are graduates who have completed a degree in just one type of engineering. There are degrees available in all the types of engineering described in the previous paragraphs. For most degrees in technical subjects you will need three A levels, although grade and subject requirements vary between institutions and subjects. Physics, maths, chemistry and other science subjects are often required. Many engineering degree courses offer the option to spend a year out in industry. Once you have completed your degree and are in employment, you are likely to work towards becoming a chartered engineer, working towards professional examinations through the relevant engineering organisation, e.g. the Institute of Mechanical Engineers.

Professional engineers are likely to have responsibility for research and development, problem solving, managing work teams and projects and bringing creative ideas to the whole engineering process.

Technician engineers

For many types of engineering, if you do not wish to study for a degree you may be able to start at technician level. This usually means you should have five GCSEs grades 9–4, including English, maths and a science subject. Your employer may give you the opportunity to train to NVQ level 3 in a relevant subject. You can also consider college courses offering City & Guilds or BTEC qualifications. The Cogent Skills and SEMTA websites offer plenty of information. You may also be able to train through an apprenticeship. Check your local Jobcentre Plus for details of what is on offer locally.

Every engineering production line, construction site, processing plant or scientific laboratory will employ a number of staff to handle the day-to-day processes, quality testing, looking after equipment, and doing all the routine work to keep systems running. For these jobs, entry requirements vary greatly, but many will not require formal academic qualifications.

Personal attributes

Professional engineers, in whatever discipline they choose to specialise, require excellent problem-solving, scientific and technical skills. They need to be imaginative in finding solutions to difficulties and they need to have a rigorous and thorough approach to research and testing. They also need good teamwork skills and good project management and human resource management skills. Working at technician or more junior levels, you may need good numeracy skills and good manual dexterity.

Earnings

Salaries for graduate entrants vary across the many fields of engineering. Starting salaries around £22,000 to £28,000 cover most branches and these rise to between £27,000 and £50,000, but can be higher with experience. Some engineers become senior project managers with higher salary potential. Technician engineers earn between £18,000 and £35,000.

Info

Institution of Engineering and Technology
01438 313 311
www.theiet.org

Engineering Council
020 3206 0500
www.engc.org.uk

The Institute of the Motor Industry
01992 519025
www.theimi.org.uk

Cogent Skills
01925 515200
www.cogentskills.com

Institution of Chemical Engineers (IChemE)
020 7927 8200
www.icheme.org

Chartered Institute of Building Services Engineers
020 8675 5211
www.cibse.org

Institution of Civil Engineers (ICE)
020 7222 7722
www.ice.org.uk

BCS, The Chartered Institute for IT
www.bcs.org

Energy Institute
www.energyinst.org

Institute of Materials, Minerals and Mining (IOM3)
020 7451 7300
www.iom3.org

Institution of Mechanical Engineers (IMechE)
020 7222 7899
www.imeche.org

SEMTA
0845 643 9001
www.semta.org.uk

The BESA (Building Engineering Services Association)
020 7313 4900
www.thebesa.com

Women into Science and Engineering
0113 222 6072
www.wisecampaign.org.uk

Women's Engineering Society (WES)
01438 765506
www.wes.org.uk

Institution of Agricultural Engineers
01234 750876
www.iagre.org

London Centre for Nanotechnology
020 7679 0604
www.london-nano.com

Nuclear Institute
020 7816 2600
www.nuclearinst.com

Institute of Physics
020 7470 4800
www.iop.org

Institute of Physics and Engineering in Medicine
01904 610821
www.ipem.ac.uk

NHS Careers (relevant for materials engineers and biomedical engineers)
0345 60 60 655
www.healthcareers.nhs.uk

Royal Aeronautical Society
020 7670 4326
www.aerosociety.com

Tomorrow's Engineers
www.tomorrowsengineers.org.uk

ENVIRONMENT AND ENVIRONMENTAL CONSERVATION

Environmental conservation and management cover activities from recycling waste to habitat management. They do not just involve green issues but are about applying scientific knowledge to produce solutions for a sustainable environment. Conservation includes the protection of rural and urban landscapes, plants and animals and countryside recreation. This includes protection and management of rivers, coastal zones and waterways, together with their fisheries and fish stocks.

There are opportunities in a range of organisations from government departments to the voluntary sector. Competition for jobs is high but many applicants lack relevant experience, so voluntary work often plays a part in moving into this career area. There are other job titles not covered here such as woodland manager or environmental education officer.

Countryside ranger/warden

Countryside rangers are responsible for the day-to-day management of areas of countryside such as common land, heaths, woodland or wetlands. They undertake practical work such as tree planting or carrying out field surveys to determine how prevalent particular species are in a specified area. Rangers patrol sites, making sure that footpaths, bridges and gates are in good order. They can also provide advice and help to members of the public, keeping an overall eye on safety. They may also have responsibility for managing budgets and for organising exhibitions, or conducting educational tours of sites.

Entry, qualifications and training

You do not need any formal qualifications to do this work, but you will almost certainly have to do some voluntary work. Some conservation organisations offer a range of short training courses to volunteers in subjects such as species identification, hedge layering, coppicing and risk management. You can also do City & Guilds courses in environmental conservation, for which you do not need any formal qualifications. An intermediate or advanced apprenticeship in environmental conservation, or a degree in environmental studies are other routes you could take to get into this role.

Personal attributes

As well as a passion for the countryside you should be very practical and confident in using tools and equipment. You need good communication skills and for many posts you also have to have reasonable office and IT skills.

Earnings

Starting salaries vary according to the type of organisation in which you are employed. Local authority salaries for rangers start at around £16,000 and can go up to £30,000. Voluntary organisations may pay around £15,000; these posts are often part time.

Nature conservation officer

Nature conservation officers are involved in the protection and appropriate development of all types of natural and rural environment. Their work is varied. They may be involved in implementing schemes to protect or improve the landscape, or they may advise on the environmental impact of proposed developments. They may put into practice schemes to protect particular plants, birds, insects and animals, or to create new habitats for these plants and animals. The work may also involve educating the public about how to use the countryside appropriately and negotiating with other land users, or preparing reports for planning committees and other formal bodies. Conservation officers are employed by local authorities, government agencies, charities such as the National Trust and the Woodland Trust and environmental consultancies.

Entry, qualifications and training

For most jobs you need a degree, preferably in a subject such as ecology, geography or environmental conservation. This is a very competitive field, so you also need some good practical skills. The majority of people who get full-time paid work of this sort have done some voluntary work first for one of the countryside organisations. Check the Info panel for the major countryside organisations in the United Kingdom. Once you are employed, there are plenty of courses you can do to increase your knowledge and skills in specific areas, e.g. woodland, birdlife, or coastal erosion.

Personal attributes

These vary according to your particular responsibilities and tasks, but a love of the countryside is always essential. Interest in geography, botany and zoology may be important. You should be good at keeping records and measuring scientific data of various kinds. You should be prepared to work outside, but also be able to communicate effectively at meetings or in an educative role.

Earnings

New entrants earn £17,000 to £22,000; some posts are offered as apprenticeships and many are part time. At management level salaries can be £22,000 to £30,000. Many of the employing organisations are charities operating on tight budgets. Salaries can be higher working for consultancies.

Info

Lantra
02476 696996
www.lantra.co.uk

Natural England
0300 060 3900
www.gov.uk/government/organisations/
natural-england

National Trust
0344 800 1895
www.nationaltrust.org.uk

Chartered Institute of Ecology and Environmental Management (IEEM)
01962 868626
www.ieem.net

The Conservation Volunteers (TCV)
01302 388883
www.tcv.org.uk

The Wildlife Trusts
01636 677711
www.wildlifetrusts.org

Environmental consultant

Environmental consultants work for government departments, local government and many industrial sectors including manufacturing and construction. The work is varied, but includes ensuring that organisations comply with environmental legislation and that the environmental impact of, for example, a new shopping development, a large dairy farm, wind turbines, a scientific laboratory, a brewery or a waste management centre is fully understood. Your work might include researching previous activities on a site to check for contaminants, conducting field surveys to collect data, interpreting data and writing reports for clients, working closely with clients, regulators, subcontractors and representatives of a local community. You could also monitor any development once work had started, to ensure that the environmental impact did not change or increase.

Entry, qualifications and training

A good honours degree is a minimum requirement and many entrants have postgraduate qualifications too. Preferred subjects include biology, chemistry, environmental science, environmental engineering, geology, geography or any combination of these. If you can get a relevant work placement this will strengthen your application and if your degree course includes an option for a project or dissertation, choosing a topic related to your environmental interests could also be useful. A postgraduate qualification, as well as experience of work or volunteering experience in an environmental setting, may help as it is increasingly common for employers to ask for a postgraduate qualification. An environmental practitioner degree apprenticeship is another option.

Personal attributes

You would need many different skills, be able to understand complex scientific and statistical data, but also be able to translate that into everyday information that clients could understand. You would need excellent report writing skills and good IT skills. You would have to be a good communicator; able to listen, to explain and to advise.

Earnings

New entrants earn £19,000 to £24,000; this rises to £25,000 to £35,000 with a few years' experience. Senior consultants can earn £60,000.

Info

Institute of Environmental Management and Assessment
01522 540069
www.iema.net

Environmental health officer/practitioner

Environmental health officers (EHOs) are enforcers, educators and advisers, and are employed in both the public and private sectors. Their responsibilities include pollution control, including noise control, environmental protection, the inspection of food and food premises, health and safety in workplaces and in the leisure industry, and the control of housing standards, particularly in the private rented sector. Much of their time is spent out of the office, dealing with the public and visiting premises of all types.

Entry, qualifications and training

The usual route to becoming an environmental health officer/practitioner is through a degree in environmental health. You can either do a three-year degree, followed by a one-year work placement, or a four-year degree that includes a third-year work-based training placement. If you have a science degree, you can also enter the profession by doing a postgraduate course in environmental health. In all cases, your course should be accredited by the Chartered Institute of Environmental Health (CIEH) in England, Wales and Northern Ireland, or the Royal Environmental Health Institute of Scotland in Scotland. Alternatively, if you have an HNC, HND or foundation degree in science, you may be able to enter directly into the second year of a degree. It may also be possible to start as an environmental health technician with a local authority, and then work towards qualification through part-time study. The minimum qualifications for this are four GCSEs grades 9–4, including English, maths and a science, but many applicants will have A levels or other equivalent qualifications.

Personal attributes

EHOs need many different skills. They have to be able to deal with complex legal and scientific information. They must be able to explain the law to members of the public or other non-lawyers. They should be diplomatic and calm, but at other times they will also have to be assertive and determined.

Earnings

Starting salaries with local authorities for those still training are between £20,000 and £23,000 (£25,000 and £32,000 in London). Salaries for experienced EHOs range from £24,000 to £35,000 (again, significantly more in London). There is some weekend and late evening work involved and this may attract additional payments. At management level salaries are £45,000 to £60,000. Salaries are often higher in the private sector.

Info

Chartered Institute of Environmental Health (CIEH)
020 7827 5800
www.cieh.org

Food Standards Agency
020 7276 8829
www.food.gov.uk

Environment Agency (EA)
03708 506 506
www.environment-agency.gov.uk

Royal Environmental Health Institute of Scotland
0131 229 2968
www.rehis.com

Pest control technician

Pest controllers control not only mice, rats, cockroaches and ants that may be damaging foodstuffs in a factory, hotel or private home, but also rabbits, moles, birds and foxes that attack farmers' crops. They work for local authorities and private firms. Service staff are employed to lay traps and set poison. There are also opportunities for graduates in research and management.

Entry, qualifications and training

Qualifications in pest control are usually preferred, although at assistant level full training is provided on the job, including day or block release to achieve a recognised qualification, such as British Pest Control Association courses. The British Pest Control Association and the Royal Society for the Promotion of Health have merged their basic pest control qualification – BPC Diploma Part 1 and RSPH Certificate in Pest Control. As part of this partnership, other BPCA examinations, including the advanced level certificate (BPC Diploma Part 2), the fumigation certification scheme and the Certificate for Surveyors – Pest Control (CSPC), are brought under the joint BPCA/RSPH umbrella.

Personal attributes

This is not a job for the squeamish and the work demands a mature outlook, an ability to get on with many kinds of people, to work in varying conditions and to work alone. The ability to drive is important.

Earnings

Pay is between £17,000 and £19,500. With experience and qualifications you can earn £20,000 to £30,000. Many pest control technicians set up their own small businesses.

Info

British Pest Control Association (BPCA)
01332 294288
www.bpca.org.uk

Royal Society for Public Health
020 7265 7300
www.rsph.org.uk

National Pest Technicians Association (NPTA)
01773 717 716
www.npta.org.uk

Recycling officer

Recycling officers work mainly for local councils, planning and developing policies to help local people recycle as much waste material as they can. Recycling officers organise schemes to recycle glass, paper, cans and plastic. They may also organise and manage schemes to encourage residents to make compost, either on their own properties or at central points set up by the local authority. Reducing waste is an important and very topical area of local authority work, so the significance of this area of work has increased. Recycling officers are also involved in organising publicity about recycling.

Entry, qualifications and training

Although there are no formal academic entry requirements, most successful applicants have either a degree or a Higher National Diploma. The most useful subjects include environmental science, earth studies, geography, or any science subject. If you don't have a degree, then plenty of useful paid or voluntary work on recycling projects strengthens your application. If you can offer relevant NVQs at levels 2 and 3, this also helps. NVQs at levels 2 and 3 are available in Recycling Operations, Waste Management and Environmental Conservation. Much of the training is on the job. You are likely to need to do frequent short refresher courses, because technology and knowledge are changing rapidly in this field.

Personal attributes

You must be a good communicator, able to present written information and oral reports. You should be well organised, good at prioritising, and you need reasonable IT skills. Being able to manage teams of people is very important.

Earnings

New entrants earn between £19,000 and £25,000. Salaries may be lower if you work for a community organisation. With experience and considerable management responsibility salaries rise to £30,000 to £40,000.

Info

Energy & Utility Skills
0121 745 1310
www.euskills.co.uk

Chartered Institution of Wastes Management
01604 620426
www.ciwm.co.uk

Waste Management Industry Training & Advisory Board (WAMITAB)
01604 231950
www.wamitab.org.uk

Waste and Resources Action Programme (WRAP)
01295 819900
www.wrap.org.uk

EVENTS ORGANISATION

Events organiser

Events organiser is a job title that covers many similar work roles. These jobs include conference or exhibition organiser; and events, conference or exhibition manager or coordinator. What all these jobs have in common is that the events organiser/manager is involved at every stage of organisation, right through from the first planning meeting to being there at the event, to ensure that everything runs smoothly and successfully. Events include trade fairs, exhibitions, festivals, fundraising events, product launches, training events and social occasions. Events can be small and local, or large and international. They may last for one evening or as long as a week. What the different job titles denote are the specific types of event for which you are responsible. These might be exhibitions, conferences or social events such as parties or weddings.

The work involves meeting clients to discuss what they want from the event, agreeing budgets and researching and booking appropriate venues, catering and entertainment. The work also involves checking health and safety issues and logistical planning. The events organiser also attends the event itself to solve any problems that arise on the spot.

Entry, qualifications and training

People move into events organisation and management from a variety of backgrounds. You don't necessarily need any formal qualifications, as relevant experience and the right blend of skills are often more important. An events assistant advanced apprenticeship is one option. There are, however, a growing number of events management courses at degree, foundation degree and HND level. The Association of Event Organisers website carries details of these courses. Other useful degree subjects include business, marketing, public relations and hospitality.

Having practical experience in organising events is really important. If you have worked in hospitality, organising conferences and banquets at hotels, for example, this gives you a real advantage. Organising social events on a voluntary basis can also be valuable.

Training is very much on the job, as you normally begin as an assistant to a more experienced organiser/manager. There is a range of relevant NVQs towards which your employer may want you to work. Professional organisations such as the Association of Exhibition Organisers (AEO) or the Association for Conferences and Events (ACE) offer training and networking opportunities.

Exhibition designer

Exhibition designers are responsible for designing the displays and stands which form part of all kinds of exhibitions. They may be working on large public exhibitions, trade fairs, or small temporary exhibitions set up by a business or a charity. The work involves discussing briefs with clients and producing sketches of ideas. These might be drawn by hand or computer-generated. Designers also have to liaise with suppliers and technical staff to ensure that the finished display matches the agreed brief.

Entry, qualifications and training

Employers prefer you to have formal qualifications in display design. It is sometimes possible to acquire these while working as an assistant designer. The British Display Society (BDS) provides details of relevant certificate and diploma courses. It is also possible to get into this work with a degree in a design-related subject such as 3D design or interior design. There are now a small number of degree courses in exhibition design being offered. Check with the BDS for details.

Personal attributes

You have to have really excellent organisational and communication skills to succeed in this work. You must be a good administrator, keeping clear records and tracking the progress of any event. You must be able to establish relationships with new people very quickly and be able to lead teams of people who may not have worked together before. You must be creative, imaginative and calm in the face of crises.

For exhibition design you need good practical, technical and creative skills, as well as all the people skills required for other aspects of events organising.

Earnings

New entrants to both events organisation and exhibition design earn between £17,000 and £24,000. Senior managers earn between £30,000 and £40,000; some employers pay staff bonuses if events are successful. Some organisers, especially those dealing with social events such as weddings and parties, are self-employed and charge a fee according to the scale of the work involved. Events organisers can earn up to £80,000 based on experience as well as other factors such as the type of events and employer. Exhibition designers start on around £18,000. With a few years' experience this rises to £25,000 to £40,000.

Info

Chartered Institute of Marketing (CIM)
01628 427500
www.cim.co.uk

People 1st
020 3074 1222
www.people1st.co.uk

Association of Event Organisers
01442 285810
www.aeo.org.uk

Association for Conferences and Events (ACE)
www.ace-international.co.uk

Association of British Professional Conference Organisers (ABPCO)
01386 858886
www.abpco.org

British Display Society (BDS)
https://britishdisplaysociety.co.uk

Wedding planner

Couples planning a wedding may choose to take on all the planning themselves, but many employ a wedding planner to take on some or all of the organisation for them. Wedding planners help choose themes or come up with imaginative ideas. They help find suitable venues, caterers, florists, photographers or musicians – in fact anything that the couple would like as part of their celebration. Wedding planners could be asked to organise anything from a very small ceremony on a remote island to a huge celebrity style extravaganza or anything in between. The role includes talking to couples to find out what they want and coming up with suggestions if they are not sure, obtaining quotes for all the various aspects of the event and being there on the day to co-ordinate and ensure that everything runs smoothly.

Entry, qualifications and training

The majority of wedding planners are self-employed and there are no specific entry requirements. It is unlikely, however, that this would be your first job. People move into wedding planning from jobs in events management, marketing or hospitality. Some events management companies may offer wedding planning as one of their services, so you might gain experience working for one of these. Some people move into wedding planning having worked in wedding shops, or as photographers and have found they have a flair for this work. However, a college course such as a Level 2 Certificate in Event Planning, or Level 3 Diploma in Hospitality will be useful in understanding the skills required for the role. An advanced apprenticeship as an events assistant may also help. Volunteering or undertaking a course run by training providers are also ways into this career.

Personal attributes

You have to be a warm and friendly communicator with excellent organisational skills. You have to be a good problem solver and be able to keep calm when other people might be getting stressed and anxious. You have to be able to pay meticulous attention to detail. You need to be a good negotiator, obtaining competitive prices for your clients.

Earnings

Working for a company you would earn from £17,000 to £20,000. If you are self-employed what you earn will depend on the fees you charge and how many weddings you plan. At the high end of the market you might earn £25,000 plus.

Info

National Association of Professional Wedding Services
www.theweddingassociation.co.uk

UK Alliance of Wedding Planners
www.ukawp.com

Facilities manager

A facilities manager is responsible for the smooth and efficient running of a building and all the systems within it, e.g. security, health and safety, buildings maintenance, catering, cleaning, computer systems, office equipment, heating, air conditioning, etc. The facilities manager allows the business or organisation to get on with its core activity, whether that be providing healthcare, business consultancy, education, publishing or administration.

Your day-to-day work would vary according to the size of your employer. Large organisations would employ several managers looking after different aspects of the facility such as a security manager, a maintenance manager and a health and safety manager. Working for a smaller company, you could be looking after several or all of these areas. Your work could involve finding and employing suitable contractors to operate various services within the building, looking at ways of making greater efficiency savings with energy or IT systems, training staff in specific areas, managing major projects such as refurbishments or moves to new premises and ensuring that buildings comply with health and safety standards.

Entry, qualifications and training

Many people entering facilities management have qualifications in either building- or business-management related subjects, either degree, HND or foundation degree level. It is possible to get into facilities management without higher education qualifications, but then you would normally start at assistant level. In all instances experience of construction, engineering or business would be of value. Once you are employed it is possible to study for relevant NVQ level 3 qualifications through the Institute of Leadership.

Personal attributes

You need a good mix of business and organisational skills plus practical knowledge of buildings and building services. You need to be a good negotiator when employing contractors and you need to be a calm problem solver. You must have good communication skills and be a good team leader.

Earnings

Facilities managers earn between £26,000 and £45,000 – although working for a very large organisation, particularly where project and contract management are important aspects of the role, salaries can reach £70,000 to £85,000.

FARMING

Farming is in a constant state of change and development and the issues affecting it are often in the news. While there are still a few small, mixed, family run farms, they have tended to become larger and often specialise in arable farming (producing crops) or one type of animal, beef or dairy cattle, pigs, sheep or poultry. Farming is also in the public eye. People have opinions on genetically modified food, food hygiene, animal welfare and whether crops should be grown as alternatives to fossil fuel. Though farms have become larger, farmers and managers have had to think of ways to diversify, such as bringing in leisure activities such as camping or horse riding, or opening farm shops or leasing land for wind turbines or solar farms on their premises. These developments have meant that jobs and work opportunities in farming have changed. Those working in farming have had to develop high levels of skill in, for example, managing a large dairy herd to maximise production or driving extremely sophisticated combine harvesters. Farmers have had to become good business people, negotiating with large buyers such as supermarkets to try to obtain the best prices for their products.

Agricultural contractor

Agricultural contractors work in many farming operations, including harvesting, crop spraying, weeding, hedging, fencing, lambing, sheep shearing and milling – in short, all those tasks where extra labour is needed for a particular task or a particular season.

Entry, qualifications and training

You don't normally need specific entry qualifications, but you do need experience of those aspects of agricultural operations in which you wish to take on contract work. There are several relevant courses available for anyone who wishes to gain qualifications. These include BTEC First Diplomas in Agriculture and BTEC National Diplomas in Agriculture, City & Guilds National Certificate in Agriculture, City & Guilds Advanced National Certificate in Agriculture, NVQ levels 2 and 3 in Agricultural Crop Production, NVQ levels 2 and 3 in Mixed Farming, and NVQ levels 2 and 3 in Livestock Production.

For some tasks, such as operating chainsaws or using pesticides, you are legally required to be trained and competent. The National Proficiency Test Council (NPTC) awards certificates of competence for chainsaw use. The NPTC offers many short courses in ploughing, crop spraying and other agricultural skills.

Personal attributes

You must be a practical problem solver, confident in handling and maintaining machinery. You need to be quick at establishing good working relationships with farmers and other landowners. You also have to be able to supervise and motivate teams of employees.

Earnings

Agricultural contractors are normally self-employed and charge for the work they do. They may charge an hourly rate; for example, for hedge cutting, or a rate per hectare for something like harvesting or crop spraying. They may also charge on herd size for milking or for sheep shearing.

Info

National Proficiency Tests Council (NPTC)
02476 857300
www.nptc.org.uk

Lantra
02476 696996
www.lantra.co.uk

Farm manager

Farm managers are employed by the landowner and are responsible for all aspects of the day-to-day working of the farm. They must plan ahead, organise the staff and work schedules, decide which crops to plant or which animals to rear, and keep a check on buildings and machinery. In addition, they must deal with the office work and accounts.

Farmworker

Farmworkers are employed by farmers, who may well be big businesses, and by landowners to carry out practical and manual tasks on farms. The work could involve working with livestock, with crops or with a combination of these two. Your work could involve milking cows, feeding and checking sheep, cattle, pigs and poultry. It could involve preparing the ground to plant crops, harvesting those crops, or maintaining farm machinery. You could also work repairing and maintaining farm buildings. Most farms in the United Kingdom are large, and each farm employs few workers; nevertheless, you are likely to become a specialist in particular work such as dairy cows, arable crops or crops for energy generation. Many farms have to diversify to generate income, so the farm on which you work may have a farm shop, horses kept at livery or a local pheasant or partridge shoot on the land. Your work may involve helping with any of these or similar enterprises.

Entry, qualifications and training

When recruiting farm managers, most employers look for candidates who have hands-on experience of farming, but most farm managers now will also have a degree in agriculture or a closely related subject. Farmworkers don't necessarily need any formal qualifications, though it may be an advantage if you have GCSEs in maths, English and a technical subject. There are many full- and part-time college courses in all the specialist areas of farm work, as well as apprenticeships such as an advanced apprenticeship in agriculture.

Personal attributes

At whatever level you are working you must have a commitment to farming and a willingness to work in all weathers at any time of the year and to put in some unsocial hours. Farmworkers need good practical skills and must be able to work alone, unsupervised or as part of a team. If you look after livestock you need a highly responsible attitude. Farm managers must be well organised, with good numeracy and communication skills. They also need to be imaginative and good at marketing. A great awareness of health and safety and potential risks is important at all levels in farming.

Earnings

New-entrant farm managers earn around £20,000 to £27,000. Managers with more responsibility on large farms can earn £30,000 to £50,000. Basic-grade farmworkers should be paid at least the minimum wage, but many are on higher grades. There may be opportunities to work overtime at certain times of year. Average salaries for farmworkers are between the minimum wage and £18,000 at the start of your career, £18,000 to £25,000 with experience.

Info

Lantra
02476 696996
www.lantra.co.uk

FASHION

(see also Clothing industry)

While much clothing manufacture is now done overseas, fashion in all its aspects is an important part of the UK economy. The fashion industry covers all aspects of clothing and accessories for men, women and children, and falls into three main sectors: *haute couture* houses, where original model garments are made for individual customers; wholesale *couture*, where trends set by the *haute couture* houses are closely followed, and limited numbers of model garments in stock sizes are made for retail; and wholesale manufacture, which occupies the largest sector of the fashion industry. Here, the latest trends are adapted to styles that are attractive to the main market, and mass produced at affordable prices.

Designer

Fashion designers design garments for all levels of the fashion market. The majority work for high street stores, or their suppliers, designing garments that will be manufactured in their thousands. Some fashion designers work for more upmarket labels, designing products that are still for a mass market but which are produced in much smaller quantities. A few designers work in *haute couture*, designing individual one-off items. Fashion designers may specialise in particular types of clothing such as baby wear, evening wear, hats or sportswear. Some choose to specialise in designing accessories or footwear. Most fashion designers start by designing garments to someone else's brief, but a small number will design original items – this is probably the ultimate goal of most people who go into fashion design. Fashion designers start by making a sketch, often using computer-aided design (CAD), and work from this to the finished product. The work also involves liaising closely with buyers, sales managers and marketing professionals.

Entry, qualifications and training

Courses at college such as a Level 3 Extended Diploma in Fashion Design and Production, or advanced apprenticeship in fashion and textiles (in order to work as a design studio assistant) are ways into this career. However, it is increasingly difficult to get into this work without a degree, and preferably a relevant one in fashion, clothing technology, knitwear, embroidery, graphic design or art and design. The British Fashion Council provides a list of relevant courses. If you have a degree in another subject, or you have not gone on to higher education, you really need to have worked in the fashion industry and have an impressive portfolio of your design ideas to show to a prospective employer. Training is rarely formal and is very much a case of 'pick it up as you go along'. Sometimes there are opportunities to undertake short training courses in new techniques or associated with new technology.

Personal attributes

Of course, a passionate interest in clothing, colour, design and fabrics is essential. In addition you need to be good at analysing trends and almost being able to second-guess what will happen next. You have to be able to work as part of a team, cope under pressure, solve problems and have good drawing skills, both freehand and with computer software. You need to have a lot of self-confidence, and be good at promoting your ideas to others.

Earnings

In London, new entrants earn between £17,000 and £25,000. Outside London, it will be much less, but there are only a few opportunities outside London. Good junior designers who have worked for three or four years in design can earn £30,000 to £42,000. Freelance designers charge per item or per collection and rates vary widely, but some can earn £60,000 to £100,000.

Info

British Fashion Council
www.britishfashioncouncil.co.uk

Screen Skills
020 7713 9800
www.screenskills.com

Textile Institute
0161 237 1188
www.textileinstitute.org

Dressmaker

Opportunities for dressmakers occur in *couture* houses that make specially designed costumes for a particular collection or customer, in wholesale fashion houses making mass-produced garments, and in theatres both making and adapting costumes. Dressmakers may also be employed by large stores to carry out alterations, or they may be self-employed, making clothes either from home or from a workshop. Teachers of dressmaking are employed in schools, colleges and by adult education centres.

Entry, qualifications and training

No formal qualifications are necessary, but City & Guilds qualifications and NVQs are available. Some degrees and HNDs in clothing design or fashion have a dressmaking option. An intermediate apprenticeship in fashion and textiles, or a garment maker advanced apprenticeship are other ways into this career. Undertaking a short course in dressmaking techniques at a private training provider or adult education centre, for example, may help to equip you with skills required for this role, although they may not give you a formal qualification.

Personal attributes

Dressmakers need to combine artistic and practical skills with an ability to follow instructions and to recognise problems as they arise and make the necessary adaptations. They may have to deal with temperamental designers and their customers.

Earnings

Earnings vary, but trainees earn around the minimum wage. With experience dressmakers can earn £17,000 to £22,000. Many dressmakers are self-employed and can earn more, especially if they make items like wedding dresses or other special-occasion wear. Some dressmakers work part time or as a second job.

Info

Chartered Society of Designers (CSD)
020 7357 8088
www.csd.org.uk

Screen Skills
020 7713 9800
www.screenskills.com

Model

Models work as 'live' or photographic models, generally showing clothes or accessories. Photographic and advertising models rely on an agent to get them work and handle the fees. Competition is intense and very few models get to the top of the profession.

Fashion models are employed full time by couturiers, wholesalers or fashion stores as 'live' models. They have the garments draped and pinned on them during the design stages, and show them to the public. Live models are usually tall, at least 1.72 m (5 ft 8 in). Photographic modelling involves posing in garments chosen to be illustrated in magazines, newspapers, catalogues or on advertising posters. This work is often out of season for the type of garments being modelled and some of the work is done abroad. Expenses include the provision of accessories, a good basic wardrobe and hairdressing.

Entry, qualifications and training

Private model schools run training courses for live and photographic modelling. Reputable schools will only take entrants whom they think will succeed, and will introduce them to agencies at the end of the training period. The London College of Fashion, a non-commercial college, offers a one-year full-time course leading to a certificate in fashion modelling. Students should have three GCSEs grades 9–4 or equivalent.

Personal attributes

A model must be able to work hard, be punctual and reliable, get on well with people, and have a great deal of common sense. Competition is intense and only those who can interpret what the stylist and photographer want will get to the top. A female model is normally at least 1.72 m (5 ft 8 in) tall and may have to meet certain body statistics requirements. A male model is normally at least 1.83 m (6 ft) tall. Models should have clear skin, good hands, nails and teeth, healthy hair and attractive features. In recent years, there has been greater emphasis on diversity within the fashion/modelling industry with models of different sizes and ethnicities represented in fashion campaigns.

Earnings

Earnings are varied. Models normally work freelance and are paid per day or per job. Rates vary enormously depending on how well established you are and what kind of modelling you do. Routine modelling for clothing catalogues may pay £50 to £60 per day. At the top end of the profession these rates are between £600 and £1,000 per day. Working for a fashion house, rates vary from £10,000 to £40,000 per year. Remember that your agent may charge up to 20 per cent of your fee.

Info

Association of Model Agents
www.associationofmodelagents.org

Alba Model Information
www.albamodel.info

Equity
020 7379 6000
www.equity.org.uk

FILM AND TELEVISION PRODUCTION

A popular and competitive field, film offers opportunities in film production, television, new media and advertising. The majority of those working in film and TV are self-employed freelancers. Film production involves both studio and location work. Anyone who is really serious about this work needs to develop personal marketing skills in addition to their creative craft skills.

Animator

Working as an animator you aim to bring drawings or models to life on screen. Your work could be used in animated short and full-length films, television cartoons, adverts, computer games, music videos, websites and movie visual effects. Producing an animation involves many stages and processes, from generating ideas to building models and editing the final piece. Each stage can involve several specific tasks and job roles, including production designers who create the look; storyboard artists who take the script or ideas and show the story in a visual way; layout artists also draw how each shot will look. In production, digital painters touch up colours; animators and modellers follow the storyboard and use computer or stop-frame animation to create movement and personality.

Announcer

Announcers work to detailed and carefully timed scripts, communicating information to the viewer from a soundproof 'behind the scenes' office. They sometimes write or adapt their own material and need to be able to work on their own.

Archivist/librarian

(see also Information science for Archivist)

Archivists and librarians collect, collate, preserve and make available collections of recorded visual, sound, written and other materials for use by various productions. Archives are valuable business resources, and some archivists are now involved in selling and marketing materials.

Art and design

(see also Art and design)

The art and design function is to create a visual effect to meet the needs of the production, creating manual or computer-generated graphics.

Camerawork

Workers in this area operate and assist with still, film and video cameras to record images as directed, using different techniques.

Costume designer

Costume designers play a key role in bringing a production to life. This could involve researching what clothing in a particular historic period was like to creating something really futuristic. Costume assistants will be responsible for the wardrobe and making sure that all the right costumes are in the right place at the right time and are ready to use.

Director

The director is responsible for achieving the creative, visual and auditory effect of a production and, equally importantly, motivating a team.

Raw tape or film is shaped to interpret the requirements of the director, either by physical cutting (film) or by selecting sequences and re-recording onto a master tape using sophisticated computer equipment.

IT specialist

IT specialists support many aspects of broadcasting, film and video, either within the companies or as consultants, providing and maintaining relevant systems and software.

Lighting technician

Lighting specialists ensure that the stage or set is correctly lit to meet the needs of the production, whether this is an outdoor scene, a dark setting for a horror film, or creating the correct lighting effects for an historical drama.

Make-up and hairdressing

(see Beauty for Make-up artist)

Marketing and sales

Marketing and sales staff work in an international marketplace to raise revenue for broadcasters or film-makers. Airtime is sold, sponsorship and co-production rights are negotiated and spin-off products, such as books, toys and DVDs are developed.

Model maker/prop maker

Model makers and prop makers work not only in film and TV but in the theatre too. They make all kinds of props from moving models to fake jewellery, replica weapons and even fake food. Model makers and prop makers use a wide range of skills, including carpentry, sculpting, casting, sewing, painting, welding and computer-aided design (CAD). It may well be that some prop makers develop experience and a reputation for being especially skilled in one or two of these areas.

Producer

Producers perform a variety of management and operational roles to bring together the many elements of a production, either in a studio or on location. Often responsible both for the initial concept and raising the essential finance, they are the team leaders.

Production assistant

Production assistants provide high-quality administrative and secretarial support to the producer and director at every stage of production, coordinating all activities and preparing schedules and scripts.

Production manager

Production managers organise all essential support facilities for the team, from accommodation and transport to on-set catering. They will also roster crews and arrange payments.

Production operative

Production operatives perform the operational duties of the production such as vision mixing and autocue operations.

Researcher

Researchers support the producer, helping to turn ideas into reality – providing and following up ideas, contacting and interviewing people, acquiring relevant factual material and writing briefings for presenters.

Runner/gofer

This job is the traditional entry-level job for the industry. Bright, highly motivated – often highly qualified – people act as general assistants, taking messages, making deliveries, being indispensable, and learning the basics of the commercial business.

Setcraft/props

People working in this area construct the scenery, sets and backdrops to meet the production brief, reflecting both historical accuracy and the required design and style. They also maintain sets during a production, and operate any mechanical features as directed. Props (hired or made) are used to dress the set.

Sound technician

Sound technicians interpret the requirements of a production in terms of sound collection. During post-production they may be involved in recording, editing and dubbing, using a range of sophisticated equipment.

Special effects designer

Special effects designers create and operate effects for a production, within technical limitations and budget, and operate the necessary machines.

Writer

(see also Writer)

Writers work to produce or edit scripts for a variety of radio, television, DVD or film productions.

Entry, qualifications and training

The film and television industry has changed rapidly over the past decade and one of the results of this has been that at all levels and whatever your specific job, you need to be multi-skilled and flexible. While formal academic qualifications are not essential, this is an exceedingly competitive field, the result being that many entrants to all jobs within the film, TV and video industry are graduates. Degrees in communications, multimedia, photography, media studies, film and television are particularly useful. These courses are also extremely popular and thus entry is competitive. Look for courses where you get the chance to use state-of-the-art technology and where there may be opportunities for work placements or at least contacts with the industry.

If you wish to get into production/direction you may have to start in research or marketing, or as a production assistant – whichever, most careers in this sector require you to work your way up from the bottom, or be prepared to make sideways transfers.

Screen Skills, the industry skills body for the creative industries, including film, provides a range of training courses and works closely with the industry to try to ensure that employees are training in appropriate skills. Some television companies offer graduate training schemes, but unsurprisingly, these are massively over-subscribed.

Personal attributes

You need either to have creative flair and imagination, or to be able to see the value of these and support them. For many roles you need good technical skills and the ability to work carefully and patiently, maintaining good powers of concentration. You need excellent people skills, as you are often working in situations where the whole team is under pressure and you have to be able to keep calm. In many situations, you need to be good at promoting yourself and your ideas.

Earnings

It is a broad industry, but here are some examples of pay to give a flavour of the range of possible earnings. Runners get between the minimum wage and £15,000, and this is great experience. Trainee production assistants earn the minimum wage to £15,000. Experienced production staff earn between £19,000 and £25,000. Technicians earn between £16,000 and £26,000. Directors' salaries are not necessarily high if they are working for small companies on low-budget productions.

Many staff work freelance and are paid on a daily basis or a fee per contract. BECTU sets rates in the industry. Your own fee-negotiating skills are often important in this field.

Info

BBC
www.bbc.co.uk

BBC Academy
www.bbc.co.uk/academy

British Film Institute (BFI)
www.bfi.org.uk

Broadcasting Entertainment Cinematographic and Theatre Union (BECTU)
020 7346 0900
www.bectu.org.uk

Screen Skills
020 7713 9800
www.screenskills.com

ITV Careers
www.itvjobs.com

FIREFIGHTER

Firefighters work to save life and rescue property in emergencies. Fighting fires is only one aspect of their work. They are called to emergencies such as road traffic accidents, plane or train crashes, explosions and chemical spillages. They also rescue people or animals stranded in high places or stuck in mud. The Fire Service also advises on fire safety through education programmes.

They offer advice on fire protection and prevention for existing properties and new buildings. They also conduct inspections of premises such as hotels and hospitals to ensure that adequate fire alarms and proper escape routes and action plans to deal with emergencies are in place.

The Fire Service is administered by local authorities, and each authority is responsible for its own recruitment and selection procedures. The armed services and the British Airports Authority also have their own fire services.

Entry, qualifications and training

No formal qualifications are necessarily required, but since each brigade sets its own entry requirements some may require GCSEs in maths and English. You must be aged 18 or over to train as a firefighter. Some brigades do offer Young Firefighter schemes allowing you to get involved in some aspects of fire service work. In order to pass the National Firefighter Selection Tests you have to fill in a detailed application form and pass a physical fitness test, a medical and a range of aptitude tests. The training is on the job, with frequent courses on new risks, better procedures, etc.

Personal attributes

As a firefighter you have to be calm and courageous, prepared to go into dangerous situations, but sensible enough to tackle things calmly. You must be good at reassuring frightened or injured people and at working as part of a team. You may also be involved in teaching about fire prevention and safety, so you must enjoy dealing with people.

Earnings

Trainee firefighters start at around £23,500. On achieving full competence, the rate for a firefighter is around £29,000. Firefighters working in London earn an additional £4,500. Crew managers earn around £32,000, and a station manager can earn up to £41,700.

Info

Skills for Justice
www.sfjuk.com

Contact local fire brigades directly – they are listed on the Skills for Justice website.

FISH FARMER

With increased concern about depleting the world's fish stocks, fish farming rapidly in recent years. Most fish are farmed for the table, but some are also produced to stock lakes and reservoirs for the leisure industry. The most commonly farmed fish are salmon and trout, but tilapia, bream and other species are also being farmed. Shellfish such as mussels, oysters and scallops are also farmed commercially. Fish farm managers, technicians and other workers are employed on commercial fish farms, private estates and by environmental organisations. The work is varied. You might buy in young fish and rear them to adulthood or breed new stock by hatching eggs from adult fish. Typical tasks include feeding fish either by hand or through automated feeding systems, checking the health of fish and the quality of the water they live in, moving fish from one tank or pond to another according to their weight and size, and finally, harvesting fish for the table or to sell to other fish producers.

Entry, qualifications and training

If you wish to join this industry as a manager or assistant manager, you normally need a relevant degree. There are a small number of fisheries degrees available in the United Kingdom. You may also be able to get into management with a degree in another subject such as agriculture or environmental management. If you wish to start at technician level, you may not necessarily need formal qualifications, although you could consider a part-time BTEC first diploma in Fisheries Husbandry or a two-year full-time BTEC National Diploma in Fisheries Management. You may also be able to train through an apprenticeship.

Once you are working in fish farming, you may want to consider taking Institute of Fisheries Management part-time certificate and diploma courses in fisheries management. You need to consider geographical location when you are thinking about this career. The majority of farms are in Scotland, although there are a few in the south of England and a scattering in other places.

Personal attributes

You need to have a real interest in the scientific aspects of what you are doing. You have to enjoy working with living organisms. You have to be prepared to work in all weathers and conditions. You may have to work as part of a team, but you also have to be happy and confident in working on your own.

Earnings

Fish farm technicians earn between £18,000 and £24,000. Assistant managers earn around £26,000 and managers of large fish farms can earn up to £40,000. For some posts accommodation may be provided, although occasionally this may only be a caravan.

Info

Institute of Fisheries Management
0845 388 7012
www.ifm.org.uk

Lantra
02476 696996
www.lantra.co.uk

British Trout Association
01722 334100
www.britishtrout.co.uk

FISHING

Fishing covers work on many kinds of commercial boats, from single-handed vessels to large factory ships employing crews of 15 to 20. The usual progression for fishermen and women is to start as deckhands, work up to mate and finally to fishing vessel skipper. Fishermen and women work on inshore vessels that stay close to the shore and on vessels that go limited distances out to sea. They also work on vessels that go far out into the ocean. In the UK most fishing vessels are based around the south-west of England, north-east Scotland and the Scottish islands.

Fishing vessel deckhand

Deckhands help with everything from gutting and cleaning the fish caught to preparing food for other crew members and keeping the boat clean and orderly. They repair nets and also help set up trawling and hauling equipment.

Fishing vessel skipper

Skippers are responsible for the management of every voyage. They have to plan where to fish and take responsibility for navigation and for health and safety aboard the vessel. They oversee the use of the vessel's fishing gear and other technical equipment. They manage the workload of the crew and deal with any problems that arise.

Entry, qualifications and training

To become a deckhand you don't need any formal qualifications, although previous experience of the sea and boating or sailing of some kind is useful. Most people train through training schemes organised around the United Kingdom; contact the Sea Fish Industry Authority for details. If you have had some useful experience, it may be worth approaching a skipper directly to see if he or she will take you on. Training is on the job, but if you progress to become a mate or a skipper you can take NVQ level 3 in Marine Vessel Operations (Mate) or Marine Vessel Operations (Skipper).

Personal attributes

As either a deckhand or a skipper you must have good eyesight and hearing and be physically fit and have a lot of physical courage. The work is often dangerous as you have to deal with wind, storms and cold seas. You must be able to tolerate working with a small group of people, often in cramped, uncomfortable conditions. You need to be able to tolerate long periods away from home, family and friends.

Earnings

There are wide variations in earnings for deckhands and skippers. Earnings are based on the size of the catch and the value of the fish caught. Salaries for deckhands and skippers are between the minimum wage and £26,000. Skippers on large commercial vessels can earn considerably more than this. Income is also affected by legal restrictions on size of catch and the number of days on which a vessel is permitted to leave port to fish.

Info

Seafish
0131 558 3331
www.seafish.org

Lantra
02476 696996
www.lantra.co.uk

Maritime and Coastguard Agency (MCA)
020 3817 2000
www.gov.uk/government/organisations/
maritime-and-coastguard-agency

FOOD SCIENCE AND TECHNOLOGY

Food scientists and technologists work in the food and drink industry developing, testing and monitoring the safety of the food and drink we consume. Food processing is often in the public eye. Concerns about healthy eating, salt and fat content, the price of products and their fitness for consumption all form part of the food scientist's daily work.

In this work you could be involved in many different roles including developing new products, ensuring that the nutritional content of products is accurately measured and described, testing entirely new ingredients, modifying products to reduce fat or sugar content and working with customers such as supermarkets to find out what customers do or do not like. You could be developing ways to process food more quickly, so that it stays fresher, or more cheaply to keep your products competitive. You could have a role in ensuring that everything produced complies with all food standard and other legal requirements. You could be working in a laboratory, at the processing plant, or in a test kitchen.

Entry, qualifications and training

There are several routes into this work. You can start as a lab technician with a food or drinks manufacturer. For this you normally need four GCSEs, including maths and a science. If you are successful, you can then study part time for higher qualifications and progress to technologist-level jobs. You could study a degree in food technology; you normally need two or three A levels, including biology or chemistry, to do this. If you have one A level there is a range of BTEC HNC and HND full- and part-time courses for which you could apply. Exact course requirements vary, so check with colleges. If you have a degree in an unrelated subject, there are some postgraduate courses in food safety and food quality management that could gain you entry. The Institute of Food Science and Technology careers website provides information on all these options.

Personal attributes

You need a real interest in food and food preparation, combined with an aptitude for, and interest in, science. You should be a good communicator, able to share ideas or enforce legislation if necessary. You must be careful and methodical and acutely aware of food safety and hygiene issues. You should be able to work well in a team, but able to work on your own too. If you are involved in recipe development you should be creative. If you are involved in research, you need an enquiring mind.

Earnings

At technician level, salaries start at around £20,000. Graduate food technologists earn between £23,000 and £29,000. If you have five to 10 years' experience and management responsibility, salaries range from £30,000 to £45,000.

Info

National Skills Academy for Food & Drink
0845 644 0558
nsafd.co.uk

Institute of Food Science and Technology (IFST)
020 7603 6316
www.ifst.org.uk

Chartered Institute of Environmental Health (CIEH)
020 7827 5800
www.cieh.org

FORENSIC SCIENTIST

Gripping TV dramas and films have probably been responsible for bringing a not always accurate portrayal of forensic science to public attention. Most forensic scientists work for independent organisations that provide forensic science services to the police, public health laboratories, universities and companies that deal with specialised areas such as fire investigation or examining questioned documents. Forensic scientists examine and try to identify, by means of analytical chemistry, molecular biology and microscopic analysis, samples of materials such as clothing, hair, blood, glass, paint and handwriting, in order to provide evidence to expose criminals, the location of a crime, the weapons used, and other relevant details.

Entry, qualifications and training

This is a fiercely competitive graduate-entry profession. The most relevant degrees are biology, chemistry, biochemistry, crop and soil science, materials science, pharmacology and physiology. While there are many undergraduate degrees in forensic science, not all of these qualify you as a forensic scientist. You should check individual course details very carefully. Choosing a university qualification accredited by The Chartered Society of Forensic Sciences may help you. Most forensic scientists also have relevant postgraduate qualifications and some laboratory work experience. Most training is on the job, but you are also likely to have to attend several short courses to improve your knowledge and skills. You could also undertake a laboratory scientist higher or degree apprenticeship, and it will be useful if the company you do an apprenticeship with provides forensic science services. Or, for example, this could be with police where there are in-house lab facilities.

Personal attributes

You must have an enquiring and logical mind. You should be patient and able to pay attention to really small details. You should have good scientific skills and knowledge and you must be persistent. Excellent written and oral communication skills are also vital.

Earnings

Trainee forensic scientists earn from £20,000 to £23,000. You may start higher up the scale if you have a postgraduate qualification. After around two years, salaries are £25,000 to £35,000. Senior forensic scientists can earn £50,000.

Info

Chartered Society of Forensic Scientists
01423 534646
www.csofs.org

Skills for Justice
www.sfjuk.com

Forensic Science Northern Ireland
www.fsni.gov.uk

FORESTRY

Trees, woodlands and forests cover some 13 per cent of the land area of Britain. Forests and woodlands have to be managed so that they can provide many resources. They are used to harvest timber for the construction industry, for furniture making and for paper production. Recreational activities such as walking, cycling and horse riding are permitted in many woods and forests and so suitable routes have to be maintained. They are wildlife havens for plants, birds, mammals, reptiles and insects. Some grazing of stock, particularly traditional breeds of cattle and ponies, is being developed in some of our forests. Forestry officers and forestry workers are employed either by private companies or environmental organisations that manage forests and woodland or by contractors.

Forestry officer

Your role as a forestry officer would depend very much on the type of forest or woodland you are managing and what its primary functions are, e.g. timber production, recreation or wildlife proliferation. Your responsibilities would almost always involve the supervision of other forestry workers and contractors. Your work may involve planning planting programmes and supervising such planting. You might have to organise both the harvesting and sale of timber. Some woods and forests have visitor centres and part of your role could be to manage this. You would be responsible for the monitoring and care of wildlife in the forest and you may have to provide information to the public on nature trails or on what tracks and paths they are allowed to use for which activities.

Forestry worker

Forestry workers take on a wide range of tasks that support all the forest's commercial and environmental activities. Forestry workers plant, prune and cut down trees. They tidy up the forest floor, perhaps removing weeds or debris from tracks and paths. They often build or maintain fences, gates and stiles.

Entry, qualifications and training

What qualifications you need depends on whether you are hoping to start as a forest worker or to get into forestry management. In either case some voluntary work with a woodland or forestry-based organisation is a very good starting point. The Woodland Trust is one such organisation, but there are others. Check the Volunteering England website to find out about local opportunities.

To become a forest worker you do not need any formal qualifications. You could choose to study full or part time at an agricultural college where you could complete a BTEC National Diploma in Forestry and Arboriculture. If you are already employed in forestry, your employer may be happy for you to do a course part time. Whether the course is full or part time, you should check with the college as it may have formal entry requirements, e.g. GCSEs including maths and science. Passing one of these courses will enable you to progress to skilled worker level and then on to management. If your work involves using a chainsaw or applying pesticides you will have to pass proficiency tests before you are allowed to do this. The National Proficiency Test Council provides information about these tests, but your employer can also help you arrange to take these.

If you prefer to go straight into forestry management, then you will need to do a degree or HND course in forestry or a related subject such as countryside management.

Personal attributes

You have to be extremely practical and very safety conscious. You must have a real love of woodlands, forests and trees and an interest in nature. You should be very happy to work outdoors in all sorts of weather conditions. You will often be working on your own and unsupervised, so you have to be comfortable with this, but also good at working as part of a team.

Earnings

Basic grade forest workers start on around the minimum wage, while skilled workers earn between £17,000 and £20,000. Supervisors earn around £22,000 and forestry managers may earn up to £35,000. Occasionally accommodation is provided, but this is by no means standard practice.

Info

Forestry England
www.forestryengland.uk

National Proficiency Tests Council
02476 857300
www.nptc.org.uk

Royal Forestry Society (RFS)
www.rfs.org.uk

Volunteering England
www.volunteeringengland.org.uk

Lantra
02476 696996
www.lantra.co.uk

Institute of Chartered Foresters
0131 240 1425
www.charteredforesters.org

FOUNDRY WORK

Foundry work supports many other industries. It makes metal-cast components such as propellers, turbines, crankshafts, all types of machinery, and domestic items such as fireplaces.

Foundry workers are employed in several specialised tasks. Pattern-makers produce template models, which are used to create moulds for casting metal. They make the models with a range of materials, such as wood, metal, plastic and wax. Moulders make moulds into which molten metal is poured to make castings. Foundry process operators are employed in one of several roles, including: mill operator; cupola attendant – looking after the furnaces; wax assembler – putting together the wax patterns; ladle person (or caster) – transferring molten metal from the furnace to the moulds; die-caster – operating die-casting machines; fettler – grinding surplus metal off castings with abrasive wheels.

There are also limited openings for foundry technologists, metallurgists, chemists and engineers in research and development. Graduate trainees are recruited to production and administrative management posts.

Entry, qualifications and training

While you don't need formal qualifications it may help if you have already worked in another area of engineering, manufacturing or production and/or if you have a forklift licence. There may be opportunities to do an apprenticeship in foundry work; what is available varies from region to region. If you want to do an apprenticeship you may need three GCSEs, including one technical subject. Much of your training will be on the job, but your employer may give you opportunities to study for engineering qualifications. If you cannot get in through an apprenticeship and do not have previous experience, a college BTEC or City & Guilds course in engineering could improve your prospects. Vocational diplomas for 14–19-year-olds have recently been introduced in the manufacturing sector. These combine school or college study with work experience and may provide a further route into foundry work. You need to be physically fit to do foundry work and some employers may require you to pass a medical as part of the selection process.

Personal attributes

You must be physically fit with good stamina. You have to be extremely safety conscious at all times. You must be able to follow instructions and work as part of a team. You may have to work on several different projects and you need a high level of concentration.

Earnings

Trainee foundry operatives earn between £13,500 and £18,000. With experience, this rises to £20,000 to £25,000. You may earn more if you have additional supervisory or other responsibilities.

Info

SEMTA
0845 643 9001
www.semta.org.uk

Tomorrow's Engineers
www.tomorrowsengineers.org.uk

Institute of Cast Metal Engineers
0121 752 1810
www.icme.org.uk

FUNERAL WORK

The key job in this field is that of funeral director, and the role of embalmer is also a significant one. Many others are employed in related work; crematorium attendants, drivers, gravediggers and administrators, for example.

Funeral director

Funeral directors collect the deceased from hospital or their residence and prepare them for burial or cremation, which may include embalming. Most funeral premises include private viewing rooms for family visits. The funeral director often makes all the funeral arrangements on behalf of the family, such as the date, time and place of any ceremony and interment or cremation. The funeral director places the relevant notice of death and acknowledgement of thanks for sympathy in newspapers, pays all the fees, arranges flowers, transports the coffin and mourners to and from church/crematorium, and will act as a collection point for flowers, or donations in lieu, if desired.

Funeral directors may be employed by large firms such as cooperative societies, or by small family-run concerns. In remote rural areas, a local carpenter or other craftsperson may also work as a funeral director.

Entry, qualifications and training

Those wishing to obtain the Diploma in Funeral Directing must register with the National Association of Funeral Directors (NAFD) and will also have student membership of the British Institute of Funeral Directors (BIFD). Full details of the diploma course are forwarded to each student. Every student must follow the foundation module – there are no exceptions.

A satisfactory standard must be reached in the foundation module before proceeding to the diploma. A student will be required to have 24 months' experience and have arranged 25 funerals before the diploma is awarded. NVQs levels 2 and 3 in Funeral Services are available for those employed within the profession.

Personal attributes

Tact, sympathy and a reassuring, helpful nature are essential to funeral directors when they are advising the bereaved. They also need to combine administrative ability with technical expertise in the varied preparations of funeral arrangements. On-call and out-of-hours work is an integral part of the job and an ability to adapt to irregular hours is essential.

Earnings

Salaries vary depending on size of firm, many of which are family concerns. Average earnings are between £16,000 and £30,000.

Info

National Association of Funeral Directors (NAFD)	British Institute of Funeral Directors (BIFD)
0121 711 1343	0800 032 2733
www.nafd.org.uk	www.bifd.org.uk

Embalmer

Embalmers work with the bodies of the deceased, working to preserve and present the body from the time of death until the time of burial or cremation. It is special work, because how a body looks to loved ones and friends of the deceased is very important. Embalmers wash, disinfect and dress bodies. They wash hair and apply cosmetics. They may use plaster of Paris or wax to preserve or restore the appearance of a body after injury or illness. They work closely with funeral directors and arrangers, so that they are aware of any special requests concerning clothing, jewellery or culture-specific practices connected with the bodies of the deceased.

Entry, qualifications and training

While you do not need formal qualifications, GCSEs in maths, English and science, especially chemistry and/or biology, are useful. You have to train with a tutor who is registered with the British Institute of Embalmers. Your training is usually through part-time or distance learning and you do this while working for a funeral director. If you successfully complete your course you can then register with the British Institute of Embalmers. At this stage you can either work for a chain of funeral directors or work freelance, offering your services to smaller, family-run firms.

Personal attributes

You have to be sensitive and aware of how those who have lost a loved one are feeling, yet you must be practical and not at all squeamish yourself. You have to have good manual dexterity for delicate work, be able to work on your own and above all have a dignified and responsible attitude to your work.

Earnings

Embalmers earn between the minimum wage and £17,000. A few with a lot of experience can earn up to £30,000.

Info

British Institute of Embalmers
01564 778991
www.bioe.co.uk

FURNITURE AND FURNISHING

Furniture manufacture

Modern furniture production for the mass market employs people in several occupations. In factories staff work on production lines, cutting, joining, finishing and assembling complete items or flat-packed products. Employees in purchasing departments source suitable materials, while sales and marketing staff with wholesalers and retailers promote and sell furniture products. In addition, there are a number of specific jobs associated with furniture production.

Furniture designer

As a furniture designer you could be designing furniture for the mass market, furniture to be made in very small quantities, or one-off items. You could be working in a range of materials: wood, MDF, even metal or plastics – think of garden and conservatory furniture, for example. You might be designing office furniture or an expensive individual item commissioned by a customer.

If you work for the mass market, your role will mainly involve drawing and designing the specifications for an item and perhaps being involved in making a prototype. If designing individual items, you may make the whole item yourself from start to finish.

Furniture restorer

Furniture restorers repair, restore and preserve antique furniture. They have to use techniques from woodwork, metalwork, cabinet making, conservation and French polishing. Restorers often need to use modern materials such as resins to repair old pieces of furniture. The work can involve anything from a minor repair, putting a handle back in place, to completely rebuilding an impressive dining room suite. One important aspect of the work is to be able to agree with a client what is realistically achievable with a particular piece of work. On large projects, say in a stately home, you may be working as part of a large conservation and restoration team.

Upholsterer

Upholsterers make the padding and soft coverings for furniture such as chairs, sofas, stools and mattresses and headboards for beds. They work with a range of materials, from natural fibres such as woollen cloth, cotton, leather or suede, to modern, synthetic materials. Upholsterers may work in mass manufacturing – including in the manufacture of cards or trains – or craft individual pieces of work. The work involves planning, advising on fabrics and estimating costs, preparing patterns and templates, cutting out fabric, fixing webbing and springs, covering frames with padding and fabric using stitching, staples, tacks or glue, making cushions and adding finishing decorations and trimmings.

Entry, qualifications and training

Most designers have a relevant degree, or HND; most appropriate subjects include furniture design, 3D design, and furniture technology and product design. Some skilled craftspeople who get into the bespoke market, making individually commissioned items, may not have formal academic qualifications but may simply have built up a reputation through work they have already completed. Many restorers also have degrees in furniture design, or other art or conservation-related subjects and there are City & Guilds courses in furniture construction offered at a small number of colleges: The British Antique Furniture Restorers Association (BAFRA) is the best source of advice. Upholsterers don't need formal qualifications, but if you choose to work in mass production, your employer may encourage you to work towards an NVQ level 1 in Supporting the Production of Furniture; building up experience via short courses run by local colleges can also be a useful starting point.

Personal attributes

Wherever you place yourself within furniture manufacture, you will have to have practical skills and some creative flair. You will need to understand the properties of various materials and be aware of costing and budgets for these materials. As a restorer, patience and the ability to pay meticulous attention to fine detail are very important. Whatever your specialism, you may have to be able to work as part of a team or, if self-employed, you will require self-marketing and business skills.

Earnings

Designers entering the mass production market start on around £17,000 to £21,000. With experience this rises to £25,000 to £50,000 – although not many reach the top end. Restorers earn between £20,000 and £40,000. Upholsterers working for the mass market earn from the minimum wage up to £36,000. Earnings can be much higher than this if you make it into expensive niche markets such as individually designed and produced one-offs in expensive and luxurious materials.

Info

Arts Council England
0161 934 4317
www.artscouncil.org.uk

The Chartered Society of Designers (CSD)
020 7357 8088
www.csd.org.uk

British Antique Furniture Restorers Association (BAFRA)
01939 210826
www.bafra.org.uk

Crafts Council
020 7806 2500
www.craftscouncil.org.uk

Creative & Cultural Skills
020 7015 1800
www.ccskills.org.uk

The Design Council
020 7420 5200
www.designcouncil.org.uk

GARDENING

Gardening involves planting and caring for flowers, trees and shrubs, cutting and tending lawns, removing weeds, clearing debris and preparing ground for planting.

Gardener

(see also Landscape architecture)

As a gardener, you might be self-employed – tending the gardens of private individuals – or you could be employed in the private or public sector – caring for the grounds of hotels, parks, hospitals, schools, residential complexes, private businesses or stately homes and heritage gardens.

Your work would be determined by who employs you, but also by the seasons and the weather. Working for yourself tending gardens of private individuals you could be involved in most aspects of garden care: weeding, planting, pruning, mowing lawns and digging out beds. Working in large gardens employing several gardeners you may be responsible for particular tasks or areas such as the greenhouses or a water garden. In all cases you would have to work closely with whoever employs you to agree on a plan for the garden, e.g. colour schemes for flowerbeds, plants to attract wildlife or overall look of the garden.

Entry, qualifications and training

You don't always need formal qualifications to become a gardener. Training is given on the job, often as part of an apprenticeship; NVQ levels 1–3 are available. Some employers will require you to have three or four GCSEs grades 9–4. Full-time training courses in horticulture are available at colleges throughout the country, from first diploma level. There may be apprenticeships available in this work.

Personal attributes

You must have a real interest in the plants you work with, whether they are commercial fruit and vegetables or ornamental flowers and shrubs. You should be very practical and happy to work in all weathers, and you must be patient – some of your work takes a long time to come to fruition. For some gardening jobs you need an eye for design and colour. You should be comfortable working on your own, but able to talk to people about their gardens, their crops and their ideas.

Earnings

Working for local authorities or private companies gardeners earn from around the minimum wage to around £25,000. As a head gardener at a heritage site garden you can earn from £25,000 to £40,000. Some jobs which involve grounds management as well as gardening can also pay up to £30,000.

Info

Lantra 02476 696996 www.lantra.co.uk	**National Proficiency Tests Council (NPTC)** 02476 857300 www.nptc.org.uk
Royal Botanic Gardens Kew 020 8332 5655 www.kew.org	**Royal Horticultural Society (RHS)** 020 3176 5800 www.rhs.org.uk
Horticultural Correspondence College 0800 083 9191 www.hccollege.co.uk	**Local Government jobs** www.lgjobs.com

GAS SERVICE

Gas service technician

Gas service technicians, also referred to as gas service fitters, work in people's homes and on business premises, installing, servicing and repairing appliances and systems such as cookers, boilers and central heating systems. They test controls and safety devices to ensure that they are working and they locate and repair gas leaks. Often they specialise in installation, servicing or repair, but some gas service engineers will work in all three areas.

Entry, qualifications and training

The usual route to qualification is through a technician-level apprenticeship lasting between three and four years. You need four GCSEs grades 9–4, including English, maths and science, and you must have perfect colour vision. Most apprentices start at age 16, but you can start up to the age of 24. Successful completion of the apprenticeship also leads to an NVQ level 3 award.

To work as a gas fitter, installer or service engineer, you must register with the Gas Safe Register, which will check your qualifications and ascertain that you have had suitable training and work experience before allowing you to register.

Personal attributes

You must be practical, able to handle tools and instruments, and you must be able to apply technical knowledge to practical problems. You have to be able to work on your own or as part of a team, and it is important that you are polite and friendly and enjoy meeting and dealing with people. Having an acute awareness of safety issues is essential.

Earnings

British Gas apprentices earn around £10,000, rising to £34,000 when fully qualified. Apprentices to smaller companies may start on considerably less.

Gas network engineer

Gas network engineers lay and service the gas pipelines that supply domestic and commercial premises. The work involves digging holes using mechanical digging equipment, using maps and plans to trace where you need to dig, laying and repairing pipes, connecting homes and businesses to the gas network and dealing with emergency leaks.

Entry, qualifications and training

You do not need formal qualifications to work as a gas network engineer, but if you train through an apprenticeship you will normally need four GCSEs grades 9–4, including maths, English and a technical subject. If you are not joining through an apprenticeship, you will have an advantage if you have experience and/or qualifications in engineering or building services. You will also need a driving licence.

Personal attributes

You need to be physically fit and you must be able to follow plans and instructions accurately. You need to have a keen awareness of safety issues and you should be good at working as part of a team. As you progress, you may need to develop supervisory responsibilities too.

Earnings

Apprentices and new entrants earn around the minimum wage. Once you have completed your apprenticeship or built up some experience, salaries rise to £18,000 to £25,000. With supervisory responsibilities earnings can be £35,000 plus.

Info

Energy & Utility Skills
0121 745 1310
www.euskills.co.uk

GEOLOGY

Geology, sometimes called geoscience or earth science, encompasses several careers. Geoscience is concerned with the understanding of the earth, its rocks, minerals and fossils, the dynamics of how the continents move, why earthquakes occur and what its 4.6-billion-year history can tell us. There are highly academic fields of geology, concerning the discovery, collection, classification and analysis of fossil remains of flora and fauna from millions of years ago. Geoscience is also concerned with very practical and current questions, advising on whether a particular site is suitable for the building of a bridge, a dam or a tunnel, working out where natural resources such as oil, gas and metals can be found and how safely they can be extracted.

Some geologists work as lecturers in higher education; others who are interested in some of the commercial rather than the scientific applications work in some of the following.

Engineering geologist

Engineering geologists analyse the underlying structure of major construction sites before tunnels, pipelines, bridges, harbours, docks and buildings are begun. They identify potential problems and advise on the best materials and construction methods to use. They analyse and assess soil, rocks, water courses and other ground conditions. They take into account environmental conditions and they work to ensure that construction projects will be safe in the short and long term.

Geotechnician

Geotechnicians support the work of geoscientists. They are based mainly in laboratories and their work involves preparing and analysing rock samples to discover their chemical make-up. Some geotechnicians work at drilling sites, logging data and monitoring activity.

Mining geologist

Whether companies are extracting rock and stone, minerals, metals, coal or precious metals and gemstones, mining geologists provide advice and expertise on the geological aspects of development and production in mining, pit and quarry sites. In overseeing drilling and surface exploration programmes, they help to determine likely directions for future development.

Palaeontologist

Palaeontologists study fossils and all the layers of rock that make up the earth's crust to try to find out more about the physical history of the planet, the pattern of past climate changes, or the movements of whole land masses, for example.

Seismic interpreter

Seismic interpreters use data generated by movements in the rocks below the earth's surface to work out exactly what quantities of oil and gas are stored beneath the surface. They use complex computer software and data from satellite stations to help them in their work.

Seismologist

These are the scientists we hear from when earthquakes and tsunamis are being reported on – why they have occurred, how powerful they were and what we might do to predict where these dangerous phenomena are next likely to occur.

Volcanologist

Volcanologists make a close study of active volcanoes and the area that surrounds them. They also look at extinct and dormant volcanoes to try to better predict when and where the next eruptions are likely to occur. They spend time working in and around craters as well as being based in laboratories. What comes out of volcanoes gives them a chance to study the structure of the core of the planet.

Entry, qualifications and training

Geoscience, except for technicians, is a graduate profession. Degrees in geology, geophysics, geo-engineering, geochemistry, earth sciences or similar subjects may all be acceptable. Many geologists also have a postgraduate qualification. To get onto one of these degree courses you normally need A levels, including maths and one science. Although this is a competitive area of work in some ways, geologists with good qualifications are likely to be in considerable demand because resources are getting harder to locate and more difficult to extract. You may be able to get a job as a junior geotechnician if you have five GCSEs grades 9–4, including English, science and maths, but some employers prefer you to have A levels, an HND or a degree. There are only a few science-based HNDs that specialise in geology and geoscience.

Personal attributes

You need a strong interest in the area of geoscience in which you want to work. You have to have a rigorous scientific approach to your work, be able to construct surveys, analyse and interpret data. You have to be good at working as part of a team, but also able to work independently. You need good powers of observation – to be quick to spot any changes in data. For some jobs you have to be able to work in physically hard conditions, on oil rigs, on the slopes of a volcano, etc.

Earnings

Geoscientists earn between £30,000 and £45,000. Project leaders and other senior geologists can earn £50,000 to £60,000, and up to £75,000 depending on experience. Salaries are highest in the oil and gas industry; this is also the work where you may have to spend long periods away from home. Geotechnicians earn between £18,000 and £29,000. The higher salaries are, once again, paid in the oil and gas industries.

Info

Natural Environment Research Council 01793 411500 www.nerc.ukri.org	**British Geological Survey** 0115 936 3143 www.bgs.ac.uk
Geological Society 020 7434 9944 www.geolsoc.org.uk	

GLASSMAKER

Glassmaking covers many types of product and hence many different production methods. Some glassmakers work on industrial processes, manufacturing double-glazed windows for buildings, glass for the automotive industry or glass containers such as milk bottles, wine bottles or jam jars. Some manufacturers produce glass fibre and tough but delicate glass for scientific equipment. A different aspect of glassmaking is based in small studios or workshops making individually blown pieces of glass such as ornaments or vases, or making stained-glass objects.

If you work in mass-production glass you are likely to work on one or more of the following processes. You could be mixing the basic ingredients of glass, silica, soda and lime. These are mixed with various additives and with scrap glass and then the whole mixture is heated to very high temperatures. The next process is to shape the glass, either by kiln forming or blowing the glass. Once the glass is cool it may have to be cut, ground or laminated to make the finished product. Finally, some objects will need to be decorated by sand blasting, acid etching or engraving.

Working in a craft studio or workshop, you are likely to be involved in the whole process of designing, mixing, heating, blowing and decorating objects made from glass.

Entry, qualifications and training

To work in mass-market manufacture you do not need formal qualifications, though GCSEs in science and/or art could be useful. To be a glassmaker in a craft workshop or studio you normally need a degree in a relevant subject such as glass and ceramics, applied art and design or decorative arts. To get a place on one of these courses, you need to have a portfolio of work, though it does not have to be in glass or ceramics but rather must show your artistic flair.

Personal attributes

In both manufacture and craft glass making you need good manual dexterity, hand–eye coordination and colour vision. In both you also need to be very health and safety conscious. In manufacture, you must be able to work as part of a team, to follow procedures and processes with great accuracy and patience. In craft work you need artistic flair as well.

Earnings

In glass manufacture, pay starts at around £14,000 rising to £18,000 to £23,000 with experience. Senior and supervisory staff can earn up to £27,000. In craft work there is great variation as many glassmakers are self-employed, but £15,000 to £24,000 is a rough guide. Earnings can be higher for successful glass artists.

Info

Heart of England Glass
www.heartofenglandglass.co.uk

British Glass
0114 290 1850
www.britglass.org.uk

British Society of Scientific Glassblowers
www.bssg.co.uk

Creative & Cultural Skills
020 7015 1800
www.ccskills.org.uk

HAIRDRESSING

Hairdresser

Hairdressers work on all aspects of hair styling, including cutting, styling, perming, straightening, colouring, applying highlights and incorporating hair extensions or other hairpieces. Salons or individual stylists may specialise in male or female hairdressing, or a niche market such as colouring, Afro-Caribbean or ethnic hairstyles. As a junior stylist in training, you may have to help out with other work in the salon, washing hair, booking appointments, cleaning and tidying. Hairdressers work in salons, hotels, airports, cruise liners, hospitals and prisons; some are self-employed, visiting clients in their own homes.

Entry, qualifications and training

You don't always need formal qualifications to become a hairdresser. You can either train at a salon, attending college on a day-release basis, or at the salon's own training centre. Alternatively you can do a full- or part-time college course in hairdressing or barbering. NVQ levels 1, 2 and 3 are available in Hairdressing. Salon and college entry requirements vary, but you may need four GCSEs grades 9–4, including English, maths and an arts subject. There may be apprenticeship schemes in hairdressing available in your area.

There are a few foundation degrees and other higher level courses available in hairdressing and the Freelance Hair and Beauty Federation offers training courses in setting up a salon and running a business.

Personal attributes

Hairdressers should have a genuine interest in people, a natural friendliness, the ability to stay calm under pressure, creative ability and an eye for detail. A presentable personal appearance is also essential. Hairdressers must not have skin conditions that can be affected by chemicals.

Earnings

Trainees usually earn close to the minimum wage and this depends on your age. Fashionable salons in busy locations may pay trainees more than this. Fully trained hairdressers earn between around £15,000 and £30,000. Top stylists can earn more than £30,000. This is work where you can sometimes make additional money from tips. It is also possible to become self-employed, visiting people in their homes to cut, colour, perm and style their hair. In this case, what you earn depends on what you charge.

Info

Hairdressing and Beauty Industry Authority
(HABIA)
08452 306080
www.habia.org

SkillsActive
033 0004 0005
www.skillsactive.com

The Freelance Hairdressers Association
01582 431783
http://thefha.org.uk

HEALTH AND SAFETY

Health and safety adviser

Health and safety advisers work for every kind of organisation, from multinationals and government agencies to small businesses. Advisers work in partnership with employers, employees, directors and trade unions, and are responsible for ensuring that all safety legislation is adhered to and that suitable policies and practices are put in place. They help organisations minimise safety risks and they are often involved in staff training.

Health and safety advisers try to ensure that workplaces are as free as possible from risks that could cause illness, accidents or even death. Construction sites, chemical plants, science laboratories, farms, foundries and oil refineries might be the kinds of business that spring to mind, but in fact any workplace can present hazards.

Health and safety advisers who work for the Health and Safety Executive (HSE) are known as HM Inspectors of Health and Safety. They visit premises to ensure that employers are complying with relevant legislation, investigate the cause of accidents that do occur, but also offer advice to help employers avoid problems, rather than deal with the consequences of them.

As well as working for the Health and Safety Executive (HSE), inspectors may work for consultancies or for large manufacturers, food retailers or construction companies.

Entry, qualifications and training

It is possible to become an adviser without a degree, if you have plenty of work experience in management, engineering, science or health, but there is a move towards making this a graduate-entry profession. Degrees in occupational health, engineering, food technology, health science and management are the most favoured; each subject has specific A level entry requirements. To train as a health and safety inspector with the HSE, you must have a degree and relevant science or engineering subjects are greatly preferred.

If you are accepted by the HSE you undergo a two-year structured training programme. This involves a combination of short courses and on-the-job training.

Personal attributes

To become a health and safety adviser or inspector you have to be extremely observant and thorough in your approach to what you see and what you are told. You have to be an excellent communicator, able to explain to someone why a workstation or a production line may be unsafe. You need to persuade people to do the right thing, but be firm enough to take action if they do not. You need to be a well-organised administrator.

Earnings

Trainee health and safety inspectors with the HSE earn around £27,000 rising to £29,000 on successful completion of the two-year training period. Senior health and safety inspectors can earn around £45,000. Health and safety advisers working with an ordinary company start on around £24,000. Senior advisers, working on large construction projects, for example, can earn up to £60,000.

Info

Health and Safety Executive (HSE)
www.hse.gov.uk

Examination Board in Occupational Safety and Health (NEBOSH)
0116 263 4700
www.nebosh.org.uk

Institution of Occupational Health and Safety (IOSH)
0116 257 3100
www.iosh.co.uk

British Safety Council
020 3510 8355
www.britsafe.org

HEALTH SERVICE (NON-MEDICAL)

(see also Medical and healthcare science)

In any healthcare system, there are a whole range of non-medical occupations which support healthcare professionals and healthcare and keep the whole system functioning. Many of these are covered below.

Some of these services are provided by the National Health Service (NHS), others such as catering, cleaning or laundry are often provided by companies that are contracted to do this work on behalf of the NHS.

Catering staff

Cooks, housekeepers and kitchen assistants working either for the NHS or for catering companies provide a range of hospital meals. They have to cater for special diets and try to provide a range of tempting food. Working within a tight budget is a key skill in this work.

Clerical and administrative staff

The NHS employs large numbers of clerks, secretaries, telephonists, receptionists and other administrative workers. Some of this work involves patient contact, e.g. receptionists at clinics, or ward clerks. Other work is more behind the scenes, ordering supplies, booking appointments and updating records.

Domestic services staff

Domestic services staff are employed either by the NHS or by private companies that have contracts to clean health service premises and also launder all the sheets, pillowcases, towels, etc.

Estates staff

Hospitals, clinics and other NHS premises need building services engineers to ensure that lighting, heating, air conditioning and other environmental management systems work at all times. Architects and surveyors are needed to design new premises or plan refurbishment of existing older properties.

Information science and technology

Computer systems of many kinds are important for keeping records, monitoring care and sharing information. All kinds of IT staff are employed, from data input clerks to systems development.

Management

This is a very broad term. The NHS employs managers in finance, human resources, strategic planning, performance monitoring and the day-to-day running of every kind of health service establishment.

Porters and messengers

Porters move patients and equipment from one part of a hospital or other healthcare centre to another. Messengers take important messages from one department to another. Even in these days of electronic communications, urgent messages are delivered by messengers.

Scientists

(see Medical and healthcare science)

Sterile services staff

Sterile services staff clean and sterilise all medical equipment. Some of this equipment is highly technical, so disinfecting it and preparing it for use is a painstaking and complex task. Applicants for this work usually need GCSEs in English, maths and a science.

Entry, qualifications and training

These vary considerably for different jobs. It is worth consulting specific career areas such as accountancy, biomedical engineering, hospitality, human resource management, information technology and secretarial work. For some work, such as being a porter or a kitchen assistant, you may not need any formal academic qualifications. For most management posts you need either a degree or professional qualifications in a relevant area such as accountancy or management studies. Posts in science, engineering or information technology will require relevant qualifications from GCSE to postgraduate level.

Personal attributes

The common thread for all these jobs is a genuine commitment to working within and for healthcare and wanting to deliver a good service to patients. For any work involving patient contact, being sensitive and caring is important. All jobs require you to be a good communicator and to be able to work very well as part of a team. Particular jobs require specific practical skills such as cooking, IT skills or being good with technical equipment.

Earnings

Apart from doctors and the most senior managers, all NHS staff are paid on a national scale. New entrants to junior posts such as kitchen assistant, porter or junior administrative assistant are paid around £15,500. Once you have supervisory functions and/or additional responsibilities, salaries can rise to £18,000. Jobs in IT, human resources and management start around £22,000 rising to more than £40,000; senior managers in all functions can earn far more than this. This salary information is a guide only, because there are so many different points on the scale.

HEALTH VISITOR

(see Nursing professions)

HEALTHCARE ASSISTANT

(see Nursing professions)

HORTICULTURE

Horticulture is the commercial production of flowering plants, shrubs, ornamental trees, soft fruit such as raspberries and strawberries, fruit trees, vegetables and herbs. Horticultural work takes place in garden centres, plant nurseries, parks and formal gardens, market gardens, community horticulture projects and large farms. The most common horticultural jobs are described below, but horticultural specialists may also teach at agricultural colleges or advise on new projects.

Arboriculturist

Arboriculturists are tree specialists with expertise in the planting, care and production of trees of every kind, from orchard fruits and native English woodland trees to exotic varieties. They study sites to assess their suitability for particular trees and carry out surveys of tree populations and attempt to analyse and solve any problems that stop the trees thriving. They often work for formal gardens, parks, local authorities or conservation bodies. Their role may cover supervising other workers carrying out activities like pruning or planting. They may also help to resolve disputes over trees on boundaries, or decisions on whether a particular tree should be preserved.

Entry, qualifications and training

You can either enter this work with a degree in arboriculture or forestry management, or work towards appropriate professional qualifications once you have had some work experience with a forestry or woodland management organisation. If you take this second route, you may not need any formal qualifications. A college course such as a Level 2 Certificate in Arboriculture would allow you to gain some of the knowledge and skills required. Or consider an arborist intermediate apprenticeship.

Personal attributes

You need a genuine interest in trees and a scientific, logical approach to your work. You must be a good communicator, able to supervise others and put across your ideas to groups or individuals. You should be physically fit and happy working in all weathers.

Earnings

New entrants earn around £16,000, but with either a degree and/or considerable experience, earnings are £22,000 to £30,000.

Horticultural manager

As a horticultural manager you will be responsible for the day-to-day care of plants and the supervision of staff. Your tasks will vary, depending on where you work, e.g. in a garden centre, a market garden or a commercial nursery. You may be involved in a lot of hands-on work, watering, feeding, pruning and planting. You may also be involved in working out costs, developing new products and markets, managing and training staff and negotiating with suppliers or dealing with queries from customers.

Entry, qualifications and training

You may not need formal qualifications to get into this work; many managers work their way up. Some employers may expect you to have three to four GCSEs, including maths, English and a science. Some managers have a degree in horticulture or a related subject. A college course in a relevant subject, such as a Level 3 Diploma in Horticulture, or a horticulture supervisor advanced apprenticeship may also be useful.

You could also start out as a horticultural worker and work your way up via promotion once you have more experience and/or qualifications.

Personal attributes

You need both practical and interpersonal skills. You should be prepared to develop specialised knowledge of the plants you care for. You must be able to motivate and supervise other workers and be confident in dealing with customers and suppliers.

Earnings

Earnings range from £18,000 to £40,000; most horticultural managers earn between £20,000 and £25,000.

Horticultural therapist

Horticultural therapists use the skills of growing and tending plants and looking after land to help people maintain or recover health and well-being, e.g. people with physical disabilities or mental illnesses or older people trying to maintain skills and independence.

Entry, qualifications and training

This is often a second career and there is no set entry route. You may already be working in horticulture, or you may be a social worker, teacher or nurse with a passion for gardening. There is no set training course, but there is useful information on the Thrive website.

Personal attributes

You must love and know about gardening. You also need to be able to work well with vulnerable people. As with all horticultural work, you must enjoy physical work in all weathers.

Earnings

Earnings are generally around £17,000 to £30,000.

Horticultural worker

Horticultural workers carry out all the tasks associated with planting, caring for, propagating and harvesting flowers, shrubs, vegetables, fruit and trees grown for commercial or amenity purposes. Your day-to-day tasks could include sowing seeds, taking cuttings, checking plants for signs of pests and diseases, and pruning, tidying and moving plants. Your job could include some landscaping work and you may also deal with customer queries if you are working in a garden centre or nursery.

Entry, qualifications and training

You don't need formal qualifications to get into this work, although some employers ask for GCSEs in maths, English and science. There are several part-time qualifications at NVQ levels 1 and 2 towards which you can work once you are in employment. You could also undertake a training course through a professional body such as The Royal Horticultural Society.

Personal attributes

You have to have a real interest in plants of all kinds and enjoy making them thrive. You need to be physically fit, with good practical skills and manual dexterity. You should be able to follow instructions and then work on your own. You may also have to work directly advising members of the public.

Earnings

Earnings range from £13,000 to £30,000. Pay starts at around the minimum wage rising to £15,000 to £17,500. You may earn more as you take on supervisory or other responsibilities.

Info

Lantra
02476 696996
www.lantra.co.uk

Chartered Institute of Horticulture (CIH)
03330 050181
www.horticulture.org.uk

Royal Botanic Garden Edinburgh
0131 248 2909
www.rbge.org.uk

Royal Botanic Gardens Kew
020 8332 5655
www.kew.org

Royal Horticultural Society (RHS)
020 3176 5800
www.rhs.org.uk

Local government jobs
www.lgjobs.com

Institute of Chartered Foresters
0131 240 1425
www.charteredforesters.org

Arboricultural Association
01242 522152
www.trees.org.uk

Thrive
0118 988 5688
www.thrive.org.uk

Chartered Institute of Horticulture
0333 005 0181
www.horticulture.org.uk/grow-careers

Association of Social and Therapeutic Horticulture Practitioners
http://asthp.org.uk

HOSPITALITY AND CATERING

Hotels, restaurants, pubs, fast food outlets, cafes and catering companies are a major source of employment – there are more than 600,000 people working in this industry. There are opportunities at all levels: bar staff, waiters and waitresses, wine waiters, kitchen assistants, kitchen porters, bar managers, general managers, banqueting managers and chefs, from junior to senior.

Chef/cook

Chefs are employed in restaurants, hotels, pubs, wine bars, cafes, corporate and banqueting catering companies, cookery schools, in hospitals, care homes, schools and workplace canteens and in the armed forces. They may also work on recipe development in the ready meals industry.

In large establishments the chef de cuisine is in overall charge, while there may be a number of chefs de partie (in charge of their part of the kitchen) and a number of commis chefs (still learning the trade).

As a head chef/cook your role would not simply be creating and supervising the preparation of all kinds of different dishes, you would also have to manage the kitchen, ensuring that health and safety and excellent food hygiene are maintained. You would have to manage the other kitchen staff, plan menus, select and order ingredients and work within budgets.

Entry, qualifications and training

No formal qualifications are necessary, but depending on which training route your employer wishes to put you through, you may need four GCSEs, including English and maths. If you want to study full- or part-time at college before you start training with an employer, you can study for BTEC National Certificates and Diplomas in Hospitality and Catering; you need four GCSEs grades 9–4 to get a place on one of these courses. You can study for NVQ courses to levels 1, 2 and 3, either full time before you start work or part time while you are training in a kitchen possibly as an apprentice. There are also some NVQ level 4 courses available in kitchen and larder, confectionery and patisserie.

If you have five GCSEs and two A levels, there are several foundation degree courses available in food preparation, including professional cookery, professional patisserie, culinary arts, culinary creativity and hospitality. There are also vocational diplomas for 14–19-year-olds in the hospitality sector, combining school or college study with work experience. An apprenticeship or gaining work experience are other routes you could take.

Personal attributes

Chefs need a real passion for food and a creative attitude to making the best use of ingredients, whether they work in a top restaurant, a country pub or a hospital canteen. Despite the impression sometimes given on TV, being able to keep calm under pressure is a great asset. Chefs must be good team leaders and motivators, able to get people to work well together.

Earnings

Trainee chefs earn between the minimum wage and £15,000. Chefs in charge of a section of the kitchen earn between £16,000 and £20,000. Second or sous chefs earn from £22,000 to £30,000 and head chefs earn up to £40,000. A head chef in a large, high-quality hotel running a large kitchen can earn £40,000 to £50,000.

Fast food/restaurant manager

The responsibilities of fast food and restaurant managers vary very much according to the kinds of outlet in which they work. Fast food managers work mainly for chains that operate burger, pizza and fried chicken eateries, for example. As a fast food outlet manager your responsibilities are mainly for organising the work of the staff team, making sure that everyone works quickly and efficiently and solving problems if they arise. You are likely to be responsible for the food preparation area, as well as the customer service and eating areas. You have a major role in training new staff. As a restaurant manager you might be working in a large hotel, a small independent restaurant, a national chain of eateries or a fast food outlet. Restaurant managers tend to work front of house, welcoming guests, and ensuring that service is good and customers are satisfied. You will certainly be liaising with kitchen staff, but management of that area is likely to be the chef's domain.

Entry, qualifications and training

You don't necessarily need formal qualifications to become a fast food manager. Many managers begin as counter service staff, then become shift supervisors and from there progress to management. A few companies do offer graduate training schemes and accept graduates from any discipline. If you are interested in food and catering there are degrees in hospitality management, culinary arts management and hotel and catering management available at several universities. In all cases a great deal of training is on the job, but your employer may send you on short courses at college or run in-house, and there is a wide variety of catering and management qualifications you could consider. You could also consider an apprenticeship, such as a hospitality manager higher apprenticeship if you already have supervisory experience in a restaurant.

Personal attributes

You have to have excellent interpersonal skills. The balance of how much time you spend with customers or managing your staff team depends very much on the kind of establishment for which you are working. In all instances you need to be polite, friendly and calm if problems arise or under pressure. In fast food management you need to be very aware of health and safety and food hygiene issues.

Earnings

Assistant managers earn £18,000 to £24,500 and managers earn £20,000 to £40,000. At the luxury end of the restaurant business, a manager may earn up to £50,000. Working for fast food chains it may be possible to move into area or head office management roles with salaries of up to £55,000.

Hotel manager

As a hotel manager, you oversee all aspects of running a hotel, from housekeeping and general maintenance to budget management and marketing. Large hotels may have several departmental managers, e.g. restaurant and catering, conferences and functions, leisure facilities and domestic services, each reporting to one overall manager. Hotel chains may also have regional management teams, providing some central services such as purchasing of goods and supplies. Managers are responsible for everything from setting and managing budgets to staff recruitment and dealing with customer complaints. The work may involve marketing and developing business plans and new initiatives.

Entry, qualifications and training

There are two main routes to qualification: attending a college or university as a full-time student, or joining a training programme operated by an employer or an organisation that works with employers to provide training, such as the Hotel and Catering Training Company (HCTC). In the latter case, entrants learn on the job and attend college or a training centre on a short-course or day-release basis. Recruits on the work-based training programme will generally acquire NVQ awards. Full-time courses are available in hospitality-related subjects, including HNDs, foundation degrees and degree courses.

Personal attributes

Managers need to be well motivated with good interpersonal and team skills. You have to be very well organised and a good problem solver. You need excellent communication skills, and must be able to get the best out of your team and to work well with customers.

Earnings

In small hotels managers earn around £20,000 to £24,000, or to £35,000 in medium-sized hotels. A manager of a large, successful hotel, or working for a chain of hotels in a head office management job, can earn up to £80,000.

Hotel receptionist

(see Business for Receptionist)

Kitchen porter

The term 'porter' is a little misleading because kitchen porters are involved in far more than the unloading of deliveries. Kitchen assistant might be a more accurate term. These staff work with food preparation staff to keep the kitchen clean, hygienic and safe. They load and unload dishwashers, put away crockery and cutlery, wash items than cannot be put in a dishwasher and generally sweep and tidy the kitchen and keep work surfaces clean.

Entry, qualifications and training

You do not need formal qualifications to become a kitchen porter or kitchen assistant, but individual employers may ask for GCSEs in English and a science subject. If you want to use kitchen porter as a step on the ladder to other work in catering, it is certainly useful to have three or four GCSEs grades 9–4. Training is on the job, though you may attend short courses such as food hygiene or health and safety awareness. A college course in cookery or hospitality such as a Level 1 Award in Introduction to Employment in the Hospitality Industry, or a Level 1 Certificate in General Cookery may also help. You could also consider an apprenticeship.

Personal attributes

You need to be very practical, quick to react to situations and see what needs to be done. You have to be able to work as part of a team and be able to cope with a fairly frantic work environment, where tempers may become frayed. You need to pay attention to detail.

Earnings

Kitchen porters/assistants earn around the minimum wage to £14,500, maybe up to £18,000 in a large kitchen where they also have supervisory responsibilities for junior kitchen porters.

Waiting staff

Waiting staff wait at tables in restaurants, cafes, wine bars, hotels and some fast food outlets. They may also work for catering companies at functions such as weddings, parties, sporting or cultural events.

Waiting staff take customers' orders and pass these to the kitchen. They bring food to the table. In fast food restaurants there may be some minimal food preparation and drinks using, for example, barista skills. Some customers will also ask advice about what to eat or how a particular dish is prepared before placing an order. Waiting staff also set and clear tables before and after meals. They may also be responsible for adding up bills and taking payments from customers. They are the main link point between the kitchen and the customer.

Entry, qualifications and training

You do not need formal academic qualifications to do this work; having the right personal approach is far more important. Many waiting staff do have formal qualifications, including GCSEs in English and maths. Qualifications are more important, though not essential, if you hope to use your waiting work as a stepping stone to more senior roles. There are also college courses such as a Level 1 Certificate in Food and Beverage Service, or apprenticeships available. Volunteering experience may also help.

Personal attributes

You have to look clean, tidy and presentable and have a friendly welcoming manner. You have to be practical, accurate in taking orders and adding up bills, good at working as part of a team and able to cope with pressure. You have to be patient; not all customers are entirely reasonable.

Earnings

Waiting staff earn around the minimum wage. Head waiters or section heads may earn £16,000 to £27,000. Many waiting staff are paid by the hour and make extra money from tips.

Info

People 1st
020 3074 1222
www.people1st.co.uk

Hotel and Catering Training Company (HCTC)
www.hotel-and-catering-training-coltd.
mytrainingwebsite.co.uk

Publican/licensee

Publicans manage licensed premises, mainly pubs and bars. They work for breweries, pub chains or for themselves running a free house. The publican/manager runs the premises, which may include a restaurant, fruit machines and overnight accommodation, and is responsible for stock control, staff management and the overall standards of drink, food and customer service. Pubs and bars vary enormously, from lively late-night city centre bars providing music and other entertainment to quiet rural pubs serving a local village clientele. The demands that these different settings make on their managers will vary considerably.

Entry, qualifications and training

Many publicans/licensees work their way up to this position by starting work as a barperson and gradually taking on more responsibility. Alternatively, pub chains and breweries may take people onto management training schemes and give them appropriate training and experience to take on a pub or bar of their own. Each employer sets its own selection criteria, but some will expect applicants to have HNDs, a foundation degree or a degree in a relevant subject such as business studies, marketing or hospitality. A good track record in work that involves customer service and taking on considerable responsibility is also a big advantage. Licensees must be aged 18 or over, have no criminal convictions and be able to satisfy the local authority that they are a suitable person to hold such a licence.

Personal attributes

You have to have excellent organisational and budgeting skills. You must be good at leading and motivating other people. You should enjoy working with members of the public, being able to provide a listening ear or a firm instruction as the need arises. You must be calm but able to react quickly in any potentially difficult situations, such as when dealing with customers who have drunk too much.

Earnings

Trainee and assistant managers earn between £16,000 and £25,000. Experienced managers generally earn between £25,000 and £50,000. Income may be related to turnover or to brewery and pub chain bonus schemes. If you are running your own establishment, your income will depend on how well that business does. In all cases, you are likely to have to work long hours to earn your living.

Barperson

Bar staff work in pubs, bars, restaurants and hotels, selling and serving alcoholic and non-alcoholic drinks to customers. In some cases they may also be responsible for taking food orders, selling snacks, etc. In some bars they will also have to know how to mix an extensive range of cocktails.

Entry, qualifications and training

You don't need formal qualifications to do this work. You must be aged 18 or over and you must have very good people skills. Some experience in retail or other customer care work is valuable. However, there are college courses you could undertake to equip yourself with some of the skills required for this job, such as a Level 1 Award in Introduction to Employment in the Hospitality Industry, or an apprenticeship.

Personal attributes

You should be friendly and helpful. You must be able to keep calm in what is often a very hectic, crowded and noisy environment. You should be able to use your initiative and work well as part of a team.

Earnings

Much of the work is part time and many bar staff are paid the minimum wage, although this can be increased through tips. Annual income works out at between £12,500 and £15,000.

Info

British Institute of Innkeeping (BII)
01276 684449
www.bii.org

Wine and Spirit Educational Trust (WSET)
020 7089 3800
www.wsetglobal.com

People 1st
020 3074 1222
www.people1st.co.uk

HOUSING OFFICER/MANAGER

Housing officers manage housing for housing associations, local authorities, charities and some groups of private landlords. The work can be very varied. Housing officers allocate properties to people waiting for tenancies and organise exchanges of properties between tenants. They carry out inspections of properties to ensure both that the tenant is looking after them as they should and that the landlord (housing association, local authority, etc) carries out appropriate repairs, maintenance or improvements. The housing officer has to deal with problems such as antisocial behaviour or rent arrears. He or she may be the one who has to instigate legal actions if problems persist. Some housing associations or charities provide accommodation for specific groups of people, such as those who are recovering from problems with substance abuse, or frail, elderly people. In these instances and in many other cases, part of the housing officer's role is to liaise with other authorities such as social services, schools and healthcare professionals. Collecting statistics and presenting reports can also form part of the role. Many people wanting to become housing officers start in customer services dealing with tenants' enquiries via e-mail or telephone.

Entry, qualifications and training

You don't necessarily need formal qualifications to work in this sector, although most housing officers do have A levels or equivalent. Individual employers may require you to have a degree or foundation degree in a relevant subject such as social policy, housing, planning or urban studies. Some housing organisations run graduate training schemes. Many housing officers work their way up from more junior roles in a housing organisation. You can work towards levels 2, 3 and 4 qualifications in housing through the Chartered Institute of Housing (CIH). You can work towards these whatever your job in housing or, indeed, if you are a tenant. You could also undertake an apprenticeship such as a housing property assistant intermediate apprenticeship, followed by a housing and property management advanced apprenticeship.

Personal attributes

An interest in improving people's living conditions, good interpersonal skills, effective organisation skills, sensitivity to an individual's needs and flexibility are all important.

Earnings

As a trainee, or working mainly in customer service dealing with telephone, e-mail and personal enquiries, salaries range from £17,000 to £22,000. As a more experienced housing officer having a caseload and dealing with more challenging problems, salaries range from £25,000 to £35,000. Senior housing managers earn £35,000 to £50,000. There is regional variation and salaries are also affected by whether you work for a local authority or a housing association.

Info

Chartered Institute of Housing (CIH)
024 7685 1700
www.cih.org

National Housing Federation (NHF)
020 7067 1010
www.housing.org.uk

Royal Institution of Chartered Surveyors (RICS)
024 7686 8555
www.rics.org

HUMAN RESOURCES

Recruiting and retaining the right people is key to any organisation's success. Human resources (HR) management covers all those functions in a business or organisation related to staffing. Recruitment is central to human resource management, but other areas of responsibility include training, handling disciplinary issues, performance monitoring and staff appraisals.

Human resources officer/manager

As an HR professional your role depends on the size and type of organisation for which you work. If you work for a small company then you might be concerned with many aspects of human resource management. Working for a large organisation you might specialise in one area such as recruitment and selection, equal opportunities, staff appraisals or planning training and development programmes.

On the recruitment side you could work with colleagues to draw up job adverts and job specifications, interview candidates, or train other staff to conduct interviews. You might also work with psychologists to devise tests to set candidates. On the daily management side you might develop systems to monitor absenteeism or to ensure that an equal opportunities policy is properly implemented. You might be called upon to deal with problems such as disciplinary issues or to resolve a situation where one employee has accused another staff member of treating them unfairly. At a senior level you could be involved in industrial relations negotiations with employee representatives and play a leading role in an organisation's strategic development.

Entry, qualifications and training

This work has become very much a graduate profession, but this is not the only route into human resource work. Places on companies' graduate training schemes are very popular and competition is fierce. Degrees which include human resource modules or placements can enhance your chance of success. It is also possible to get into this work by taking on an administrative role in a human resources department and working your way up. You can also take professional qualifications part-time to develop your career. Most middle and senior managers in human resources have relevant professional qualifications. You could also consider a college course such as the Level 5 Diploma in Business Management and Human Resources, or an apprenticeship.

Personal attributes

You have to have a broad range of management skills for this work. You should be highly organised, with good administrative and basic IT skills. You need to be good at building relationships with people; you must have integrity and sensitivity, but also be assertive. You need to be able to interpret and explain legal and statistical information.

Earnings

Salaries for graduates are between £22,000 and £27,000. At senior levels salaries range from £35,000 to £80,000. This range reflects the varied nature of the role and the part it plays in organisations of such different size and type.

Training officer/manager

Training officers work in medium-sized and large firms and organisations, national and local government, emergency services and voluntary organisations. They are responsible for identifying training requirements, designing training programmes, delivering training to individuals or groups and evaluating the success of training.

Entry, qualifications and training

This is an area of work that people move into after gaining experience in other posts or following general HR experience. A professional qualification is advisable. The CIPD offers a certificate in training practice for those new to the profession or with limited experience. NVQs in training and development at levels 3–5 are available.

Personal attributes

You need to be happy and confident presenting to or facilitating groups of people. You need to be a good problem solver and able to get people to change their attitudes. You must also be well organised, positive and enthusiastic. Sometimes you will have to be creative and imaginative, developing your own training materials.

Earnings

Salaries start at between £19,000 and £22,000, sometimes a little more in London. Training managers can earn between £30,000 and £45,000.

Info

Chartered Institute of Personnel and Development (CIPD)
020 8612 6200
www.cipd.co.uk

ILLUSTRATION

(see Art and design and Medical and healthcare science for Medical illustrator)

IMAGE CONSULTANT

Politicians, pop stars, sports personalities, business people, fashion specialists – even whole businesses – all of these and others might choose to employ an image consultant. An image consultant looks at the kinds of visual impression made by someone in the public eye and helps them work out how to create maximum impact and appear in a style that supports the message they want to put across. This might be flamboyant or serious, dynamic or thoughtful. Image consultants advise on appropriate clothing to wear, what colours suit a person, what hairstyle(s) they might use, what style of make-up to apply, where to shop, how to stand, sit, etc. They may recommend to a client that he or she get some voice coaching, or be seen taking part in a particular activity. Image consultants normally work from their own homes, so they need to have a suitable office area. They will also visit clients and accompany them on shopping trips, to hair salons, manicurists, etc. They help clients prepare for photography sessions or press conferences. They might also work with a client who is about to give a presentation of some kind.

At a more everyday level, many stores employ fashion stylists/image consultants to help shoppers choose clothing, shoes, make-up etc, to best develop a particular look, or a sense of individuality.

Entry, qualifications and training

There are no specific entry requirements and not that many job opportunities. It is likely to be a second career after a background in one or more of the following areas: fashion, hairdressing and beauty, public relations or marketing.

Personal attributes

You need to be a confident communicator with a real sense of style – of what works and what does not. You need a good eye for colour and an interest in fashion. You have to be good at establishing your clients' trust and confidence, since you are advising them on very personal aspects of their appearance and how they come across. You also have to listen to them and work with them so that they are comfortable and effective when they use your suggestions.

Earnings

Stylists working for stores earn £14,000 to £19,000. Most image consultants are self-employed. People who can afford to employ image consultants are generally reasonably wealthy, though, and successful image consultants earn between £30,000 and £45,000 a year.

Info

The Institute of Image Consulting
0800 781 1715
www.inst.org/image-consulting-courses

IMMIGRATION

Immigration officer

Immigration officers and assistant immigration officers work for UK Visas and Immigration (previously the UK Border Agency), which is part of the Home Office. They work at the nearly 50 air- and seaports checking passports, visas and work permits and interviewing any travellers who are non-EU or non-British citizens entering the United Kingdom. Immigration officers have to try to establish why people are visiting the United Kingdom and check that the reasons given are really the case. They may be involved in surveillance work and in arranging to remove people from the United Kingdom who do not have the right to remain.

Entry, qualifications and training

You may not need formal entry qualifications, although a good general education is an advantage. UK Visas and Immigration sets its own selection tests, which are designed to assess your powers of written and spoken communication and your ability to take responsibility. You must be aged between 18 and 64. Having a foreign language can also be an advantage. For many roles you need a driving licence and for most posts you must be a British citizen. Training is on the job and there is a clear career development and promotion structure in UK Visas and Immigration. Check the UKBA website for the current recruiting situation.

Personal attributes

You need good powers of observation, a calm but firm manner and the ability to work closely as part of a team. You may need to take quick decisions and you must be able to take responsibility.

Earnings

New entrants earn £21,500 to £26,000, rising to £36,000 for senior officers. There may also be additional payments for working unsocial hours.

INFORMATION SCIENCE

Information science is an interdisciplinary field concerned with the analysis, collection, classification, manipulation, storage, retrieval, movement, dissemination, and protection of information. Practitioners in this field work to create, replace, improve or understand information. They develop systems that can be used by other people, e.g., the general public in a library, other company staff in an organisation's own information centre or academic researchers in a specialist learning centre.

Archivist

Working as an archivist, you manage and preserve collections of historical records and documents. The collections you work with are of all types, from books, photographs and maps to audio, film and electronic files. Collections may belong to government, hospitals, universities, businesses, museums, libraries, families or individuals. Your day-to-day work is likely to include making sure materials are stored correctly and kept in good condition, identifying, dating, cataloguing and indexing archive materials, helping people to use the archives and carrying out research. You may also be expected to give talks about the collections you manage and to seek out and negotiate the purchase of new material to help extend or complete your collections.

Entry, qualifications and training

The main qualification is the postgraduate diploma in archive management, which is run at six UK universities. To be accepted on to one of these programmes you need a good honours degree, usually a 2.1. Any discipline is acceptable, but history, or a subject where you have had to research original source material, will be particularly useful. Many entrants start as records clerks or assistant archivists. In fact, such work experience is very important if you want to complete a postgraduate diploma. Many applicants also do quite a lot of voluntary work to strengthen their applications. Your paid or voluntary experience must be in an archive or records management department, not a library. The Archives and Records Association website is a useful source of information. Tracking down employers who can provide experience can be quite hard – universities and local government offices have some of the largest archive and records departments.

Personal attributes

A passionate interest in history and in original source material is essential. You should be logical, well organised and good at paying attention to detail. You meet all sorts of people in this work, so good communication skills and a real commitment to customer service are very important. At senior level you also need to be good at managing members of a team.

Earnings

New entrants earn around £20,000. Higher salaries tend to be paid in academia. Senior archivists earn between £35,000 and £60,000.

Info

The National Archives
020 8876 3444
www.nationalarchives.gov.uk

Archives and Records Association
01823 327077
www.archives.org.uk

Analysts

Business has become an environment that is driven by large amounts information in the form of data. The role of data is to empower business leaders to make decisions based on facts and trends in a marketplace. To make the right strategy decisions, business leaders must be able to sift through large amounts of data to extract useful information. There are two key roles in an organisation that make this possible – data analysts and business analysts – and a growing demand for both. Data analysts gather and analyse data to identify useful information, which can then be presented in an easy-to-read way, such as charts. In smaller organisations this allows management to evaluate the data and use it to make decisions. Larger organisations often also have business analysts who use the data to help organisations make more effective business decisions.

Entry, qualifications and training

Both roles tend to be graduate roles at entry level. Data analysts tend to have a degree such as maths, statistics or computer science. They also need technical skills and knowledge of software, such as Excel and SQL databases and programming skills, and this is often gained through on-the-job training. Business analysts often have a degree, and relevant degrees include business or economics, but are not limited to these. An MSc in data science or business analysis is available as a direct route into data analysis and business analytics respectively.

Personal attributes

Both roles need strong communication skills. Business analysts need fewer technical skills, but need strong decision-making skills. An interest in business and ongoing learning is needed as there is continuous change in technologies.

Earnings

Entry level data analysts earn from around £21,000, and with experience the average salary is around £33,000. Entry level business analysts earn from around £23,000. The average salary for business analysts is around £53,000, with many experienced business analysts earning more than this.

Information scientist

Rather like librarians, information scientists organise, manage and develop information systems. Working with IT- and paper-based systems, they store, analyse and retrieve information and distribute it to interested clients. They work for many types of organisation and with all kinds of information, including scientific, technical, legal, commercial, financial and economic. As well as cataloguing and indexing information and dealing with enquiries, information scientists often have to analyse statistics or write reports summarising highly technical or specialised information.

Entry, qualifications and training

This is a graduate profession and unless your degree is in librarianship or information science/management, you also have to do a one-year postgraduate qualification. Competition for places on these courses is fierce, and you need a year's experience in a library or information centre of some kind before you start your course.

Personal attributes

You must be able to get on well with people and enjoy dealing with enquiries. It is important for you to have good IT skills: experience of handling databases is particularly useful. You should have a good memory and either a breadth of knowledge or highly specialist knowledge in a particular field such as law or science.

Earnings

Trainees earn between £18,000 and £20,000. Newly qualified professionals earn £22,000 to £28,000. With further professional experience information scientists earn between £30,000 and £40,000 – a few more than this.

Info

BCS, The Chartered Institute for IT
01793 417417
www.bcs.org

Chartered Institute of Library and Information Professionals (CILIP)
020 7255 0500
www.cilip.org.uk

AIIM (Association for Information and Image Management)
www.aiim.org

Librarian/information manager

Librarians and information managers anticipate the information needs of their clients, acquire that information by the most efficient means possible on behalf of their clients, and may well analyse it and repackage it for the client. Information may come in the form of a book or journal, or may be extracted from databases in-house, on CD-ROM or online. Librarians and information managers need to be able to use the internet and show others how to do so.

Information needs to be organised to make it accessible to users by indexing, cataloguing and classifying. Librarians and information managers promote and exploit the library's collection to users of the library or information source and assist them with any enquiries. They work in public libraries and schools, universities and colleges, in government, in the law, in hospitals, business and industry, and also in accountancy, engineering, professional and learned societies and in virtually all areas of economic activity.

Entry, qualifications and training

Library assistants are usually required to have four to five GCSEs or equivalent, to include English language; training is on the job. Part-time or distance-learning vocational courses leading to City & Guilds and SQA qualifications are available to library assistants in post. NVQs levels 2–4 in Information and Library Services are also available. To qualify as a professional librarian or information officer and gain Chartered Membership of the Library Association, a degree or postgraduate qualification accredited by the association is necessary.

First degree courses, postgraduate diplomas and Masters are jointly accredited by the Library Association and the Institute of Information Scientists. A full list of the courses offered by 17 universities is available through the Library Association website. The Library Association and Institute of Information Scientists have joined together to create a new organisation, the Chartered Institute of Library and Information Professionals.

Personal attributes

Librarians and information managers need to be well educated, with an outgoing personality, and able to communicate with people at all levels with clarity, accuracy and tact. They need intellectual curiosity, breadth of knowledge and a logical and methodical approach to seeking out, organising and presenting information. A good memory is also useful. Management skills and an interest in working with computers are important assets.

Earnings

Salaries vary from sector to sector: posts in large university libraries tend to be the best paid. The Chartered Institute of Library and Information Professionals (CILIP) produces annual salary guidelines for the different sectors. Library assistants earn from £18,000 to £24,000. Newly qualified librarians earn £20,000 to £25,000. Senior librarians can earn up to £40,000.

Info

Chartered Institute of Library and Information Professionals (CILIP)
020 7255 0500
www.cilip.org.uk

INFORMATION AND COMMUNICATION TECHNOLOGY

Information and communication technology (ICT, often just IT) is part of all our daily lives, both business and personal. Computers, tablets and mobile phone apps are used in all sorts of ways. While millions of us use technology as a tool at work, there are many jobs where knowledge of various aspects of IT forms the core of the job. The sector is continuing to expand, new careers are emerging, and employers report shortages in key areas: there are plentiful opportunities for those with the right skills. Some employers are now working in partnership with universities to offer fees-paid Bachelor's and Master's degree apprenticeships in IT-related subjects, which enable you to study while a full-time employee – see the Tech Partnership website (note that this organisation has now closed, but many of its activities are being taken forward by others, as set out on www.tpdegrees.com/tech-partnership-legacy).

Computer games developer

(see also Art and design for Graphic designer, Broadcasting for Broadcast engineer, Writer)

Computer games developers are involved in creating and producing games for PCs, games consoles, mobile phones, tablets and other hand-held devices. Development of games is very much a team effort, where professionals with different areas of expertise, e.g. animation, design, graphics, sound engineering, programming, quality assurance, all have to work together. The developer writes the code for the computer programs that make the game work.

Entry, qualifications and training

Apprenticeships are available for an entry level role as a games tester within quality assurance. Opportunities exist for games testers to move across into other areas of games development. Most games developers will have a foundation degree, HND or degree qualification;

apprenticeships are available. You could undertake a course such as a T level in Digital Production, Design and Development, which may lead to more advanced qualifications or a higher apprenticeship.

Personal attributes

You will need to be able to work happily in a team with other professionals. You will also need to be creative and adept at solving problems, disciplined about meeting deadlines and enthusiastic about the games industry.

Earnings

Games testers earn the minimum wage (unless fluency in a language other than English is required) but pay increases to between £18,000 and £22,000 for those taking on responsibility within quality assurance. Programmers, artists and animators in games development earn between £19,000 and £25,000 initially. With experience, however, you can earn between £35,000 and £50,000 – more, in senior positions.

Database administrator

Organisations obtain and store information about their customers, accounts, orders or stock levels on computers. The database administrator (or database manager) takes responsibility for maintaining these and for security, access and the legal use of information held. It is a specialised role and you could work in many different types of organisation – from a bank, to a hospital, to a membership organisation or charity. You will ensure the database serves the needs of its users and is secure. Alternatively, you may be employed by a company that builds databases for other organisations and so work with a variety of clients. You might be involved in establishing a new database, or upgrading an existing one. Many experienced database administrators choose to work as freelance contractors or consultants.

Entry, qualifications and training

You will need to know how to use database management systems and structured query language (SQL) but opportunities exist for those with good all-round IT skills. Apprenticeships are available which include qualifications in database administration. Alternatively, you could study for an HNC/HND or a degree, and then join a company's graduate trainee scheme. Relevant subjects include: computer science, information science, software development and maths – but some employers are happy to accept high-quality graduates from other disciplines.

Personal attributes

You will need to be organised and good at solving problems, as well as having a high level of accuracy and the discipline to meet deadlines. You will also require business and budget awareness, good communication and negotiating skills, an understanding of data protection issues and a willingness to keep up to date with developments in technology. Being a good team worker is very important, too.

Earnings

Junior database administrator salaries start at around £22,000. With experience, this can rise to £35,000. Senior database administrators can earn £45,000 to £70,000 and beyond. Contractors can earn £300 to £400 a day.

E-learning developer

(see Software developer)

Forensic computer analyst

Forensic computer analysts investigate crime involving the use of computer systems. They may work for the police or various government agencies helping to tackle IT crime (cyber crime), or for a private company. The work may involve recovering deleted files, investigating computer hacking and data theft, internet fraud, the downloading of pornography, terrorist networks and industrial, commercial and political espionage. Specialists working in this type of role will often provide evidence in court. Depending on the exact nature of your role, you may be restricted in what you can say about your job outside of work hours or may have to view images and information that you find distressing.

Entry, qualifications and training

It may be possible to move into forensic computing with a general background in IT, having begun in an entry level position, such as IT user support. By taking professional development courses and applying for opportunities as they come up, you may eventually be able to move into a specialised analyst role. Apprenticeships in cyber security are also available. In addition, it is possible to follow degrees specifically tailored to forensic computing, with some courses offering work placements as part of your study. As well as more general degrees in IT or computer science, maths, physics and other STEM subjects are also welcomed by employers, who will offer you further training once you start work. It is possible to undertake certified industry training with a professional body such as The Chartered Institute for IT.

Personal attributes

You will need a creative approach to solving problems, and the ability to pay attention to detail and spot trends and patterns in large amounts of data. A well-organised and methodical approach to work, excellent communication skills combined with discretion, the ability to work under pressure and a willingness to keep pace with fast-changing technology are also essential.

Earnings

Salaries for graduates start at between £20,000 and £25,000 a year, but with a year's experience you could be earning up to £35,000. After five years and working in more senior roles, your salary could be between £40,000 and £60,000 a year.

Information security manager

Information security managers protect networks against unauthorised access to prevent cyber crime. IT security managers work for software manufacturers, for government departments, large business organisations, financial institutions or companies that specialise in IT security. Their role is to protect IT systems from potential threats such as viruses or hackers that can result in the corruption or loss of data; or denial-of-access attacks. Your work could involve assessing potential risks, testing security procedures and products, planning for disaster, investigating security breaches and training staff to ensure that security procedures are followed.

Entry, qualifications and training

It may be possible to move into information security with a general background in IT, having begun in an entry level position, such as user support or operations technician; apprenticeships are available. However, there are increasing numbers of graduates in junior information security positions and it is now possible to follow degrees specifically tailored to information security. As well as more general degrees in IT or computer science, maths, physics and other STEM subjects are particularly welcomed by employers.

Personal attributes

Excellent problem-solving, analytical and technical expertise, an understanding of confidentiality issues, good project manager skills and the willingness to develop with technological advances are all essential. Being able to work under pressure and communicating well are important, too.

Earnings

You can expect to earn between £25,000 and £28,000 a year initially but pay can rise rapidly with experience. Salaries for information security managers working for a large company are often in excess of £60,000.

IT architect

An IT or technical architect is responsible for the overall structure of an organisation's IT network or system, including an organisation's communication and security. They create the system identified as necessary by the systems analyst. Depending on the services they provide, different organisations will require different IT systems, the levels of interconnectivity between different sectors of the organisation, and the digital shape of the framework itself such as cloud computing and virtualisation. An IT architect therefore needs both an understanding of IT systems, the software used, and compliance with regulations, as well as an understanding of how best to create IT solutions for specific organisational needs. You'll work closely with project managers, systems analysts and software developers.

Entry, qualifications and training

This is not an entry level job. You will need industry experience in systems analysis and development, following on from an initial apprenticeship, HND or degree in computer science or a related subject. You'll need knowledge and experience of relevant programming and processes. Experience of project management methods like PRINCE2, Agile and ITIL will also be helpful.

Personal attributes

As well as a creative approach to problem solving, you will need excellent communication and presentation skills, the ability to explain technical ideas clearly and good negotiating and team working skills. You will also need to be organised and able to manage a project, with budgeting skills and an appreciation of wider business demands. You must be willing to keep up to date with developments in technology.

Earnings

This is a shortage area and salaries reflect this. IT architect salaries start from around £35,000 and can rise to in excess of £70,000, depending on your level of experience.

IT operations technician

Operations technicians (also known as service and repair technicians) maintain computer systems that are already up and running, and the individual computers within a system. They are employed by retailers, manufacturers and organisations that make extensive use of computers in their business. Regular upgrading of office systems means that a substantial amount of time is spent on installing and checking new systems, the rest being spent on diagnosing and correcting faults. You could also be employed as a field technician by a specialist IT operations company providing services on contract to businesses, especially those too small to have their own IT department. Alternatively, you could run your own PC repair and upgrade business, working with other local businesses and individuals who experience problems with their home PC.

Entry, qualifications and training

With sufficient self-taught knowledge of computer hardware and software, you may be able to find a job without formal qualifications. Courses in IT systems maintenance are available, however, such as Level 1 ICT or a Level 2 Certificate/Diploma in ICT Systems and Principles. Courses and qualifications certified by CISCO and Microsoft in the operation of their particular systems are often requested by employers. Many companies offer apprenticeships in computer system maintenance.

Personal attributes

As well as a sound knowledge of hardware, operating systems and commonly used software, you will also need to be a good communicator skilled at customer service. Other requirements include an ability to solve problems, meet deadlines and keep up to date with developments in IT, patience, and an awareness of electrical safety issues.

Earnings

Salaries start at around £17,000. With experience, you can earn between £12,000 and £25,000 a year. Senior technicians with management responsibility can earn up to £35,000 a year.

IT project manager

An IT project manager (also known as IT project lead, IT programme manager, IT consultant) oversees the overall implementation of an organisation's IT project, for example putting a whole area of its activity online for the first time, or revamping its existing systems, or integrating two or more areas of its activity. This will involve finding out what the client needs and working out and agreeing timescales, budgets and quality at the start, then using project management software to plan and resource stages, co-ordinating the project team, keeping clients and managers informed of progress, solving problems as they arise and adjusting plans. The project manager may also provide documentation and training for users of the new system as part of ensuring a smooth transition, and will need to confirm the organisation is satisfied with the new system before signing off and evaluating the project's success. You may work for a business, in the public sector or for a charity, or as a consultant for an IT specialist company.

Entry, qualifications and training

This is not an entry level job. You will need industry experience in systems analysis and development, following on from an initial apprenticeship, HND or degree in computer science or a related subject. You'll need knowledge and experience of relevant programming and processes. Experience of project management methods like PRINCE 2, Agile and ITIL will also be helpful.

Personal attributes

You'll need advanced IT skills, the ability to understand complex information and explain it to others, as well as excellent organisational and leadership skills.

Earnings

This is a shortage area and a senior role. Average salary is around £50,000 with earnings potentially rising to in excess of £70,000.

IT user support technician

IT user support technicians (also known as system support staff or computer help desk advisers) provide technical support to customers by telephone, e-mail and online. They are the first line of support for customers who are experiencing difficulties with hardware and software. The technician works with the computer user to identify what the problem is and suggest solutions, often by having remote access to the computer. If the technician cannot help the computer user to solve the problem, they may refer them to a second line of support. IT user support technicians work for suppliers of software and hardware, internet service providers and in-house for many large organisations such as businesses, universities or government departments.

Entry, qualifications and training

If you have an excellent working knowledge of computer systems and software, you can become a trainee user support technician without formal qualifications; apprenticeships are also available. Recognised computer support qualifications include BTEC and City & Guilds certificates, as well as those certified by companies such as Cisco and Microsoft. You can also become a user support technician with an HNC or HND in computing, and with a degree you can gain a place on a graduate trainee scheme.

Personal attributes

In addition to having good IT skills, you also need to be a patient and sympathetic communicator, well-organised and adaptable.

Earnings

Pay for user support technicians starts at between £18,000 and £22,000 a year. With experience, you can expect to earn £22,000 to £24,000. If you take on managerial responsibilities, your salary will rise to £25,000 to £35,000 a year.

Network engineer

Network engineers ensure that an organisation's network – its system of computers and other communication equipment linked to exchange information – is always running smoothly. When a new system is required, network engineers are responsible for installing and testing the equipment. When a system is in place, network engineers diagnose faults and maintain the hardware, software and cabling systems. This work can often involve being on-call and available to get the network up and running again, whatever the time of day or night. In a large organisation, you may be responsible for just one part of the system; in a smaller set-up, you may be responsible for any and all IT-related problems that arise. Alternatively, you may work for an IT specialist company which has contracts to service the networks of a variety of organisations, or work on your own as a self-employed freelance contractor.

Entry, qualifications and training

Apprenticeships are available and you can also take IT courses such as a Level 2 Diploma in ICT Systems Support. Employers also welcome higher education computing qualifications, such as an HND or degree. Large companies, e.g. retailers and banks, often recruit graduates directly into their IT department, usually favouring a degree in some sort of computer science, electrical/ electronic engineering, maths or physics.

Personal attributes

You will need to be a good communicator – including with those who are not technically trained but whose work depends on the smooth working of the network, as well as having analytical and organisational skills, with the ability to prioritise your workload.

Earnings

An entry level network engineer can expect to earn in the region of £18,000. With experience, this can go up to between £35,000 and £55,000. Senior network engineers can earn £50,000-plus.

Software developer

(see also Web developer)

Software developers (also referred to as software engineers, programmers, applications programmers, applications developers or software engineers) develop programs for use in other sectors – e.g. a sales and stock control system for retail, robotics for manufacturing, money transfers for banking, the storage of medical records for the NHS, an e-learning system for a university, and so on. Software developers write the code that makes up the program or software – the back-end of what appears on the screen for those using the system. They develop detailed knowledge of particular computer languages, e.g. Java, JavaScript, Python, SQL, and often specialise in a specific development environment, such as e-commerce or banking. As a software developer, you may work for an IT specialist company, or in the IT department of an organisation in another sector. Software developers' main activities involve creating supplementary code to adapt and improve pre-existing software, but may also be involved in developing and implementing a new system from scratch, working with an *IT architect and systems analyst*.

Entry, qualifications and training

Some firms offer apprenticeships providing hands-on experience and training in software development. Standard requirements are at least five GCSEs grades 9–4 including maths, English and either computer studies or science, as well as solid technical experience in programming either self-taught or gained through school/college, work experience or voluntary employment. Otherwise, you will require a HND, foundation degree or a degree. If your degree is not in IT, there are postgraduate IT conversion courses and many larger companies accept graduates in other subjects, e.g. maths and physics, provided you show the necessary aptitude and enthusiasm.

Personal attributes

You need to have excellent problem-solving, analytical and technical expertise and the willingness to develop with technological advances. Being able to work under pressure, work productively as a member of a team and communicate well are also important.

Earnings

Pay for beginners starts at £20,000 a year, with experience rising to £30,000 to £40,000, and in senior roles increasing to more than £50,000 a year.

Systems analyst

Systems analysts ensure that an organisation's information technology – its system of computers and other communication equipment linked to exchange information – meets its particular needs. Analysts identify the organisation's needs and suggest a new or redesigned computer-based system to fulfil them. They examine how and where computerised systems would be of benefit, assess the hardware and software needed and look at the most cost-effective solutions.

They advise clients on the options and benefits of particular systems and can also oversee their installation. Systems analysts work with an IT architect and software developers to ensure the system and software are developed to meet the needs identified.

Entry, qualifications and training

You will usually need an HND or degree, plus industry experience – this is not usually an entry level job. Relevant subjects to study include computer science, information management systems, business information systems, maths and physics. Employers welcome graduates with business skills as well as technical ability. Some degree courses include industry placements alongside your studying.

Personal attributes

As well as a creative approach to problem solving, you will need excellent communication and presentation skills, the ability to explain technical ideas clearly and good negotiating and team working skills. You will also need to be organised and able to manage a project, with budgeting skills and an appreciation of wider business demands. You must be willing to keep up to date with developments in technology.

Earnings

Systems analyst salaries start from between £20,000 and £27,000 a year. With more experience, you can earn between £30,000 and £45,000. Senior staff can earn up to around £62,000.

Telecommunications engineer

Telecoms engineers work on satellite, digital TV and fibre optic systems, and install broadband, mobile and landline phone networks. As well as broadband or mobile phone operators and satellite installers, telecoms engineers are also employed by rail companies or public bodies like the emergency services. Day to day, you may be installing aerials or satellites, setting up communications and data networks, laying and testing underground and underfloor cabling, finding and fixing faults, or designing, building and testing components and equipment.

Entry, qualifications and training

There are no set entry requirements. Apprenticeships are available. Experience in electronic or electrical engineering is useful. Although not essential, you can get a college qualification in a subject like communications cabling, ICT systems and principles, or electrical and electronic engineering. You must have colour-normal vision. You may need a full driving licence.

Personal attributes

You need good analytical and communications skills, a methodical approach and attention to detail, and an ability to read technical drawings, circuit diagrams and cabling plans.

Earnings

Starting salaries are around £18,000. More experienced telecoms engineers earn up to £28,000; £30,000 with management responsibilities.

Web developer

(see Art and design for Software developer and Web designer)

Web developers design and plan websites either for their own company or for clients. They are concerned with the software that makes the website work, rather than how the site looks to its users (which is the job of a web designer). The complexity of the task varies according to the nature of the site, and can include extensive use of multimedia or implementing secure systems for financial transactions. A considerable amount of time is spent testing sites and checking they are user-friendly.

Entry, qualifications and training

You'll usually need a foundation degree, HND or degree in an IT-related subject. You may be able to start in a junior position with other IT qualifications if you can demonstrate good skills in web development technologies such as graphics and web design, common operating systems and servers, databases and web programming or networking and security. Apprenticeships are available at all levels. You'll also need an understanding of World Wide Web Consortium (W3C) web development standards.

Personal attributes

You'll need excellent problem-solving skills, the creativity to turn clients' ideas into workable plans and a good appreciation of design and how people use websites.

Earnings

Salaries start at between £20,000 and £24,000, rising to £35,000 with experience. A highly experienced web developer with management responsibilities can earn in excess of £50,000.

Info

BCS, The Chartered Institute for IT
01793 417417
www.bcs.org

British Interactive Media Association (BIMA)
020 3538 6607
www.bima.co.uk

Tech Partnership Degrees
https://www.tpdegrees.com

Institution of Analysts and Programmers (IAP)
020 8004 9085
www.iap.org.uk

Skills Framework for the Information Age (SFIA)
www.sfia-online.org

TechUK
020 7331 2000
www.techuk.org

Screen Skills
020 7713 9800
www.screenskills.com

INSURANCE

The insurance industry is a significant employer in the United Kingdom. Many large insurance companies, providing insurance cover for every kind of item, situation and mishap, are based in the United Kingdom or have large operations here. There are many different career pathways open to people who have an interest in working with people and with financial information.

Account manager

As an insurance account manager your key role would be to ensure that your company's insurance policies are recommended by brokers and financial advisers to their clients. You would arrange meetings with brokers and advisers to ensure that they are aware of new products that you are developing. You might work with other members of the insurance team to develop new products as a result of requests from brokers on behalf of their clients. You could be involved in producing marketing literature or in training customer service staff to provide appropriate information on your insurance products. You could be responsible for monitoring brokers and advisers to see that they sell your products according to industry codes of practice.

Broker

Insurance brokers are the link between customers and insurance providers. They have a detailed knowledge of insurance products, whether this is life assurance, motor insurance, buildings insurance or any other specific field. They do not work for one insurance company – they work for customers trying to find the most appropriate insurance cover at the best possible price.

Claims administrator

Claims administrators, sometimes known as claims settlers or claims technicians, deal with policyholders who are making claims. Administrators issue forms, explain procedures to customers, gather further information and issue payments where claims are simple. If there is some dispute or the claim is very complex, they may have to refer it to their managers. Claims administrators work for brokers or for insurance companies. They normally specialise in a particular type of insurance, e.g. motor or household.

Claims inspector

When anyone makes a claim on their insurance, the claims inspector assesses the claim to ensure that it is truthful and also to check that the insurance company is liable for payment. Inspectors carry out detailed inspections of damaged goods or property and their work often involves interviewing claimants either in person or by telephone.

Insurance technician

Insurance technicians provide all the day-to-day administrative and clerical back-up that keeps the insurance industry going. They are often referred to as insurance clerks or insurance administrators. The work includes sending out routine correspondence such as policy renewal reminders, entering data onto computer systems or sending out marketing information. Exact tasks and responsibilities vary according to what kind of insurance organisation and for what department they are working.

Loss adjuster

Loss adjusters carry out very similar work to that of the claims inspector – the key difference is that they are independent. They investigate claims on behalf of insurance companies. They assess the causes of loss or damage, and make sure that the insurance claim is valid and covered by the policy. They can deal with all kinds of insurance claim, including damage by fire, flooding, theft or accident.

Risk surveyor/analyst

Insurance risk surveyors, also known as insurance risk analysts, work for general insurance companies, brokers, or firms of specialist surveyors. Their main role is to advise about risk, based on technical knowledge, experience and good practice. They visit sites such as commercial premises or engineering works and produce detailed reports on any particular risks associated with the site. They can also advise people on how to reduce the impact of these risks.

Underwriter

Underwriters assess the financial risk involved in insuring particular items, premises or projects. They calculate the prices for insurance premiums, aiming to fix on a price that will be profitable for the insurer but also competitive for potential customers.

Entry, qualifications and training

Insurance claims administrators and technicians usually need four or five GCSEs grades 9–4, including English and maths. Exact requirements vary from firm to firm. Accounts managers often start as technicians and work their way up. For brokers and underwriters, different firms set their own entry requirements. These vary from five GCSEs grades 9–4 to two A levels or a degree in a mathematical subject. Many firms like you to have had some experience in insurance or other financial work. Study for examinations from the Chartered Insurance Institute while working is usual and takes two to five years depending on the level you are working towards.

Brokers are regulated by the Financial Conduct Authority (FCA) and need to meet the FCA's training and competency standards. Brokers who deal in long-term investments such as pensions and life assurance need an approved qualification from the FCA.

Loss adjusters normally have several years' experience in the insurance industry or in other professional fields such as accountancy, law or surveying.

Personal attributes

People working in insurance must have excellent written and spoken English, be able to talk to people and write concise accurate reports. Some roles require good negotiating skills and the ability to deal with sensitive situations. Some degree of numeracy skill is important for all jobs. To be an underwriter, you need to be able to analyse complex statistical information.

Earnings

New-entrant brokers earn £16,000 to £25,000 – £20,000 to £80,000 with experience. For jobs that involve the sale of insurance products, part of your salary is earned through commission or bonuses. Claims managers earn around £19,000 to begin with – up to £60,000 if managing a large department. Loss adjusters start on £19,000 to £25,000, possibly rising to £50,000. The picture is very similar for underwriters. Technicians start on around the minimum wage to £19,000. In all cases achieving professional qualifications is likely to boost salaries.

Info

Chartered Insurance Institute
020 8989 8464
www.cii.co.uk

London Institute of Banking & Finance
01227 818609
www.libf.ac.uk

Discover Risk
www.discoverrisk.co.uk

INTERIOR DECORATION

(see Construction for Interior and finishing trades)

Interior designer/inscape designer

Interior designers work for commercial organisations as well as undertaking private commissions. They are responsible for the interiors of buildings (whereas an architect is responsible for its shell). Interior design can cover materials for floors and ceilings, fitments and fittings, and colour schemes, along with electrical and spatial planning. The commercial organisations may be offices, hotels, pubs, stores or banks. Interior designers may work with architects, have their own consultancies, or work in design units within large organisations.

Entry, qualifications and training

Most interior designers have a degree in one of the following subjects: fine art, fashion and textile design, product design, interior design or graphic design. It is possible to get into this work without a degree if you have really demonstrable creative flair or a lot of relevant experience. A Level 3 Diploma in Interior Design is available, but most training is on the job, working closely with more experienced and established designers. It can be valuable to do short courses on photography, desktop publishing and new product knowledge, in order to remain current.

Personal attributes

As well as an eye for colour and a feel for fabric, you need considerable technical and product knowledge and technical drawing skills, either on paper or with computer-aided design (CAD). You need to be able to work closely with other people and, if you work freelance, you should be confident enough to promote your own work.

Earnings

Salaries start at between £18,000 and £23,000, but if you have established your reputation you may earn far more. If you work freelance you can charge £30 or more an hour. What you can charge depends upon geographical location and upon personal recommendations of your work.

Info

Design Council
020 7420 5200
www.designcouncil.org.uk

British Institute of Interior Design
020 7628 0255
www.biid.org.uk

Chartered Society of Designers (CSD)
020 7357 8088
www.csd.org.uk

Creative & Cultural Skills
020 7015 1800
www.ccskills.org.uk

JEWELLERY

(see Crafts)

JOURNALISM

Journalists write and produce material for print, broadcast and digital media. Twenty-four-hour news and new ways of receiving that news have had a great impact on this sector. Newspapers, magazines, radio, television and internet news channels offer myriad opportunities for journalists, though every one of these opportunities is hotly pursued by many applicants. New technologies have blurred some of the demarcation lines between jobs in journalism. In national media there may still be clear distinctions between editors, reporters, subeditors, production editors, features editors, etc, but in smaller business-to-business (trade) magazines one person can be concerned with editing, commissioning, subediting and production-editing tasks.

Editor

The editor of a publication is responsible for its policy, content and the appointment and organisation of staff. An editor will prepare schedules for content and build up key relationships with external bodies. An editor of a publication will become the spokesperson for the title and will be expected to speak at conferences and to comment publicly on issues of importance. The editor works closely with the different groups within the team, including writers, production staff, advertising sales team, marketing and the publisher (*see Publishing*). The editor will hold regular editorial meetings to discuss current work and to plan forthcoming features. The editor will also oversee the editorial budget. Section editors (newspapers and magazines) specialise in specific areas, run their own teams of journalists and commission articles for their sections. Typical newspaper sections include home affairs, foreign affairs, health, media, education and travel.

Entry, qualifications and training

Most editors have come from a background in journalism and have worked their way up to the job, and so may have journalism qualifications.

Personal attributes

The mix of skills you need depends partly on how large a publication you are working for, but certainly team leadership, good planning skills and the ability to meet deadlines are essential. Being able to create and maintain a 'house style' in both appearance and content is very important.

Earnings

Earnings vary according to whether you edit a trade magazine, a local free newspaper, a paid-for regional paper, a popular weekly or monthly magazine, or a national daily newspaper. At the lower end, editors of trade magazines or free local newspapers earn between £25,000 and £35,000. At the top end, editors of national daily papers may earn £80,000 to £90,000. Editors of regional newspapers and well-known magazines earn between £40,000 and £60,000 – more for some magazine titles.

Journalist

Journalists/reporters find, research and write news articles and features for newspapers, magazines, special-interest periodicals, news agencies, radio, television and the internet (*see Broadcast journalist*). Most reporters start out on local papers where they cover a mix of stories, from weddings to council meetings. Local reporters are generally expected to multi-skill and might be expected to write the local news or features, subedit or take photographs. They work irregular hours and must be able to produce accurate, interesting and readable copy quickly, often in noisy offices or even public places. Editors look for trainees with an interest in current affairs and events, an accessible writing style and a good use of grammar, and an understanding of the role of the local newspaper within its community. Good time management and being able to work under pressure are also important qualities as journalists have to work to strict deadlines.

Inexperienced journalists are expected to work their way up, starting with more routine jobs. Regional and local newspapers recruit trainee reporters and photographers under a training contract and some newspaper groups run trainee schemes. These schemes are open to school or college leavers who have not taken a specialist university or college course. Applications for traineeships should be made direct to the editor. Direct entrants to these schemes will be expected to attend block-release or day-release courses and to sit the National Council for the Training of Journalists (NCTJ) National Certificate or a National (Scottish) Vocational Qualification.

National papers generally employ reporters with some experience, and will look to journalists who have had experience on local newspapers. Trade magazine experience, where knowledge of a specialist area has been developed, is also a route to entry into the national press. Occasionally national newspapers advertise for trainee recruits, but these opportunities are rare.

Trade magazines are also a route into the industry. Many magazines are produced on a monthly or fortnightly basis and specialise in particular subjects. Reporters on trade magazines are able to develop a specialist subject that can then be used to transfer to writing for national newspapers or to develop into a freelance career.

Experienced journalists have the opportunity to become feature writers or columnists for national newspapers. Feature writers suggest subjects for research, and produce longer than average articles dealing with topics not necessarily of current news value but of general interest. Feature writers will have developed an expertise or specialism within the subject they write about, and may have come originally not from a journalistic background but from the specialist area on which they write. Columnists often write about subjects from a personal point of view. Feature writers and columnists tend to be freelance writers working for a number of different newspapers, magazines and publishers, and will also work in broadcast media.

Entry, qualifications and training

There is always lively competition for every job in journalism. You can either train as a direct entrant with a newspaper, working while obtaining experience and qualifications, or you can get in through what is termed pre-entry, completing a relevant degree or postgraduate course before taking up training. In reality, journalism is becoming very much a graduate profession and direct entry training is becoming rare. There are several journalism degree and postgraduate courses run at universities and colleges and there are some short courses offered by private trainers. Many of these courses are expensive, so it is important to check them out carefully before signing up to one. Courses accredited by the National Council for the Training of Journalists are highly respected in the industry. You need to do as much as you can to strengthen your application. Write articles for local newspapers or student magazines/websites and try to get some voluntary work experience on a local newspaper. Journalism courses allow you to take the NCTJ preliminary certificate as part of your studies. Whether you enter journalism through a course or as a direct entrant, much of your training will be on the job, learning from more experienced colleagues.

Personal attributes

To be a good journalist you must have excellent writing skills and be able to adapt these to suit your particular audience. You should be good at researching information, talking to people, listening and encouraging them to talk to you. You need very good IT skills and you must be able to meet a deadline without fail.

Earnings

Trainees earn £15,000 to £22,000. Once you have completed your training, earnings are between £20,000 and £40,000, depending on whether you work for a magazine, a local or regional newspaper or a national daily. The most successful journalists can earn £100,000, but few reach this level.

Subeditor

Subeditors or 'subs' work for national daily or weekly newspapers, local and regional newspapers, magazines and websites. They process all the copy that will appear in their publication to ensure that it is accurate, free of typographical errors and spelling mistakes, makes sense and reads well. Subeditors take the stories written by journalists and reporters and rewrite the copy to make it fit the 'house style', adhere to word counts and remain within the law. The subeditor is responsible for putting the story on the page and is often responsible for designing and laying out pages. Subeditors write headlines, picture captions and summaries.

Entry, qualifications and training

Many subeditors will have been trained as reporters and then specialised. The NCTJ runs short courses and distance-learning qualifications for subeditors.

Personal attributes

Subeditors must be meticulous in their work. They are required to make quick decisions and to have the confidence to rewrite or cut the work of others. They must be able to work under pressure and to meet deadlines.

Earnings

Subeditors start on between £18,000 and £24,000, depending on the title they work for. Senior subeditors earn from £25,000 to £55,000. Top salaries are paid only to chief subeditors on national newspapers.

Info

HoldTheFrontPage
01332 895972
www.holdthefrontpage.co.uk

Screen Skills
020 7713 9800
www.screenskills.com

National Council for the Training of Journalists (NCTJ)
01799 544014
www.nctj.com

News Media Association
020 3848 9620
www.newsmediauk.org

Broadcast journalist

Broadcast journalists work in radio, television and online. Unlike print journalists, almost all broadcast journalists take a postgraduate pre-entry course. Some journalists still make the transition to broadcasting from newspapers, but it is increasingly regarded as a specialist branch of the profession in its own right. As in print, broadcast journalists will need to have good communication skills, an enquiring mind, knowledge of current events and a sense of what makes a news story. The ability to speak clear, standard English is important. Both the BBC and ITN run traineeships for entrants into broadcast journalism.

Experience in radio journalism can be found in hospital, community and college radio. This can be used as evidence of interest and experience when applying to courses – many postgraduate courses will require a recorded news story as part of their application procedure.

Entry, qualifications and training

You can move into broadcast journalism from newspaper or magazine journalism and join a new-entrant training scheme with a TV or radio broadcaster – this is referred to as direct entry. You can complete a degree or postgraduate qualification in broadcast journalism – this is known as the pre-entry route. You can also get details of courses from the Broadcast Journalism Training Council. If you have a degree in journalism, media studies or politics this may strengthen your application for a training position. This is a fiercely competitive field and any voluntary work for community radio could be helpful.

Personal attributes

You have to be an excellent communicator, able to speak clearly and with confidence. You need to be able to listen and to question and to be sensitive or persistent as required. You also need good writing and research skills. You have to be able to work under pressure and to meet deadlines.

Earnings

Salaries on training schemes are between £18,000 and £20,000. Once you are qualified, these rise to £25,000 to £40,000. Top broadcast journalists who are household names can earn far more than this – some in the region of £100,000 plus.

Press photographer

(see Photography)

Web content editor

Web content editors research, write, edit, proof and update material on websites. They may also be referred to as web content producers. This material includes images as well as text. Just like any magazine or newspaper journalist or editor, web content editors try to ensure that what they produce is appropriate to their target readership. Web content might include local and national news, opinion, information about products and services, factual information or entertainment. Editors work closely with technical staff who develop and design websites. Web content editors also liaise closely with the clients for whom they are writing, editing and updating material *(see also Marketing)*.

Entry, qualifications and training

There is no one route for entry into this work. Many web content editors have worked as journalists. Some have worked in IT or marketing, and many have considerable experience in the profession or subject with which they are going to work. Knowledge of desktop publishing, photo imaging packages and different web content management sytems can greatly increase your employability, as can a basic understanding of HTML (the language/code that is the basic building block of the web). A degree in a subject such as English may give you an advantage. A college course such as an A level in English or Level 3 Diploma in Creative and Digital Media may help to equip you with some of the skills required. You could also complete an advanced apprenticeship in creative and digital media or as a junior content producer, for example.

Personal attributes

You need excellent writing skills, with a good grasp of English grammar. You should be creative, but not lose sight of the importance of detail and accuracy. You should be able to write to very specific word counts or house styles and you should be able to communicate really well with other members of your team.

Earnings

New entrants earn between £19,000 and £23,000. With three or four years' experience, and depending on the size of the organisation you work for and where you live, this can rise to well over £30,000.

Info

Society for Editors and Proofreaders
020 8785 6155
www.sfep.org.uk

Screen Skills
020 7713 9800
www.screenskills.com

World Wide Web Consortium (W3C)
www.w3.org

Tech Partnership Degrees
www.tpdegrees.com

National Union of Journalists (NUJ)
www.nuj.org.uk

LABORATORY WORK

Laboratory technician

(see also Medical and healthcare science)

Assisting with research, helping to diagnose diseases, measuring pollution levels and developing new products – these are some of the tasks you would undertake as a lab technician. Laboratory technicians ensure that equipment is clean and in working order. They set up experiments and investigations and record data. They may also be involved in stock control, monitoring and ordering chemicals, equipment and other supplies. Laboratory technicians work in education, in medicine, in the pharmaceutical industry, in food science and in research laboratories of every kind. Those working in education help school and college students to use equipment safely and record results correctly, and they may be involved in demonstrating how to conduct experiments.

Entry, qualifications and training

You can get into laboratory technician work with four GCSEs grades 9–4 including maths, English and a science. You may also be able to enter laboratory work through an apprenticeship (see the SEMTA website). However, many employers now expect applicants to have higher-level qualifications such as HND, foundation degree or degree in a science subject, e.g. biotechnology or chemistry. There are several qualifications to choose from: NVQ levels 2, 3 and 4 in Laboratory and Associated Activities or NVQ levels in Clinical Laboratory Support. You could also study part time for a BTEC HND/HNC or foundation degree while working, rather than before joining this profession. If you work in a school science laboratory, CLEAPSS, the School Science Service, offers several professional development courses. Because technology is changing fast, your employer, whether you work in healthcare, education or research and development, is likely to send you on short courses to keep you up to date with changes and developments. An advanced apprenticeship as a laboratory technician may also help you to get into this career.

Personal attributes

You need a genuine interest in science and in the kinds of projects on which you are working. You need to have a very thorough and careful approach to all your work, be able to follow procedures and record results accurately. You will need a range of technical and IT skills, though the precise nature of these varies from job to job. You have to be good at working as part of a team. If you are working in schools or colleges, you may have to explain and demonstrate experiments and procedures to students and assist them in their work, so good training and information-giving skills are important.

Earnings

Laboratory assistants earn £14,000 to £22,000. Laboratory technicians earn between £15,500 and £23,000. Senior technicians earn £20,000 to £27,000. Private sector laboratories tend to pay the highest salaries, especially in 'cutting edge' fields of biotechnology.

Info

The Science Council
020 3434 2020
www.sciencecouncil.org

NHS Careers
0345 60 60 655
www.healthcareers.nhs.uk

SEMTA
0845 643 9001
www.semta.org.uk

CLEAPSS Science – supporting practical science and technology in schools and colleges
science.cleapss.org.uk

Animal technician

A very specific role in a laboratory is that of the animal technician. Animal technicians are the staff responsible for the care and welfare of animals used in biomedical, pharmaceutical and other fields of research. Governments around the world require that new medicines have been extensively tested on animals before allowing human clinical trials. Testing is also undertaken on veterinary medicines and other products that may have an effect on human health. Animal technicians are responsible for caring for the animals, undertaking observations, sampling for the scientific studies, and ensuring that the strict laws controlling their use are followed at all times. Applicants should have a genuine desire to work with animals and must demonstrate concern and respect for their well-being.

Entry, qualifications and training

The minimum entry qualifications are five GCSEs at grade C or above (grade 4 or above, if in English or maths), but some entrants have A levels or a degree. The Institute of Animal Technology (IAT) offers five levels of qualification, from a basic one-year certificate to a postgraduate MSc. You can get exemption from certain modules of these courses if you can offer sciences at A or degree level. These qualifications can be taken as distance-learning modules or at local colleges through day-release courses. There are also a number of college courses you could undertake, or an apprenticeship such as an animal technologist advanced apprenticeship.

Personal attributes

You have to be comfortable handling animals and you must be kind, caring and calm when doing so. You also have to accept that you will have to do things that are stressful for animals, so you need to be prepared for this. You must be practical, thorough and meticulous, since you have to record scientific information accurately.

Earnings

Trainees earn £13,000 to £15,000 and from £15,000 to £23,000 for qualified technicians, but there is no national agreed rate for this work. A senior laboratory manager can earn up to £40,000.

Info

SEMTA
0845 643 9001
www.semta.org.uk

Lantra
02476 696996
www.lantra.co.uk

Institute of Animal Technology (IAT)
0800 085 4380
www.iat.org.uk

LAND AND PROPERTY

The land and property sector covers many occupations connected with both the daily management of and sale and purchase of land and property.

Estate agent

Estate agents are responsible for the sale, letting and management of any kind of property – factories, shops, offices and farms as well as residential property. In many cases they also deal with valuation and survey work, and offer other services such as auctioneering and financial services advice. Large firms provide a wide range of these services through specialist departments employing qualified professionals, particularly in the area of surveying and valuation. Dedicated sales staff fulfil the role of property negotiators, and in the majority of smaller firms with just one or two branches a combination of these functions will be found.

Entry, qualifications and training

You don't necessarily need formal qualifications to become an estate agent. Relevant experience and the right skills are extremely important. At the moment there are not many graduates in this profession, but some large estate agent chains do run graduate training schemes. Where this is the case, a degree in a relevant subject such as surveying or business may put you at an advantage. Many people start work in an administrative role with an estate agent and work their way up. In this case, each agent sets its own entry requirements, but many expect you to have GCSEs in English and maths.

You normally start as a trainee sales negotiator and receive on-the-job training from more experienced agents. The National Association of Estate Agents (NAEA) offers a range of distance-learning professional qualifications for estate agents. Qualifications cover residential property agency, commercial property agency, property letting and management, and property auctions.

Personal attributes

You must be outgoing, with very good people skills. You should be a good negotiator. You should be well organised, able to keep track of several things at the same time. You should have good written as well as spoken English and you should have a genuine interest in property.

Earnings

Trainees earn between £14,000 and £22,000, and once you handle sales you earn commission on properties sold. This can take earnings to £20,000 to £50,000 plus. Estate agents' earnings are very sensitive to fluctuations in the property market.

Gamekeeper

Gamekeepers work on large country estates for private landlords, management firms and private syndicates that wish to raise game birds such as pheasant or partridge. Gamekeepers known as river keepers may also manage fish stocks such as salmon or trout for sport fishing. They rear the game birds and fish, and protect them from poachers and predators. They must ensure that the proper environment for the game is maintained, and on shooting days they organise the beaters.

Entry, qualifications and training

Competition for jobs is strong. There are no formal entry qualifications, but gamekeepers must have a driving licence, be good at handling a dog, and be suitable to apply for a shotgun licence. Practical skills such as carpentry and experience on a shoot, as a beater, for example, may be useful. There are part- and full-time City & Guilds and BTEC courses in gamekeeping and countryside management. Some of these courses may set specific entry requirements. The training is on the job and most gamekeepers start as an assistant or under-keeper. An intermediate or advanced apprenticeship in game and wildlife management is also a route you could consider.

Personal attributes

You have to love being outside in all weathers and have a real interest in nature. You need to be very practical, good with your hands and physically fit. It is important that you are very observant, both of animal and plant life and of safety issues. You are on your own for a great deal of the time, but you must be able to communicate well with other people when shoots or other events are taking place.

Earnings

Gamekeepers earn between £14,000 and £20,000. Many posts include free or subsidised accommodation, and a suitable motor vehicle.

LANDSCAPE ARCHITECTURE

Landscape architecture includes three distinct areas: design, management and science.

Landscape designer

Designers are trained in the planning and design of all types of outdoor spaces. They use design techniques based on their knowledge of the functional and aesthetic characteristics of landscape materials, and of the organisation of landscape elements, external spaces and activities. Their work ranges from large-scale landscape planning to the preparation of schemes for the short- and long-term development of individual sites. It also includes preparing detailed designs, specifications, contract drawings and letting and supervising contracts. Some practitioners are also qualified in other disciplines such as planning and architecture, and the landscape designer draws on many fields in order to promote new landscapes and sustain existing ones.

Landscape manager

Landscape managers employ management techniques in the long-term care and development of new and existing landscapes, and also in determining policy and planning for future landscape management and use. They have particular expertise in the management and maintenance of landscape materials, both hard and soft, based on established principles of construction, horticulture and ecology. In addition, the landscape manager will have a thorough knowledge of budgetary control procedures, property and resource management, especially related to labour requirements and machinery, and the letting and administration of contracts.

Landscape scientist

Landscape scientists explore and investigate the flora, fauna and geology of an area to be landscaped or which has already been landscaped. They survey areas to find out what impact landscape projects will have on wildlife. They suggest strategies to encourage new wildlife into an area. They are involved at all stages of a project, from initial planning through to monitoring wildlife and other natural phenomena in an area once a project has been completed.

Entry, qualifications and training

The recognised professional qualification for those working in all aspects of landscape architecture is Member of the Landscape Institute (MLI), which confers the title of chartered landscape architect. There are three divisions: design, management and science. Associate membership, the first step towards achieving this, is gained after completing an accredited degree. Two years' relevant work is required as an associate member before taking the Institute's professional practice examination and progressing to full professional membership. A list of accredited courses is available from the Landscape Institute.

Personal attributes

Those working in design need creativity, imagination, a practical outlook, interest in the landscape and an enthusiasm for working outdoors. Those in management require good organisational and interpersonal skills, consistent application and a practical outlook. Scientists need enthusiasm for the subject, technical commitment and good communication skills.

Earnings

New graduate landscape architects and scientists earn between £18,000 and £26,000. For fully qualified and chartered landscape architects, salaries range from £30,000 to £47,000. Some landscape specialists earn £50,000 plus. There is much variation according to whether you are working for a corporate development company landscaping gardens of expensive commercial premises, or working on a project funded by a voluntary body, for example.

Info

Lantra
02476 696996
www.lantra.co.uk

Landscape Institute
0330 808 2230
www.landscapeinstitute.org

Chartered Institute of Ecology and Environmental Management (CIEEM)
01962 868626
www.cieem.net

LAW

The legal profession includes many occupations, all concerned with aspects of the law: from the high-profile role of prosecuting or defending a case of public notoriety in the courts, to helping individuals in the purchase and sale of property. The term 'lawyer' is used to describe a solicitor or a barrister. There are other roles supporting solicitors and barristers and ensuring the smooth running of the court system.

Barrister

Barristers have a detailed knowledge of the law. They represent their clients in court. They are independent sources of legal advice and can advise clients on their case. Usually, they are hired by solicitors to represent a case in court and only become involved once advocacy before a court is required. They plead the case on behalf of the client and the client's solicitor. Barristers usually specialise in particular areas of law, such as criminal, chancery (estates and trusts), commercial, and common law, which includes family, housing and personal injury law. Most barristers are self-employed, working from offices referred to as chambers. Some work for government departments or agencies such as the Crown Prosecution Service. An increasing number of employed barristers work in private and public organisations such as charities or trade unions. In Scotland the role and responsibilities of an advocate are similar to those of a barrister in England and Wales. The work of a barrister or advocate is likely to include taking instructions from solicitors, studying and working out how to proceed with each particular case, answering complex legal questions raised by solicitors or by cases through researching complicated points of law and writing opinions on legal matters. If a case is to go to court the barrister will have to prepare for this and then appear in court speaking and questioning on behalf of either the defence or the prosecution.

Entry, qualifications and training

This is a graduate profession open to graduates with a good degree (2.1 or above in any subject). If your degree is not in law, then you have to take a one-year full-time or two-year part-time law conversion course. This course can be either a Common Professional Exam (CPE) or a Graduate Diploma in Law (GDL). After this, all entrants must take a further one-year full-time or two-year part-time Bar Professional Training Course (BPTC). Applicants for the BPTC also have to join one of the four Inns of Court before starting the course. On completing the BPTC, hopeful barristers apply for a pupillage in a set of barristers' chambers (their word for offices). After completing a pupillage, the next stage is to get a tenancy to practise in a set of chambers. All stages are exceedingly competitive.

In Scotland, advocates need to pass a postgraduate diploma in law and spend two years practising as a solicitor before being called to the bar.

Personal attributes

As it will be necessary to understand and interpret complex legal wording into clear basic English, barristers must have an excellent command of the English language and a meticulous understanding of the use of words. Barristers must understand and talk knowledgeably about technical matters in order to be able to cross-examine the most expert witness, for example on complex aspects of technology. It is also useful if barristers present a highly confident and self-assured manner and can put on a 'good performance' in court. Since the work is confidential, a barrister needs to be trustworthy and discreet.

Earnings

Earnings are very broad, ranging between £12,000 and £250,000. Most barristers' earnings are based on the fees they charge. Trainees during pupillage earn a minimum of £12,000 – many earn more than this. After this the range is from £25,000 to £300,000, depending on your area of specialisation. Salaries in the Crown Prosecution Service are between £30,000 and £70,000.

Info

The Bar Council
020 7242 0082
www.barcouncil.org.uk

Bar Standards Board
020 7611 1444
www.barstandardsboard.org.uk

Law Careers
020 7939 4002
www.lawcareers.net

All About Law
020 3651 4919
www.allaboutlaw.co.uk

Barristers' clerk/advocates' clerk

The barristers' clerk is the administrator or manager of the business of a set of barristers' chambers, deciding which briefs to accept and which barrister to allocate them to and negotiating fees with clients. The accounts, the barristers' appointment books and the efficient day-to-day running of the office are all part of the job of an experienced clerk.

Entry, qualifications and training

The minimum qualification is four GCSE pass grades at 9–4 in academic subjects. Training is on the job and juniors can apply through the Institute of Barristers' Clerks to attend a two-year part-time Edexcel (BTEC) national certificate course studying organisation, finance, management, law, marketing and chambers administration. On obtaining the certificate, juniors may apply, after five years' service, for qualified Membership of the Institute of Barristers' Clerks.

Personal attributes

In order to manage efficient chambers and the barristers who work from them, a barristers' clerk needs good organisational skills, the ability to lead a team as well as be part of a team, and to get on with the general public. A good command of written and spoken English and an appreciation of the necessity for absolute confidentiality at all times are vital to success in this career.

Earnings

Clerks start on £15,000 to £18,000. Junior clerks with two or three years' experience earn £20,000 to £35,000; senior clerks may earn £60,000 to £80,000 plus a performance-related bonus.

Info

Institute of Barristers' Clerks
020 3763 8999
www.ibc.org.uk

Coroner

Coroners have the job of inquiring into the circumstances of and determining the cause of any deaths that don't appear to be through natural causes. Sudden deaths, deaths in prison or in police custody – in fact any unexplained deaths are those which coroners must investigate. The work involves talking to other professionals such as doctors or police officers and/or talking to relatives of the deceased. Coroners can decide whether a post mortem needs to be carried out. They decide whether an inquest into the death needs to be held and if so they preside over that inquest, draw conclusions, write reports, inform appropriate authorities and ensure that the law is adhered to at all points.

Entry, qualifications and training

All coroners must already be qualified as lawyers, barristers, solicitors or fellows of the Society of Legal Executives. In whichever of these professions they have qualified, they must have had at least five years' experience before they can apply to work as a coroner. Some coroners have medical as well as legal qualifications. Most would start as assistants or deputies. Coroners are appointed by local authorities, but every appointment must also be approved by the Lord Chancellor. Some coroners work part time and still continue with other legal work.

Personal attributes

Coroners must have excellent communication skills. They need be able to explain highly complex information, ask questions in a way that can be easily understood and be able to question people who may be very upset or anxious. They need enquiring minds, and an ability to think rationally in highly emotional situations. They need a good knowledge of the law and an ability to follow procedures rigorously.

Earnings

Coroners' earnings are based on the size of population they serve and current salaries range from £85,000 to £115,000. Part-time coroners are paid according to the number of cases they cover.

Info

Coroners' Society of England and Wales
www.coronersociety.org.uk

Chartered Institute of Legal Executives
01234 841000
www.cilex.org.uk

Ministry of Justice
020 3334 3555
www.gov.uk/government/organisations/
ministry-of-justice

Court staff

Court administrative officer

Court administrative officers and court administrative assistants ensure the smooth day-to-day running of the courts. They book cases, allocate cases to courtrooms, prepare lists of the day's cases and send out correspondence. They may also be involved in the collection of fines and providing information to members of the public. More senior administrative officers lead teams of assistants, ensuring that all the tasks listed above are carried out efficiently.

Entry, qualifications and training

To work as an administrative assistant you need two GCSEs grades 9–4 and to be an administrative officer you need five GCSEs grades 9–4. If you have other useful administrative experience, you may be considered without these formal qualifications.

Personal attributes

You must be able to deal calmly and politely with people. You should have good organisational skills and be able to stay calm in a busy environment. You should be able to pay attention to detail and work well as part of a team.

Court legal adviser

Court legal advisers, sometimes referred to as court clerks, are legal advisers who give advice to unpaid (non-stipendiary) magistrates who are trying cases in the magistrates' courts. They are qualified lawyers, but they do not take part in the decision making about judgments and sentencing. As magistrates do not have to be legally qualified, it is the court clerks who ensure that magistrates interpret and apply the law correctly.

Entry, qualifications and training

Court legal advisers have to be either qualified solicitors or barristers, who themselves must have either a law degree or an approved postgraduate legal qualification. Court legal advisers follow a set training programme and also learn by working with more experienced clerks, finding out about the many different areas of work – road traffic, licensing, fines enforcement, sentencing, etc.

Personal attributes

As well as a real interest in and broad knowledge of the law, court legal advisers must be logical thinkers, capable of undertaking fairly detailed research. They must be discreet, sensitive and calm, but also able to remain detached when dealing with stressful and upsetting situations.

Court usher

Whether you are a defendant, a witness, a jury member or a lawyer, it is the responsibility of the court usher to ensure that you know where you should be, what you should do and how you should do it. Ushers ensure that the courtroom is prepared and that everyone is present. They call witnesses and defendants, label evidence and administer the taking of oaths. At Crown Court, where a jury trial is taking place, court ushers escort members of the jury to and from the courtroom. They remain on duty outside the jury room while the jury is in discussion and they take messages between the jury and the judge.

Entry, qualifications and training

You do not necessarily need any formal qualifications to become a court usher, although you would be expected to have a good general level of education. Previous work experience of dealing with the public and handling difficult situations is more important than professional qualifications. Your training will be on the job and you start by shadowing another usher. You will probably be sent on several short in-house courses. Skills for Justice has recently introduced NVQ levels 2 and 3 qualifications in Court Operations, so you may have the opportunity to work towards one of these.

Personal attributes

These are really important. You have to be trustworthy and truthful and you must have excellent people skills, be able to remain calm, reassure and explain, but be confident if people are hostile or difficult. You have to be well organised and pay attention to detail.

Earnings

Court administrative assistants and ushers are paid between £15,000 and £21,000, while court administrative officers earn between £17,000 and £22,000. Trainee court legal advisers start on £20,500 rising through five tiers to £43,000.

Info

Skills for Justice
www.sfjuk.com

Her Majesty's Courts and Tribunals Service
www.gov.uk/government/organisations/
hm-courts-and-tribunals-service

Northern Ireland Court Service
www.justice-ni.gov.uk

Court reporter

Court reporters attend court sittings and take down a complete report of all the evidence, the summing-up or judgment and, on occasions, the speeches of counsel in the various cases. Formerly, the proceedings were taken down in shorthand; now a palantype or stenograph is used. This is a typewriter-like machine that enables the reporter to achieve 200 words per minute. In addition, computers may be used to prepare transcripts, with all the advantages of on-screen editing and speed of preparation. The work sometimes involves travelling to a number of different courts. The majority of verbatim reporters begin their careers in the courts but can also work for Hansard, producing reports of proceedings in the House of Commons and the House of Lords. Television subtitlers also use the skills of verbatim reporting.

Entry, qualifications and training

While there are no formal academic entry requirements, the reality is that most court reporters have A levels or equivalent. Applicants need to have proven ability in written or machine shorthand (usually over 180 words per minute), good typing speeds and excellent spelling, grammar and punctuation. Legal experience can also be an asset. Details of full-time, part-time and distance-learning courses are available from the British Institute of Verbatim Reporters. In Scotland, there are no college courses but training is provided on the job by working alongside an experienced reporter.

Personal attributes

Like anyone concerned with the courts, reporters must be discreet, honest and trustworthy, as most of the work is confidential. Reporters must show a high degree of accuracy.

Earnings

Pay is from £16,000 to £20,000. Many court reporters work freelance and can earn anything from £60 to £325 a day. What you earn depends on how complex and demanding your work is.

Info

All about law
020 3651 4919
www.allaboutlaw.co.uk

British Institute of Verbatim Reporters
020 8907 8249
www.bivr.org.uk

Ministry of Justice
020 3334 3555
www.justice.gov.uk

Legal executive

A legal executive is a professional lawyer employed in a solicitor's office or in the legal department of commerce and central and local government. The training and academic requirements in a specified area of law are at the same level as those required of a solicitor. Consequently, with few exceptions, a legal executive is able to carry out tasks that are similar to those undertaken by solicitors. The main areas of specialisation are conveyancing, civil litigation, criminal law, family law and probate. In addition to providing a worthwhile career in its own right, the legal executive qualification provides access to those wishing to qualify as solicitors via the Chartered Institute of Legal Executives (CILEx) route. In Scotland, the term 'legal executive' is not used, but solicitors engage assistants to do similar work.

Entry, qualifications and training

The minimum entry requirement is four GCSEs, including English, but A-level students and graduates are welcome. As an alternative, the Institute accepts a qualification in vocational legal studies, and has special arrangements for students who are over 21. In the main, training is on a part-time basis so that there is potential for trainees to 'learn while they earn'. The CILEx website provides more information on qualifications and apprenticeships.

Personal attributes

An ability to communicate, both verbally and in writing, with people at all levels, absolute discretion and trustworthiness, together with meticulous attention to detail, are all essential.

Earnings

Trainees earn between £15,000 and £28,000. Qualified legal executives earn around £35,000. Large city firms pay the highest salaries, which may include bonuses.

Info

Chartered Institute of Legal Executives (CILEx) 01234 841000 www.cilex.org.uk	**Skills for Justice** www.sfjuk.com **All About Law** 020 3651 4919 www.allaboutlaw.co.uk

---

Paralegal

Paralegals work for firms of solicitors, commercial companies and public sector bodies. They are not qualified solicitors or legal executives, but they develop considerable specialist knowledge. They normally specialise in a specific area of the law, such as conveyancing, probate or family law. Their work involves researching information, drafting and managing documents, attending client meetings, and some general clerical work. Paralegals also have to keep up to date with legal developments in their specialist field.

Entry, qualifications and training

While there are no specific entry qualifications for paralegals, many hope to become solicitors, barristers or legal executives. This means that many applicants for these posts have a law degree. In any case, some firms ask for four or five GCSEs grades 9–4 or two A levels. Training is on the job. You could also consider a college course such as Level 2 Diploma in Legal Studies before you look for a role, or a paralegal advanced apprenticeship. The Chartered Institute of Legal Executives (CILEx) also offers part-time and distance-learning courses for paralegals.

Personal attributes

You must be very well organised, able to manage your time and prioritise your work well. You need excellent written English skills and should be interested in legal matters.

Earnings

Salaries for paralegals are between £19,000 and £25,000. In large city law firms earnings can be much higher – up to £70,000 plus large bonuses.

Info

Chartered Institute of Legal Executives (CILEx)
01234 841000
www.cilex.org.uk

Institute of Paralegals
020 3034 1487
www.theiop.org

Skills for Justice
www.sfjuk.com

National Association of Licensed Paralegals
020 7112 8034
www.nationalparalegals.co.uk

All About Law
020 3651 4919
www.allaboutlaw.co.uk

Solicitor

The role of the solicitor is to provide clients with skilled legal representation and advice. The clients can be individual people or companies, or any type of organisation or group. A solicitor may work on all kinds of legal matters, from house purchases to defence of people accused of crimes; from selling a corporation to drafting a complicated will or trust. Solicitors may also represent clients in all courts, but will often brief a barrister (see *Barrister*) to represent the client, and then act as a liaison between them.

Scottish solicitors can appear in all courts and tribunals in Scotland up to and including the Sheriff Court. They can also gain rights of audience, enabling them to appear in the higher courts by becoming a solicitor-advocate, or may brief an advocate to represent their clients.

While some solicitors may deal with a variety of legal problems, others specialise in a particular area, such as shipping, planning and construction, financial services or social security. Specialisation within the profession is increasing. The majority of solicitors work in private practice, with firms made up of several partners. Many others work as employed solicitors in commerce, industry, local and central government and other organisations.

Solicitors are instructed directly by clients and have a lot of contact with them. They have rights of audience in the magistrates' court and the county court. Unlike barristers, solicitors do not wear wigs but do wear gowns if they appear in the county court. Solicitors are governed by a professional body called the Law Society.

Entry, qualifications and training

The Law Society governs the training of solicitors in England and Wales, which takes place in two stages – the academic and the professional. Most, but not all, entrants to the profession are graduates. Some universities offering law degrees require applicants to take the National Law Aptitude Test (LNAT). Fellows of the Chartered Institute of Legal Executives (CILEx) over the age of 25 with five years' qualifying experience do not need to complete the academic stage. Non-law graduates take the Common Professional Examination (CPE) or a postgraduate diploma in law; those with qualifying law degrees are exempt from this. The next stage, the vocational stage, is taken via the legal practice course, available at a number of colleges and universities. It is a one-year full-time or two-year part-time course. The trainee solicitor then has to undertake a two-year training contract with an authorised firm or organisation. There is always strong competition for these since there are more applicants than available places.

The Law Society of Scotland governs the training of solicitors in Scotland. It is possible to study for a Bachelor of Law degree at five Scottish universities: Aberdeen, Dundee, Edinburgh, Glasgow and Strathclyde. Alternatively, it is possible to take the Law Society's own examinations by finding employment as a pre-diploma trainee. After completion of the LLB degree or professional examinations, all graduates who would like to become solicitors must take the diploma in legal practice – a 26-week postgraduate course, which also offers training in office and business skills. After successful completion of the degree and the diploma, those who wish to become solicitors then serve a two-year training contract with a Scottish solicitor. Trainees must undertake a further two-week course of study, keep training records that will be examined and monitored by the Society, and take a test of professional competence. The trainees can then apply to the Law Society of Scotland for a practising certificate. All Scottish solicitors must hold a Law Society of Scotland practising certificate.

Personal attributes

A high level of academic achievement, integrity, good communication skills, patience, discretion, a good command of language and problem-solving skills are all required.

Earnings

The recommended minimum salary on a training contract is £19,619 (£22,121 in London). Many London firms may pay more – £30,000 to £32,000. Once qualified, starting salaries in a smaller firm outside London will range between £25,000 and £40,000. Starting salaries in larger firms and in London can be significantly higher. Salaries are higher if you specialise in commercial law – £60,000 to £150,000. In non-commercial law, salaries are between £40,000 and £80,000.

Info

The Law Society
020 7242 1222
www.lawsociety.org.uk

Law Society of Northern Ireland
028 9023 1614
www.lawsoc-ni.org

National Admissions Test for Law (LNAT)
www.lnat.ac.uk

Law Careers
020 7939 4002
www.lawcareers.net

All About Law
020 3651 4919
www.allaboutlaw.co.uk

LEISURE AND AMENITY MANAGEMENT

(see also Sport and exercise)

Leisure and amenity management shares many aspects of arts administration, sport and recreation, tourism and management of the natural environment and there is not always a clear distinction between some careers in these fields. Leisure activities could include anything from taking a stroll in a park, visiting a country house or historic monument to learning to kite surf at an outward bound centre.

Leisure centre manager

Leisure centre managers are responsible for the day-to-day running of their centres. These health clubs and leisure facilities may be run by local authorities, private companies or form part of hotel leisure and spa facilities. Your work will depend on what range of activities your particular centre has to offer. It is always likely to include drawing up timetables of activities, coordinating special events, recruiting and training staff, developing marketing material and marketing strategies, and managing budgets.

Entry, qualifications and training

You could enter this profession by starting as either an assistant manager or a management trainee. Each employer sets its own entry requirements, but a good standard of education including GCSEs in English, maths and a science are usually necessary. A strong interest in sport and leisure and a track record of working with people are also important. While working as an assistant or trainee, the Institute of Sport and Recreation Management offers a number of qualifications for which you can work on a part-time basis.

Alternatively, you can take a degree in sports and leisure management, sports science, sports studies or similar and start work as a graduate manager or management trainee. Degrees in business, psychology or tourism may also be useful entry qualifications. College courses include the Level 3 Diploma in Leisure Management. You could also enter the leisure industry by completing an advanced apprenticeship as a leisure duty manager.

Personal attributes

You should have a genuine interest in sport and fitness. You need excellent interpersonal skills and to be good at motivating other people. You should be very well organised and have a flair for marketing and publicity. You should have some grasp of financial management and reasonable IT skills.

Earnings

Earnings range from £18,000 to £25,000 for assistant or trainee managers. Managers earn between £21,000 and £26,000, and senior managers running large facilities can earn £35,000 to £40,000.

Info

The Chartered Institute for the Management of Sport and Physical Activity
0343 836 0200
www.cimspa.co.uk

SkillsActive
033 0004 0005
www.skillsactive.com

LINGUISTICS, LANGUAGES AND TRANSLATION

Interpreter

Interpreters communicate between people who do not share a common language. They use two main techniques: simultaneous and consecutive interpreting. Conference interpreters usually work using the simultaneous method in a booth with headphones and communicative technology, allowing them to hear the speaker and interpret to their audience.

Very few openings are available for interpreters, even worldwide. Conference interpreters work at international conferences such as the United Nations or the European Commission and at the International Court of Justice, using simultaneous or consecutive interpreting. Some work for international agencies, others are freelance. Demand for conference interpreters in particular languages may fluctuate depending on the political and economic requirements of the day. Interpreters with specialist knowledge, such as engineering or economics, may have the chance to work at conferences on their subject. Interpreters may also work as guides in tourist centres, and to do this they must usually be accredited and trained as guides.

Demand for interpreting in the public services (police, courts, public health and local government) has led to the creation of the National Register of Public Service Interpreters, which covers a wide range of African, Asian, European and Far Eastern languages. This register is supported by the Home Office and the UK legal agencies. The Institute of Translation and Interpreting (ITI) can also help source qualified public service interpreters from its membership, as can numerous other commercial agencies.

Entry, qualifications and training

Most interpreters have a degree in one or more modern language(s) and there are some degree courses available in translating and interpreting. To gain a place on a language degree you need A level(s) in the language(s) you intend to study. It is also possible to become an interpreter if you have expert knowledge of a language and a degree in a subject such as science, business or engineering. Most interpreters also undertake a Master's degree or other postgraduate diploma in interpreting before they enter the profession.

Personal attributes

Fluency in two or more languages should be allied with a natural feeling for words and phrases and a good ear. It is necessary to be able to think quickly, to remain alert for long periods and to be socially confident. Subject knowledge is essential, especially for simultaneous interpreting, which requires a degree of understanding and anticipation of subject matter and context.

Earnings

Earnings vary and there are few salaried jobs for interpreters. The majority work freelance and earnings vary from £30 to £70 per hour. The languages you interpret, the complexity of information and the situations in which you work affect daily pay rates and the best-paid work is often outside the UK.

Info

Institute of Translation and Interpreting (ITI)
www.iti.org.uk

Chartered Institute of Linguists (CIOL)
020 7940 3100
www.ciol.org.uk

Sign language interpreter

British Sign Language (BSL) interpreters help deaf and hearing people to communicate effectively through the use of signing. They work for social service departments or organisations working for or with deaf people, while some work freelance or for agencies. As a sign language interpreter you might use your skills in many different kinds of setting and on different types of assignment. You could be aiding communication at business meetings, at police stations, in court, in a hospital, at a parents' evening, at a conference or at a theatre. Your work would involve preparing for your assignment by ensuring that you are aware of any specialised vocabulary you may need to sign. During an assignment you would have to listen or watch carefully as appropriate, to ensure that you communicate meanings as accurately as possible.

Entry, qualifications and training

To become a BSL Interpreter you must achieve interpreter and BSL qualifications recognised by the Registration Department of Signature. You can qualify in either of the following ways: you can either do a degree or postgraduate diploma, or alternatively work towards a level 6 award in both British Sign Language and interpreting (BSL/English). You can work towards this while you are already working in some other role with deaf people.

Personal attributes

You must have excellent communication skills and be able to listen carefully, work with speed and accuracy, and maintain intense concentration. You must be able to establish a good rapport with people very quickly. You will sometimes be working with clients who are in stressful situations such as courts or hospitals.

Earnings

As an employed BSL interpreter you can earn £20,000 to £35,000 a year. Freelance interpreters charge £25 to £30 an hour and can also claim travel expenses.

Info

Signature
0191 383 1155
Textphone: 07974 121594
www.signature.org.uk

Association of Sign Language Interpreters (ASLI)
01244 573644
www.asli.org.uk

Translator

Translators work freelance from home, as staff translators in a commercial organisation whose main business is not translation, or with a translation agency. Normally, they only translate from another language into their mother tongue. The work translated varies from whole books to business letters and documents. Translators, especially those who specialise in work for publication, must be able to express themselves very well. In areas where the subject matter of the text is specialised, for example computing, maths or mountaineering, expert knowledge is required of the translator. A broad-based general knowledge is always an advantage. Translators may be responsible for finding their own work but may also be registered with a translation company or agency.

Entry, qualifications and training

Proficiency in a foreign language is obviously necessary, as is the ability to write well in the target language. An understanding of the culture of the relevant countries is important. Most translators have a postgraduate qualification or a diploma in translation. First degree courses in translation are available at a number of universities and diplomas are available via the Chartered Institute of Linguists.

Personal attributes

Translators must be meticulous, conscientious, creative and persistent. The ability to carry out research, as and when necessary, and good interpersonal skills are also required.

Earnings

Starting salaries for in-house translators are between £18,000 and £25,000 – 25,000 to £40,000 for experienced translators. Most translators work freelance, in which case they are usually paid a fee per thousand words translated. This fee ranges from £80 to £250. The rate depends on the language(s) being translated. Translating Chinese characters commands the highest fees. Both the European Union and the United Nations pay some of the best rates.

Info

Association of Translation Companies (ATC)
01787 221298
www.atc.org.uk

Chartered Institute of Linguists (CIOL)
020 7940 3100
www.ciol.org.uk

Institute of Translation and Interpreting (ITI)
www.iti.org.uk

International Federation of Translators
www.fit-ift.org

LOCAL GOVERNMENT

Local government is responsible for developing local policies and delivering local services. In addition to the specific local government roles described below, local government provides education, social care, environmental health, leisure facilities and public protection. These departments employ appropriately qualified professionals, including teachers, social workers, lawyers, architects, trading standards officers, housing officers, engineers, environmental health officers and many more. Local authorities also employ specialists in finance, human resources and business management, and some specialised administrators such as registrars of births, deaths and marriages, and clerks to council committees. The local government jobs website gives details of the range of jobs on offer.

There is currently a decline in numbers of local government jobs and many local government functions may be undertaken by private contractors, looking for staff with similar skills to those required by local government departments.

Local government administrative assistant

Local government administrative assistants provide support in all council departments, e.g. housing, social services or planning. Your work will vary depending on where you work and what your specific role is, but many tasks are common to most administrative assistant posts. As an administrative assistant your work could include processing forms, answering queries on the telephone or at a help desk, sorting mail, filing, photocopying, inputting and updating information on computers, finding information and taking notes at meetings.

Local government officer

Local government officers are responsible for putting council policy into practice. Your day-to-day tasks will vary according to your particular role and responsibilities, but are likely to include supervising and training administrative staff, keeping records, dealing with enquiries, presenting and preparing information for committees or other meetings, monitoring performance, overseeing projects and managing budgets.

Entry, qualifications and training

Many local authorities are cutting staff numbers, so competition for jobs is strong. Entry requirements vary between councils. For some administrative assistant posts you may need GCSEs, including maths and English; formal qualifications are often not required. Administrative officers usually need four or five GCSEs, including maths and English. You could also consider a college course such as a Level 2 Certificate in the Principles of Business Administration, to gain some of the skills and knowledge needed. Entry requirements for local government officers vary widely, depending on the job, and can be anything from four GCSEs, including maths and English, to a degree or equivalent qualification. Local authorities provide training on the job and support for part-time study for relevant professional qualifications. A public service operational delivery officer advanced apprenticeship, or an advanced apprenticeship in business and administration, are also routes you could consider.

Personal attributes

While every role demands particular knowledge and skills, there are some common threads that are essential for all employees. You must have a genuine interest in and commitment to serving your local community. Most jobs require a good level of communication skills, as they involve direct contact with members of the public. You should be flexible and able to work well as part of a team. You should also be prepared to take on responsibilities. Some jobs require good IT or numeracy skills.

Earnings

Administrative assistants are paid between £15,500 and £21,000, and local government officers are paid from £16,000 to £37,000 – more if you move into senior management. Salaries are higher in London than elsewhere and many councils pay performance-related bonuses.

Info

Local Government jobs
www.lgjobs.com

LOGISTICS

(see also Road transport)

Logistics is the management of the moving of goods or materials from one place to another.

Freight forwarder

A freight forwarding firm will arrange for the most efficient means of the international transport of goods, and will ensure that all documentation, legal and insurance requirements are met, and customs duties paid. Freight forwarders may be individuals or firms; they may specialise in a particular method of transport, certain goods or countries. They may arrange for a number of different shipments to be grouped together for more economical transport. Some very large organisations have their own freight forwarding department or a subsidiary company.

Freight forwarders are usually located near ports or airports and in provincial centres. They employ people to deal with a wide range of clerical and administrative tasks, such as sales, personnel, timetabling, accounting and computer work.

Entry, qualifications and training

School leavers can enter the industry through the apprenticeship route. NVQs are available in International Trade and Services, Distribution and Warehousing Operations, and Organising Road Transport. There are several degree courses in international trade, logistics, supply chain management, transport, export studies and overseas business. Large companies may offer graduate training schemes for those with relevant degrees.

The Institute of Freight Forwarders offers an Advanced Certificate in International Trade that can be studied full or part time or by correspondence. The Institute of Logistics and Transport offers a range of professional qualifications, which can be studied by distance learning.

Personal attributes

People working in freight forwarding need excellent problem-solving and communication skills. Accuracy and clarity are essential, as misunderstandings can cause major problems. IT skills are essential with the growth in internet trading and greater use of technology such as global positioning satellite (GPS) systems to plan and manage journeys. Geographical, cultural and religious awareness are also important.

Earnings

School leaver trainees earn £15,000 to £17,000. Graduate trainees working for larger companies start on £19,000 to £24,000. Senior managers in freight forwarding departments can earn £30,000 to £40,000.

Info

Skills for Logistics
0117 927 8800
www.skillsforlogistics.org

British International Freight Association (BIFA)
020 8844 2266
www.bifa.org

Chartered Institute of Logistics and Transport (CILT UK)
01536 740100
www.ciltuk.org.uk

Institute of Export
01733 404400
www.export.org.uk

Supply chain manager

Supply chain managers (also known as logistics or distribution managers) are the ones who ensure that food, drink, clothing, electrical equipment, in fact anything that you can buy from a retail outlet, arrives where it should when it should. The manager has to ensure that supplies neither run out nor build up in overlarge quantities in warehouses, shops or anywhere along the supply chain. You can work either for a large retailer that has its own logistics department or for a logistics contractor that organises all the transport and distribution on behalf of retailers and wholesalers. Your responsibilities are likely to include planning delivery timetables, monitoring stock levels using computer databases, tracking the movement of goods through depots, and overseeing the ordering and packaging process ready for dispatch. You also have to monitor performance and try to come up with ways of making the whole process more efficient and cost effective, and you are also responsible for recruiting and managing staff in the distribution department. Your work would involve close liaison with purchasing officers, warehouse managers and transport staff.

Entry, qualifications and training

There are two ways to get into supply chain management. Some people take a foundation degree, HNC, HND or degree in a relevant subject such as transport management, supply chain management or international transport. Other subjects such as geography and business subjects may also include relevant modules. Some large companies prefer to recruit graduates for their management training programmes. However, it is possible to join a company in its distribution or logistics department and work your way up into a management role. You may also choose to take some relevant qualifications on a part-time basis if you choose this second route. Supply chain advanced or higher apprenticeships are available.

Personal attributes

You need good planning skills and you must also be able to pay attention to detail. You need to be numerate with good IT skills too. You have to be able to work under pressure and solve problems quickly and calmly. You must have a good range of people skills, be excellent at leading and motivating, good at soothing ruffled and agitated managers somewhere else along the supply chain and able to liaise effectively with others.

Earnings

Graduate trainees earn between £18,000 and £22,000. If you start by working your way up, your salary will depend very much on what job you are doing, but once you get into supply chain management your earnings are similar to those of a graduate trainee. In either case, once you have completed some training and built up a year or two of experience, salaries rise to £25,000 to £30,000. For very large operations, the most senior managers can earn £40,000 to £60,000.

Info

Chartered Institute of Logistics and Transport (CILT UK)
01536 740100
www.ciltuk.org.uk

Skills for Logistics
0117 927 8800
www.skillsforlogistics.org

MANAGEMENT

Management is necessary in every kind of business and organisation and will be part of many people's jobs, especially through career development and promotion. There are some roles which require you to look very specifically at the art and science of management and help others manage more successfully.

Management consultant

Management consultants advise businesses and organisations of many sizes and types on all aspects of problem solving or improving the way that the business or organisation operates. They may, for example, offer financial advice, suggestions about recruitment and ideas on improving levels of staff motivation or methods of conflict resolution. They may advise on ways of reshaping the actual structure of a business.

The work could involve interviewing members of staff, observing activities, looking at written information about the company, accounts, future projections, etc. After having drawn various conclusions, the consultant will then suggest actions that the business could take to change things. This advice could involve working with key members of staff as well as providing written reports.

Entry, qualifications and training

Becoming a management consultant is often a second career after time spent in finance, marketing, project management, human resources or the armed services. The other route in is through a graduate training scheme offered by a management consulting firm. Preferred degree subjects include business, management, IT, economics and psychology. If you specialise in a particular area of consultancy, such as marketing or human resources, a relevant degree is helpful. You should have a 2.1 and an A level tariff of 320 points. Training is on the job, but many consulting firms provide extensive in-house courses. A junior management consultant higher apprenticeship is also something you could consider; with experience, you could progress. After about two years in the profession you are likely to have the option to take either a Master's in Business Administration (MBA) or a professional qualification linked to your area of expertise, for example finance, marketing or human resources.

Personal attributes

You need to be an excellent communicator, one-to-one, with groups and on paper. You should have good IT and numerical skills and the ability to analyse problems and suggest solutions. You should have a broad knowledge of business issues.

Earnings

New entrants earn between £25,000 and £35,000, depending on location and the type of consulting. Experienced consultants earn between £35,000 and £90,000. Earnings for the most successful can be much higher than this and may include performance bonuses.

Info

Management Consultancies Association 020 7645 7954 www.mca.org.uk	**Instructus Skills** 01536 738631 www.instructus-skills.org
Institute of Consulting 01536 207480 www.iconsulting.org.uk	

MANUFACTURING

Manufacturing encompasses many occupations, all concerned with the large-scale production of goods, parts and packaging.

Factory worker

Factory work (often referred to as production or process work) is all about the manufacture of products of every kind: food, furniture, paper, concrete, cars, toiletries, clothing, computers, pharmaceuticals – in fact, all those products that we all use. Many different roles support any manufacturing process: administration, research, engineering and marketing, and they are covered elsewhere.

The term 'factory worker' refers to workers who are involved in the production process – and specific tasks and duties vary depending on what is being produced. Workers may operate special machinery for building cars, work on a conveyor belt filling cans of drink, wash and grade raw fruit and vegetables to be processed, assemble complete items by putting components together, or monitor the quality and consistency of any product. The range is really very wide.

Entry, qualifications and training

For most jobs there are no specific academic requirements, although some employers may like you to have GCSEs in maths, English and technology. Many employers set their own entry tests to measure how well you are likely to perform the tasks you will be expected to do. There are now some NVQs level 2 available in Performing Manufacturing Operations, and you may find some apprenticeships available in your local area.

Personal attributes

You need to be good at practical work and quick with your hands. It is important that you don't mind carrying out repetitive tasks and that you can keep your concentration while doing this. You must be able to follow instructions, pay close attention to safety and work well as part of a team.

Earnings

Starting pay is between the minimum wage and £16,000, and if you take on some supervisory responsibility it can rise to £20,000. Many jobs include shift-work allowances.

Info

Cogent Skills
01925 515 200
www.cogentskills.com

National Skills Academy for Food & Drink
0845 644 0558
www.nsafd.co.uk

Vacancies are advertised in local papers and
through Jobcentre Plus offices.

Instrument technician

Instrument technicians, sometimes called measurement and control technicians, work with engineers to ensure that the production systems used in manufacturing are working efficiently and safely. They may use control panels to check that a production line is running correctly or carry out routine checks on equipment to ensure that it is properly maintained. They will identify preventative repairs to be carried out and highlight any potential problems that could be dangerous or cause a breakdown.

Entry, qualifications and training

Employers offer apprenticeships for instrument technicians, but you will need to check what is available. You will need four or five GCSEs grades 9–4, including maths, English, science and/or engineering, or equivalent qualifications. Alternatively, you can take a course at your local college in a relevant subject, e.g. a certificate or diploma in electrical or electronic engineering, or in manufacturing practices.

Personal attributes

You will need to be able to work methodically and precisely, be confident in solving problems and have a good understanding of computer engineering applications. You will need to be able to work both alone and as part of a team.

Earnings

Instrument technician pay starts within a range of £19,000 to £22,000. With more experience, you can expect to earn between £25,000 and £35,000 a year.

Info

Institution of Engineering and Technology (IET)
01438 313311
www.theiet.org

Tomorrow's Engineers
www.tomorrowsengineers.org.uk

SEMTA
0845 643 9001
www.semta.org.uk

Packaging technologist

There are opportunities for packaging technologists with manufacturers of packaging materials, with companies that produce packaging and with companies that have a product to be packed.

Many small firms do not have their own packaging adviser/technologist, and hire a consultant when the need arises.

The purpose of packaging is to protect, preserve, contain and present its contents. It also has a vital function in branding and brand awareness. The environmental impact of packaging is also important, so developing products that can be recycled or composted, or that can be made from already recycled material, is a growing challenge for packaging technologists.

There are career opportunities developing materials for packaging purposes, for designing equipment to manufacture or fill packaging, for structural design of parts, for graphic design on packs, for physical and chemical testing, and for quality assurance.

Entry, qualifications and training

Most applicants have either a degree, foundation degree or HND in a relevant subject. This could be a course that specialises in packaging technology and design or a relevant scientific or technical subject such as physics, chemistry, food technology or materials science/engineering. There are some postgraduate courses in packaging design and technology, but these are not essential entry requirements. Training is on the job and through further short courses, so that you can keep up with new developments in the field. You could also consider an apprenticeship such as a packaging professional degree apprenticeship.

Personal attributes

Technologists and scientists must be able to look at problems in a practical way and have the ability to communicate their ideas to others both verbally and on paper.

Earnings

New entrants earn between £16,000 and £20,000; senior technologists can earn £25,000 to £40,000, with research and development work attracting the higher salaries.

Info

The Packaging Society
01476 513882
www.iom3.org/packaging-society

Sheet-metal worker/plater

Sheet-metal workers/platers are engaged in shaping, cutting and joining together pieces of metal. Sheet-metal workers work with thin metal sheets up to 3mm thick, using a wide range of hand and power tools. They make such items as aircraft sections and car prototypes. Platers work with metal plates from 3mm thick upwards. As well as hand and power tools, heavy presses are needed to bend the plate. Products include ship and submarine parts and industrial boilers.

Entry, qualifications and training

You may not need academic qualifications, though many employers will look for GCSEs in maths, English and a technical subject. Some companies offer apprenticeships to train you in the specific skills they require and there are college courses in several sheet-metal working skills.

Personal attributes

You must have good manual dexterity and be able to concentrate for long periods of time. You should be good at following instructions, but able to work without direct supervision. Normal eyesight is essential and good colour vision is important.

Earnings

Starting salaries range from £14,500 to £17,000. With experience you can earn between £17,000 and £25,000.

Toolmaker

Toolmakers work in engineering, making a wide range of jigs used to guide cutting tools and to hold the work in position; fixtures, to hold metal for bending or welding or to hold parts together; press tools in different shapes and sizes for cutting parts; mould tools to make items such as fridge interiors or mobile phone cases and measuring gauges. Toolmakers are often involved in making small quantities of a new product when it is at the design and development stage. Toolmaker machinists make the tools, often specialising in just one kind. Toolmaker fitters work on large structures that are constructed from many parts. They check all the parts, number them and then fit them together.

Entry, qualifications and training

If you are between 16 and 24 years old and want to do a NASEC apprenticeship, you need GCSEs grades 9–4 in maths, English and a science. If you have engineering drawing, metalwork or other practical subjects as well you may have an advantage. Applicants without the required entry grades may also be considered. These apprenticeships take up to three years and you train on the job, working alongside experienced toolmakers. This apprenticeship leads to an NVQ level 3 award in Engineering Production. Older applicants can do BTEC Certificates in Manufacturing Engineering. Other college courses you could consider to learn and equip yourself with some of the skills needed include the Level 1 Certificate in Engineering Technologies, Level 2 Certificate in Engineering Operations, and Level 2 Diploma in Engineering.

Personal attributes

You must have good manual dexterity and be able to understand engineering drawings. You should be good at following instructions, but able to work without direct supervision. Normal eyesight is essential and good colour vision is important.

Earnings

Starting pay ranges from £15,000 to £18,000. With experience you can earn between £19,000 and £30,000.

Welder

Welders join pieces of metal together by applying intense heat and melting the edges so that two pieces become one. The sorts of items welded are metal sections of aeroplanes, ships, oil rigs, cars and power turbines. Welders work in light and heavy engineering firms, in foundry work and in shipbuilding. Some plastics are also welded.

Welders work on all types of fabrication, from the manufacture of metal-frame chairs to high-quality, complex applications such as building a submarine.

Entry, qualifications and training

If you are aged between 16 and 24 you can do an engineering apprenticeship. There are no set entry qualifications for this, but many employers prefer you to have GCSEs in English, maths, technology and a science subject. If you have these GCSEs, this also offers a wider range of further qualifications you can take part- or full-time at college. These qualifications are also open to people of any age. There are several different NVQ awards related to welding, including fabrication and welding, performing engineering operations and welding with pipework.

Personal attributes

You must have good practical and technical skills and be able to concentrate for long periods of time. You should be good at following instructions, but able to work without direct supervision. Normal eyesight is essential and good near vision is important.

Earnings

Pay starts at between £14,500 and £17,000, and with experience you can earn £20,000 to £26,000. Highly skilled specialist welders may earn up to £30,000.

Info

ECITB
01923 260000
www.ecitb.org.uk

Tomorrow's Engineers
www.tomorrowsengineers.org.uk

TWI (The Welding Institute)
01223 899000
www.twi-global.com

MARINE SCIENCES

Marine scientist

Marine scientists study the life of the planet's oceans – plants, fish, plankton, mammals and seabirds. They study the geology of the seafloor and of coastal regions. Marine science encompasses many disciplines, including biology, botany, environmental science, geology and zoology. Marine scientists' work involves research and analysis of what is happening in the oceans and forecasting of what could happen. They may study the impact of climate change, underwater volcanic activity, fishing and water sports. They also study the impact of offshore developments such as oil platforms or wind turbines and the effects of pollution on the seas and the shoreline. Marine scientists work for a range of organisations, including those dealing with energy exploration for oil and gas, fisheries, renewable energy sources, marine conservation and wildlife protection.

Your work as a marine scientist could involve analysing samples, designing experiments, building computer models to simulate certain situations and writing detailed reports. In many cases you would conduct some of your work based on seagoing vessels and might even incorporate diving in your work routine. You would also be responsible for managing research budgets and junior members of the research team.

Entry, qualifications and training

There are a few degrees and postgraduate courses in marine science or oceanography. This is a degree-level career, but it draws on many other subjects, including biology, biochemistry, geography, geology and environmental sciences.

Personal attributes

Marine scientists need the same characteristics as all scientists: patience and the willingness to repeat experimental work and measurements to check results, a methodical way of working, good observation and accuracy.

Earnings

Research assistants earn £17,000 to £27,000, depending on your job title, role and what type of organisation you work for – public, private or voluntary body. PhD entrants earn between £25,000 and £35,000.

Info

The Centre for Environment, Fisheries and Aquaculture Science (CEFAS)
01502 513865
www.cefas.defra.gov.uk

Institute of Marine Engineering, Science and Technology (IMarEST)
020 7382 2600
www.imarest.org.uk

Lantra
02476 696996
www.lantra.co.uk

The Marine Biological Association (MBA)
01752 426493
www.mba.ac.uk

Marine Conservation Society
01989 566 017
www.mcsuk.org

Natural Environment Research Council (NERC)
01793 411500
www.nerc.ukri.org

Scottish Association for Marine Science (SAMS)
01631 559 000
www.sams.ac.uk

MARKETING

Digital marketing officer

As digital marketing officer (increasingly called digital marketing executive or marketer), your role will be to promote your employer's services, ideas or products online. You'll use your extensive knowledge of social media to market your products via the channels and on the platforms that best enable you to reach your chosen customers. You will create marketing campaigns across the different channels and platforms and brief other professionals, e.g. web designers, to help implement them. You will use appropriate tracking tools, e.g. Google Analytics, Hootsuite and Tweetdeck, to measure the effectiveness of your campaigns and adapt your techniques accordingly.

Entry, qualifications and training

Most digital marketing officers have a degree in a relevant subject such as marketing or a business-related subject, as well as a sound understanding of social media. Alternatively, you can gain experience in another area of marketing, sales or customer services. The Chartered Institute of Marketing (CIM), among others, offers short, specialist courses in the use of digital media for marketing. There are also a number of college courses such as the Level 2 Certificate in the Principles of Marketing, or Level 3 Diploma in Digital Marketing to help you enter the profession, as well as apprenticeships you could consider.

Personal attributes

You need to be creative as well as a capable organiser and planner. In particular, you need to be an enthusiastic user of social media, as well as being a good all-round communicator, both in writing and in person, and able to work well as a member of a team.

Earnings

Digital marketing officers earn between £20,000 and £24,000. Senior digital marketing officers can earn up to £40,000. Managers responsible for a company's online marketing strategy can earn in excess of £50,000.

Market researcher

Market research is the collection and analysis of information about markets, organisations and people, so that businesses, charities, media and other organisations can target products, services, publicity at potential customers. It is used to discover gaps in the market, to measure customer satisfaction and to plan effective marketing strategies.

Depending on your seniority and experience your work could include meeting clients to agree a brief for a research project, conducting background research on a topic and commissioning specific pieces of research. You might be involved in the design and distribution of surveys and questionnaires including the use of online and social media and in the recruitment and training of market research interviewers. You could also be responsible for both analysing the information and data collected and presenting those results to your client. At a junior level, you might be the person who stops people in the street to ask them to complete a questionnaire, or telephones them to gather research information.

Entry, qualifications and training

Field workers do not need qualifications but must be articulate, persuasive and presentable. Applicants for research and executive positions will be expected to hold a degree. The majority of market research graduates are drawn from disciplines that require strong communication or analytical skills, such as languages, English literature, maths, psychology, geography, history, politics, science and IT. However, graduates with degrees as contrasting as zoology and theatre studies are also welcomed by the industry.

The Market Research Society offers a range of qualifications that are linked to the UK's National Qualifications Framework and are designed to suit a wide range of candidates, from those with no experience to practitioners seeking continuous professional development. You could consider a college course such as a Level 2 Certificate in Principles of Marketing which may be useful, or an apprenticeship.

Personal attributes

Excellent communication skills and the ability to get on with people of all types are necessary. Analytical skills, numeracy and data interpretation are important.

Earnings

Market research analysts who interpret the data and results, or managers who plan and develop research, start on £21,000 to £28,000. Experienced research executives earn between £35,000 and £60,000. Market research interviewers working on a casual basis earn £6 to £9 per hour. Interviewers who are permanent employees earn between the minimum wage and £17,000.

Info

Chartered Institute of Marketing (CIM)
01628 427500
www.cim.co.uk

Direct Marketing Association
020 7291 3300
www.dma.org.uk

Institute of Direct and Digital Marketing (IDM)
020 8614 0255
www.theidm.com

Ipsos
020 3059 5000
www.ipsos.com/en/careers

Market Research Society (MRS)	Social Research Association (SRA)
020 7490 4911	020 7255 0695
www.mrs.org.uk	www.the-sra.org.uk

Marketing executive

Marketing is the process of persuading us to buy, or of raising the profile of products, services or causes. The role of marketing executive can be varied and demanding, since marketing covers many activities, including advertising, promotion, sponsorship, public relations, media relations and research. As an executive you could be involved in planning, developing and managing any of these activities. Marketing executives work either for specialist marketing consultancies or for in-house marketing departments working to sell, promote or increase market share of that business's products or services. Day-to-day tasks can include writing press releases, planning campaigns, liaising with customers, training sales staff, writing brochures or website entries, writing content for social media, attending meetings, building up and maintaining good contacts in the media and, more elusively but very importantly, coming up with new ideas.

Entry, qualifications and training

There are two main routes into marketing. You either need a degree in a relevant subject such as marketing or a business-related subject, or you can get into marketing if you already have relevant experience in sales or customer services. You would normally start as a marketing assistant if you come into the profession straight from education. The Chartered Institute of Marketing (CIM) offers several professional qualifications towards which you can work while employed. These courses cover all aspects of marketing and are pitched at several levels, from introductory to postgraduate diplomas. You could also consider an apprenticeship.

Personal attributes

You must be an enthusiastic and energetic communicator, able to motivate staff and persuade customers and clients. You also need to be a good team member, able to listen to the ideas of others. You have to be a good organiser and great planner. You have to be a creative thinker, imaginative and able to come up with something new.

Earnings

Marketing assistants earn between £19,000 and £24,000 – geographical location and the sector you work in affect pay. Senior marketing managers earn between £25,000 and £55,000. Some senior marketing executives can earn £100,000.

Social media analyst

Social (or digital) media analysts carry out research to support marketing campaign planning, to ensure that new strategies are based on detailed, accurate insight. Social media analysts examine huge amounts of data using social media monitoring software in order to write post-campaign reports for clients. They also research new products and emerging digital trends that could be used in future campaigns. They keep up to date with the latest 'social listening' software. They often work for specialist digital marketing agencies.

Entry, qualifications and training

Social media analysts are usually graduates – employers usually ask for 'a degree or equivalent'. An analytical or mathematical degree is useful, but a keen understanding of social media is also essential. The job requires a high level of skill with both numbers and words.

Personal attributes

A social media analyst needs to be curious, emotionally intelligent, commercially astute, organised and able to manage several projects at once. They also need to be confident about reporting on insights gained from their analysis.

Earnings

Pay for social media analysts starts at around £27,000 but with a few years' experience they can earn £40,000 plus.

Social media manager

(see also Journalism for Web content editor)

A social media manager is responsible for communication with an organisation's customers or clients across all social media platforms, and ensures that the company's social media builds their brand's reputation. The social media manager creates and oversees the social media strategy and produces content – or oversees others who are producing content – to implement that strategy. You will use tools such as Hootsuite, Tweetdeck and Buffer to monitor and measure the strategy's success. You will probably also manage the budget that makes all this activity possible. Some social media managers work freelance or for an agency, in which case you will probably be managing the online presence for several companies at any one time.

Entry, qualifications and training

Many social media managers have a degree in a relevant subject such as marketing or a business-related subject, as well as experience of and an acute understanding of how people engage with social media. Social media managers are also required to have strong analytics skills and will often have taken a specialist short course in this. Without a degree, entry is possible with experience in related areas such as marketing, advertising and public relations. If you have sound project management and communication skills and the required understanding of social media, you may be able to start as an assistant manager and work your way up. You could also consider a digital marketer advanced or degree apprenticeship, or a digital community manager higher apprenticeship.

Personal attributes

You need to be a versatile and empathetic communicator to engage with different online communities. You also require the ability to analyse and reflect on your findings, and to adapt your strategy accordingly.

Earnings

Social media manager salaries start at around £22,000. With more experience, this can rise to between £25,000 and £35,000 a year. For a senior social media manager for a large company, pay can be in excess of £70,000. As a freelancer, you will negotiate your fee with each company separately.

Info

Chartered Institute of Marketing (CIM)
01628 427500
www.cim.co.uk

Institute of Direct and Digital Marketing (IDM)
020 8614 0255
www.theidm.com

Communication Advertising and Marketing Education Foundation (CAM)
01628 427120
www.camfoundation.com

Arts Marketing Association (AMA)
01223 578078
www.a-m-a.co.uk

MEAT INDUSTRY

The meat industry extends from work in a small retail shop through to supermarkets; from meat buying for large organisations such as hotels and caterers to the manufacture of meat and poultry products. There is also work connected with health and meat hygiene and with the slaughtering of animals for meat production.

Butcher

Butchers prepare and sell meat, poultry, game and meat products. They work in small shops, supermarkets, markets, farm shops and farmers' markets. Some butchers also make their own products, such as pies or sausages. As well as cutting and preparing meat for sale, they deal with customers, offering advice on how best to prepare and cook meat and poultry. They are responsible for ordering and buying products and have to have a good knowledge of food safety and food hygiene.

Entry, qualifications and training

A good general education is necessary but there are no formal educational requirements. Training is on the job and courses are available at further education establishments and technical colleges. NVQs are available at levels 1–4, and Higher National Diploma/Certificate qualifications. Modern Apprenticeships are available. Apprenticeships may be an option if you wish to train as a butcher – employers set their own entry requirements, but five GCSEs grades 9–4 may be required. The Food and Drink Training and Education Council website is a useful source of information, including information on apprenticeships and courses.

Personal attributes

Butchers need to be very practical, with good manual dexterity, and not squeamish. They must ensure that they and their work environments are really clean and hygienic and they must enjoy talking to people and giving advice. A good business sense is also useful.

Earnings

Trainee butchers earn around the minimum wage. Skilled butchers earn from £14,000 to £19,000. Skilled butchers who are also section managers and who have responsibilities for sourcing and buying produce can earn £25,000 or more.

Info

Worshipful Company of Butchers Guild
020 3931 8350
www.butchershall.com

Food and Drink Training and Education Council
0113 397 0398
www.foodtraining.org.uk

National Skills Academy for Food & Drink
0845 644 0558
www.nsafd.co.uk

MEDICAL AND HEALTHCARE SCIENCE

Many scientific disciplines play a key part in medicine – in the development and testing of drugs and the monitoring of the performance of these drugs. Scientists contribute to the understanding of the processes of disease and damage to tissue, organs and systems, as well as to the development of equipment and techniques to improve diagnosis and treatment. There are very many jobs in medical and healthcare science, and those described here are examples from some of the different areas of science in medicine.

Life scientists and pathologists

Life scientists work in hospital laboratories, in community health and for other national agencies concerned with blood, health protection and organ transplant. Life scientists work in three broad areas: pathology, investigating causes and development of diseases; genetics, looking at genetic components of illness; and embryology, investigating the development of life and treatments for infertility. Some examples of these scientific roles are listed below.

Clinical embryologist

This is a rapidly developing field. Clinical embryologists are involved in research and investigation of various aspects of in vitro fertilisation (IVF) treatment and other programmes of assisted reproduction. This work involves the collection of eggs from patients for examination, checking fertility levels of individuals and the application of 'cutting edge' and sometimes controversial technologies.

Clinical immunologist

Clinical immunologists use sophisticated laboratory techniques to examine the effects on the immune system of syndromes such as AIDS and allergic conditions such as hay fever or asthma. They apply the knowledge they acquire to developing better treatments of these conditions. This is a fast-moving and developing area of medical science.

Clinical microbiologist

Clinical microbiologists work to diagnose all kinds of infections – bacterial, viral, fungal or parasitic. What they discover about the infections a patient has plays an important role in how that patient is treated: what antibiotics are given, for example. They also work for the Health Protection Agency helping prevent the spread of diseases.

Phlebotomist

Phlebotomists take blood samples from patients so that these samples can be analysed to diagnose diseases and other disorders. They have to take great care when collecting blood to disturb the patient as little as possible, to label the blood taken correctly and to ensure that it is taken to the correct laboratory. Phlebotomists also work for the blood donor agency, collecting healthy blood from volunteers.

Physiological scientists

Physiological scientists monitor the body's systems: breathing, hearing, sight, heart, liver, kidneys, brain, etc. They help investigate problems and produce information that will assist doctors in making diagnoses. In some roles they work to maintain many of the body's systems and functions during surgery. Many physiological scientists work directly with patients in outpatient clinics and on hospital wards.

Cardiographer

Cardiographers work in hospitals, operating the electrocardiograph (ECG) machines that monitor the functioning of the heart. They reassure patients and explain the procedure to them before fitting electrodes to the patient's body, ensuring they are correctly connected to the machine, and take readings that a doctor uses to make decisions about diagnosis and treatment.

Neurophysiology technologist

Neurophysiology technologists, also referred to as clinical physiologists (neurophysiology), work in hospital outpatient departments, in intensive care units and in operating theatres. Their work is concerned with monitoring and measuring activities in the central and peripheral nervous systems. They use highly sophisticated equipment to obtain their readings. They work closely with patients of all ages – a child who has suffered a brain injury, or an older person who has had a stroke, for example. They also work closely with other members of the healthcare team.

Perfusionist

Perfusionists (or perfusion scientists) work in operating theatres where patients are undergoing open heart surgery. The term 'perfusion' refers to the movement of liquid through tissue. The perfusionist ensures that oxygen is circulated through the patient's blood even when the action of the heart and lungs is temporarily stopped in order to carry out the surgery. Perfusionists use a range of complex machinery and monitoring equipment to carry out their work. They must alert fellow members of the operating team if they have any causes for concern.

Physical scientists and biomedical engineers

Physical scientists working in medicine develop ways to measure what is happening in the body, new ways of diagnosing and treating diseases and new equipment to aid in treatment. They also have to ensure that such equipment works safely.

Medical physicist

Medical physicists are involved in developing highly sophisticated equipment for measuring the effects of illnesses and disabilities. Medical physicists have developed X-ray and ultrasound scanning equipment and they use their research skills to refine and improve these techniques and technologies. They often work closely with radiographers in the field of nuclear medicine, treating cancer cells with the correct dose of radiation.

Clinical engineer

Clinical or bioengineers design equipment for monitoring, diagnosis, treatment and rehabilitation or research. They may design laser equipment or electronic aids for patients with disabilities. They examine the mechanics of the human body to see how to replicate the functions of particular organs or systems. They develop a detailed knowledge of materials and of engineering processes, and apply this technical knowledge in a medical environment.

Medical laboratory technician

All the scientific research and development work that goes on throughout the health service and in medical schools needs the support of medical laboratory technicians and assistants. Laboratory technicians work in all aspects of medical and clinical sciences, whether it is testing blood, screening cells for disease, or developing a new material to treat burns or wounds. Medical laboratory technicians assist scientists in setting up experiments, monitoring these experiments and recording the results.

Entry, qualifications and training

There are three levels of entry. For most healthcare science professions there is also a range of assistant roles that form an important part of the clinical science team. For these roles there are no set academic requirements, though many applicants have GCSEs grades 9–4 in maths, English and a science. These roles can be a stepping stone to further career development and eventual professional qualification. You can start work as a trainee or assistant, combining on-the-job training with study so that you learn as you earn.

If you have A levels or equivalent qualifications you can join as a trainee, combining work and practical training with part-time study for a degree or professional qualification in a specific area of healthcare science. Opportunities for graduates who wish to work in healthcare science are open to graduates from many science disciplines. There are some vocational degree courses that are specific to particular healthcare science roles and accredited by the relevant regulatory body. With most other science degrees you will need to undergo a period of further study, typically 18 months to two years, on the NHS Science Training Programme (STP) to extend your knowledge in your chosen specialism. This will lead to a postgraduate diploma or MSc and professional registration. You need a 2.1 honours degree in pure or applied science to qualify for this programme.

Personal attributes

If you are engaged in research and development you must have a rigorous and questioning scientific approach to your work – be good at problem solving and coming up with imaginative solutions. If your work involves contact with patients, you must have an understanding and reassuring manner, but you must also be able to avoid becoming too emotionally involved in your work. Many roles require you to have good practical skills, manual dexterity and the ability to be meticulous and highly observant. Many roles will also require you to use complex instruments and take careful recordings of results.

Earnings

Most NHS jobs are on a graded, structured pay scale. Medical laboratory technicians earn from £16,900 to £19,800. Most scientists start on the scale between £22,100 and £28,700, though senior scientists earn between £40,000 and £57,600. Assistant roles earn around £17,000 to £19,000.

Info

NHS Careers
0345 60 60 655
www.healthcareers.nhs.uk

Health and Care Professions Council (HCPC)
0300 500 6184
www.hcpc-uk.org

Institute of Biomedical Science
020 7713 0214
www.ibms.org

Association of Clinical Scientists
020 7940 8960
www.assclinsci.org

Learn Direct
www.learndirect.com

Institute of Physics and Engineering in Medicine (IPEM)
01904 610821
www.ipem.ac.uk

Microbiology Society
020 3034 4870
www.microbiologysociety.org

Association for Science Education (ASE)
01707 283000
www.ase.org.uk

SEMTA
0845 643 9001
www.semta.org.uk

Medical illustrator

Medical illustrators employ a range of artistic and technical skills to produce photographs, drawings, videos and other digital images in healthcare settings. They produce material to help assess the effectiveness of treatment regimes by photographing patients at different stages of their treatment. They may produce material for medical textbooks, websites, lectures and other training and teaching activities. Some specialise in forensic work, taking pictures of non-accidental injuries or copying evidence from X-rays and slides.

Because medical illustrators use a combination of photography, video and drawing skills, there may be some opportunities to take work that allows you to develop special expertise in one or other of these areas. You are likely to spend your time working in hospital wards, operating theatres and clinics, as well as studios and technical laboratories.

Entry, qualifications and training

Although it is not always necessary to have formal qualifications, it is now very difficult to get into this work without a foundation degree, HND or degree in a relevant subject. The most useful subjects are graphic design and photography. It is likely that in the near future medical illustrators will only be able to practise if they are state registered. The exact date for this has not been finalised. However, when this does happen, all new entrants to this profession will have to have a relevant degree that meets the standards for registration. It is very useful if you can gain some relevant work experience with an NHS trust medical photography department. You should also be able to produce a portfolio of your work at interview.

Personal attributes

This work demands a wide range of qualities and skills. You should have artistic and photographic ability and be competent working with technical equipment. You must have an interest in and some knowledge of biology, physiology, diseases and medical conditions. You have to have excellent interpersonal skills, and be sensitive and empathic when dealing with people who are anxious or vulnerable. You should be good at working as part of a team, but be able to get on with your own work unsupervised.

Earnings

Pay for new entrants is between £22,100 and £28,700. Senior medical illustrators earn between £28,000 and £37,400. Large teaching hospitals have much bigger medical illustration departments so these offer more scope for management jobs, which pay up to £41,700.

Info

Medical Artists' Association
www.maa.org.uk

Medical Artists' Education Trust (MAET)
www.maet.org.uk

NHS Careers
0345 60 60 655
www.healthcareers.nhs.uk

Institute of Medical Illustrators
www.imi.org.uk

British Institute of Professional Photography (BIPP)
01772 367968
www.bipp.com

MEDICINE

Doctors work in many healthcare settings in both the National Health Service (NHS) and the private healthcare sector. In the NHS they work in GP practices, health centres, polyclinics and hospitals of every size and type. They can choose, through training, to work in one of very many different fields of medicine. In private practice doctors work in hospitals, clinics and medical centres.

General practitioner

Family doctors, or GPs, may offer healthcare to everyone in a particular geographical location. They will see children, adults and older people. They must be able to diagnose and deal with a broad spectrum of illnesses and disorders, mainly those common within the community, but also to recognise those that are rare. Increasingly, doctors also help their patients to cope with personal and emotional problems. They have to be aware of and take into account physical, psychological and social factors when looking after their patients. About 90 per cent of GPs now work together in group practices, allowing some specialisation.

GP practices are offering a greater range of treatments on their premises, including minor procedures, testing and screening. It seems likely that they will soon have greater administrative and financial responsibility if they become the health professionals responsible for commissioning the majority of healthcare for their patients.

Hospital doctor

Hospital doctors treat hospital inpatients and patients who come to the hospital through outpatient clinics. Hospital doctors work in one of 50 different specialist areas within medicine, treating illness, disease and infection. The specialisms fall into three main groups: medicine, surgery and psychiatry. During training they will learn about every aspect of health and with more experience choose a specialist area that interests them. Doctors choosing to work in medical areas can specialise in such fields as cardiology or paediatrics. They prescribe treatments or organise further investigations, and they monitor patients' progress. Surgeons perform operations of many kinds. They can choose to specialise in such areas as orthopaedics, repairing damaged and broken bones. Psychiatrists treat patients with mental illnesses such as anxiety or depression, prescribing drugs or behavioural or talking therapies.

Research and teaching

Research work is carried out in universities, hospitals, public health laboratories and other research establishments and pharmaceutical manufacturing companies. There are opportunities too for teaching in universities. Teaching may involve very little or no contact with patients, or it may be similar in content to hospital doctors' work. An academic career in medicine through either teaching or research is possible in practically all hospital specialities, general practice and public health medicine.

Entry, qualifications and training

To become a doctor in the United Kingdom you must take a degree course in medicine recognised by the General Medical Council (GMC). To be accepted onto one of these courses you must have three A levels, normally two As and a B, including maths and two sciences. In Scotland you need five H grades and two Advanced Science Highers, one of which must be chemistry.

The GMC also approves some six-year degree courses in medicine designed for applicants who do not have the appropriate science grades. The additional year is a pre-medical course in science. In some cases, an Access to Higher Education course may be accepted. It is important to check carefully with the GMC, to ensure that you embark on an approved course. There are also some four-year medical degrees designed for graduates who already have a degree in science.

As part of the selection process for a degree you may be asked to take a UK Clinical Aptitude Test (UKCAT). This test assesses behavioural and mental attributes relevant to people working in medicine. Check the UKCAT website to find out about participating universities and how to apply to take the test. All medical degrees combine practical training and clinical experience with academic learning. Having completed your medical degree you then undertake a two-year foundation programme gaining further experience and consolidating your learning.

Personal attributes

All doctors must have excellent interpersonal skills – these qualities have become increasingly important in selecting appropriate students for medical school.

Earnings

Junior doctors in postgraduate foundation training earn £27,689 to £32,050. Doctors in specialist training earn between £37,935 and £48,075. Hospital doctors earn from £45,000 and specialists earn £70,000. Senior NHS consultants earn between £79,860 and £107,668. Some consultants supplement their NHS salary with private work and can earn more than £150,000 a year. GPs earn from £59,000 on qualifying to £89,000, but there is no upper limit.

Info

NHS Careers
0345 60 60 655
www.healthcareers.nhs.uk

Royal College of Surgeons of England
020 7405 3474
www.rcseng.ac.uk

General Medical Council (GMC)
0161 923 6602
www.gmc-uk.org

UK Clinical Aptitude Test (UKCAT)
0161 855 7409
www.ukcat.ac.uk

Royal College of General Practitioners
020 3188 7400
www.rcgp.org.uk

British Medical Association
www.bma.org.uk

MERCHANT NAVY

The Merchant Navy refers to all non-military shipping and comprises cargo ships, tankers, ferries and cruise ships. The Royal Fleet Auxiliary also employs civilian crew. While different ships will carry different ranges of personnel – for example more engineers on a tanker, more cooks and hospitality staff on a passenger cruise liner – there is still a clear staffing structure on every ship and below are the main job titles and the work associated with them. In addition to the jobs outlined, ships employ catering staff and administrative staff. Cruise liners employ a whole range of additional personnel, including medical staff, hairdressers, activities coordinators and entertainers of many kinds.

Deck officer

Deck officers are responsible for every aspect of the ship, from its navigation to the management of the crew and the safety of passengers and crew. There are four grades of deck officer: captain or master; chief officer; second officer; and third officer. The captain is in overall charge of the ship. The other three levels of officer share a range of responsibilities for navigation, cargo handling, safety of crew and passengers, supervision of crew, and management of overall maintenance. The levels of responsibility become greater for each deck officer grade.

Entry, qualifications and training

You can join as an officer cadet or marine apprentice if you have four GCSEs grades 9–4, including English, maths and physics or combined science. You must also be sponsored by a shipping company or another training provider. There are also some opportunities to be sponsored through a foundation degree or degree programme in science. These industry-sponsored courses include practical training on board ships as well as your academic studies.

Personal attributes

You must have good leadership skills and be able to motivate people and work as part of a team. You should have good technical ability and enjoy learning about equipment and systems. You have to be able to tolerate long periods away from home and sometimes work in rough and uncomfortable conditions.

Earnings

After the first year of training, trainees earn £20,000. Once you are qualified as a junior officer you are paid between £24,000 and £28,000. Senior officers, that is, chief officers and captains on large ships, earn between £30,000 and £55,000, but can also earn more than this.

Merchant Navy rating

Merchant Navy ratings are the crew members who work on the decks, in the engine room, handling the cargo and providing catering services on board ships. Exact duties vary according to the size and type of vessel and depending on what special skills or training you have. Work might include loading and unloading cargo, cleaning every part of the vessel and routine maintenance jobs.

Entry, qualifications and training

To train as a Merchant Navy rating you have to be sponsored for training by a shipping company or train with the Royal Fleet Auxiliary (RFA). You need to apply directly to shipping companies or to the RFA. Each company sets its own entry requirements, but three or four GCSEs are a good guide. These should include English, maths and a science subject. If you have previous experience in engineering or in catering, this can give you a real advantage. Training is through a combination of college-based training and experience on board. You can work towards NVQs in marine support. You then have to make a choice between deck work, catering or engineering. If you continue with your studies you can go on to train as an officer. An able seafarer (deck) intermediate apprenticeship or advanced apprenticeship in maritime occupations are also options to consider.

Personal attributes

All ratings have to have a real interest in shipping vessels and in being at sea. You need to be physically fit and comfortable working in harsh conditions. The atmosphere is very different on a large tanker compared to an upmarket cruise liner – so you need to consider this when you decide what jobs to apply for. Teamwork is very important indeed. You need to be practical for all Merchant Navy work, but you will also need particular skills depending on whether you specialise in catering, engineering or deck management.

Earnings

Merchant Navy rating pay is low during training, although college fees and all living expenses on board ship are paid by the employer. Experienced ratings earn between £17,500 and £30,000.

Info

Merchant Navy Training Board
www.mntb.org.uk

Royal Fleet Auxiliary Service (RFA)
www.royalnavy.mod.uk/The-Fleet/
Royal-Fleet-Auxiliary

Careers at Sea
www.careersatsea.org

Marine Society & Sea Cadets
020 7654 7000
www.ms-sc.org

METALLURGIST

Metallurgists study the physical and chemical properties of metals and alloys, such as iron and steel, aluminium, copper, nickel and precious metals. There are three different types of work for metallurgists. Chemical metallurgists are concerned with the extraction of metals from ore. They also study metal corrosion and fatigue. Physical metallurgists study the performance of metals under stress. Process metallurgists shape and join metals and select the best metal to use for particular jobs. Metallurgists work in research and development, design and manufacture, production management and quality assurance. Metallurgists may be at the forefront of new technologies, developing metals for new applications, or involved in the traditional manufacture of anything from razor blades to washing machines.

Entry, qualifications and training

This is almost always a degree-level career with preferred subjects being metallurgy, chemistry, physics, manufacturing engineering or similar. Occasionally you can join this profession if you have an HND in a relevant subject. For research and development posts, employers sometimes expect you to have a postgraduate qualification such as an MSc in metallurgy.

Personal attributes

Metallurgy demands an interest in scientific and technological subjects, an ability to solve practical problems and to work with other people on specific projects.

Earnings

Graduate entrants earn between £22,000 and £27,000. With a few years' experience earnings rise to between £30,000 and £45,000.

Info

Institute of Cast Metal Engineers (ICME)
0121 752 1810
www.icme.org.uk

Institute of Materials, Minerals and Mining (IOM3)
020 7451 7300
www.iom3.org

METEOROLOGY

Meteorologist

Meteorologists are the people who tell us what the weather is going to do. While we are all aware of weather forecasts on TV, the internet and radio, meteorologists provide information for many other clients too. Accurate weather forecasts are important for agriculture, air transport, shipping, public service, the media, the armed forces and retail businesses. People involved in air travel or water sports or outdoor pursuits such as climbing, or sporting organisations – all of these can plan more effectively if they know what weather to expect. Meteorologists collect data from satellites all over the world. They use computer and mathematical models designed to make short- and long-range forecasts concerning weather and climate patterns. They also study the impact of weather on the environment, taking measurements, recording results and looking at patterns over time. Meteorology is one of the sciences most frequently used in the study of climate change.

The largest employer of meteorologists in the United Kingdom is the Met Office, but meteorologists are also employed by agriculture and fisheries organisations, the oil and gas industry, research organisations and the Environment Agency. Some work for small consultancies contracted to provide information for the kinds of organisations just listed.

Entry, qualifications and training

Meteorology is a graduate profession – many meteorologists also have postgraduate qualifications. The most useful degree subjects include maths, physics, meteorology, environmental science and oceanography. The Met Office usually takes entrants with a First or 2.1 degree. It is very unusual to get in with an HND or a foundation degree. The Met Office has a Mobile Met Unit (MMU) and it is possible to apply to be a forecaster for this unit if you have good A levels in maths and physics. Technical support staff and administrative staff employed by the Met Office do not need degrees, but from these roles it is not possible to become a meteorologist. The Met Office provides a structured training scheme for new entrants.

The Met Office offers a small number of highly sought-after summer placements, which can provide really useful experience. Experience of computer modelling, even if it is not weather related, is also extremely useful.

Personal attributes

Of course, you must be interested in the weather – who isn't? In addition you have to have very good observational skills and the ability to generate and interpret highly complex data. You must be able to work as part of a team, and be able to communicate scientific information in such a way that it can be easily understood by the non-scientist.

Earnings

Graduate trainees in the Met Office earn around £23,000 rising to £27,000 on completing training. Experienced forecasters earn £25,000 to £35,000, but can earn more. Shift-work allowances may also be paid. Private weather consultancies may pay higher salaries, but they do not usually provide initial training.

Info

The Met Office www.metoffice.gov.uk	**Royal Meteorological Society** www.rmets.org

MILK

Milk delivery roundsperson

(see Roundsperson)

MOTOR INDUSTRY

The motor industry provides job opportunities from technical to sales and management roles. Whatever your particular role, you need a genuine interest in motor vehicles. The following section gives details of the most commonly found job titles and training routes in this industry.

Auto electrician

Auto electricians are motor vehicle technicians who have highly specialised knowledge of and skill in the complex electrical and electronic systems that are part of modern motor vehicles.

Entry, qualifications and training

To be an auto electrician, you need to do an apprenticeship. To start an apprenticeship you must have five GCSEs grades 9–4, including maths and English. The apprenticeship combines on-the-job training with your employer and college-based learning. Through your apprenticeship you can gain an NVQ certificate. Relevant college courses that include/cover auto electrical work are Level 1 Award in Motor Vehicle Studies, Level 2 Certificate in Light Vehicle Maintenance and Repair Principles, and Level 2 Diploma in Auto Electrical and Mobile Electrical Competence.

Personal attributes

You must be good at working with your hands and able to solve problems. You must be good at working as part of a team.

Automotive engineer

(see Engineering)

Body repairer and refinisher

Body repairers and refinishers restore cars, vans, trucks and motorcycles to their original condition after accidents, damage or other wear and tear. This includes replacing windscreens and other glass, removing dents and rubbing away patches of rust. Repair and refinishing cover several different roles, including body repair, electrical, mechanical and trim repair, and vehicle valeting.

Entry, qualifications and training

For any job in body repair and refinishing, apart from car valeting, you need to do an apprenticeship. To be accepted for an apprenticeship you must have five GCSEs grades 9–4, including maths and English. The apprenticeship combines on-the-job training with your employer and college-based learning. Through your apprenticeship you can gain relevant NVQ certificates. You could also consider a relevant college course such as a Level 2 Certificate in Vehicle Body and Paint Operations, for example.

Personal attributes

These vary according to exactly which aspect of body repair and refinishing you have chosen, but they all demand that you pay great attention to fine detail, that you can find ways to solve problems and that you are able to work as part of a team.

Roadside assistance and recovery technician

Roadside assistance and recovery workers are called to the scene of vehicle breakdowns. They have to make quick, accurate assessments as to whether they can repair the vehicle on the spot or whether it will have to be towed away. They also have to reassure vehicle drivers and passengers and explain to them clearly what the best course of action is.

Entry, qualifications and training

For this work you must be 21 years old and hold a full, clean driving licence. Most successful applicants will already have worked for three years or more with motor vehicles, usually as a vehicle technician. Most technicians qualify through an apprenticeship.

Personal attributes

You need to be extremely responsible, with good technical skills and knowledge. You must be able to take decisions on your own and to solve problems. You must have good people skills, be polite, friendly and reassuring, and good at explaining technical problems.

Vehicle parts person

Vehicle parts operatives deal with the ordering and management of the hundreds of separate parts that need to be replaced in every type of vehicle. Vehicle parts operatives have to be able to recognise any vehicle part and know that part's place in a vehicle. They have to liaise with customers, with technicians, with manufacturers and with distributors. The work involves ordering and finding stock, controlling stock levels and advising customers.

Entry, qualifications and training

You don't necessarily need formal qualifications for this work, though experience working in a car spares store could be useful. You may be able to train through an apprenticeship. To be accepted on an apprenticeship you must have five GCSEs grades 9–4, including maths and English. The apprenticeship combines on-the-job training with your employer and college-based learning. Through your apprenticeship you can gain relevant NVQ certificates.

Personal attributes

You must be really interested in vehicles, be very well organised, able to work under pressure and good at dealing with people. You must be good at handling a lot of detailed information.

Vehicle salesperson

People working in vehicle sales, often called sales executives, sell cars and other vehicles to private and business customers. They have to know a great deal about cars, not just those they are trying to sell, but those they may be purchasing or taking in part exchange.

Entry, qualifications and training

There are no formal entry qualifications for this job. Many vehicle salespeople have worked as vehicle technicians or in other roles in the automotive industry. Some have come from a selling background in other sectors.

Personal attributes

Sales executives have to combine good technical knowledge with excellent people skills. You must be polite, friendly, prepared to answer detailed questions and able to offer clear explanations.

Vehicle technician

Vehicle technicians work to repair and maintain cars, vans, trucks and motorcycles. It is usual for technicians to specialise in just one of these groups of vehicles. Vehicle technicians also work at the many fast-fit centres that fit tyres, exhausts or other parts and systems. Some technicians specialise in MOT testing or in converting petrol cars to run on liquid petroleum gas (LPG).

Entry, qualifications and training

To become a motor vehicle technician (with the exception of fast tyre fitting) you need to do an apprenticeship. To start an apprenticeship you must have five GCSEs grades 9–4, including maths and English. The apprenticeship combines on-the-job training with college-based learning. Through your apprenticeship you can gain relevant NVQ certificates.

Personal attributes

All motor vehicle technicians have to have a real interest in working with vehicles and be good at working with their hands. You often need to be a good problem solver and patient too – sometimes why something won't work is not obvious.

Vehicle valeter

Vehicle valeters clean and polish vehicles for individual customers and for car showrooms, and vehicle leasing and rental companies. Valeters clean the inside and the outside of vehicles. They may have to vacuum, clean windows and other glass, steam clean, wash, use high-pressure hoses and wax and polish vehicles. Some vehicle valeters combine vehicle pickup and delivery with their valeting work.

Entry, qualifications and training

There are no formal entry qualifications for this work, but if your job involves driving, you must have a full, clean driving licence. A mature attitude is important, and some experience in customer care work can be an advantage.

Personal attributes

You must be very thorough, good at paying attention to detail and you should be reasonably physically fit. You should be polite, friendly and trustworthy.

Earnings

Apprentices earn around the minimum wage, rising to £16,000 to £20,000 on completing training. Experienced technicians can earn £25,000 plus. Car valeters earn between £14,000 and £16,500. Sales people normally earn a basic salary plus commission on each vehicle they sell; the basic salaries start at around £15,000 with a possible £5,000 in commission and bonuses. Many people with technical qualifications and experience go self-employed.

Info

Institute of the Motor Industry
01992 519 025
www.theimi.org.uk

Autocity
01992 511521
www.autocity.org.uk

Driver & Vehicle Standards Agency
01372 383056
www.gov.uk/government/organisations/driver-and-vehicle-standards-agency

Retail Motor Industry Federation
020 7580 9122
www.rmif.co.uk

MUSEUM WORK

(see Art and design for Arts administration)

MUSIC

Working in music – popular, classical, jazz, world, folk, blues, etc – appeals to many people. Becoming a performer in any genre is highly competitive. In addition to the roles described here, the music industry employs people in marketing, finance and events management. It also crosses over with other industries such as arts administration and theatre.

Composer

Composers and songwriters either write original pieces or devise new arrangements for pieces that have already been written, orchestral arrangements of piano pieces, instrumental versions of songs, jazz arrangements of classics, etc. It is very hard to make a living purely from composition, unless you have a really well-established reputation or can get a position as composer-in-residence – and there certainly aren't many of these. Once established, you may be commissioned to write pieces: film scores, for example. The nature of composition has changed with the impact of powerful software which enables you to cut out some of the basics of writing out music or structuring chords. No software, however, can replace flair, talent and imagination.

Entry, qualifications and training

For most people who wish to compose music, it is not a full-time job. There are no specific entry requirements, but many composers will have studied music, been through music college and are likely to play at least one instrument.

Personal attributes

A passion for music, creative energy and determination are the key qualities you need. If you want to have work commissioned, marketing what you do and getting yourself known are also very important.

Earnings

It is hard to say. Many composers make only part of their income from writing compositions. If they gain commissions they will charge a set fee for each particular piece of work. They can also earn money from royalties if recordings or sheet music of their work is sold.

Info

Incorporated Society of Musicians (ISM)
020 7221 3499
www.ism.org

Associated Board of the Royal Schools of Music (ABRSM)
020 7636 5400
www.abrsm.org

Disc jockey

Disc jockeys (DJs) select, play and mix music at clubs, private parties and on radio stations. They use a variety of high-tech equipment for mixing, pitch control and cross-fading, and may also be responsible for lighting and multimedia effects. A DJ's personality may be the key to success or otherwise of a radio show. At live events it is up to the DJ to create the right atmosphere and read the audience. What is required at a family party is going to be very different from what makes a successful club or dance venue.

Entry, qualifications and training

A strong interest in and enjoyment of different music styles is essential, and it is useful to have an interest in technology and electronics. Some DJs specialise in specific music genres such as soul, funk, hip-hop and pop. Most are self-taught and usually begin their career by volunteering their services at clubs, radio stations or to friends. It is useful to send a tape demonstrating DJ skills when asking for work. You could also consider a college course which could equip you with some of the skills needed to work with sampling equipment and decks, for example. Relevant courses might include a Level 2 Certificate in Music Technology.

Personal attributes

DJs must have a lively personality, a sense of fun and natural creativity. They need to have a good knowledge of and genuine interest in music and be able to interact well with an audience.

Earnings

Sometimes you have to start off doing unpaid work. Very often you are paid by the session, anything from £50 to £300, most sessions lasting a few hours. Really experienced club and radio DJs with an established reputation can earn up to £1,000 per session.

Info

Creative & Cultural Skills
020 7015 1800
www.ccskills.org.uk

Screen Skills
020 7713 9800
www.screenskills.com

RadioCentre
020 7010 0600
www.radiocentre.org

The Radio Academy
www.radioacademy.org

Music promoter

Bands, solo artists and other musical performers need their music to be heard and talked about. It is the job of music promoters (also referred to as music promotions managers) to manage and publicise recording and live artists who are their clients. Music promoters work for record companies and for performers. Music promoters could be involved in many different activities, including organising tours, planning media interviews, issuing press releases, attending publicity events, negotiating airtime on TV, radio or new media, working with designers and printers to ensure that publicity is just right. They can also be involved in negotiating contracts for their clients.

Music promoters may also listen to new acts before deciding whether they should be offered a contract. This aspect of the work is referred to as 'A and R' (artiste and repertoire).

Entry, qualifications and training

There are no set qualifications to get into this work, but it is highly competitive and being persistent as well as being in the right place at the right time are going to be significant. You may start in an administrative position with a record company, or at a music venue. There are a few foundation, BTEC and degree courses which cover music industry management, and these could help you to build up some contacts. Voluntary work such as organising local gigs, writing gig reviews or getting involved with student or local radio and press could also help you. An apprenticeship, such as an intermediate or advanced apprenticeship in live events promotion may also be a good starting point.

Personal attributes

Your personality, knowledge and enthusiasm for the music industry are all crucial here. These are going to count for more than any academic qualifications. You do, however, need extremely good spoken and written English. You must be really well organised and be able to cope with a great deal of pressure.

Earnings

Administrative assistants in record companies earn £16,000 to £19,000 and senior managers earn between £30,000 and £60,000. Some promoters working for top acts earn £100,000 plus.

Info

Creative & Cultural Skills
020 7015 1800
www.ccskills.org.uk

Creative and Cultural Skills
www.ccskills.org.uk/index.php?/careers/advice/any/music

Musical instrument maker/repairer

Musical instrument makers and/or repairers build, repair, restore and maintain musical instruments of all kinds, from modern electric guitars to ancient pianos. Most repairers specialise in a particular instrument or family of instruments, such as woodwind, string, brass or pianos. Some develop special skills in restoring very old instruments, others make and build instruments using modern materials such as plastics and carbon fibres. One specialised field in musical instrument repair is piano tuning.

Entry, qualifications and training

You do not need specific qualifications to get into this work, but you do need careful training. You should certainly have excellent manual dexterity and a good ear. There are a few courses in musical instrument making and repair. These include the ASET Certificate in Classical Musical Instrument Technology at levels 2 and 3 and BTEC HNC/HND in Instrument Technology. London Metropolitan University offers foundation degree and degree courses in musical instrument technology. You can find out about short courses in instrument repair from the National Association of Musical Instrument Repairers website. If you are interested in piano tuning, the Association of Piano Tuners provides details of training courses.

Personal attributes

As well as manual dexterity and a love of the instrument or instruments on which you wish to work, you need a range of people and business skills. Many instrument makers and repairers are self-employed, so you must be able to market your services and deal with potential customers.

Earnings

Salaries vary, but start at £14,000 to £18,000. Instrument repairers and makers with experience and a good reputation can earn more than £30,000. If you are self-employed, you will set an appropriate fee for the level of work involved and the length of time the job is likely to take.

Musician (classical)

Whether you play an instrument or sing, musical training leading to a degree or equivalent qualification opens the door to a wide range of careers in music, including performing, teaching, administration, management, broadcasting, recording, journalism, publishing, promotion, librarianship and the retail trade.

Many professional musicians work on a freelance basis as soloists, orchestral players, commercial session musicians and in a variety of chamber music ensembles, including classical, rock, dance and jazz groups. A performer's working life often includes some teaching, master classes or community education work alongside regular and vital practice.

Some musicians arrange their own engagements, others have an agent or use a diary service to find work. For all performers, membership of a professional association or union is desirable.

There are opportunities, particularly for those who already play an instrument, to join the Army, the RAF or Royal Marines as a bands person.

Entry, qualifications and training

Entry to undergraduate courses of study usually requires a minimum of five GCSEs and one or more A levels, preferably including music. Full-time courses of study over three or four years, usually leading to a degree, are available at conservatoires (performance-based), universities (more academic) and colleges of higher education (broader spectrum). Singers require a longer training, often over six years. Conservatoires and universities also offer a range of postgraduate courses. Details of courses in performance, composition, musicology and teaching are available from the ISM website. The government introduced a training scheme for the music industry under the 'New Deal' initiative; details are available from Jobcentre Plus.

Personal attributes

A love of music, a positive and persuasive personality, robust physical and mental health, stamina, patience and excellent communication skills are essential for any career in music. Competition is fierce for performers, and only a very few talented musicians can establish a successful solo career. The ability to get on well with others helps to ensure good relationships with colleagues, managers and promoters to support career development.

Earnings

There is wide variation in earnings. Most musicians are self-employed and either have short contracts or are simply paid for individual jobs. There are some permanent salaried posts in orchestras, but many members of orchestras and bands of all types, as well as session musicians working in recording studios, are self-employed. What you earn depends on how much work you get, how good you are and how much your particular instrument or style is in demand. The Musicians Union (MU) can offer detailed guidance on what you might expect to be paid for work at your level and your instrument.

Musician (pop)

This career is desired by so many but achieved by only a few. Pop covers many styles – rock, heavy metal, folk, jazz, indie, etc – with trends for what is most popular shifting all the time. Pop musicians may be singers or play any instrument. The day-to-day work consists of practising your instrument or your singing, composing material, recording material and preparing for or going on tour. Not every pop musician is going to front a band or become a household name. Many singers and instrumentalists work as session musicians for bands either in the recording studio or on tour.

Entry, qualifications and training

There are no specific entry requirements – although a passion for your music is a good starting point. Being able to read music is useful, especially if you are going to work as a session musician. Many people learn the instrument they wish to play from a young age and hours of practice are a vital part of getting into this profession.

Personal attributes

You have to be enormously resilient and determined as well as talented. Many people will not achieve their dreams, or will work for a long time to achieve success. Success, if it comes, also brings demands on your time, your energy and your emotional resilience. You have to be able to cope with being very much in the public eye. How you look and how you present yourself are often very important too.

Earnings

Many pop musicians have to do other work to make ends meet, while the most successful earn enormous salaries. Equity, the performers' union, provides guidance on what session musicians can expect to be paid.

Music teacher

If you love music and want to pass on that passion, or the skill of playing an instrument, music teaching offers a range of possibilities. Opportunities range from private instrumental or vocal tuition to class teaching at primary schools, guiding secondary school students through GCSE and A levels in music, or working as a visiting teacher to schools, taking individual lessons with school students.

Private teachers set up and develop their own independent, studio-based business. The Incorporated Society of Musicians (ISM) sets professional standards for members who are listed in their Register of Professional Private Music Teachers. They set minimum hourly tuition fees, so that a reasonable income can be assured, and advise on business matters such as tuition contracts.

Entry, qualifications and training

To teach in a school you need an appropriate teaching qualification which confers Qualified Teacher Status. There are many routes to this and you should consult the 'Teaching' section of this guide. In all cases to teach in schools you will need five GCSEs, you will need to pass selection tests and you will have to have an enhanced background check by the Disclosure and Barring Service.

Private music teachers do not need specific qualifications, though they must be exceptionally good musicians, and there are several music teaching courses available at universities and music colleges which could help you develop your teaching skills if you already have great musicianship.

Personal attributes

A love of music, a positive and persuasive personality, robust physical and mental health, stamina, patience and excellent communication skills are essential for any career in music.

Earnings

In state schools teachers earn £22,000 to £27,000 – more in London. Private music tutors normally charge by the hour and the average range for this is £25 to £35 an hour. Guidance on rates of pay is available from the Incorporated Society of Musicians (ISM).

Info

Creative & Cultural Skills
020 7015 1800
www.ccskills.org.uk

Incorporated Society of Musicians (ISM)
020 7221 3499
www.ism.org

Associated Board of the Royal Schools of Music (ABRSM)
020 7636 5400
www.abrsm.org

Musicians Union
www.musiciansunion.org.uk

Equity
020 7379 6000
www.equity.org.uk

RSL (Rockschool)
0845 460 4747
www.rslawards.com

Music therapist

(see Therapy specialisms (arts-based))

Piano tuner

(see Musical instrument maker/repairer)

NANOTECHNOLOGIST

Nanotechnologists work with tiny particles; a nanometre measures one billionth of a metre. Nanotechnologists design and develop devices and materials using these tiny particles. Nanotechnology is a growing area of science and engineering and nanotechnologists work for many organisations including universities, research institutes and companies engaged in energy production, biotechnology, medical equipment manufacture, IT and electronics. The work is usually laboratory based and the nanotechnologist's role is one of research and development.

Entry, qualifications and training

You will need a relevant degree if you wish to work as a nanotechnologist. There are now some degrees and postgraduate courses specifically in nanotechnology, but other relevant subjects include maths, physics, chemistry, electronics and materials science. Many nanotechnologists undertake paid PhDs or postdoctoral studies funded by industry.

Personal attributes

As well as a thorough grounding in scientific method and research techniques, you need an enquiring mind, the ability to solve problems, think clearly and work well as part of a team. You should have excellent writing skills, as you will often be presenting your findings or ideas to colleagues. Because this scientific discipline is changing fast, you need to be prepared to update your knowledge.

Earnings

PhD students doing paid research earn £14,000 to £15,000, postdoctoral researchers earn £25,000 to £37,000 and research scientists working in industry earn from £25,000 to £45,000.

Info

Nanowerk
www.nanowerk.com

SEMTA
0845 643 9001
www.semta.org.uk

Future Morph
www.futuremorph.org

NAVAL ARCHITECT

A naval architect is an engineer who specialises in the design, construction and repair of seagoing craft, including cruise liners, Merchant Navy vessels, warships, submarines, ferries, pleasure craft and high-speed boats. Shipbuilding has declined as an industry in the United Kingdom, but there are opportunities to build and design small craft, especially in coastal towns. Some naval architects also work for the Maritime and Coastguard Agency inspecting ships in port to ensure that they are seaworthy. They also work on the design and construction of offshore installations such as oil and gas drilling rigs. As a naval architect you would work with construction and project teams checking specifications and coordinating work. Your work could involve consulting with lawyers, scientists and accountants.

Entry, qualifications and training

Most naval architects have a relevant degree or postgraduate qualification recognised by the Royal Institute of Naval Architects (RINA). Its website gives an up-to-date list of the courses it recognises, but they include naval architecture, marine engineering, ocean engineering and ship science.

Having completed your academic training you would then go on to a work-based training programme, again approved by RINA. Many companies offer their own schemes, but if they do not, RINA can help you develop an individual training programme.

Personal attributes

A genuine interest in ships, boats and other vessels is a good starting point. You must have good technical engineering knowledge and a creative attitude to problem solving. Naval architects need good report-writing skills and the confidence and clarity to explain technical problems to non-technical people. If you are onboard vessels, you may have to deal with bad weather or working at heights.

Earnings

Trainees start on £25,000 to £28,000. Qualified and experienced naval architects earn around £30,000 to £60,000. Experienced and senior naval architects can earn £75,000.

Info

SEMTA
0845 643 9001
www.semta.org.uk

British Marine Federation
01784 473377
www.britishmarine.co.uk

Royal Institution of Naval Architects (RINA)
020 7235 4622
www.rina.org.uk

Institute of Marine Engineering, Science and Technology (IMarEST)
020 7382 2600
www.imarest.org.uk

NURSING PROFESSIONS

Nurses, healthcare assistants, midwives and health visitors work in many settings, including hospitals, health clinics, GP practices and the community. They work in the NHS, and for independent healthcare providers including business and not-for-profit organisations.

Healthcare assistant

Healthcare assistants work alongside nurses and provide care for patients. Healthcare assistants help wash and dress patients, help with treatments, help patients with mobility problems to move around, talk to patients, keep wards tidy and complete basic paperwork. They work on general hospital wards, in clinics and outpatient departments, psychiatric hospitals, hospices and care homes. There are also opportunities for community-based work, providing physical care to individuals who might otherwise have needed to go into hospital or a residential care home.

Entry, qualifications and training

No formal qualifications are needed to start work as a healthcare assistant, but hospitals, care homes and other organisations do provide training and many healthcare assistants work towards NVQ level 2 in health and social care. Applicants also have to have a background check through the Disclosure and Barring Service to ensure that they are suitable to work with children and/or vulnerable people. In some areas, you may be able to train as a healthcare assistant through an apprenticeship, or take a full-time college course in health and social care. Previous experience of working with people can strengthen your application. There are opportunities to do voluntary work with the NHS and other organisations, if you have not had any previous, relevant experience. You could also consider an apprenticeship such as an intermediate apprenticeship as a healthcare support worker.

Personal attributes

Like qualified nurses, healthcare assistants must have patience, tact, tolerance and an ability to communicate with the patients in their charge. Physical fitness is essential as the job sometimes involves heavy work (such as lifting and turning patients).

Earnings

Newly qualified healthcare assistants earn from £15,000 to £18,000, more in London. Experienced healthcare assistants who have taken additional qualifications earn up to £20,000.

Info

NHS Careers
0345 60 60 655
www.healthcareers.nhs.uk

Skills for Health
020 7388 8800
www.skillsforhealth.org.uk/nsahealth

Health visitor

Health visitors promote health and contribute to the prevention of mental, physical and social ill health in the community. This involves educating people in ways of healthy living and making positive changes in the environment. Education may be achieved by teaching individuals or families in their own homes, in health centres, clinics, in informal groups, or through campaigns for the promotion of good health practices through local or national mass media.

The health visitor may work with people who are registered with a GP or who live within a defined geographical area. The work includes collaboration with a wide range of voluntary and statutory organisations.

Entry, qualifications and training

You have to have qualified as a nurse or midwife to train as a health visitor. There is currently a shortage of health visitors and there is no minimum period after qualifying as a nurse or midwife before you can start health visitor training. Most trainees are seconded onto courses by their employers – usually the local health authority. Training is one year full-time or its part-time equivalent and covers all aspects of health visiting.

Personal attributes

Health visitors must be excellent communicators, able to convey information to all types of people without being patronising. They must have self-confidence, tact and a lot of common sense. They must be able to work alone, yet know when to seek advice. They should be confident, articulate public speakers.

Earnings

Health visitors earn between £30,400 and around £43,700. Newly qualified health visitors may earn less, and salaries may depend on experience and if they are team leader or manager health visitor roles, for example.

Info

Community Practitioners and Health Visitors Association
www.unitetheunion.org

(see also the Info panel at the end of the Nurse section)

Midwife

Midwives (who may be female or male) provide care and advice to mothers and fathers before, during and after birth; they are employed by the NHS in hospital and/or community settings, including home births, by private hospitals, or work independently. The midwife provides care during normal pregnancy and birth, and up to 28 days following the birth. The midwife will also care for women who have complications. The midwife is an integral part of the multidisciplinary team responsible for delivering care, working closely with obstetricians and other health professionals in ensuring the well-being of mothers and babies.

Entry, qualifications and training

To qualify as a midwife you need to complete a degree or diploma course in midwifery that is approved by the Nursing and Midwifery Council (NMC). Institutions running courses can set their own academic entry requirements, but there are broad general guidelines. For nursing diploma courses you need five GCSEs grades 9–4, including English, maths and a biological science. For degree courses the same GCSE requirements apply, but you also need two A levels. Applicants must be aged 17.5 in England and Wales, 17 in Scotland and 18 in Northern Ireland. In England you must apply through the Nursing and Midwifery Admissions Service (NMAS) – the contacts for Scotland, Wales and Ireland are listed in the Info panel. Applicants who do not meet these entry requirements may be successful if they can demonstrate literacy and numeracy skills and provide some evidence that they have recently undertaken successful study of some kind. If you have a nursing degree or diploma (adult branch) you can do a 12- to 18-month midwifery diploma.

Personal attributes

Midwives must have extremely good interpersonal skills, and be caring, practical, friendly and encouraging. They must be able to work as part of a team, but also to take responsible decisions on their own.

Earnings

Midwives earn between £24,000 and around £43,000. Newly qualified midwives may earn less, and salaries may vary depending on whether midwives are community midwives, senior midwives or those involved in research and management.

Nurse

Nurses care for people of all ages who are ill, injured or suffering from mental, emotional or physical disabilities. They are based in hospitals, in clinics, in local GP practices, in schools, in the community and in industry. While there are many settings in which nurses work, there are four main branches that determine your career path: adult nurse, children's nurse, mental health nurse and learning disabilities nurse.

Adult nurses care for patients aged 18 and over in hospitals, clinics and other settings. They work with people who have long-term illnesses, who are recovering from surgery or who have suffered injury and trauma. Your daily tasks could include checking temperatures, blood pressure and respiratory rate, giving drugs and injections, cleaning and dressing wounds, administering blood transfusions and drips, and using hi-tech equipment. Once qualified, adult nurses may choose to specialise in fields such as operating theatre work, accident and emergency, coronary care and many more.

Children's nurses undertake the same variety of work as adult nurses, but their patients are all aged under 18 years. The work might involve caring for premature or newborn babies, or nursing older children who have long-term or terminal illnesses. Babies and young children may not be able to explain what is wrong, so children's nurses must develop good powers of observation.

Learning disabilities nurses work with people of all ages who need help with aspects of everyday living. These nurses may work in hospitals, in day care or residential settings, special schools and the community. The work normally involves assessing clients to see what they can do and where they need help, and then teaching, advising and developing programmes that help those people to reach their potential.

Mental health nurses work in hospitals, psychiatric units and the community. They work to support people who experience difficulties caused by conditions such as depression or anxiety. They work with people who have phobias, or who have suffered traumas through accidents or illnesses. Mental health nurses also work with people who have become dependent on alcohol or other substances. The work involves helping people to live and cope more effectively, whether this is through medication, talking problems through, or developing programmes of beneficial activities.

Entry, qualifications and training

You have to choose which of the branches of nursing interests you most, since the courses are each tailored to one of these branches. Having made this choice, the entry route for each branch is very similar. From 2013 all nurse training has been through a degree course, but there are currently a few remaining diploma courses. To get onto a diploma course you need five GCSEs grades 9–4, including maths, English and one science. For a degree course you need the same

GCSEs plus two A levels. Some institutions run advanced diplomas, which are pitched between the diploma and the degree-level course. There are other routes in. If you have graduated in another subject you may be able to do a two-year fast-track course. All courses combine academic learning with practical experience. If you are a healthcare assistant and have NVQ level 3 qualifications you may be able to get full nursing qualifications on a part-time basis. All applicants for courses must have a criminal records check (Dislosure and Barring Service – DBS) check. Once qualified, there are many opportunities for further training and developing specialist skills and knowledge in particular fields of nursing.

Personal attributes

While the balance of required skills and qualities may vary between the different branches of nursing, there are many requirements common to all. Nurses must be caring and compassionate and enjoy working with people. They have to be emotionally resilient, often dealing with distressing situations. Nurses must be practical and have good manual dexterity and confidence in handling specialised equipment. They need an interest in the science, anatomy and physiology that underpins health and illness. They must be very observant and also good at working as part of a healthcare team. In senior roles they must also be able to motivate, train, supervise and monitor the work of others.

Earnings

Newly qualified nurses earn between £24,000 and £30,000. With experience, specialist knowledge and management responsibilities, salaries are between £31,600 and £41,700. Staff in inner London earn an extra 20 per cent, and an extra 15 per cent in outer London.

There are opportunities to work overtime, which is paid at time and a half. These figures are based on working for the NHS. Some private sector salaries are higher, and some charity sector salaries are lower.

Info

Nursing and Midwifery Council (NMC)
020 7637 7181
www.nmc.org.uk

Health in Wales
0300 060 4400
www.wales.nhs.uk

Northern Ireland Practice & Education Council for Nursing & Midwifery
0300 300 0066
www.nipec.hscni.net

Nursing Careers Centre (NCC)
www.nursingcareers.ie

NHS Careers
0345 60 60 655
www.healthcareers.nhs.uk

Skills for Health
020 7388 8800
www.skillsforhealth.org.uk

OCCUPATIONAL THERAPY

Occupational therapist

Occupational therapists work with people who have physical, mental or social problems, either from birth or as the result of accident, illness or ageing. Their aim is to enable people to achieve as much as they can for themselves. They start with a thorough assessment of each client and his or her lifestyle to establish what the person wants to achieve. Treatment can involve adapting living and working environments, teaching coping strategies and discovering the most beneficial therapeutic activities.

Although occupational therapists often work as part of a team, they have more autonomy than other healthcare workers in the way they apply their knowledge and expertise. They work in hospitals, social service departments, individuals' homes, residential and nursing homes, schools, universities, charities and prisons. They may also work in private practice.

Employment and promotional opportunities are excellent and all UK-educated occupational therapists receive a qualification that is recognised by the World Federation of Occupational Therapists, giving them opportunities to work abroad.

Entry, qualifications and training

Entry to the profession is normally on completion of a full- or part-time degree in occupational therapy. Most courses require three A levels or equivalent; mature students will be considered without these academic requirements. Accelerated two-year full-time courses are also available to graduates of other disciplines. Part-time in-service programmes are also available for those employed as occupational therapy support workers or technical instructors. Some part-time courses can be studied irrespective of employment status. Although courses vary, all include the principles and practice of occupational therapy, behavioural, biological and medical sciences, and periods of clinical practice in a variety of hospital and community settings. You could also consider an occupational therapist degree apprenticeship.

Personal attributes

You must be a good problem solver and be flexible, patient and sensitive. You have to be a very good communicator, encouraging and supporting clients, but also liaising effectively with other members of the health and social care team.

Earnings

Newly qualified occupational therapists earn between around £22,000 and £29,000, with experience and responsibility this rises to £26,300 to around £42,000. Working in inner London you earn an additional 20 per cent and 15 per cent in outer London.

Info

Health and Care Professions Council (HCPC)
0300 500 6184
www.hcpc-uk.org

NHS Careers
0345 60 60 655
www.healthcareers.nhs.uk

Royal College of Occupational Therapists
020 3141 4600
www.rcot.co.uk

OIL/GAS RIG WORK

Extracting oil or gas from wells on land or on the ocean floor, or fracking (extracting oil and gas trapped in certain types of rock) requires many different skills. Fossil fuel companies need to locate oil and gas deposits, and then assess the best ways of extracting these resources. Research and development are a significant part of this industry – with companies developing new techniques such as fracking to extract oil and gas from shale deposits, or finding ways to drill safely in ever-deeper parts of the ocean. As well as those roles specific to oil and gas extraction, an oil rig is a whole community, needing people to provide catering, hotel services, medical support, health and safety and helicopter transport.

Diver

(see also Diver)

Divers are employed in exploration and production work, as well as underwater repair work such as welding.

Drilling crew

The drilling crew is responsible for the drilling of wells, and the operation and maintenance of a variety of heavy machinery. The crew consists of a toolpusher who manages the team and is responsible for the safety and integrity of the operation, and a team of people including a driller, assistant driller and derrickman – who works on the tapering steel superstructure above the drill – roughnecks and roustabouts. A typical drill crew will number around 10 people. Progression to the role of driller is hierarchical, with people working through general labouring jobs (roustabouts), working on the drill floor (roughnecks) or at the top of the derrick (derrickman). The work is physical, from the operation of the drilling equipment to the cleaning and maintenance of pumps and equipment. A graduate drilling engineer and a range of other specialists, such as logging engineers, directional drilling specialists and mudloggers, will also work with the drill crew.

Engineer

A production engineer supervises activities ranging from production and storage, gas compression and injection (to assist in the recovery of the oil), to tanker loading. The reservoir engineer is concerned with the behaviour of the oil accumulation or reservoir, and has to attempt to discover how much oil remains below ground and what the most effective methods of recovery are. Economics plays an important role. The maintenance engineer must ensure that all equipment is functioning properly, selecting and monitoring the companies under contract.

Geologist

(see also Geology)

The oil companies employ technical experts such as geologists, geophysicists, drilling and petroleum engineers, and seismic interpreters. Geologists collect and analyse data from a variety of sources to determine whether drilling might prove successful at a particular site, and to optimise production from existing oilfields. There are opportunities around the world.

Entry, qualifications and training

Engineers and geologists need relevant degrees. To join a drilling crew you do not necessarily need formal qualifications, but you must be aged 18 or over and are likely to have to pass a medical. Many people join through an apprenticeship scheme, and employers are likely to require four GCSEs grades 9–4. Job security in the industry is volatile because of the fluctuating oil price, the demand for oil and the unpredictable nature of finding new oil and gas supplies.

Personal attributes

You need to be physically fit, geographically mobile and emotionally resilient. It can be hard working for long periods, especially on offshore rigs. You need to be able to work really well as part of a team and have acute health and safety awareness.

Earnings

The harsh nature of this work leads to relatively high rates of pay. Derrickmen earn around £30,000. Drillers and assistant drillers earn from £35,000 to £50,000. Drilling engineers start on between £28,000 and £35,000, increasing to £35,000 to £45,000. Geologists and geophysicists are paid similar salaries to those earned by engineers. Annual leave is usually very generous if your job involves a lot of time working offshore.

Info

Cogent Skills
01925 515200
www.cogentskills.com

Institute of Materials, Minerals and Mining (IOM3)
020 7451 7300
www.iom3.org

Oil and Gas UK
01224 577250
www.oilandgasuk.co.uk

SEMTA
0845 643 9001
www.semta.org.uk

Society of Petroleum Engineers
020 7299 3300
www.spe.org

Rigzone
www.rigzone.com/oil/jobs

OPTOMETRY

Dispensing optician

Dispensing opticians supply and fit spectacles and contact lenses prescribed by optometrists (also known as ophthalmic opticians) and eye specialists. They can advise clients on different types of lens, such as varifocals or prescription sunglasses. They take precise measurements to ensure that the lenses work properly for individual clients and they also fit, adjust and repair spectacle frames. Most dispensing opticians work for high street chains or independent opticians in the retail sector and part of your role would be to sell and market your company's products and services. There are also some opportunities to work in hospitals and other healthcare settings.

Entry, qualifications and training

To practise as a dispensing optician you must complete a training course approved by the General Optical Council (GOC) and pass a professional examination administered by the Association of British Dispensing Opticians (ABDO). There are three routes to qualifying: a two-year full-time diploma; a three-year day-release course; or a three-year distance-learning course. Whichever route you choose you need GCSEs grades 9–4 in English, maths and a science. Many course providers like you to have two A levels, including maths, biology or physics. The GOC provides a list of course providers, so check individual requirements. ABDO offers access courses for applicants who do not have the required GCSEs.

Personal attributes

You must be pleasant, friendly, approachable and patient. You must also be good at handling delicate equipment and have reasonable mathematical skills for taking measurements and making calculations. It is also useful to have a grasp of fashion and style, since this is very important to many of your clients when they choose spectacles or lenses.

Earnings

Trainees and assistants without full qualifications earn £16,000 to £22,500. Qualified opticians earn £23,000 to £40,000. Many opticians run their own businesses, where earnings may be higher, but it is a competitive market.

Info

General Optical Council (GOC)
020 7580 3898
www.optical.org

Association of British Dispensing Opticians (ABDO)
020 7298 5100
www.abdo.org.uk

Optometrist

Optometrists (also referred to as ophthalmic opticians) are trained to examine eyes and test sight, detect and measure defects in healthy eyes and prescribe spectacles, contact lenses or other appliances to correct or improve vision. They must carry out whatever tests are clinically necessary to detect signs of injury or disease to the eye or elsewhere, and must refer these patients to a medical practitioner. Most optometrists work in general practice in a variety of arrangements, including independent businesses, partnership, as an employee of corporate bodies, as a franchisee or in the hospital eye service. There are also job opportunities in research organisations, academic departments, ophthalmic hospitals and clinics.

Entry, qualifications and training

Optometrists must be registered with the General Optical Council (GOC) before being permitted to practise in the United Kingdom. To obtain registration they must pass the professional qualifying exam run by the College of Optometrists. The exam is in two parts. For Part I you must gain a BSc honours degree in optometry. You can take Part II after completing a pre-registration year of supervised practice. The professional qualifying exam combines practical and oral assessment of the candidate's ability to manage patients and practise safely as an independent optometrist.

For a place on the degree course you normally need three A levels, two of which must be maths and science.

Personal attributes

Opticians need mathematical and scientific skills to make accurate observations and calculations. They also need an ability to get on with, and communicate effectively with, patients of all ages and backgrounds and to be able to put them at their ease.

Earnings

In the pre-registration year most optometrists earn around £18,000 to £22,000. If you do your pre-registration year in an NHS hospital the salary is around £19,400. Optometrists in private practice can earn between £28,000 and £60,000 plus. In the NHS, they start on £26,500; salaries for specialist optometrists start at £31,600 and for consultants can go up to £83,000.

Info

College of Optometrists
020 7839 6000
www.college-optometrists.org

General Optical Council (GOC)
020 7580 3898
www.optical.org

Orthoptist

Orthoptists diagnose and treat various abnormalities and weaknesses in the eye, such as a squint or double vision. Many patients are children, and special equipment and exercises are used to help correct any defects while they are still young. Orthoptists work closely with medical eye specialists and, where operations are necessary, with ophthalmic surgeons. Most orthoptists work within the NHS, in hospitals and clinics (including school clinics). There are also opportunities in private practice and teaching.

Entry, qualifications and training

To practise as an orthoptist you must hold a degree approved by the Health and Care Professions Council (HCPC). Details of approved degree courses are available from the HCPC and also from the British and Irish Orthoptic Society. For these degree programmes you normally require five GCSEs grades 9–4, including English, maths and two sciences. You also need two or three A levels, one of which must be biology.

Personal attributes

You need to enjoy working with people, be good at putting them at ease, and be patient and reassuring, especially when working with children. You need good powers of observation, good manual dexterity and good numeracy skills.

Earnings

Newly qualified orthoptists earn between £22,100 and £28,700. With experience you can earn up to £41,700. These figures are based on working for the NHS where you also earn an extra 20 per cent if you work in inner London and an extra 15 per cent in outer London. In private practice, initial salaries may be lower than the NHS, but this gap is likely to close with experience.

Info

NHS Careers
0345 60 60 655
www.healthcareers.nhs.uk

Health and Care Professions Council (HCPC)
0300 500 6184
www.hcpc-uk.org

British and Irish Orthoptic Society (BIOS)
0121 728 5633
www.orthoptics.org.uk

PAINTER AND DECORATOR

(see Construction for Interior and finishing trades)

PATENT ATTORNEY

A patent is a legal document that gives an inventor the right to claim an invention as his or her own work and to produce, sell or make the invention. It also protects the inventor from having his or her work and/or ideas copied by others.

Patent attorneys have expertise in the field of intellectual property. They advise individual clients and companies on matters relating to patent law, and act on their behalf if they wish to patent an invention, or to register a trademark or a design in the United Kingdom or abroad. First, records are searched to gauge the likelihood of a patent being granted. The patent agent then draws up the particulars of the client's invention clearly and concisely, ensuring that it neither infringes another patent nor is liable to be copied without infringing its own patent. In cases where a client's patent has been infringed, the agent advises as to the best course of action. Patent attorneys are employed by private practice firms of patent consultants, industrial companies with a patent department, and the government.

Entry, qualifications and training

The minimum educational requirement for an attorney is a degree in a science or a technology-related subject. It is usually necessary to register as a patent attorney in the European Patent Office. This involves taking the European qualifying exams, for which a degree is necessary. Training is provided by your employer, and some patent agents choose to become patent examiners or work in-house for companies involved in research and development.

Personal attributes

You need a broad mix of skills: curiosity; the ability to assimilate new ideas; good analytical and critical skills; clear and concise thinking; and the capacity for logical and clear expression both in speech and in writing are all essential.

Earnings

Trainee patent attorneys earn around £30,000. Once qualified, salaries are between £53,000 and £80,000. Experienced patent attorneys can earn up to £100,000.

Info

Chartered Institute of Patent Attorneys
020 7405 9450
www.cipa.org.uk

UK Intellectual Property Office (UK-IPO)
0300 300 2000
https://www.gov.uk/government/organisations/
intellectual-property-office

European Patent Office
00 800 80 20 20 20
www.epo.org

PERFORMING ARTS

(see also Music)

Dance, circus, theatre and music – all significant fields in the world of entertainment encompass a wide range of careers. Performing arts is always a competitive career area, with only a few reaching the very top in terms of money, fame and success, but there are many different occupations to choose from.

Circus performer

Circus performers entertain in many ways designed to be spectacular, amusing or both, from skilled high-wire acrobatics, trapeze work and tightrope walking, to juggling, fire eating and performing as clowns. They work in circuses that travel from place to place and in fixed venues such as theatres. Circus acts often form part of major events designed to impress, such as opening ceremonies for sporting or cultural events. Some circus performers may also get work as stunt performers in film or theatre. As a circus artist you may work on solo performances or on team displays.

Entry, qualifications and training

Having a real talent for what you do is far more important than academic qualifications. There are many courses in circus arts available, from short weekend courses, part-time courses at local adult education institutes, through to full-time two-year foundation degree courses in London and Bristol. Some circuses and circus companies also run training courses. A full list of courses is available on the Circus Development Agency website.

Personal attributes

Of course, these very much depend on the particular circus craft you wish to pursue. For many you will need to be physically fit, agile and flexible and have a fair degree of physical courage. You will have to be prepared to learn and work hard at very specific sets of skills. You need to be confident and at ease in front of a crowd, and you must be able to work well with other people.

Earnings

Earnings vary widely as a lot of work is part time. Performers earn between £150 and £200 a show, minimum recommended rates are £440 a week. Equity can provide advice on what you should be paid.

Info

Creative & Cultural Skills
020 7015 1800
www.ccskills.org.uk

Screen Skills
020 7713 9800
www.screenskills.com

National Centre for Circus Arts
www.circusarts.org.uk

Get Into Theatre
020 7939 8492
www.getintotheatre.org

Equity
020 7379 6000
www.equity.org.uk

Dance

There are many genres of dance – ballet, contemporary, stage dance, jazz, tap, ballroom, folk, street, world dance, etc. As well as opportunities for professional dancers there are opportunities for teachers, choreographers and dance notators.

Choreographer

Choreographers create and plan dance routines and oversee the execution of their plans by the dancers. Choreographers are often former dancers.

Dance notator

Notators are employed by dance companies to record their repertoire, and assist choreographers and rehearsal staff in the revival of choreographic works. Most notators are graduates of vocational dance schools or ex-professional dancers, as the work involves close and informed observation of the choreography, the ability to demonstrate the movement accurately and the ability to work effectively with professional dancers.

Dance performer

Dancers use movement and gesture to portray situations, characters, stories or abstract ideas to their audiences. They work for ballet companies, theatres, cabaret clubs, on cruise ships and for street theatre and dance groups. Dancers sometimes work for companies overseas in order to find work. Many dancers combine a career as a performer with some teaching, or other related work.

Dance teacher

Teachers of dance can specialise in one area of dance teaching or teach in a variety of areas. The demand for teachers is high, especially as dance is now seen as a form of recreation. Teachers may work in commercial dance studios and professional dance schools both in the United Kingdom and abroad.

Entry, qualifications and training

If you want to dance professionally, the earlier you make the decision the better, since you will face competition from people who have trained in techniques such as ballet since early childhood, but some dancers begin their careers later than this. The Council for Dance Education and Training (CDET), now known as the Council for Dance, Drama and Musical Theatre (CDMT), provides details of accredited courses in many dance genres. Most courses last three years, but there is a lot of variation in the style and content of courses. Some university degree courses cover dance, either on its own or with other cultural and performing arts subjects.

Dancers who want to become teachers must obtain the relevant qualifications, for which full-time and part-time courses are available. These generally have an entry requirement of four or five GCSEs at grade C and above (grade 4 and above, if in English or maths). The Royal Academy of Dancing offers certificates, diplomas and degrees in classical ballet teaching. The courses are available on a part- and full-time basis.

Personal attributes

Dancers need to be hard working, self-disciplined both physically and mentally, dedicated and determined. They must be imaginative, able to express themselves artistically, and have a good sense of timing and an ear for music.

Earnings

Equity, the trade union for actors and performers, negotiates minimum rates for its members per performance or per week. Non-Equity members are often paid less than this, but dancers often accept these lower rates while they are trying to establish their careers. Experienced dancers can earn £500 a week and in London's West End rates are often closer to £700 to £800 a week.

Info

British Association of Teachers of Dancing
0141 427 3699
www.batd.co.uk

British Dance Council
020 8545 0085
www.british-dance-council.org

Council for Dance, Drama and Musical Theatre (CDMT)
020 7240 5703
www.cdmt.org.uk

Foundation for Community Dance
0116 253 3453
www.communitydance.org.uk

One Dance UK
020 7713 0730
www.onedanceuk.org

National Resource Centre for Dance
01483 689 316
www.surrey.ac.uk/nrcd

Royal Academy of Dance
020 7326 8000
www.rad.org.uk

Creative & Cultural Skills
020 7015 1800
www.ccskills.org.uk

Equity
020 7379 6000
www.equity.org.uk

Music

(see Music)

Stunt performer

When you see a fight, a high-speed car chase, a fall, a daring dive off the top of a cliff, or a horse rider negotiating a plunging mountain path at breakneck speed as part of a film or TV drama, it is highly likely that it is a stunt performer who is taking on these potentially hazardous challenges. Stunt performers stand in for film and TV actors, where a high degree of specialised skill is essential. They may also perform live stunts as part of shows, big public events or in circuses. The work can involve precision driving, gymnastics, fighting with or without weapons, diving, swimming and horse riding. The work also involves planning and setting up the stunt in great detail, so that every step is clearly understood by the performer and the rest of the crew.

Entry, qualifications and training

While there are no formal academic qualifications, stunt performers must be really enthusiastic about and have reached a high level of attainment in at least six of the following activities: boxing, martial arts, gymnastics, rock climbing, high diving (for falls), advanced driving, cars and/or motorcycles, swimming, diving, sub-aqua and horse riding. Fighting skills have to be one of your six and you cannot include two martial arts. Contact Equity for further details.

Personal attributes

Of course you have to be physically fit, full of physical courage, balanced with the common sense and meticulous planning skills that you need to succeed. You have got to be a communicative member of a team, ensuring that everyone knows what to expect. In the end, however, you must be able to take personal responsibility for your own actions and decisions.

Earnings

Stunt performers are normally self-employed earning a daily rate. Daily rates are recommended by Equity.

Info

Screen Skills	**Equity**
020 7713 9800	020 7379 6000
www.screenskills.com	www.equity.org.uk

Theatre

(see also Film and television production)

Many jobs, such as director, producer, lighting technician, prop maker, make-up artist and wardrobe manager, are common to television, film and in some instances (for example, sound technician) radio as well as theatre. There are also jobs in administration, front of house, taking bookings and selling programmes. There are jobs in marketing, advertising a theatre's activities or looking for sponsorship. There are practical opportunities such as carpentry. There are, however, some jobs that are specific to live theatre.

Actor

Acting mainly involves the interpretation of someone else's work and the communication of it to an audience, although there are opportunities for actors to write their own material. Actors are employed in various types of theatre (commercial, subsidised, community, fringe and theatre-in-education), and also in television, film, radio, and television and radio commercials.

Competition is keen and, because it is such a precarious profession, those entering it must be prepared for long periods of unemployment.

Entry, qualifications and training

Most people who want to act go to drama school. The National Council for Drama Training provides information on accredited courses. A good general education is important, and some schools require GCSEs and A levels or equivalent. Training courses at established schools usually last two or three years. Entrance is by audition and is competitive. Further experience may be gained from working in a repertory company or in fringe theatre. This may be an alternative way of entering the profession, but it is becoming increasingly difficult to enter solely by this method. You may also find it useful to complete a college course such as a Level 2 Technical Certificate in Performing Arts, or a Level 3 Extended Diploma in Performing Arts (Acting).

Personal attributes

Acting requires a combination of intelligence, sensitivity and imagination, together with a good memory, determination and physical stamina.

Earnings

Many actors struggle to make a living through acting, especially in their early careers. Only 6 per cent of actors earn more than £30,000 a year. Equity, the actors' union, sets minimum rates for its members – contact them for information. Actors are paid either per performance or per run of a play.

Stage hand

Stage hands, also referred to as stage technicians or crew, play an essential role behind the scenes, helping to ensure that props, scenery and special effects are exactly where they should be at just the right moment. Daily tasks vary, but can include helping carpenters to build, erect and paint scenery; moving scenery and furniture during a performance, either manually or with automated equipment; opening and closing stage curtains; and clearing and tidying the stage, studio or backstage area after a performance. Stage hands also have to attend rehearsals to become familiar with a performance so that they know exactly what they have to do and can time it perfectly.

Entry, qualifications and training

You do not need formal qualifications – practical experience is more important. Many stage hands start as casual workers helping with large productions before they are able to get full-time work. Having experience of backstage work through school, college, university or other amateur dramatics is extremely helpful. Having practical woodwork skills can also give you a good start. It is often worth approaching local theatre stage managers direct to see if they can offer you casual work. After this, training is very much on the job. Completing a college course such as a Level 2 Certificate in Technical Theatre Support may also be useful, and you may also be able to enter the profession by completing an apprenticeship such as a creative technician or technical theatre advanced apprenticeship.

Personal attributes

You must be physically fit and happy to work at evenings and weekends. You must be able to maintain a good level of concentration, and work quickly, quietly and calmly during a performance. You should have a real interest in theatre and you must be able to work as part of a team.

Earnings

Full-time stage hands earn between the minimum wage and £15,000, but there is not always full-time work available. Experienced theatre technicians with large companies can earn up to £27,000.

Stage manager

Stage managers are responsible for ensuring that all the technical and practical sides of rehearsals and live performances run smoothly. The stage manager is in charge of all stage hands and technicians and he or she has to ensure that everyone, including the performers, is in the right place at the right time. Typical activities for a stage manager include organising rehearsals, managing the props budget and the props themselves; liaising with other departments, e.g. lighting, set designers and wardrobe; cueing performers to go on stage, cueing sound and lighting staff; working closely with front-of-house staff; and keeping the 'prompt copy' of the script (which details the performers' positions on stage, script changes, and the props, lighting and sound needed for each scene).

Entry, qualifications and training

Most new entrants to stage management have degrees or professional diplomas in stage management and technical theatre. You can take a degree or diploma in this subject at drama school. Alternatively, you could take a degree in drama, stage management or practical theatre at a college or university. Some people who have worked as actors move into the stage management side of the profession. It is also possible to work your way up from a behind-the-scenes job such as a stage hand, but this route is becoming increasingly difficult. Practical experience is as important as formal qualifications. You must have had some experience of stage management through amateur dramatics, school, college, or university drama groups.

Personal attributes

You must be an excellent communicator with outstanding organisational skills. You should be able to liaise with people at every level in theatre. You need to be calm, quick at solving problems, able to take responsibility, good at motivating or pacifying others and easily able to think about several different things at once – a true multi-tasker.

Earnings

Salaries for assistant stage managers are from £16,000 to £25,000. Stage managers earn £21,000 to £40,000 or more. High salaries are few and far between because theatres often work on very tight budgets.

Info

Get Into Theatre
020 7939 8492
www.getintotheatre.org

Conservatoire for Dance and Drama
020 7387 5101
www.cdd.ac.uk

Creative & Cultural Skills
020 7015 1800
www.ccskills.org.uk

Equity
020 7379 6000
www.equity.org.uk

Independent Theatre Council
020 7403 1727
www.itc-arts.org

London Academy of Music and Dramatic Art (LAMDA)
020 8834 0500
ww2.lamda.ac.uk

National Association of Youth Theatres
www.nayt.org.uk

Federation of Drama Schools
www.federationofdramaschools.co.uk

PHARMACY

Pharmacists dispense and give advice on drugs prescribed by doctors or bought over the counter. They work either in the retail sector (community pharmacy) or in hospitals and other healthcare settings such as GP surgeries. A few pharmacists work in research for the pharmaceuticals industry.

Community pharmacist

Community pharmacists work for high street retail pharmacies and local health centres. They dispense prescriptions and ensure that medicines ordered on prescription or bought over the counter are supplied correctly, safely and in compliance with the law. They give advice to customers on what over-the-counter medicines might be suitable for their complaint, or they may recommend that the customer consult a doctor. They act as a link between doctors, patients and the pharmaceutical industry.

Hospital pharmacist

They dispense drugs for hospital in- and outpatients and work side by side with nurses, doctors and other health professionals to ensure that NHS patients receive the most appropriate medicines in the most effective way. In addition, in some hospitals, pharmacists manufacture their own products, take part in research work and come into direct contact with inpatients by accompanying medical staff on their ward rounds.

Entry, qualifications and training

Pharmacists must complete a four-year Master of Pharmacy degree, followed by one year's paid competency-based training and a registration examination. Entry to degree courses is with A level chemistry plus two other A levels or equivalent; maths and biology are preferred.

Personal attributes

As well as excellent relevant medical knowledge and the need to be very careful and accurate, it is also important that you get on well with people and can be patient and understanding. Pharmacists already have responsibility for handling dangerous drugs, and it seems likely that they will be given greater prescribing rights in the near future, when responsibility and decision making will be extremely important aspects of their skills mix.

Earnings

In the NHS newly qualified pharmacists earn between £22,100 and £28,700, with experience and responsibility this rises to £26,500 to £41,700. A consultant pharmacist can earn more than £80,000. Working in inner London you earn an additional 20 per cent and 15 per cent in outer London.

Salaries for retail pharmacists are between £24,000 and £40,000.

Info

Royal Pharmaceutical Society
020 7572 2737
www.rpharms.com

NHS Careers
0345 60 60 655
www.healthcareers.nhs.uk

Association of the British Pharmaceutical Industry (ABPI)
020 7930 3477
www.abpi.org.uk

General Pharmaceutical Council
020 3713 8000
www.pharmacyregulation.org

Skills for Health
020 7388 8800
www.skillsforhealth.org.uk

Skills for Health
020 7388 8800
www.skillsforhealth.org.uk/nsahealth

Pharmacy technician

Pharmacy technicians work as part of the pharmacy team and are supervised by a pharmacist. Their duties can include the dispensing of medicines from prescriptions, preparing sterile medicines, assessing stocks of drugs, patient counselling, advising on health promotion issues and collecting and collating information on drugs from a variety of sources. Pharmacy technicians can work in pharmacies, hospitals, the armed forces, the prison service, or within the pharmaceutical industry.

Entry, qualifications and training

Your first step is to find a job as a pre-registration pharmacy technician with an approved employer and then complete two years on-the-job training for the NVQ level 3 diploma in pharmacy service skills or a similar qualification. After this you can register with the General Pharmacy Council as a pharmacy technician. To get a job at the pre-registration stage you need at least five GCSEs grade 9–4, including maths, English and a science. If you have the appropriate GCSEs, you may be able to find an apprenticeship which offers pre-registration pharmacy training.

Personal attributes

As a pharmacy technician you should have a real interest in science and the ability to be accurate and careful. You should be able to deal sensitively and tactfully with people, be good at working as part of a team, and in some posts you may have to use sales skills as well.

Earnings

In the NHS, pharmacy technicians earn £19,400 to £22,600, rising to £28,700 with experience. The NHS also employs pharmacy support workers, who earn £15,400 to £18,700. In the private sector pharmacy technicians can earn up to £30,000.

Info

General Pharmaceutical Council
020 3713 8000
www.pharmacyregulation.org

Royal Pharmaceutical Society
020 7572 2737
www.rpharms.com

NHS Careers
0345 60 60 655
www.healthcareers.nhs.uk

Association of the British Pharmaceutical Industry (ABPI)
020 7930 3477
www.abpi.org.uk

PHOTOGRAPHY

Photographers produce visual images of many kinds, either working to a brief set by a client or employer, or exploring subject matter they have chosen themselves. Photographers use a range of photographic equipment, including digital cameras (a few still use conventional cameras), lighting systems and computer programs developed to manipulate photographs. Some photographers also develop their own work, using either traditional darkroom methods or digital processing. The subject matter you work with is determined by the field of photography in which you work. Typical aspects of the job include choosing locations and subjects, selecting appropriate cameras and accessories, and setting up lighting and background. Photographers also have to compose the picture, whether this is discussing a pose with a model or arranging still-life objects.

Advertising/editorial photographer

Advertising photographers take pictures for magazines and brochures. These pictures either advertise a product or illustrate a story. Many advertising photographers specialise in particular subjects such as food, cars, portraiture or landscapes.

Corporate photographer

Corporate photographers work for large businesses and other organisations taking pictures for annual reports, promotional brochures or in-house journals. Some people working in this field become specialist industrial photographers, taking pictures of the manufacturing process as well as finished products.

Fashion photographer

Fashion photographers take pictures of models promoting clothes, shoes, jewellery, cosmetics and hairstyles. At the top end of the market they work for well-known magazines, taking pictures of famous models. At the other end of this market, photographers take hundreds of pictures for mail order catalogues.

Food photographer

Food photographers produce images for magazines, menus, food packaging and promotional brochures. They have to create colourful, appealing images and often have to work very quickly as the food they are photographing begins to melt, dry out or collapse. They must have a good eye for detail and colour. They might be photographing just one apple, or an elaborate dining table set with everything for a festive banquet.

General practice photographer

General photographers take pictures for a range of clients in their local community. A great deal of the work involves wedding photography, but these photographers often cover community events and family occasions. Many do some work for local newspapers that don't employ in-house press photographers. Those photographers who do specialise mainly in weddings or other special occasions are sometimes described as social photographers rather than general practice photographers.

Medical photographer

(see Medical illustrator)

Press photographer

While some reporters and journalists take their own photographs, there is still a specific role for a press photographer. Press photographers either work for a particular newspaper or magazine, or they work freelance, selling their images to whoever wishes to buy them. They take photographs that reflect everything from serious news and current affairs to sport and lifestyle pictures. A press photographer works to take images that best document an event or capture a moment. Some press photographers specialise in particular types of picture, e.g. sport, entertainment, celebrity or news events.

Scientific/technical photographer

Some photographers specialise in taking pictures for scientific journals and research papers. They may have to work with microscope slides as well as living subjects. The work of the wildlife photographer is a highly specialised aspect of this type of photography.

Entry, qualifications and training

While there are no formal entry requirements, this is a very competitive field. There are several courses you can do, and being able to combine a course with a good portfolio of your work and some relevant work experience is the best way to improve your chances of success. Courses are available at many levels, including City & Guilds, BTEC Certificates and Diplomas, A levels and degree courses. Many people start work as a photographer's assistant to gain basic skills and knowledge. The British Institute of Professional Photography (BIPP) awards the Professional Qualifying Examination (PQE) to photographers – the award is based on assessing a photographer's portfolio to ensure that it is of a good professional standard.

Personal attributes

These vary according to your chosen specialism, but all photographers must have the ability to perceive and recreate visual impact in a creative way. They must all be competent with technical equipment and normally need great patience. For most jobs, photographers must be able to work well with people, whether it is as subjects or as fellow members of a work team. They also need good business management skills.

Earnings

Initial earnings are between the minimum wage and £22,000. Many photographers have to start as photographer's assistants. Successful photographers earn between £20,000 and £30,000; a few may earn up to £60,000. Many photographers work freelance or are self-employed.

Info

Association of Photographers
020 7739 6669
www.the-aop.org

British Institute of Professional Photography
01772 367968
www.bipp.com

Creative & Cultural Skills
020 7015 1800
www.ccskills.org.uk

Screen Skills
020 7713 9800
www.screenskills.com

Master Photographers Association (MPA)
01325 356555
www.thempa.com

Photographic technician

Photographic technicians work either in large photographic laboratories or in mini labs in high street stores. If you work in a professional laboratory, you may use traditional darkroom techniques developing films. Much of the work now on the high street and in traditional laboratories involves using computerised equipment producing prints or CDs from images taken on digital cameras. In both cases the work involves producing pictures of the best possible quality. Technicians check for quality, analyse problems and may give feedback to customers on what could have gone wrong. Based in high street stores, the work also involves dealing directly with customers, packaging pictures, and taking orders and payments.

Digital imaging technician

Digital imaging technicians work for professional photo finishing laboratories and picture libraries. The work usually involves discussing the format and finish of an image with a client, scanning images into a computer, using specialised software to manipulate the images, change colour, resize or crop a picture where appropriate, printing the finished image onto paper, saving it on CD or uploading it to a website. Digital imaging technicians are often responsible for building up banks of images that can then be purchased by clients.

Entry, qualifications and training

You may not need formal qualifications to work in a high street mini lab, although some employers may ask for GCSEs, including maths and a science. To work in a professional laboratory you are far more likely to need qualifications in photography, such as an HND, a foundation degree, or a degree. If you want to work in digital imaging, it may also be helpful to build up a portfolio of images on which you have worked; you also need to be competent with relevant computer software packages such as Photoshop.

Personal attributes

In all cases you need a genuine interest in photography. For all positions you need good basic IT skills. To work for a professional digital imaging lab you need a high level of desktop publishing skill. You need good communication skills, to be able to explain problems to customers, or to clarify a brief from a client. You have to be good at working as part of a team.

Earnings

For photographic technicians, starting salaries are between the minimum wage and £16,000 on the high street, possibly more in professional laboratories. Digital imaging technicians earn from £20,000 to £35,000.

Info

British Institute of Professional Photography (BIPP)
01772 367968
www.bipp.com

Screen Skills
020 7713 9800
www.screenskills.com

Association of Photographers
020 7739 6669
www.the-aop.org

PHYSICIST

Physicists study the world around us; they try to understand and explain why and how objects, from the universe itself to the smallest atomic particle, exist and behave in the way they do. As well as tackling these profound questions, physicists apply their knowledge in many practical ways – anything from the development of the next generation of mobile phones to the forecasting of climate change. Using mathematical techniques and computer modelling, they can have useful input into many industries. Physicists could be involved in the development of new medical instruments, the exploration of new methods of power generation or the investigation of artificial intelligence and robotics. Physicists work closely with many other scientists and engineers, including materials engineers, biomedical engineers, astronomers and information technologists. Physicists also work in teaching, academic research and scientific publishing.

Entry, qualifications and training

This is a complex and intellectually challenging profession. Employers normally require at least a good honours degree in physics, applied physics or engineering, but many applicants will also have a Master's degree or a PhD. To gain a place on a physics degree course you need five GCSEs and A levels in maths and physics. If you do not have these A levels you may be able to do a bridging course or a foundation degree in science to meet these requirements.

Personal attributes

Above all, you need an enquiring mind and the ability to think in new directions and find imaginative ways of tackling problems. You also have to be logical and methodical in your thinking and you must be a good communicator. You have to be patient – you may be working on something for a long time before you get any answers, or the answers you would like. You have to be able to work successfully on your own, or as part of a team.

Earnings

New entrants earn £24,000 to £30,000. Research physicists who have just completed PhDs earn around £30,000. In industry, physicists earn from £30,000 to £55,000 plus. Senior researchers and project leaders in academia earn £35,000 to £70,000.

Info

SEMTA 0845 643 9001 www.semta.org.uk	**Institute of Physics** 020 7470 4800 www.iop.org

---

PHYSIOTHERAPIST

Physiotherapists treat patients suffering from a wide variety of diseases, conditions or injuries by physical means. They help people who have had a stroke to regain the use of lost functions, treat sports injuries and people with arthritis, and help children with cerebral palsy to learn to walk. The techniques used include massage and manipulation, developing and prescribing exercise, electrotherapy and hydrotherapy. Most physiotherapists work in the NHS but there are many opportunities now for employment in industry, sports clinics, schools and private practice.

Sports physiotherapist

The increasing number of opportunities to work with sportsmen and women, both professional and amateur, has become a rather specialised and growing area within physiotherapy. Sports physiotherapists must hold a first-aid certificate and be a chartered physiotherapist. There is a special-interest group within the Chartered Society of Physiotherapy (CSP) for therapists who specialise in treating sporting injuries. There are also several postgraduate diplomas and Master's courses available in sports physiotherapy.

Entry, qualifications and training

To be registered with the Health and Care Professions Council and the Chartered Society of Physiotherapy you must complete an approved degree in physiotherapy.

Entry requirements for these degrees in England, Wales and Northern Ireland usually include three A levels at grade C or above, including a biological science. You also need five GCSEs grades 9–4, including maths, English and a range of science subjects. In Scotland, you need five H grades (AABBB) with at least two science subjects. Appropriate Access to Higher Education courses may also be accepted.

Personal attributes

You must enjoy working with people, putting them at ease, explaining treatments and teaching exercises. You must have a good grasp of physiology and have good manual dexterity. You should be good at observing people and you also need to be able to work well as part of a team.

Earnings

Newly qualified physiotherapists earn between £22,100 and £28,700, with experience and responsibility this rises to £26,500 to around £41,700. Working in inner London you earn an additional 20 per cent and 15 per cent in outer London.

Info

Health and Care Professions Council (HCPC)
0300 500 6184
www.hcpc-uk.org

NHS Careers
0345 60 60 655
www.healthcareers.nhs.uk

Chartered Society of Physiotherapy
020 7306 6666
www.csp.org.uk

PLUMBER

(see Construction for Interior and finishing trades)

PODIATRIST

Podiatrists used to be known as chiropodists. There are still some chiropodists in practice, but new entrants to this profession will train as podiatrists. Podiatrists are concerned with the health of feet. Those working in the NHS deal with problems caused by diabetes or arthritis and may work with those suffering from sports injuries. Ailments such as corns, bunions and malformed nails are more likely to be dealt with by those in private practice.

Podiatrists perform minor operations under local anaesthetic. They may work in the NHS in hospitals, clinics or health centres, or in private practice or large organisations. Many undertake postgraduate training to specialise in areas such as sports medicine, biomechanics or podiatric surgery.

Entry, qualifications and training

To practise as a state registered podiatrist you must take a degree in podiatry approved by the Health and Care Professions Council (HCPC). You then register with the HCPC and The Society of Chiropodists and Podiatrists. To do a degree in podiatry you usually need five GCSEs grades 9–4, including maths, English and a biological science. You also need three A levels, including one biological science. If you already have a degree in a biological science you can gain exemption from part of the degree course. Once you are in practice you must undertake annual continuing professional development activities monitored by the HCPC.

If you do not wish to study for a degree, you can work in the private sector as a foot health practitioner and you can take a diploma in foot healthcare. Foot care practitioners can register with Foot Health Care Practitioners but you are not obliged to do so to practise. A similar role in the NHS is that of chiropody or podiatry assistant. Qualifications for these roles vary, but many employers and NHS Trusts require you to have three or four GCSEs grades 9–4, including a science subject. Some NHS areas offer cadet or apprenticeship schemes in this work.

Personal attributes

You have to be good with people, able to reassure them and provide them with information. You need good practical skills with good manual dexterity. You should be able to work on your own, but also as part of a healthcare team. You need to be well organised and good at managing your own time. If you are in private practice you will also need good business skills.

Earnings

Newly qualified podiatrists earn between £23,000 and £29,600, with experience and responsibility this rises to £28,000 to £43,000. Working in inner London you earn an additional 20 per cent and 15 per cent in outer London. Private practitioners set their own charges, but generally earn between £20,000 and £30,000. Assistants or foot health practitioners earn between £15,500 and £22,200.

Info

Institute of Chiropodists and Podiatrists 01704 546141 www.iocp.org.uk	**Health and Care Professions Council (HCPC)** 0300 500 6184 www.hcpc-uk.org
NHS Careers 0345 60 60 655 www.healthcareers.nhs.uk	**British Chiropody and Podiatry Association** 01628 632440 www.bcha-uk.org

POLICE SERVICE

Police forces employ staff in many roles other than those of police officer. As well as the roles mentioned here, they employ staff to handle telephone calls from members of the public, and staff to handle the general administration and finance of local police services.

Police community support officer

Police community support officers (PCSOs) are civilians, rather than serving police officers. They support and report to local police. They patrol public areas, providing a visible presence to reassure the public. In some areas they have powers to direct traffic or issue arrest warrants, and they often work at events such as football matches or public demonstrations.

Entry, qualifications and training

There are no formal academic requirements or age restrictions for applying to become a PCSO. Applicants must be UK, EU or Commonwealth citizens. Foreign nationals who have indefinite leave to remain in the United Kingdom and the right to work here are also eligible. While each police force sets its own entry requirements for PCSOs, they all tend to use similar selection criteria. You apply via an application form and after an initial screening of these forms you will be invited to an interview. You will also have to sit a written test and take part in role-play exercises to assess how you would cope with the range of situations the job throws up. Many forces set fitness tests, because you may have to undertake long foot patrols. Thorough background and security checks are made on all successful applicants. Having a criminal record does not necessarily exclude you from applying, but any convictions for violent or public order offences will certainly disqualify an applicant. Training takes between three weeks and three months, and is mainly classroom-based; it covers many aspects of the work, including using computer systems, first aid, radio communications and patrolling.

Personal attributes

You need very good people skills, and to be confident dealing with difficult or sensitive situations. You need to be able to work on your own or as part of a team, to take decisions or seek support as appropriate. You must be able to keep calm in pressured situations and you should be able to remain alert and observant.

Earnings

Pay starts at £18,000 rising to £20,000 to £23,000 with experience. In London salaries are higher – up to £26,500. The average salary for a police community support officer is around £25,700.

Fingerprint officer

At any scene of crime, accident, or other unexplained event, many objects, clothing, weapons, doors, windows, furniture or weapons will carry fingerprints of people who have touched those objects. Fingerprint officers work as part of the police team checking the fingerprints as part of the attempt to solve a crime. They compare fingerprints of suspects with those found on objects and against fingerprints already held in the national database. They also add fingerprints to that database. While much of the work is analytical and based in a laboratory or a fingerprint bureau, fingerprint officers also visit scenes of crime to offer expert advice or take fingerprints. They may also have to take fingerprints of deceased persons. Part of the work would include writing reports or presenting evidence in court.

Entry, qualifications and training

In all cases you will need four GCSEs grades 9–4, including English, maths and a science. Applicants also have to pass aptitude tests. Some police forces prefer you to have A levels and to have had some experience of analytical work in a laboratory. Fingerprint officers start as trainees and through a combination of residential courses and learning on the job become fully qualified. The first residential course lasts four weeks and is at foundation level; you can then work through intermediate and advanced levels to fully qualify. A degree in a relevant subject such as forensic science will give you an advantage.

Personal attributes

You need to be calm, patient and meticulous in your approach. You have to be good at working as part of a team, sharing information with others. You may have to be emotionally resilient and have a strong stomach if, for example, you are taking prints from a decomposing body. You have to be well organised with your record keeping. If you appear in court you need to be calm and clear and be able to express yourself accurately.

Earnings

Trainees earn £17,000 to £21,500 – once qualified pay is £24,500 to £35,000. When qualified you may also receive extra pay for working shifts or weekends.

Police officer

Police officers are recruited as trainee police constables (PCs). PCs work in all aspects of policing, including preventing and investigating crime, maintaining public order and protecting people and property. PCs work from police stations or out on the beat, either on foot or in patrol cars. There are many opportunities to specialise in particular areas of police work once you have completed your probationary period.

There is a separate British Transport Police Force, which operates on passenger transport services to prevent crime, protect public safety and maintain public order.

Entry, qualifications and training

Each police force does its own recruiting, but they all work to a nationally agreed competency framework. While there are no formal educational requirements for joining the police service, there is a demanding selection procedure. Joining the police service is open to British or Commonwealth nationals and also to other foreign nationals who have no restrictions on their right to work in the United Kingdom. Applicants must be aged 18 or over. The first stage is to complete an application form and a medical questionnaire. If you are successful at this stage, you are invited to a selection centre to sit a variety of physical and psychometric tests. The physical fitness tests relate to tasks you would have to perform as a serving police officer. Sessions to help you prepare for these tests and to know what to expect are run throughout the United Kingdom several times a year.

The psychometric tests include written numeracy, literacy, information handling and reasoning tests, plus personality tests to assess your suitability for the demands of the job. The selection procedure also includes an interview and a full medical, with eyesight and hearing tests. You must have good vision and colour vision and be physically fit. If you pass the selection procedure, references are followed up and security checks, including your financial status, are made. Minor convictions or cautions do not necessarily preclude you from joining the police, but you must declare these.

New recruits work a probationary period of two years. During this time, training is a mixture of on the job with the local police service and college-based learning. Everyone goes through the Initial Police Learning and Development Programme. During this period, trainees work towards the NVQ level 3 in Policing and either during or shortly after this two-year period they are also expected to complete the NVQ level 4 in Policing.

As a probationer or serving officer you may be able to join the High Potential Development Scheme (HPDS), which offers accelerated training and development and helps your promotion prospects.

All police officers will undergo a wide variety of training throughout their career, enabling them to cope with changes in the law, social policy, information management and technology.

Personal attributes

You need a mature attitude and the ability to assess and weigh up situations quickly and then take appropriate action. You must be able to follow orders and have the confidence to instruct others. You must be able to stay calm in difficult situations and you must be emotionally resilient. You need excellent and varied people skills, to be able to be confident, assertive, diplomatic, reassuring, patient or firm as the occasion demands. You must be effective as part of a team, but also capable of working on your own.

Earnings

Salaries are set by individual police forces – the average starting salary is around £21,000 to £23,000. Constables earn between £21,000 and £40,000. Sergeants earn from £41,500 to £45,000 and Inspectors and Chief Inspectors between £51,000 and £61,000.

Info

College of Policing (Recruitment)
recruit.college.police.uk

Police service UK (for details of local forces)
www.police.uk/forces

Skills for Justice
www.sfjuk.com

Police Scotland
www.scotland.police.uk

Police Service of Northern Ireland (PSNI)
www.joinpsni.co.uk

POLITICAL WORK

Although politics offers relatively few career opportunities, there are a number of jobs in politics associated with supporting the work of politicians, political parties, undertaking political research and lobbying political bodies on behalf of interest groups. There are also positions in administrative, human resource, information technology and financial roles with political organisations of every kind.

Elected politician

Politicians for the House of Commons, the Scottish Parliament, the Welsh Assembly, the Northern Ireland Assembly and the European Parliament are all elected, so they don't 'apply' for their jobs in the traditional sense. Their work involves representing the concerns of their constituents and contributing to the process of decision making by joining in debates, asking questions and voting.

Political researcher

Many different kinds of organisations employ political researchers; MPs, political parties, trade unions, public relations consultancies and non-government organisations are the most likely employers. The work involves detailed research, by monitoring the media, the daily work of both Houses of Parliament and the institutions of the European Union. Researchers also provide detailed answers to questions on almost every topic imaginable.

Entry, qualifications and training

Politicians do not need specific qualifications and come from many different career backgrounds; law is one of the more common. There is a trend towards more people being 'career politicians' who work their way up through such jobs as political researchers or political party administrative staff. Most political researchers have at least a degree and may start by doing voluntary work.

Personal attributes

Politicians have to be good communicators who are well organised and able to balance the needs of their constituency work with demands in Westminster, or wherever they are based. Good organisational and interpersonal skills as well as a rigorous attitude to information research are essential for other political jobs.

Earnings

Junior research staff earn between £17,000 and £20,000; up to £23,000 in London. If you work for a politician, there are no general guidelines on what you should be paid. Senior researchers earn from £20,000 to £35,000. MPs earn £79,468.

POSTAL DELIVERY WORKER

Postal delivery workers deliver mail to private and business addresses. They each have a round including several hundred addresses they visit on foot, by bicycle or by van. Postmen and women also sort the mail for their own rounds; some mail is still sorted by hand. Postmen and women may also be responsible for collecting mail from postboxes, local post offices and from business addresses.

Some postmen and women work at district or central offices, sorting mail to be sent to other areas of the United Kingdom or overseas.

There are many other delivery and administrative opportunities within the Royal Mail, including work behind post office counters.

Entry, qualifications and training

There are no formal entry qualifications, but applicants have to pass an aptitude test that assesses their suitability for postal work. Once employed, it is possible to work towards NVQ level 2 in Mail Delivery Services. This covers mail sorting, mail handling and working with automated systems. Apprenticeships are available for applicants aged 16–18, but many postal delivery workers are taken on at age 18 or over. If your job involves driving, you must have a full, clean driving licence.

Personal attributes

You need good basic literacy and numeracy skills and you must not mind doing repetitive tasks. It is essential to be physically fit, reliable and honest. You need to be polite and friendly, but not mind working on your own.

Earnings

Earnings range between £13,500 and £25,000 for this role. It is also possible to earn more through working unsocial hours, taking on driving duties, or other responsibilities.

Info

Royal Mail Group plc
www.royalmailgroup.com

Skills for Logistics
0117 927 8800
www.skillsforlogistics.co.uk

PRINTING

In the world of electronic communication we are still surrounded by many examples of hard-copy printed material. Printing is all about communication, including books, magazines, newspapers, posters, greetings cards, forms, business cards or address labels. Printers are also involved in other products, from wallpaper and floor coverings to advertising slogans on food packaging. The printing industry employs people in several roles – in total it employs more than 200,000 people.

Camera/scanner operator

Camera/scanner operators are part of the pre-press department scanning photographs, drawings, graphics and other visual images that are to appear on the finished printed product, be it the cover of a book, the page of a newspaper or the design on a business card.

Finishing department

Printed products are usually produced in large flat sheets or reels. To convert and finish sheets or reels into books, brochures or magazines, the material must be folded, stitched, sewn and trimmed. A range of specialised machinery is used to produce the finished product at high speed. Great care is needed at this stage to avoid faults, which could result in scrapping the product and financial loss to the company.

Graphic design

(see also Art and design)

This is the most artistic job in the printing industry. Designers liaise with clients, understand their needs and transform ideas into high-quality printed products. A mastery of computers and a complete understanding of processes, techniques, typography and colour are required. Applicants normally enter the industry after a National Certificate diploma or higher-level course in graphic design.

Pre-press department

Most setting is via electronic transfer or CD. The pre-press operator uses a computer keyboard and mouse to set type and arrange the page, which is output to film or direct to the printing plate. An error in the pre-press department could result in the scrapping of thousands of books or products.

Printing department

This is where ink is applied to paper or other materials, by a variety of large and small printing machines. Such machines are complex and often computer controlled. They are managed by one or more craftspeople who control the physics and chemistry of the press to ensure that each copy produced is perfect.

Entry, qualifications and training

Although you don't always need academic qualifications to get into printing, most companies do ask for GCSEs grades 9–4 in English, maths, science and IT. The range of qualifications acceptable for office and management jobs is wide. Some jobs require GCSEs; others are open to applicants with A levels or a degree. Training is mostly on the job, and the British Printing Industry Federation runs a number of short courses and also provides information on companies offering training. You can work towards a range of different NVQs, depending on what work you do and what is of special interest. Possibilities include Machine Printing levels 2 and 3, offering several options, such as lithography, web offset and screen printing; Digital Print Production levels 2 and 3, with units on machine operation, digital artwork and pre-press work; and Mechanised Print Finishing and Binding, covering finishing methods in general print and newspapers.

Personal attributes

For many roles in print you need good colour vision and excellent manual dexterity. You need to have a real interest in the finished product and how it looks. You should be keen to learn new skills and be able to adapt quickly as technology changes fast in this field. You should be able to work well as part of a team, but also to take responsibility for your own work.

Earnings

The variety of jobs leads to a wide range of salaries. On the machine operating and finishing side, salaries start at £16,000 to £22,000. Where jobs are more technically demanding, earnings can reach £40,000. Managers earn £18,000 to £40,000. Many posts include shift-work allowances and opportunities to earn overtime.

Info

British Printing Industries Federation (BPIF)
01676 526030
www.britishprint.com

PRISON SERVICE

The prison service includes many types of institutions, from high-security prisons to open prisons and young offenders' institutions. As well as prison governors and prison officers the prison service employs staff in catering, healthcare and education. The roles described below are those which are specific to the prison service.

Prison governor/manager

As prison governor (often referred to as manager these days), your role is to manage the day-to-day running of your establishment. Each establishment may have one or more assistant governors to take on particular areas of responsibility. As a governor or assistant governor you could be involved in many aspects of running your prison. These include security, ensuring that inmates and staff are safe and having plans in place in case of emergencies, dealing with the prison's budget, recruiting and training staff, dealing with disciplinary issues and carrying out inspections. Governors have to ensure that government policies on all aspects of prison life are adhered to. It is the governor who has to talk to the press if something does go wrong. Governors and assistant governors plan how the prison might best be developed to reduce the likelihood of inmates reoffending once they return to society.

Entry, qualifications and training

There are two routes to becoming an assistant governor. Serving prison officers who have been identified as demonstrating great qualities of leadership may be invited to apply to join the National Offender Management Scheme (NOMS), which is an intensive management development programme. Graduates can apply to go straight on to the NOMS, but there are only around 20 places each year, so competition is strong. Your degree subject is not important; it is possessing the right mix of skills that is vital. Graduates go through a series of rigorous selection tests to try to gain a place.

Personal attributes

This is a challenging career. You need excellent leadership skills and self-confidence. You must be able to react quickly and calmly in potentially difficult situations. You must be firm and assertive and yet a good listener too. You need really good administrative and financial skills and must possess the ability to work under pressure.

Prison officer

Prison officers are employed in prisons, detention centres, young offender institutions and remand centres. The work involves supervising prisoners inside the place of detention, escorting them to courts and other prisons and, if relevant, teaching a skill or trade. Officers also deliver programmes that help prisoners address their offending behaviour. Some specialist prison officers are employed as hospital officers, dog handlers, security experts and caterers.

Entry, qualifications and training

Five GCSEs, including maths and English, are required and applicants must pass an aptitude test and an interview. Training is a mixture of time spent at a local prison and residential courses at an officers' training school. In Scotland, the requirement is five standard grades (1, 2 or 3) or equivalent (including maths and English) or three years' experience managing people. A good level of physical fitness is required. NVQs in Custodial Care are available at levels 2 and 3, as is Custodial Healthcare level 3 and Youth Justice levels 3 and 4. There is special training for caterers, dog handlers, physical education instructors and medical staff. An accelerated promotion scheme exists for graduate entrants.

Personal attributes

Officers should be positive thinkers with humanity and common sense; they must be good listeners, assertive, have excellent communication skills and the ability to mix with a wide range of people.

Earnings

In England and Wales, new entrants earn around £20,545 With experience this rises to around £31,000. Senior officers earn around £31,000 to £33,000. The manager of a large prison can earn £60,000 plus.

Info

Skills for Justice
www.sfjuk.com

Police Service of Northern Ireland (PSNI)
www.joinpsni.co.uk

HM Prisons Service
www.justice.gov.uk/jobs/prisons

National Offender Management Service
www.nomscareers.com

PRIVATE INVESTIGATOR

Private investigators work with individuals, businesses, insurance companies, solicitors and other organisations. They are often self-employed, but may be employed by organisations such as law firms or insurance companies. The work is very varied, including tracing missing persons, investigating insurance claims and presenting legal or financial documents to private individuals and to businesses. Private investigators also investigate commercial piracy and fraudulent activities. Work activities are varied, including interviewing people, carrying out detailed research and surveillance operations.

Entry, qualifications and training

There are no formal entry qualifications, but many private investigators have worked in other security roles – it is normally a second career. A good standard of general education is important. All private investigators must be licensed by the Security Industry Authority (SIA) and the SIA is in the process of developing both the licensing system and appropriate qualifications. The Academy of Professional Investigation runs a level 3 advanced diploma in private investigation. The Academy also offers advice on where you might obtain some training.

Personal attributes

You must have excellent powers of observation and concentration. You need good people skills to be able to talk to people and encourage people to share information with you. You need good research and information-gathering abilities and some knowledge of IT. You should be self-confident, with good business awareness.

Earnings

Earnings vary. New entrants earn around £13,000. Private investigators on regular salaries earn between £15,000 and £25,000. It is harder to predict incomes for those who are self-employed, but £20,000 to £25,000 is a reasonable estimate. Top investigators can earn £50,000 to £100,000.

Info

Security Industry Authority (SIA)
www.sia.homeoffice.gov.uk

World Association of Professional Investigators (WAPI)
08709 099 970
www.wapi.com

Institute of Professional Investigators (IPI)
01707 371144
www.ipi.org.uk

Academy of Professional Investigation (API)
01444 441 111

Association of British Investigators (ABI)
020 8191 7500
www.theabi.org.uk

PROBATION OFFICER

In England and Wales probation officers are employed either by the National Probation Service (NPS) or by one of the 20 or more private sector criminal rehabilitation companies (CRCs). The NPS is responsible for supervising the higher risk offenders, while the CRCs manage lower risk offenders.

Probation officers work with people who have committed criminal offences. They work with prisoners both while they are serving sentences and after release, to try to ensure that they do not reoffend. They supervise offenders who have community rather than custodial sentences. They interview offenders and try to help them understand the impact and consequences of what they have done. They supervise group activities of various kinds and they prepare reports for courts, magistrates and prison officials.

Probation services officer

Probation services officers (PSOs) work with probation officers. Your work could involve supervising offenders on community projects, helping offenders address some of the issues that led them to offend (drug dependency, lack of a job, family strife, etc). You could also be visiting offenders in prison and helping them to readjust to life after their sentences have been completed.

Entry, qualifications and training

A college course, such as a diploma in public services, a qualification in youth and community work, or A levels may help a direct application. You could also consider a probation services practitioner advanced apprenticeship. For up-to-date information check the National Probation Service website.

Personal attributes

You need a mature and calm approach to your work. You must have excellent written and spoken communication skills. You must have an understanding approach to people and their problems, but you also need firm confidence to challenge and question behaviour. You must be caring, but also emotionally resilient. You need to be able to work well as part of a team and you must have excellent organisational skills. You have to develop a good understanding of the law and legal processes.

Earnings

PSOs on full-time contracts earn £22,000 to £27,000. PSOs on temporary contracts earn less than this. Probation officers can earn up to £40,000.

Info

Skills for Justice
www.sfjuk.com

National Probation Service
0300 047 6325
www.gov.uk/government/organisations/
national-probation-service

Probation Board for Northern Ireland
028 9052 2522
www.pbni.org.uk

Ministry of Justice
020 3334 3555
www.justice.gov.uk

PROJECT MANAGER

'Project manager' is one of those job titles that can leave you feeling perplexed. What industries do project managers work in? What do they do? A project manager can work in any industry and it is his or her job to see that any kind of project is completed according to a client's requirements, within budget and on time. The project manager liaises with all the people working on the project and keeps the client informed of progress or notified of any unforeseen problems. The types of projects managed might include setting up a new department within a business, introducing a new IT system, developing a new market for products, overseeing a construction project, devising a consultation process with a local community or redeveloping a piece of land that has fallen into disuse. These are just a few examples.

Entry, qualifications and training

These may be as varied as the projects themselves, but generally project management is a fairly senior job. Most project managers are graduates and have experience in the sector in which they are managing, e.g. finance, human resources, engineering, construction or information technology. There are some degree courses in project management, but other useful subjects include business, engineering, accounting, construction, science or technology. Most project managers develop their skills while working and the Association for Project Management offers professional qualifications towards which you can work.

Personal attributes

Being a good leader, able to motivate people from different work teams, is very important. You must be an excellent communicator and have very good problem-solving skills. In fact, you need the knack of anticipating possible problems before they arise. You must be very good at working to deadlines yourself and ensuring that other people do the same. In addition, you need a good knowledge of the particular sector in which you are project managing.

Earnings

Starting salaries are from £25,000 to £50,000 – the variation results from project management being a part of so many industries. Project management is rarely someone's first job. Senior project managers can earn up to £75,000.

Info

Association for Project Management
0845 458 1944
www.apm.org.uk

Chartered Management Institute
020 7497 0580
www.managers.org.uk

PSYCHOLOGY

Psychologists work in many different settings: in hospitals and healthcare, in schools and for local education authorities, in industry, in marketing and business, for the police and criminal justice system, and in sport. While these settings may be very different, all psychologists work to measure, understand, predict and assess human behaviour.

Entry, qualifications and training

For most branches of psychology, you must obtain Graduate Basis for Registration (GBR) with the British Psychological Society (BPS). This means completing a three- or four-year degree in psychology, accredited by the BPS, and it is important to check the status of any psychology degree before you begin your studies, if you think you may wish to register as a chartered psychologist. If your undergraduate degree is not in psychology you can start by doing a BPS-approved conversion course and sitting a qualifying examination. Consult the BPS website for details of these courses. Further detail on specific qualifications for the different branches of psychology is given in the following sections.

Clinical psychologist

Clinical psychologists work mainly in health and social care settings with clients of all ages who are facing a variety of mental health and emotional problems. Clinical psychologists work as part of a multidisciplinary team devising programmes to help people who are suffering from such conditions as severe anxiety or phobias, depression, addictive behaviour, or behaviours resulting from neurological or physical injury. They assess their clients' mental and emotional states and may offer advice, counselling or therapy.

Entry, qualifications and training

In addition to a BPS accredited degree, clinical psychologists must complete a three-year NHS-funded doctorate programme in clinical psychology. Places on these programmes are highly sought after, so you normally need a First or 2.1 degree plus some relevant work experience. Work as an assistant in a clinical psychology department is most useful, but course providers will give you advice on what work experience is suitable.

Consumer psychologist

Consumer psychologists do not have to be chartered with the BPS. They work in marketing in commercial businesses and other organisations, trying to understand and make use of the psychological basis of the choices that consumers make and why they choose to buy a certain product or service. Much of their work involves interviewing people or organising focus groups. They interpret the results of these interviews and discussions to help marketers understand and exploit trends in consumer behaviour.

Entry, qualifications and training

Most consumer psychologists have a degree either in psychology or in a marketing discipline where the course has covered consumer psychology in some depth. Some consumer psychologists start their career in other roles in marketing departments.

Counselling psychologist

Counselling psychologists work with children and adults of all ages, helping them to deal with difficulties of many kinds. These could include psychological conditions such as anxiety or depression. Problems may be associated with life situations such as domestic violence or bereavement. Sometimes the problems are associated with substance abuse or eating disorders. Counselling psychologists advise their clients on ways of coping with situations and moving on.

Entry, qualifications and training

In addition to the BPS accredited degree, counselling psychologists need to complete a postgraduate qualification in counselling psychology, also approved by the BPS.

Educational psychologist

Educational psychologists work with school students and other young people who are experiencing difficulties in learning and making progress with their education. Students may encounter difficulties because they have a learning disability, a sensory impairment or some emotional problem that is getting in the way. Educational psychologists work with individual students, with parents, teachers and other professionals, to try to find ways round the problem. They may advise students on new ways to learn, encourage them to talk about problems or set up particular programmes of study and activities.

Entry, qualifications and training

In addition to a BPS accredited degree, educational psychologists in England, Wales and Northern Ireland must complete a three-year doctorate in Educational Psychology; in Scotland they must complete a two-year Master's in Educational Psychology plus one year of supervised practice.

Forensic psychologist

Forensic psychologists work mainly in the prison and probation services. The aim of their work is to try to develop interventions that stop offenders from reoffending and help them find ways to change their behaviours. Work may be one-to-one or in groups. They also advise prison governors and other prison and probation staff on what treatment programmes and institutional policies might be most effective in helping reduce offending. They work closely with the court system, with victims and with witnesses. They have to evaluate the programmes they have set up to measure their effectiveness.

Entry, qualifications and training

In addition to a BPS accredited degree, forensic psychologists must complete a Master's degree in forensic psychology (one year full time, two years part time) and then undergo two years' supervised practice.

Health psychologist

This is a new and evolving area, and is the practice and application of psychological methods to the study of behaviour relevant to illness and healthcare. Health psychologists work in community, social care and healthcare settings examining the psychological aspects of illness. They help people implement programmes of behaviour that might prevent health problems and they also work with people learning to cope with various aspects of chronic and acute illnesses. At present, only a small number of health psychologists are employed by the NHS.

Entry, qualifications and training

In addition to a BPS accredited degree in psychology, health psychologists must complete a Master's degree in health psychology and two years' supervised work experience.

Occupational psychologist

Occupational psychologists work in organisations of many kinds or for private consultants. They examine how particular work tasks affect the well-being or performance of workers and they also determine which personal characteristics allow someone to perform tasks well. A major part of their work is in designing recruitment tests that will help employers select the most likely candidates to succeed in particular work roles. Occupational psychologists also work with organisations to solve issues of conflict within a work team, or to identify possible new management strategies.

Entry, qualifications and training

In addition to a BPS accredited degree in psychology, occupational psychologists need to complete a Master's degree in occupational psychology plus two years' supervised practice. An alternative route is to undertake three years' supervised practice and study for the BPS Certificate in Occupational Psychology.

Sports and exercise psychologist

Sports psychologists work with sportsmen and women, helping them to improve their performance by examining the psychological aspects of their games and strategies. Sports psychologists teach techniques like relaxation and visualisation, to help people to perform better. They also undertake research on the general effects of taking part in sport and physical exercise. Sports psychologists are often self-employed, though some are employed by sports teams or by umbrella organisations for particular sports.

Entry, qualifications and training

This is a fairly new branch of psychology, so there is no formal training route in place yet. Most entrants will have a degree in psychology or in sports science, followed by a Master's degree in sports psychology. This is followed by a period of supervised work experience.

Personal attributes

Psychologists have to have excellent interpersonal skills, and be easily able to work with and listen to people who may be very distressed. They have to be good at observing and highly perceptive. In many roles they need good numeracy skills and the ability to write good reports.

Earnings

Outside the NHS, salaries vary. Some counselling psychologists are self-employed. Educational psychologists receive a bursary from their placement provider during training, but amounts vary. Newly qualified educational psychologists' salaries start at around £30,000. Trainee forensic psychologists earn between £25,520 and £28,776; senior forensic psychologists can earn up to £48,000, and more with specialist experience. Occupational psychologists earn between £25,000 and £45,000. Many sports and exercise psychologists are self-employed; earnings to start with are normally £20,000 to £27,000, but higher with experience and a good reputation. Most experienced psychologists in all branches of the profession earn between £25,000 and £50,000.

Info

British Association for Counselling and Psychotherapy (BACP)
01455 883300
www.bacp.co.uk

British Psychological Society (BPS)
0116 254 9568
www.bps.org.uk

NHS Careers
0345 60 60 655
www.healthcareers.nhs.uk

Health and Care Professions Council (HCPC)
0300 500 6184
www.hcpc-uk.org

PSYCHOTHERAPIST

Psychotherapy is a generic term within which there are many specialist disciplines. People may practise as psychoanalytic psychotherapists, as cognitive or behavioural psychotherapists, or as counsellors, with varying degrees of training and experience; however, there are plans to introduce greater regulation.

Psychotherapists may work with individuals of any age, couples and families, or groups, resolving problems such as over-shyness, over-aggression, sleeping disorders, separation difficulties, behavioural problems, eating difficulties, self-harm and depression. They work in hospitals, in- and outpatient clinics, child and family consultation centres, GPs' surgeries, special schools for disturbed children, and in private practice.

Entry, qualifications and training

The picture is very different depending on whether you want to go into private practice or work for a recognised public body such as the NHS or HM Prison Service. At present, for private practice there are no specific entry requirements and a wide range of courses of varying quality is available. If you are aiming for salaried employment with a public institution the situation is very different. You must have a degree, preferably in psychology or a healthcare subject. Training that conforms to standards set by the UK Council for Psychotherapy (UKCP) or the British Psychoanalytic Council is normally required. To complicate matters, prospective employers often state which of these they require, so it may well be worth perusing job adverts before you embark on training. The British Association of Counselling and Psychotherapy produces a directory of approved training courses. Approved training courses usually require you to undergo personal therapy as part of your training, and this can prove expensive. Many psychotherapists have worked in other social service, social care or medical professions and take on psychotherapy as a second career. You could consider completing a diploma in counselling before undertaking study at undergraduate level.

Personal attributes

You must be a really good listener and able to encourage someone else to talk. You have to be sensitive, patient and calm; able to cope with your clients showing signs of distress. You need to be able to offer understanding and encouragement without becoming overly emotionally involved in your clients' problems. The training and the work can be personally very challenging, so you need emotional resilience. You also need to be well organised and good at working as part of a team.

Earnings

The national average salary for a psychotherapist is around £36,000. Some psychotherapists are employed by the NHS. Trainees earn from around £28,000 a year; qualified psychotherapists can earn between £31,700 and around £43,000. Many psychotherapists work in private practice and their earnings are linked to what they charge – anything from £30 to £120 per hour; £45 to £60 is the most likely.

Info

British Association for Counselling and Psychotherapy (BACP)
01455 883300
www.bacp.co.uk

The Guild of Psychotherapists
020 7401 3260
www.guildofpsychotherapists.org.uk

UK Council for Psychotherapy (UKCP)
020 7014 9955
www.psychotherapy.org.uk

PUBLIC RELATIONS OFFICER

As a public relations (PR) officer/executive/consultant, your main role is to maintain and improve a company's, organisation's or high-profile individual's image with customers, or with the general public. Some PR officers work in-house for a particular company or organisation and are often known as media officers or managers. Many work for specialist PR consultancies providing services for a range of clients such as businesses that are too small to do this work in-house. Wherever you work, your responsibilities are likely to include a mix of the following: writing brochures, leaflets, press releases, speeches and articles, as well as content for social media; monitoring the public and media perception of a person, organisation, service or product; organising publicity campaigns and press launches; making presentations; developing and maintaining good relations with the media; and representing your client/company at a wide range of events.

Entry, qualifications and training

This is a very competitive industry and, while not absolutely essential, most entrants are graduates. Degrees in advertising, business, English, marketing, journalism or public relations are all relevant and give you some advantage, but any subject is acceptable. There are also some postgraduate courses in PR. The Chartered Institute of Public Relations (CIPR) is currently developing a course – the Introductory Award in Public Relations, which is aimed at students considering PR as a career. It is possible to join a PR company or department in an administrative role and work your way up. Many PR professionals move into a career in PR following on from work in advertising, marketing or journalism. Most of the training is on the job or through a variety of short courses, many run by the CIPR. You could also consider a public relations assistant higher apprenticeship.

Personal attributes

You must be excellent at all aspects of communication, able to write fluently and at the correct level. You must be confident at speaking in public, dealing with awkward questions and building good one-to-one relationships. You have to be a good problem solver and an excellent organiser. You must be able to work as part of a team and to cope with pressure.

Earnings

Trainees earn between £18,000 and £22,000. Experienced PR executives earn between £28,000 and £40,000. Someone running a PR consultancy can earn up to £80,000 to £100,000.

Info

Chartered Institute of Public Relations (CIPR) 020 7631 6900 www.cipr.co.uk	**Screen Skills** 020 7713 9800 www.screenskills.com

PUBLISHING

Publishers produce and sell books of every kind: fiction, biography, travel, cookery, sport, or academic books – name a subject and someone will have published a book about it. E-readers, downloads, self-publishing, educational technology and global online booksellers have had a huge impact on this sector, but many of the roles in publishing remain the same. Most have editorial and production/design departments employing staff in a range of roles. Of course, they will also have sales, marketing and finance departments, but described here are some of those jobs that are specific to publishing.

Book publishing

Editor

Editors liaise with those involved in the design, planning and production of each book. They read and edit the manuscript, prepare it for the typesetter, check the proofs and are responsible for assembling all the various parts, paginated in the correct order, for the printer. There is no automatic promotion system or salary structure. In a small company the only way to move up may be to move out.

The editorial director or managing editor runs a centralised copy-editing department, and commissions and supervises freelance editorial workers.

Commissioning editor

Commissioning editors are responsible both for identifying new authors and new titles likely to be successful and for monitoring the performance of the current titles being published by their company. A commissioning editor's work can include identifying possible future market trends, setting out proposals and costings for new book titles, deciding whether to accept manuscripts and proposals submitted by hopeful authors and overseeing the progress of any book, from the initial idea to the finished product being on sale.

Copy-editor

Copy-editors check the manuscripts submitted by authors and prepare this material for publication. They have to ensure that the text makes sense and that it is in the right 'house style'. Copy-editors work closely with authors, discussing and agreeing necessary changes. Copy-editors need to be alert to any possible legal questions that the text may raise. They also keep commissioning editors informed of progress and problems.

Editorial assistant

Editorial assistants support the whole publishing process in many ways. They often act as personal assistants to commissioning editors or senior copy-editors. They carry out general office duties, such as maintaining databases or filing systems. They are often the contact point on any project for authors, editors, design and production staff, and marketing and sales departments.

Proofreader

Proofreaders check written text after it has been edited and typeset, but before it is printed and published. Their role is to check for basic errors such as spelling and typos, but also to check for consistency or continuity. They check that page numbers follow on correctly, that contents and chapter titles match up and that the text follows the 'house style' if there is one.

Entry, qualifications and training

All jobs in editorial are very popular. The most usual career route is to work your way up from editorial assistant through copy-editor or development editor and then commissioning editor. It is sometimes possible to join a publisher as a commissioning editor in academic or professional publishing, if you have highly relevant knowledge of particular topics. There is fierce competition for entry-level editorial jobs, so you may well find it useful to do some work-shadowing or voluntary work. This also helps you build up a network of contacts. Editorial work is almost exclusively a graduate career. Degrees in English or publishing are especially useful. If you are interested in a specific area such as scientific publishing, then a degree in a subject relevant to this may also be helpful. Proofreaders and copy-editors often work freelance or on individual contracts, normally working from their own homes.

Personal attributes

All editorial staff need excellent written and spoken communication skills. To be successful you must be able to work to strict deadlines and work well as part of a team. You have to pay close attention to detail and have an eye for good presentation. Commissioning editors must be good negotiators, planners and project managers. Proofreaders may need qualifications in particular fields if they are working on highly specialised technical or scientific texts.

Earnings

Commissioning editors earn between £18,000 and £25,000 to begin with, rising to £35,000 plus with a few years' experience. Senior commissioning editors earn £45,000 plus. Copy-editors earn between £16,000 and £35,000 if they work in-house. Freelance copy-editors negotiate a fee per contract, often based on an hourly rate. This is around £20 to £30 an hour, but some publishers pay less, or more, than this. Editorial assistants usually start on between £16,500 and £23,000.

Production controller

The production controller draws up an accurate specification for the book and invites tenders from typesetters, printers, paper suppliers and binders. When all the estimates have been received, the production controller places orders and ensures that all the production stages are carried out to the required standard and on schedule. Undemanding production work on, for example, leaflets or reprints is often given to a production assistant, who is regarded as a trainee.

Designer
(see also Art and design)

Designers prepare layouts, sketches, specimen pages and dummies, and mark up the manuscripts for the typesetter after they have been edited. All the activities of the design department are managed by the design director. Directors discuss illustrated or complicated technical books with the author and the editor, commission freelance artwork, arrange the in-house preparation of artwork and impose a visual style on the company product.

Entry, training and qualifications

Production and design staff tend to be graduates and will be expected to have a vocational diploma or relevant qualification.

Personal attributes

Production and design professionals will need to be able to work under pressure and to tight deadlines. Being able to work well in a team and to interpret editorial briefs is also a quality expected in this area. Good planning skills are also essential. Production staff will also be expected to negotiate with printers and freelance designers for good deals.

Earnings

For production assistants, starting salaries are from £16,000 to £20,000, rising to around £27,000 after a few years' experience. Senior production staff earn around £30,000.

Indexer

Indexers provide a systematic arrangement of the terms appearing in a book, journal or other publication, which could be electronic or paper-based. They also work with page numbers or other locators in order to ensure that the information can be easily found. Indexers are generally employed by publishers or authors. Most are freelancers working from home.

Entry, qualifications and training

No formal qualifications are required but a good education, normally to degree level, is necessary, plus subject knowledge in the case of specialist books. Training is by open-learning course leading to accreditation. Registered indexers prove their experience and competence through an assessment procedure and admission to the Register of Indexers.

Personal attributes

An ability to analyse a text and meticulous attention to detail are essential, plus the ability to work to set requirements and time limits.

Earnings

Indexers are usually self-employed and charge either by the hour or a fixed rate for a particular contract. The Society of Indexers can give you advice on what you should charge. They recommend a basic hourly rate of £25.90 per hour for straightforward work, but for more complex indexing work you may well be able to negotiate a much better rate.

Magazines and newspapers

(see also Journalism)

The main career opportunities for those employed by newspaper and magazine publishers, but not on the editorial side, are connected with sales, advertising and production.

Advertisement sales representative

Commercial magazines depend on advertising revenue for survival. Graduates are often recruited straight from university to sales posts and are trained on the job. Sales staff must know the magazine's readership and build up advantageous contacts with potential advertisers. They spend a lot of time researching, analysing and planning, and need a persuasive manner and numerical skills.

Entry, qualifications and training

Requirements for trainees vary and many sales reps learn through work experience.

Personal attributes

Sales staff need an outgoing personality and good communication skills, and the ability to work under pressure and to meet deadlines.

Earnings

Many advertising reps earn a basic salary of approximately £14,000 and then earn more through commission. Successful advertising sales reps can earn £40,000+.

Designer

The range of work includes cover design, typographical design, layout, design of advertisements and direct mail material. Entrants will need a design qualification. Entrants need to have a good working knowledge of current design software used within the industry.

Production manager

Production staff are trained in the printing trade. It is their responsibility to see that the magazine is available at point of sale on publication day, and this involves meticulous planning and a tolerance of stress.

Entry, training and qualifications

Production and design staff tend to be graduates and are expected to have a vocational diploma or relevant qualification.

Personal attributes

Production and design professionals need to be able to work under pressure and to tight deadlines. Being able to work well in a team and to interpret editorial briefs is also a quality expected in this area. Good planning skills are also essential.

Earnings

Salaries for new entrants range from £15,000 to £19,000. In London, salaries are a little higher and this is where many jobs are based. Production managers' salaries vary very much according to the range they are producing and how large a team they have to manage, but a general guide is £22,000 to £35,000.

PURCHASING OFFICER/INDUSTRIAL BUYER

Purchasing careers exist in all large organisations, whether profit-making or not. Essentially, purchasing and supply management involves identifying the requirements of the company's internal customers and then obtaining the necessary products and services by negotiation and agreement with suppliers. The primary objective is to obtain value for money. This does not always mean achieving the very lowest price – sometimes other commercial considerations are more important. For example, the flexibility and speed of response of the supplier might be the deciding factor, or the need to minimise risk by choosing a vendor with a good business record.

In a manufacturing environment such as a car plant, the purchaser is directly involved in buying components such as wheels, lights and shock absorbers for the production line. In a financial services company, purchases might well be for telecommunications systems, catering services and marketing services, including advertising and design. In retail purchasing the role is slightly different as buyers are more involved in merchandising, selecting product lines that appeal to the consumer and sell quickly.

Entry, qualifications and training

Most companies require a minimum of four or five GCSE passes. Graduates or individuals with A levels usually enter as trainee buyers, working with experienced personnel and continuing their training in the workplace. The minimum requirement for individuals wishing to study for the Foundation Stage of the Chartered Institute of Purchasing and Supply (CIPS) Graduate Diploma is two A levels and three GCSEs (or equivalent). The Certificate in Purchasing and Supply Management is offered to those with no A levels.

Personal attributes

You need good written and spoken communication skills and a high level of numeracy. You have to have the confidence to negotiate firmly and the temperament to take risks at times. You should be able to build good relationships with people and you need good all-round business awareness.

Earnings

New entrants earn between £21,000 and £27,000. With a few years' experience salaries are £25,000 to £40,000. Senior purchasing managers with large organisations can earn £65,000.

Info

Chartered Institute of Procurement and Supply (CIPS)
0845 880 1188
www.cips.org

Skills for Logistics
0117 927 8800
www.skillsforlogistics.co.uk

QUARRYING (TOPSOIL)

There are more than 2,000 sites in the UK where quarrying (extracting material from just below the earth's surface) takes place. Many different materials are extracted from these sites, including clay and stone for the building industry, or sand and gravel to help construct flood defences or improve the quality of beaches.

Quarry operative

Quarry operatives are involved in the operations connected with this extraction process. Modern quarrying involves using very heavy machinery to excavate, transport, cut and crush the different products, and quarry workers operate this machinery.

Entry, qualifications and training

There are no specific academic entry qualifications, but you must be fit, and having a light goods vehicle (LGV) driving licence or experience of using heavy plant and machinery can be an advantage. If you are between 16 and 24 years old you may be able to do an apprenticeship; availability of these varies according to locality. Some employers will expect you to have four GCSEs to do an apprenticeship; these should include English, maths and technology. The industry offers the chance to do NVQs at levels 2 and 3 in Drilling Operations, Plant Operations and Process Operations. There is also an NVQ level 3 in Working with Explosives, and there are higher-level courses in Sampling. Most of the training is on the job.

Personal attributes

You need to be physically fit and confident in handling highly specialised technical equipment. You should have good numeracy skills for calculating quantities and you must be able to work as part of a team. You should have an acute awareness of health and safety issues and thrive on working outdoors.

Earnings

New entrants earn around the minimum wage, rising to £19,000 after two or three years' experience. Senior quarry workers earn between £20,000 and £26,000. There are often opportunities to increase earnings with overtime and shift-work payments.

Info

Mineral Products Qualifications Council
www.mp-qc.org

Careers in Quarrying
020 7963 8000
www.careersinquarrying.co.uk

Radiographer

Radiographers are healthcare professionals who use different kinds of radiation, such as X-rays or ultrasound, to diagnose or treat injuries and diseases. There are two branches: diagnostic radiography and therapeutic radiography.

As a diagnostic radiographer, you would use highly specialised equipment to produce and interpret images of the body, which could help doctors diagnose the extent of an injury or the progress of a disease. You could also be involved in screening people to check for early signs of conditions such as breast cancer.

As a therapeutic radiographer you would be part of the healthcare team treating patients, many of whom have cancer, using X-rays and other radioactive sources. You would help plan the most appropriate treatment, deliver that treatment and monitor the patient to check what impact your treatment was having on the diseased tissue, but also to check the patient's health.

Entry, qualifications and training

For both branches of the profession, you must take a degree in radiography. You must choose your preferred branch before you start your degree as they are different disciplines. These courses combine academic study with practical placements in radiography departments. You need three A levels, including a science, to get a place on one of these degree courses.

On graduation, entrants are eligible for State Registration with the Health and Care Professions Council (HCPC).

Other health professionals or graduates in science or healthcare-related subjects can train through a postgraduate diploma in radiography – though these are fewer in number than the degree course.

Personal attributes

As well as having an interest in science, radiographers should be caring and compassionate but sufficiently level-headed not to get upset when dealing with sick people. They need to be patient and calm when faced with patients who may be frightened or difficult. Good health and reasonable strength are needed for lifting people and heavy equipment. In addition, radiographers should be good humoured, and able to work well in a team and take on responsibility.

Earnings

The average salary for a radiographer is around £26,000. Newly qualified radiographers earn between around £22,000 and £29,000, with experience and responsibility this rises to £26,300 to around £43,000. Working in inner London you earn an additional 20 per cent and 15 per cent in outer London.

Info

NHS Careers
0345 60 60 655
www.healthcareers.nhs.uk

Society and College of Radiographers
020 7740 7200
www.sor.org

Health and Care Professions Council (HCPC)
0300 500 6184
www.hcpc-uk.org

RAILWAY WORK

An important part of infrastructure, the rail industry employs more than 150,000 people in many roles: drivers, conductors, revenue protection inspectors, customer service assistants, station staff, signal operators, engineers, fitters, clerical workers, technicians, timetable planners, and managers. The latter are responsible for the day-to-day running of the railways or are in charge of departments such as planning, engineering, marketing and accounts. Some specific roles are described below.

Train conductor

Train conductors, also known as guards, are responsible for the passengers on the train. A conductor's duties include checking that carriages are clean and tidy before the start of a journey and that door controls, etc are working properly. Once passengers are on the train conductors check and issue tickets, answer passengers' queries, ensure that passengers have safely boarded or alighted from the train before it leaves stations. Conductors also deal with unexpected problems that arise such as missing luggage, or travel delays.

Train driver

Driving a train involves more than driving from A to B. A driver must check equipment before setting out, stop at the appropriate stations for that particular route, pay attention to signals, operate automatic doors, liaise with control centres, keep passengers informed if there are delays or problems and make passenger announcements.

Entry, qualifications and training

Train drivers must be aged 20 or over, with a good general education. Train companies set their own entrance requirements but often use aptitude tests, including tests on train cab simulators. Training takes between 9 and 18 months and includes work towards NVQ level 2 in Rail Transport Operations (Driving). It is likely that a licensing system for train drivers will be introduced in the near future.

Electricians, fitters and mechanics often have experience as technicians or electricians in other sectors before they join the railway. Apprenticeships may be an option for school leavers; those with four or five GCSEs grades 9–4, including maths, English, are able to join. All technicians and engineers are put through Personal Track Safety (PTS) training by their employers before they are allowed to work on railway tracks.

Station assistants, booking clerks and other customer service staff need no formal entry qualifications. Engineers and managers normally have a degree in a relevant subject: electrical or mechanical engineering, or business subjects, respectively.

Personal attributes

An interest in railways is a good starting point. Roles such as driving and signal work require good concentration, and safety awareness at all times is essential. Many positions entail a great deal of customer contact or teamwork, so good interpersonal skills are extremely important.

Earnings

Trainee drivers earn around £20,000 to £30,000, and from £35,000 to £60,000, including benefits such as free train travel, once training is completed. Trainee fitters/electricians start on £18,000, less for apprentices. After training, earnings can go up to £30,000 a year. Station staff earn from £17,000. Experienced workers can earn up to £27,000.

Info

Network Rail
www.networkrail.co.uk

People 1st
020 3074 1222
www.people1st.co.uk

The National Skills Academy for Railway Engineering
0203 021 0575
www.nsar.co.uk

Careers that Move
www.careersthatmove.co.uk

RECRUITMENT

Recruitment consultant

Recruitment consultants work to fit the right people to the right jobs. Recruitment agencies deal with many types of staff, from office and secretarial, driving, production line work, IT, sales, technical and scientific through to headhunting specialists looking for people to fill senior executive and managerial posts. Much of the work involves selling recruitment services to potential clients, finding out what their staffing needs are, matching these needs with candidates on the agency's books, and interviewing and shortlisting candidates for particular posts. Consultants also keep in touch with clients to ensure that they are happy with the staff they have recruited.

Entry, qualifications and training

Many recruitment consultants have come into the industry after some experience of another job, for example sales, human resources or administration or technical work. Training is either in-house or on courses run by the Recruitment and Employment Confederation (REC). The REC offers two levels of qualification: the Foundation Award, suitable for those in their first year in the industry, and the Certificate in Recruitment Practice for those with more than one year's experience. Both qualifications can be studied by distance learning or through a part-time course. A degree is not essential, but some employers do prefer graduates. They may prefer a relevant discipline such as marketing, or a technical or scientific subject if this is a specialist recruitment area that they offer to clients. There are also college courses, and you may be able to undertake an apprenticeship such as an advanced apprenticeship as a recruitment consultant.

Personal attributes

Recruitment consultants must be able to relate to people at different organisational levels, have good communication skills, work quickly and calmly under pressure and be organised and resilient.

Earnings

Trainees earn around £18,000 to £25,000, plus commission for successful placing. With some experience, consultants earn between £25,000 and £45,000, but a tough job market makes commission harder to earn.

Info

Recruitment and Employment Confederation (REC)
020 7009 2100
www.rec.uk.com

Chartered Institute of Personnel and Development (CIPD)
020 8612 6200
www.cipd.co.uk

RELIGION

Religious leader

Religious leaders work with faith communities and with people who do not subscribe to any religious belief system. As a religious leader your role includes offering spiritual and moral leadership to your followers. Your work encompasses leading groups of people in acts of worship or in specific ceremonies. These might include religious festivals or significant occasions for individuals and families such as births, deaths, marriages, or ceremonies for new members who join a particular faith. The Church of England is the established church in the United Kingdom, but as well as other Christian faith groups there are significant numbers of members of other faiths – Buddhism, Islam, Hinduism, Judaism and Sikhism are the largest groups. Your work normally involves pastoral care, visiting people who are sick, who have been bereaved, or who have relationship problems. Religious leaders also talk to those who are having a crisis of faith, or those who want to find out more about a particular belief system. Some faith groups would expect their leaders to go out and actively try to recruit new members, but this would not always be the case. For many religious leaders, part of their work would also include taking part in interfaith discussions or giving advice to government departments, charities and voluntary organisations. Many religious leaders work full or part time in hospitals, universities, prisons or for charities, voluntary or faith-based organisations.

Entry, qualifications and training

Each faith has its own particular entry qualifications, but these are usually based on a commitment to and understanding of a particular faith rather than purely academic qualifications. Your best starting point is to check with your own religious leader about how to begin to work towards becoming one yourself. Do remember that religious groups do not have to comply with all the normal equal opportunities legislation, so in some instances it is not possible, for example, for women to become religious leaders. There may be other restrictions. There are many degree courses available in theology, religion and comparative religion, and if this career really interests you, taking such a course could be a useful way for you to explore the subject more deeply.

Personal attributes

A commitment to your own faith and an understanding of the problems that people encounter are essential. The skills mix you might need would vary somewhat not just between different faiths, but also between different jobs within that faith. The work of a prison chaplain is quite different from that of someone working in a rural parish, or an inner city area, for example.

Earnings

Pay varies greatly. Some religious leaders are paid a full-time salary and/or are provided with accommodation and other benefits. Many religious leaders have other jobs and do their religious work on a voluntary basis. You need to check with the faith group that interests you exactly what financial benefits may be available.

Info

Board of Deputies of British Jews
020 7543 5400
www.bod.org.uk

Buddhist Society
020 7834 5858
www.thebuddhistsociety.org

Churches Together in Britain and Ireland
020 3794 2288
www.ctbi.org.uk

Hindu Council UK
www.hinducounciluk.org

Church of England
www.churchofengland.org

Muslim Council of Britain
0845 262 6786
www.mcb.org.uk

Network of Sikh Organisations (NSO)
020 8540 4148
www.nsouk.co.uk

REMOVALS WORK

If you have ever moved house, you are probably familiar with the role of removals companies. Whether you're going just around the corner or to the other side of the world, it is the remover's job to see that all your belongings are professionally packed and transported to their destination. The work may involve packing fragile objects quickly and efficiently, as well as travelling long distances. Some large companies have their own storage facilities, so employees may be involved in ensuring that furniture is stored safely.

Estimators are the technical salespeople in a removals company. They visit customers' homes and estimate the amount of packing space needed, the time it will take and the price.

Entry, qualifications and training

Employees can work towards NVQs for the removals and storage industry. Progression is also possible to supervisory level. A large goods vehicle (LGV) licence would be beneficial, but is not essential when starting out. Estimators should have a good standard of education, with good passes preferably in English, maths, geography and modern languages, hold a full car driving licence and be able to express themselves clearly and persuasively. Training is on the job.

Personal attributes

Removers should be fit and strong. They must be honest and have a sense of responsibility towards other people's possessions. Common sense and the ability to work in a team are important.

Earnings

Earnings and job security are highly dependent on an active property market. Generally, starting salaries are fairly low: from around the minimum wage to £15,000, rising to £16,000 to £22,000 for more experienced staff. Drivers may earn up to £21,000. All employees may earn more for shift work, weekend work, etc.

Info

Skills for Logistics
0117 927 8800
www.skillsforlogistics.co.uk

British Association of Removers
01923 699480
www.bar.co.uk

Delivering Your Future
www.deliveringyourfuture.co.uk

RETAILING

We are surrounded by retail stores of many kinds in city shopping centres, local high streets, large retail parks – and online. Retailers can be small shops specialising in a particular type of product: shoes, car spares or speciality foods, for example. Supermarkets, department stores and discount stores are just some of the other examples of retail outlets. Much retail is now done online and this is where many of the jobs now are.

Retailing offers many different career opportunities. As well as the careers outlined in this section, retailing offers opportunities in distribution management and warehouse work, in finance, in marketing and in human resource management. There are openings at school-leaver level (including apprenticeships), through to graduate and senior management opportunities.

Buyer

The merchandise that you find in all kinds of shops – clothes, shoes, food, furniture, electrical goods, jewellery, etc – will have been selected by a retail buyer whose job it is to source the most appropriate goods to sell in retail outlets. As a buyer your role would include finding the right goods at the right price and ensuring that they are available at the right time in your store. You may be the one who has to come up with ideas on new lines that you could sell. You have to work very closely with wholesalers, manufacturers and suppliers at every stage, from negotiating a price and placing an order to monitoring the quality of the supplied products. You have to monitor stock levels to ensure continuous supply and sales levels to confirm that you are choosing the right kinds of goods to sell successfully. Much of your time will be spent visiting suppliers, producers and wholesalers. Buyers work for department stores, chain stores and some smaller independent retailers. In the latter case, you might combine the role of buyer with other management duties.

Entry, qualifications and training

Although you don't have to have a degree or HND, many people who get into buying work have higher education qualifications. Useful subjects include supply chain management and business studies. In some cases employers may prefer a degree in a subject closely related to the products you are buying, e.g. fashion for clothing retailers, information technology for a store that sells computers or food science for food and drink. Some people have worked in other areas of retail such as store management before they move into buying. Training is mostly on the job and there are NVQ level qualifications at levels 2, 3, 4 and 5 towards which you can work.

Personal attributes

You need a broad range of skills, including negotiating, organising and working to deadlines. You need to be able to write reports and also have good numeracy skills when you are negotiating prices. You need to be able to establish relationships with people very quickly and be good at working as part of a team. You need a good understanding and feel for the kinds of products in which you specialise.

Earnings

Assistant buyers earn from £15,000 to £25,000. Buyers earn from £25,000 to £45,000. Buyer managers can earn up to £90,000.

Checkout operator

Checkout operators work at the tills in supermarkets and other large retail stores. They scan the prices of all the items customers have purchased, process payments whether by cash, cheque or card, and they may also offer some assistance with packing, e.g. wrapping delicate items or putting frozen foods into separate bags.

Entry, qualifications and training

No specific qualifications are necessary, although individual stores may request a good standard of education. Training is provided on the job and it is possible to obtain NVQ level 1 in Checkout Operations and NVQ levels 2 and 3 in Customer Service and Sales. Career progression is to supervisory roles.

Personal attributes

You must be polite and friendly and able to talk to people without losing your concentration or slowing down. You need good numeracy skills in order to spot errors. You must have good stamina and be able to work under pressure in a hectic environment.

Earnings

New checkout staff earn around the minimum wage, rising to £14,800 with some experience. Many work part time. Supervisors earn around £17,000 to £24,000. A few stores include all staff members in profit-sharing schemes.

Display designer/visual merchandiser

Display designers are responsible for shop windows and displays inside stores. These may be to attract customers into a shop, promote a new product or reinforce a company image. Displays are often seasonal or themed. Some designers work to instructions from head office, others create their own designs. The work may include making props, arranging lighting and general care of the display areas. Some shops also employ visual merchandisers who arrange products according to an organisation's display policy.

Entry, qualifications and training

Although there are no standard, formal entry qualifications, in practice most entrants have a relevant qualification. There are several three- or four-year degree courses in Design Merchandising Management and Exhibition and Retail Design. There are also some two-year foundation degrees available in display design or visual merchandising. Other art-based qualifications may be accepted by some employers. A great deal of training is on the job.

Personal attributes

You need real artistic flair and to be good at working with colour and with three-dimensional design. You should be imaginative and practical, able to work as part of a team and able to relate design ideas to commercial impact. You also need good IT skills and preferably to be able to use computer-aided design (CAD).

Earnings

Trainees earn between the minimum wage and £14,000, while experienced display designers earn up to £35,000. It is possible for a display manager with a large store or a retail design agency to earn more than £45,000.

E-commerce assistant/executive/manager

E-commerce or online retailing is still very much evolving and retailers differ as much online as they do in the high street. Some retailers were born with the internet, e.g. Amazon, while others have had to adapt fast and move their business online in order to survive, e.g. big brands like Marks & Spencer and the supermarkets. For some, such as Burberry, the possibility of selling worldwide has transformed them into a global brand. For niche, one-off shops, on the high street of a small town, the internet allows them to sell enough of their goods to become a going concern. E-commerce assistants, executives and managers are the people who make this happen, combining traditional retail knowledge and experience with an understanding of the internet and social media that enables them successfully to sell their merchandise online. They will, on the whole, be based in an office rather than a shop.

E-commerce assistants may provide support to customers by phone or email and be responsible for updating the e-commerce database. They may help with stock management for website orders as well as contributing to social media content. They will need to be as confident with using the basic office functions of a computer as they are with stock and customers.

E-commerce executives may spend even more time at the keyboard, analysing and reporting on the performance of products and the website.

E-commerce managers are responsible for strategic planning for both merchandise and website and in setting budgets and targets.

Entry, qualifications and training

There is no set route of entry into e-commerce. A background in retail is usually essential. Although no formal qualifications are required, a reasonable level of English, maths and basic computer literacy are essential. Courses such as a degree in Fashion Marketing offered by the London College of Fashion together with the Chartered Institute of Marketing will be useful for fashion retail. Other routes of entry are through marketing and IT.

Earnings

Because of the particular combination of skills required, pay in this sector of retail is often higher than in store. An assistant may earn between £17,000 and £20,000 while an executive can expect to earn between £25,000 and £30,000. An e-commerce manager for a larger brand earns between £38,000 and £45,000.

Retail store manager

Retail store managers work in department stores, in supermarkets and in small, individually owned stores. In a small store they will run the whole operation. In a supermarket they may be responsible for one area; fresh produce or the checkouts, for example. In a department store they may run one or several departments. Managers are responsible for ensuring that everything runs smoothly. They have to organise work rosters, ensure that sales targets are met, that customer service is of a high standard and that sales staff are fully trained.

Entry, qualifications and training

There are several ways to become a retail store manager. Large stores or chains may run graduate management training programmes or programmes open to school leavers with two or three A levels. Many stores also offer apprenticeships in several aspects of retailing, and some of these could lead to management roles. Experience, however, is often as important as qualifications, and many managers start out as sales assistants and work their way up to management positions. You could also consider college courses which may give you an understanding of the skills and knowledge required. Courses include a Level 3 Diploma in Retail Skills Management, or a Level 4 Diploma in Retail Management.

Sales assistant/manager

There are many opportunities for sales staff in retailing. Your responsibilities and tasks depend on what kind of retail outlet you are working in, as well as your level of experience. In general, sales staff are expected to sort stock, sell goods, ensure these goods are attractively displayed and deal with payments for goods. They also answer customers' queries, give information about products and offer advice. Some sales staff process orders for new stock.

Entry, qualifications and training

Although no formal academic qualifications are necessarily needed, GCSEs grades 9–4 in English and maths are helpful, as is some experience of working with people. Training is on the job, and large stores or chain stores may offer some structured training programmes including apprenticeships. It is possible to work towards several NVQs at levels 2 and 3 in retail, including Sales, Retail Operations and Customer Service. Many people who start as sales assistants become supervisors for a section of a store, or progress to become store managers.

Personal attributes

You must be polite, friendly and enjoy working with people. You need good basic literacy and numeracy skills and must be reasonably physically fit. Being smart and tidy is important, especially in fashion retailing. If you are interested in management, you have to be well organised, good at solving problems and at leading and motivating other staff.

Earnings

Trainee store managers earn £18,000 to £25,000; the higher rates are more likely if you are on a graduate training scheme. As your career progresses, into management, earnings can increase up to £60,000. Pay depends on the size and type of store. Sales assistants earn between the minimum wage and £25,000, but there are often opportunities to move into supervisory or management roles.

Info

People 1st
020 3074 1222
www.people1st.co.uk

ROAD TRANSPORT

(see also Driving for Bus/coach driver, Large goods vehicle driver, and Logistics)

Road transport includes passenger transport and road haulage. Passenger transport covers bus and coach travel. Haulage is the transport and distribution of all goods that are carried by road – food and drink, cars, household electrical goods, building materials and much more. While many functions such as administration, financial management, human resources, information technology and marketing are not specific to road transport, there are some particular roles involved. In addition to those described below, passenger transport and haulage firms employ drivers and customer service staff on the passenger side, and drivers and warehouse staff in haulage.

Road haulage load planner

Load planners work to ensure that goods transported throughout the country and to overseas destinations are moved in the most efficient and cost-effective way possible. Load planners decide on the size, type and number of vehicles to be used for any job. They monitor progress as loads are moved, and work out back-up plans in case anything goes wrong, such as traffic hold-ups or breakdown of refrigeration equipment. They discuss plans with clients and they may be involved in working out costs. Load planners often use specialised computer software to aid planning, but may have to resort to pen and paper.

Entry, qualifications and training

To start as a trainee you don't always need formal qualifications, although many employers do ask for GCSEs grades 9–4, including maths and English. There are sometimes opportunities to do an apprenticeship, in which case you are likely to need three or four GCSEs. A background in transport and distribution is also useful. Most of your training is on the job, and you may be able to work towards NVQ levels 2 and 3 in Distribution and Warehousing Operations.

Road transport planner/manager

Managers work in passenger and goods transport, planning routes, organising schedules, managing staff, liaising with customers and calculating costs. It is the manager's job to ensure that whatever is transported – goods or people – is carried in the safest, most efficient and most cost-effective way. Managers have to ensure that all operations comply with UK and EU legislation on health and safety and employment. They have to know about transporting particular types of load, such as dangerous chemicals, live animals or perishable foods. They are also likely to be involved in training and recruitment of staff.

Entry, qualifications and training

Many managers work their way up from administrative, driving or warehouse posts. Some companies run management training schemes and entry requirements vary, but may be an HND, foundation degree or degree in a relevant subject. Acceptable subjects include business, logistics, supply chain management and transport. Most training is on the job. Every transport operator has to have at least one employee who has achieved the Certificate of Professional Competence (CPC), so as a trainee manager you would be expected to work towards this. There may be an opportunity to complete a passenger transport operations manager higher apprenticeship if you are working for a passenger transport company.

Personal attributes

Planners and managers need to be logical, well organised and careful in their work. Good IT and numeracy skills are important. They also have to be good communicators, able to manage staff and deal with clients. Managers have to be able to understand and apply relevant legislation. Planners and managers have to be good problem solvers.

Earnings

Trainee planners earn £15,500 to £19,000, rising to £20,000 to £24,000 with experience. Managers earn £20,000 to £30,000 when they are training; £25,000 to £45,000 with experience. In large passenger transport organisations, salaries for senior managers can be £50,000 to £70,000.

Info

Skills for Logistics
0117 927 8800
www.skillsforlogistics.co.uk

Chartered Institute of Logistics and Transport (CILT UK)
01536 740100
www.ciltuk.org.uk

ROOFER

(see Construction trades)

ROUNDSPERSON

The roundsperson we are all most familiar with is probably the person who delivers milk and other dairy products to people's doorsteps on a daily basis. In fact, working as a roundsperson can involve delivering and selling goods and services of many kinds to private homes and business premises. Examples include doing a sandwich round to businesses, selling ice cream or fast food, and running mobile shops selling many different kinds of goods. Usually, you work for yourself or you operate a franchise for a franchising company.

Entry, qualifications and training

You do not need any formal qualifications to do this work, but some companies set their own entry tests, and you need good basic maths skills for calculating prices and making out bills. You need a full driving licence and many companies prefer applicants to be over 21 years old. If you are selling fast food, you will need a licence to trade from your local environmental health department. You could do a number of relevant NVQs in customer service and sales. If you are employed by a retailer or a franchising company, it usually provides specific training about its own products and services.

Personal attributes

For most of the time you are working on your own, but you have to enjoy and be good at dealing with customers. You must be well organised, with good numeracy skills and usually some computer skills these days. You have to be highly motivated and not mind working some antisocial hours or being out in all weathers.

Earnings

Initial earnings are between the minimum wage and £15,000. With experience these can rise to £15,000 to £20,000; there are only a few types of round (milk and sandwiches, for example) where you are likely to receive seasonal tips.

Info

People 1st
020 3074 1222
www.people1st.co.uk

National Skills Academy for Food & Drink
0845 644 0558
www.nsafd.co.uk

British Franchise Association
www.thebfa.org

ROYAL AIR FORCE

(see Armed forces)

ROYAL MARINES

(see Armed forces)

ROYAL NAVY

(see Armed forces)

S

Sales representative

A sales representative, often referred to as a 'rep', may work for a manufacturer, wholesale distributor or service industry, persuading potential customers to buy the firm's products and also looking after the needs of existing customers and providing after-sales advice and support. Sales reps sell many products including pharmaceuticals, office supplies and catering equipment to business customers, or double glazing, utilities, wine and fitted kitchens to private customers. As a 'rep' you are usually assigned a geographical area and travel around it on the firm's behalf.

One distinctive area of work is that of the medical sales rep. Medical sales reps sell drugs and other medical products to GPs and hospitals on behalf of pharmaceutical companies.

Entry, qualifications and training

Requirements for trainees vary, but most firms look for four GCSEs grades 9–4 or equivalent and in some companies prefer graduates. Medical sales reps nearly always need a degree and most companies prefer this to be in a science-based subject. Sales reps may study for examinations set by such bodies as the Chartered Institute of Marketing (CIM) or the Managing and Marketing Sales Association (MAMSA). Diplomas and certificates are also issued by various trade associations representing particular types of product. Technical sales representatives usually have a degree or equivalent in the relevant subject. You could also complete an intermediate or advanced apprenticeship in sales and telesales, or vehicle sales, before progressing to a sales executive higher apprenticeship.

Personal attributes

An outgoing, friendly personality, a manner that inspires confidence and the ability to be persuasive are essential. How 'pushy' you need to be depends on the products you are selling and your employer's attitude. You will have to be resilient, with plenty of stamina to cope with disappointment, and you also need to be well organised and a good time keeper.

Earnings

New entrants earn £17,000 to £25,000, rising to £30,000 to £40,000 with experience. In most cases, salary comprises a basic rate of pay plus on-target earnings (OTE), meaning you have to achieve the sales targets your employer sets. Adverts for sales jobs often give the salary including commission, and some sales jobs pay on commission only. Senior, successful reps can earn £50,000 to £100,000. The highest salaries are paid in the pharmaceuticals sector.

SCIENTIFIC RESEARCH

Research scientists work in medicine, physics, chemistry and life sciences. They are employed in industry and in academia. The topics and issues they research are extremely wide ranging and are of course determined by the particular field of science in which they work. They may be involved in developing new products, materials or medicines, examining the effects of chemicals on behaviour, or of climate upon plants. Research scientists may be involved in the development of drugs, the study of genetics or stem cell research. In astrophysics they may be tackling questions about the nature of the universe or the structure of asteroids. In whichever scientific specialism researchers work, their main role is to design, carry out and analyse the results of scientific experiments.

Entry, qualifications and training

Scientific research is a graduate-entry profession. While job titles vary, there are basically three levels at which you can get into research. Technician-level posts require an undergraduate degree in a science discipline relevant to the field of research. Research assistants usually need to have a Master's degree in the appropriate area of science, and research associates have usually completed a PhD.

Personal attributes

Regardless of which field of science you enter, you must have a rigorous and questioning approach to whatever you do. You need good numeracy skills and the ability to interpret data accurately. Many posts require good IT skills and/or the ability to work with highly specialised equipment. You need to be able to work on your own and as part of a team. You may well have to negotiate for funds and you have to be an imaginative problem solver with a real fascination for your subject.

Earnings

Typical starting salaries are around £17,000 to £21,000 at technician level; £20,000 to £25,000 for research assistant level (usually with an MSc or MPhil); £25,000 to £33,000 at postdoctoral research associate level. Research scientists working in industry or leading a research project or team may earn considerably more than this – in the region of £45,000 to £70,000.

SECURITY WORK

Security guards/officers work for all kinds of organisations and businesses, where buildings, property and people need protection. They work to prevent theft and other criminal activities and to alert the police when the need arises. Typical tasks for security guards and officers include door supervision, checking people who enter a premises to confirm identity, patrolling buildings on foot or monitoring them from a control room, guarding cash and other valuables as they are delivered or removed or when they are in transit, and checking individuals and observing behaviour at airports or other public places. Many security staff begin as security guards and then progress to becoming security officers or supervisors with responsibility for coordinating security arrangements and training other security staff.

Entry, qualifications and training

You don't need formal qualifications, but many employers do ask for a good standard of education including GCSEs in English and maths. You have to pass security checks and your work and personal history is checked for the previous 10 years prior to your seeking employment. Whether you need to be licensed by the Security Industry Authority (SIA) depends on whether you work in-house or for a security contractor. If you are employed by the company for whom you are providing security services, you don't need a licence – if you are employed by an agency or contractor you do. The training to obtain a licence takes four days. The SIA is currently looking into licensing all security staff, including in-house employees. Whoever employs you, you may be expected to do training courses in dog handling, first aid, or other specialist skills. You may be able to enter the profession by completing an intermediate apprenticeship in providing security services.

Personal attributes

You need to be polite and helpful, but also able to challenge people assertively when this is appropriate. You should be able to write clear, short reports detailing an incident. You may have to handle technical equipment of various kinds. You should be confident, with a mature attitude to your work, and you must be able to use your initiative. You must be reasonably fit and in many instances you will have to work shifts or do night work.

Earnings

New security staff earn between the minimum wage and £16,500 a year. With experience you can earn £21,000 to £26,000.

Info

British Security Industry Association (BSIA) 01905 342020 www.bsia.co.uk	**Skills for Security** 01905 744000 https://skillsforsecurity.org.uk

Security service personnel

Security service personnel work for the three government security services, MI5, MI6 and Government Communications Headquarters (GCHQ). These services work to protect the United Kingdom from a range of serious threats, including terrorism, espionage and serious crime.

There is not one typical job in the security services. People may work as surveillance officers watching particular individuals or observing what takes place at particular premises. Others are employed as intelligence officers, gathering, analysing and assessing secret intelligence, perhaps working under cover. The security services also employ linguists to translate information gathered from various sources in the United Kingdom and abroad. They also employ computer specialists who can follow information leads found on computers or decode information on seized computers.

Entry, qualifications and training

To work as a surveillance officer you do not necessarily need formal qualifications. Trainee intelligence officers have to be graduates with at least a 2.1. Any subject may be acceptable, but history, economics and politics are good for general intelligence roles. Modern languages are very much sought after, as are IT specialists.

In all cases applicants must fulfil strict nationality criteria and pass rigorous security and background checks. The selection procedure is challenging.

Training for most roles includes an initial induction programme, then a combination of on-the-job training and continuing professional development. Surveillance officers undergo a 10-week training course.

Personal attributes

While specific roles require particular attributes, there are many qualities that are important whatever your role. You must possess absolute integrity and discretion. You must be able to work on your own or as part of a team. You should be a good problem solver and a calm thinker. For many roles you need excellent analytical skills, to be highly observant and have the ability to make decisions and take responsibility.

Earnings

Starting salaries are from £21,000 to £36,000 depending on your role. Salaries for senior staff are from £45,000 to £80,000.

Info

MI5 Careers
www.Mi5.gov.uk

SHIPBROKER

Shipbrokers act as go-betweens for shipowners looking for cargo to fill their vessels, and charterers seeking to ship their dry cargo and tanker requirements. The sale and purchase of vessels are also an important service offered to clients. Brokers are paid commission on the contracts arranged. The Baltic Exchange in London is the centre of the chartering market. It is a self-regulated market and the Exchange maintains a register of those seeking employment, which its member companies may consult. Vacancies are also advertised on the website. Additionally, shipbrokers/ ship's agents in ports make arrangements when a ship calls for customs clearance – loading and discharging cargoes, meeting crew requirements and so on. Port agents who attend to cargo liners may also be involved in marketing and documenting cargo. In order to maintain contact with the international scene, shipbrokers tend to work long hours and to travel abroad frequently.

Entry, qualifications and training

There are no fixed entry requirements to get into shipbroking, but different companies set their own entry criteria. A few will accept you with GCSEs grades 9–4, but it is common for companies to recruit applicants who have at least A levels or their equivalent. Some employers prefer graduates. Any subjects are acceptable, but business studies, modern languages and courses that include modules on transport and/or logistics will be particularly appreciated. A background in administrative work of any kind can also be very useful. There are sometimes opportunities to do an apprenticeship in International Trade and Service (ITAS) and you may also be able to study to NVQ levels 2 and 3 in this subject. You can also work through e-learning and distance-learning courses towards membership of the Institute of Chartered Shipbrokers. The majority of training, however, is provided on the job.

Personal attributes

You have to be very well organised and pay especial interest to being very clear and accurate in what you write and what you say. You should be a good communicator, able to talk to customers, importers and exporters, and good at communicating with people whose first language is not English. You must have good IT skills, and command of any modern language can be really useful. You have to have a good knowledge of geography and to be sensitive when working with people of other cultures.

Earnings

New entrants earn £18,000 to £24,000. With a year or two's experience this rises to £26,000 to £35,000. Senior shipbrokers can earn £35,000 to £50,000.

Info

Institute of Chartered Shipbrokers
020 7357 9722
www.ics.org.uk

British International Freight Association (BIFA)
020 8844 2266
www.bifa.org

Institute of Export
01733 404400
www.export.org.uk

Skills for Logistics
0117 927 8800
www.skillsforlogistics.co.uk

SOCIAL CARE AND SOCIAL WORK

Social care and social work covers several careers, all of which involve working with people who need support of some kind. This could mean working with families facing problems, older people who have become ill, young adults involved in substance abuse, adults of all ages with serious physical or learning disabilities, children at risk or people with mental health problems.

Care assistants

Care assistants, also called care workers or social care workers, are employed in many settings with many client groups. The overall job of a care assistant is to help and support people in their daily lives with tasks such as getting up in the morning, bathing and showering, getting dressed, preparing and eating meals, going out shopping or taking part in activities. Some care workers work with clients in their own homes, visiting frail elderly people each day to help them get up and dressed or to go to bed in the evenings. These care workers are usually referred to as domiciliary care workers. Care assistants also work in residential homes for elderly people or for people who have learning disabilities, physical impairments or mental health problems. An important part of the work is also simply to talk to and reassure people.

Entry, qualifications and training

You may not need formal qualifications; experience of working with people is very valuable, especially if this has been in a caring role. Once you are employed you will receive training on the job, including taking part in a 12-week induction programme. There are also several relevant NVQ awards towards which you can work. Before you can work as a care assistant you will have to undergo a Disclosure and Barring Service (DBS) check. If you are providing care to people in their own homes you are likely to need a driving licence.

Personal attributes

You need to be caring, compassionate and patient. You need very good communication skills, to be able to listen and to encourage people to communicate with you. You need to be practical and physically fit. You need to be a good problem solver and you must be able to work as part of a team.

Earnings

Earnings start at around the minimum wage. With experience, pay can be £16,000 to £18,000 and there may be some opportunities to earn overtime payments.

Info

The National Skills Academy for Social Care
020 3011 5270
www.nsasocialcare.co.uk

Northern Ireland Social Care Council
www.niscc.info

Skills for Care and Development (England)
0113 241 1240
www.skillsforcareanddevelopment.org.uk

Social Care Wales
www.socialcare.wales

Scottish Social Services Council (SSSC)
www.sssc.uk.com

Health and Care Professions Council (HCPC)
0300 500 6184
www.hcpc-uk.org

Care home managers

Care home managers manage care homes that are registered to provide care. The majority of homes provide care for elderly people who are too unwell or too frail to continue living in their own homes. There are also care homes for adults with learning and physical disabilities. The majority of care homes are in the independent (private) sector, but some are run by local authorities, and many are run by not-for-profit organisations. Care home managers are responsible for all the day-to-day running of the home – everything from seeing that appropriate nursing care is delivered to ensuring that catering and laundry services run well. Care home managers also look at ways to make care more effective, for example by introducing programmes of activities that could help people with dementia to enjoy a better quality of life. Managers also have to respond to complaints and concerns raised by residents or their relatives. They also have to ensure that the home complies with all appropriate legislation and standards. They also have to be business managers – homes are businesses and have to be financially viable – so it is the manager's job to ensure that rooms are occupied and that the home is well marketed and builds links with its local community.

Entry, qualifications and training

Many care home managers will move into this work as a second career, having started in nursing or in some other management role. It is also possible to work your way up to a management role if you have started as a care assistant. Many companies operating care homes run management training schemes and set their own entry requirements. Managers are often required to work towards the level 5 diploma in leadership in health and social care. This course offers several pathways, so that you can choose the one most appropriate to your work setting. You could also complete an apprenticeship such as a higher apprenticeship for children, young people and families managers, or care leadership and management, before further training on the job.

Personal attributes

You need a wide range of skills, although the balance of these depends on the size and type of home you manage. You need to be caring and compassionate. You also need to be a good team leader and able to motivate staff. You need good business skills, and to be able to handle budgets and market the home. You need excellent communication skills, to be able to listen sympathetically to a resident and to deal effectively with other healthcare professionals, the media or the wider community.

Earnings

Salaries depend not only on your level of experience, but on the size and type of home you manage and whether your employer is in the independent, public or not-for-profit sector. Generally salaries start at between £20,000 and £30,000, but can reach £45,000 and above if you work for one of the larger care provider organisations.

Skills for Care and Development 0113 241 1240 www.skillsforcareanddevelopment.org.uk	**The National Skills Academy for Social Care** 020 3011 5270 www.nsasocialcare.co.uk

Social work assistant

Social work assistants are part of the social work team. They support qualified social workers who are involved in helping and advising many different clients in the community, in day-care establishments, residential homes, hospitals, schools and their own homes. The work can be varied but might include making contact with clients, booking appointments and following up on enquiries, making routine visits to people to monitor situations, advising clients on what services and resources could be available to them, and conducting routine interviews. A key part of the role is to refer situations to qualified social workers if you have any concerns about a client you have spoken to or visited. Your work is also likely to involve keeping records, attending meetings and updating yourself on changes in social care legislation.

Entry, qualifications and training

While you don't necessarily need formal academic qualifications, many employers expect you to have two or three GCSEs grades 9–4. You could also consider an intermediate or advanced apprenticeship for the children and young people's workforce, or in youth work or care work as a starting point. What is most important to employers is whether you have had experience of working with vulnerable people. You may find that your application is strengthened by doing some voluntary work. There are also several full- and part-time BTEC certificate and diploma courses in health and social care. These normally include work placements, so this could also be a way of strengthening your application. You will have to pass a Disclosure and Barring Service (DBS) check to do this type of work. Once you have started work, your employer has to provide induction training to approved national standards, and you may also be able to study part time for further qualifications such as a foundation degree in health and social care.

Personal attributes

You need excellent communication skills, to be able to listen to and explain things to people who may be coping with high levels of stress. You have to be highly observant, too. You must be calm in tense situations and, while you have to take responsibility, you must be very clear about when to refer a situation to other professionals. You must be well organised, a good administrator and excellent at working as part of a team.

Earnings

New entrants earn between the minimum wage and £17,000, more in London. With experience, further qualifications and management responsibilities you can earn £19,000 to £25,000.

Social worker

Social workers are qualified professionals who work in the same settings as social work assistants – in someone's home, schools, hospitals, day centres, residential homes, and specialist units such as drug dependency centres. They may also do outreach work in the wider community. They work within a framework of relevant legislation and increasingly they work as part of multidisciplinary teams with healthcare workers. Each social worker has an allocated caseload to deal with. More than half of qualified social workers work with children and young people. This can include working with young offenders, pupils who have poor school attendance records, or children whose families are in a crisis of some kind.

Much of a social worker's job is to carry out assessments of any service user's situation to see what kind of support they might need, or whether some intervention is required. Can an elderly person continue to cope living in his or her own home, or might he or she be better off in a residential home? Is it appropriate to leave a child with his or her family, or should he or she be placed in care? What treatment programme might help an adult with mental health problems to cope more easily with daily life? These are just a few examples of the kinds of questions that social workers tackle. They have to attend meetings, prepare reports, conduct interviews, monitor progress and review cases on a regular basis.

The majority of social workers are employed by local authorities, but some voluntary and not-for-profit organisations employ their own social workers. Senior social workers are also involved in the purchasing of care packages, the training of staff and the development of strategy.

Entry, qualifications and training

To qualify as a social worker in England you need either a three-year degree or a two-year postgraduate degree in social work approved by the Health and Care Professionals Council (HCPC) if you already have a degree in another subject. For acceptance on a degree course you normally require five GCSEs and two A levels. An alternative to A levels could be an NVQ level 3 in health and social care. Mature applicants with other relevant experience may be accepted without these qualifications – check with course providers. You could also consider a social worker degree apprenticeship, which takes around three years to complete.

Once qualified, social workers must register with the Health and Care Professions Council (HCPC) and they must re-register after three years, during which time they must continue learning and professional development. The HCPC has developed three post-qualifying awards towards which social workers can work; these are certificates in specialist and advanced social work. There are five possible areas of study that link into these awards, focusing on mental health; adult social care; children, young people and their families; education practice; and management and leadership.

Personal attributes

Social workers must be patient, understanding and able to empathise with people. They must also have the emotional resilience to cope with distressing situations and clients who are angry, upset or frightened. They must be able to keep calm and assertive when taking decisions that service users may strongly disagree with. They have to be able to take difficult decisions and be responsible for these decisions. Social workers must be able to work alone, but also as part of a social and healthcare team. They must be good organisers and able to manage a demanding caseload.

Earnings

On qualifying, you earn between £24,000 and £25,000. Once you have had a few years' experience, salaries range from £26,000 to £40,000.

Info

Health and Care Professions Council (HCPC)
0300 500 6184
www.hcpc-uk.org

Skills for Care and Development (England)
0113 241 1240
www.skillsforcareanddevelopment.org.uk

Northern Ireland Social Care Council (NISCC)
www.niscc.info

Social Care Wales
www.socialcare.wales

Scottish Social Services Council (SSSC)
www.sssc.uk.com

Step Up to Social Work
www.gov.uk/guidance/step-up-to-social-work-information-for-applicants

SOCIAL RESEARCH/SOCIAL SCIENCE

(see also Anthropology)

Social researcher/social scientist

Social researchers and social scientists work in academia, for government and for many independent organisations. Their role is to acquire knowledge about human behaviour, values and attitudes looking at society as a group, rather than as individuals in the way that a psychologist might. The kinds of issues they study could include demographics, crime, education, the impact of economic changes, welfare, morality and culture. These are just examples; many other topics could be relevant. Their work could be used to inform policy or to try to predict trends in behaviour and attitudes.

As a social researcher/scientist you would use a variety of methods to conduct your studies. You would have to select the population group to be studied and then work out the best way to obtain the sort of information you are seeking. This could mean conducting interviews, or training others to carry these out on your behalf. You might design questionnaires or put together focus groups to discuss an issue. You would be likely to have to write up your findings, perhaps as a piece of academic research or as a report to be read and studied by a wider audience.

Entry, qualifications and training

This is often highly academic work, so most entrants would have at least a degree and very often a postgraduate qualification in one of the social sciences. These could include sociology, social policy, social administration or anthropology. Many people would get into social science research by working towards a PhD and conducting a piece of original research as part of their doctorate.

Personal attributes

You need a really strong interest in the social sciences and a strong intellectual curiosity. You need to have very good writing skills, and often need to be good at talking to people, getting them to relax and speak freely about attitudes and ideas. You may well need some facility with statistics in order to process, manipulate and manage the data you gather for some of your research work.

Earnings

Junior research assistants earn around £23,000. If your work is combined with teaching in higher education then you could be on a lecturer's salary earning £28,000 to £45,000. Working for other organisations, salaries would probably be around £25,000 to £30,000.

Info

Economic and Social Research Council
www.esrc.ukri.org

SPEECH AND LANGUAGE THERAPY

Speech and language therapist

Speech and language therapists (SLTs) identify, assess and treat people who have communication and/or swallowing disorders. A large proportion of these will be children, but SLTs also help adults who may have communication or swallowing problems caused by disease, accident or psychological trauma. Some SLTs specialise in a particular patient group, for example in the area of severe learning difficulties, hearing impairment or neurological disorders, while others choose more general, broad-based practice. The NHS is the largest employer of SLTs, working in community clinics, hospitals, special schools and homes for the mentally or physically disabled. Some of the larger voluntary organisations also employ SLTs. Often the SLT works closely in a team that may include members of the medical, teaching, therapeutic, psychological and other caring professions.

Entry, qualifications and training

Speech and language therapy is a degree-entry profession. Courses leading to professional qualifications are offered at 15 universities and colleges of higher education throughout the United Kingdom. There are a number of two-year postgraduate diploma and Master's courses available to candidates with a relevant degree.

Entry qualifications for courses vary from one institution to another, but the minimum is five GCSEs and two A levels or equivalent. A good balance of language and science is expected. Other equivalent qualifications are considered on merit. All courses will consider applications from mature students (over 21), who are encouraged to apply in the normal way.

Students who successfully pass all academic and clinical components of an accredited course are eligible to obtain a certificate to practise and to enter the professional register of the Royal College of Speech and Language Therapists as full professional members.

You could also consider a speech and language therapist degree apprenticeship. Opportunities also exist to work as a speech therapist's assistant. An NVQ in care at level 3 is available.

Personal attributes

It is essential that speech therapists themselves should have clear speech and be able to listen actively. In addition, they must have an interest in people as individuals, as well as an enquiring mind, initiative, patience, imagination and a willingness to take responsibility.

Earnings

Newly qualified speech and language therapists earn between around £22,100 and £28,700, with experience and responsibility this rises to around £26,500 to around £43,700. Working in inner London you earn an additional 20 per cent and 15 per cent in outer London.

Info

Royal College of Speech and Language Therapists
020 7378 1200
www.rcslt.org

NHS Careers
0345 60 60 655
www.healthcareers.nhs.uk

Health and Care Professions Council (HCPC)
0300 500 6184
www.hcpc-uk.org

SPORT AND EXERCISE

(see also Leisure and amenity management)

Sport at all levels is popular in the UK, and many people dream of a career in sport. It also has a high profile because levels of fitness among all age groups are of concern to government and health professionals. While not every keen amateur is destined to become a sporting legend or even a professional sportsperson, there are other roles associated with sport; for example, coaching, training, managing facilities or teaching.

Coach

Coaches help individuals and teams identify areas for improvement in physical fitness levels and for specific sports skills. They also plan and implement training programmes in a wide variety of sports provided by sports centres, clubs, schools, hotels and swimming baths.

Much coaching is done on a voluntary basis; however, there are opportunities for paid work, and many coaches work in a self-employed capacity. Some local authorities employ coaches to offer facilities for local schools at one or more centres in the authority. Such coaches are expected to be able to coach in most of the following sports: badminton, basketball, climbing (on indoor walls), ice skating, squash, swimming, tennis, trampolining and weight training. Increasingly, there is a need for coaches in the summer months to work in outdoor activity centres.

Entry, qualifications and training

Formal academic qualifications are not needed to become a coach. You should check the qualifying route with the national governing body for your chosen sport; they will all have their own approved coaching schemes. These vary in length and some are full time, some part time, while others can be done via distance learning. The key to qualifying for any of these is to have demonstrable skill in your chosen sport and to be able to show that you have the ability to teach others. There are several degrees available in sports science or sport and exercise. While a degree is not necessary to become a coach, these courses may provide useful background on the psychology of performance. Some of them also offer the opportunity to work towards coaching qualifications in conjunction with studying the academic programme. The various sporting governing bodies have designed qualifications equivalent to NVQs levels 1 to 4. You cannot become an assistant coach until you are aged 16, but beginning as soon as you are able to do so, in the sixth form for example, can be very beneficial. You could consider completing a qualification at college like a Level 3 Diploma in Coaching, or an advanced apprenticeship in sports coaching.

Personal attributes

In addition to a passion for and understanding of your own sport, you must have excellent communication skills. You must be able to motivate an individual or help a group of players function effectively as a team. You have to be physically fit yourself and aware of the rules and regulations governing your sport. You need lots of enthusiasm, but you must be sensitive enough to work with people of different abilities.

Earnings

Many coaches work part time and earn £10 to £30 an hour. Full-time work at a basic level pays around £13,500 to £24,000 a year. Senior and experienced coaches may earn £25,000 to £35,000. In professional sport, coaches working with national teams or top athletes and sports stars earn considerably more than this.

Info

UK Coaching
www.ukcoaching.org

Sports Leaders UK
01908 689180
www.sportsleaders.org

SkillsActive
033 0004 0005
www.skillsactive.com

Sport England
www.sportengland.org

Exercise/fitness/martial arts instructor

Many people attend fitness and well-being classes of all kinds, which offers full- and part-time opportunities for instructors, teachers and trainers. Techniques taught are yoga, pilates, circuit training, aerobics and exercise based on dance moves. Instructors may also teach aquacise or train clients to use gym equipment, or instruct in one of the martial arts that are now very popular. Instructors work either at leisure or fitness centres and clubs or with individual clients in their own homes. Their job is to ensure that whatever the form of exercise being taught, clients learn to do it correctly so that it is beneficial rather than harmful.

Entry, qualifications and training

Since many different forms of exercise and activity are involved, there is no one entry and training route for everyone. Most instructors or teachers specialise in one or maybe two exercise disciplines. In all cases you need to achieve a level 2 nationally recognised qualification approved by the Register of Exercise Professionals (REP). You also need to obtain a first-aid certificate and you cannot teach unless you have public liability insurance. You can start as an assistant instructor and train while working for professional certificates. You could also consider completing a diploma or undertaking an intermediate apprenticeship in exercise and fitness or as a leisure team member.

Personal attributes

You have to be physically fit yourself, well able to demonstrate all the techniques you are teaching to others. You have to be a really good communicator, explaining things carefully and realising when people have not caught on. You must be observant and pay attention to detail. You need good organisational skills if you are working at several different locations.

Earnings

Employed instructors earn £13,000 to £18,000, and can earn up to £30,000. If you work freelance, hourly rates range from £10 to £225 per hour.

Info

Register of Exercise Professionals
0113 279 1645
www.exerciseregister.org

OCR Information Bureau (for information on appropriate qualifications)
024 7685 1509
www.ocr.org.uk

SkillsActive
033 0004 0005
www.skillsactive.com

YMCA Fitness Industry Training
www.ymcafit.org.uk

Active IQ
01480 467950
www.activeiq.co.uk

Outdoor activities instructor

Outdoor activities or outdoor pursuits instructors work at centres providing a range of activities such as hill walking, climbing, abseiling, canoeing, horse riding and sailing. Clients using outdoor activities centres could be people seeking an adventurous holiday combined with an opportunity to learn new skills. Purchasing a day of outdoor activities as a gift for someone has also become very popular. Many businesses send their staff on outdoor activities courses as a method of team building. Sometimes groups of young people identified by social services or other agencies are offered outdoor activities courses to try to help them cope with stress and learn new techniques for dealing with problematic situations. Your work would include planning activities and then briefing participants before you set out. You would check that all equipment to be used is safe and in good working order. During the activity you would explain to participants exactly what to do. You would observe participants to make sure they understood and were doing everything correctly and in accordance with safety procedures. You may have to deal with emergencies – say if someone falls, or a boat capsizes.

Entry, qualifications and training

There is no one specific qualification for this work because so many different activities could be involved. You would normally need experience of and qualifications in one or more of the activities your centre offers. If your work involved instructing children you would have to pass appropriate Disclosure and Barring Service (DBS) checks. Being involved on a voluntary basis with outdoor activities of some kind could also be an advantage. You may find it useful to undertake a qualification in a relevant subject such as a Level 2 or 3 Diploma in Skills and Activities for Sport and Active Leisure (Outdoor Education). You could also consider an apprenticeship such as an advanced apprenticeship as an outdoor activity instructor.

Personal attributes

You must have good leadership qualities, and be able to motivate and encourage people. Some participants are overenthusiastic and could put themselves or others in danger. Others may be timid and require more help and encouragement. You have to be highly observant, good at anticipating situations and thinking quickly if something goes wrong. You must be an excellent communicator possessed of practical common sense.

Earnings

Junior instructors earn around the minimum wage to £15,000. Senior instructors earn £18,000 to £30,000.

Info

UK Coaching
www.ukcoaching.org

SkillsActive
033 0004 0005
www.skillsactive.com

Institute for Outdoor Learning
01228 564580
www.outdoor-learning.org

Physiotherapist

(see Physiotherapist)

Sports centre manager

Sports and recreation facility managers are responsible for the efficient running of leisure centres, swimming pools, health clubs, sports and leisure facilities at hotels, etc. Managers usually start their career as a recreation assistant and progress through supervisory and assistant manager positions via on-the-job training and professional development.

Entry, qualifications and training

There are two routes into this career. You can either start as a junior or management trainee and work for professional qualifications, or you can do a BTEC qualification, foundation degree or degree course. The Chartered Institute for the Management of Sport and Physical Activity (CIMSPA) runs relevant certificate and diploma courses that can be studied on a part-time basis. There is also a wide choice of BTEC, foundation degree and degree courses available in sports and leisure management, leisure studies, sports science and recreation management. Whether you work your way up or join as a graduate trainee, there is a lot of on-the-job training. You could consider entering the profession via an advanced apprenticeship such as a leisure duty manager, which normally takes 18 months to complete, and will involve on-the-job training and time at a college or training provider.

Personal attributes

You need excellent interpersonal skills, to be able to motivate staff and to work well with members of the public. You must be well organised, energetic and able to take responsibility.

Earnings

Trainee and assistant managers earn £15,000 to £18,000. Newly qualified managers earn between £18,000 and £25,000. An experienced manager of a large facility can earn more than £35,000.

Info

SkillsActive
033 0004 0005
www.skillsactive.com

**Chartered Institute for the Management of Sport
and Physical Activity (CIMSPA)**
www.cimspa.co.uk

Sports professional

There are opportunities in sport for professional sportspeople and for careers in coaching. Not all sports allow players to be professionals and there are some where there is room for only a very few professionals. Sports attracting professionals in relatively large numbers are football, cricket, golf, horse racing, rugby (league and union) and tennis.

Sportspeople's careers are generally short but if, during their careers, they have made a name for themselves, there may be opportunities in journalism, broadcasting or consultancy.

Entry, qualifications and training

Professional sportspeople naturally need to be excellent at their sport. Those in team games generally begin by playing for their school, town or county side. In this context, a young player may be noticed by professional selectors. In the case of football, it is not necessary to join a local football league club; apprentices are taken on from all over the country. Because a club apprentice has no guarantee that he or she will ever play for the first side, some clubs allow apprentices time off to obtain academic qualifications.

Personal attributes

As well as talent, professional sportspeople must possess dedication, perseverance and commitment and be highly competitive.

Earnings

Salaries for professionals are often low initially, but the rewards for top performers may be very high. The amount of money earned varies enormously depending upon the sport. Coaches' salaries vary according to whether the work is full or part time, what type of work they are doing and the number of hours.

Info

Sport England
www.sportengland.org

Talented Athlete Scholarship Scheme (TASS)
0191 607 8270
www.tass.gov.uk

SkillsActive
033 0004 0005
www.skillsactive.com

Swimming pool attendant/lifeguard

Swimming pool attendants and lifeguards work at swimming pools in hotels with leisure facilities, private sports clubs, public swimming pools and local authority leisure centres. Their key responsibility is to ensure the safety of everyone in the pool, watching to make sure no one is getting into difficulty and rescuing and providing first aid to anyone who needs assistance. They also make sure that people are behaving safely and sensibly in the pool. This is very much the lifeguard side of the work. Some swimming pool attendants are also responsible for monitoring the water quality in the pool and checking for levels of chemicals or bacteria. At some facilities, pool attendants may also supervise dry activities such as a gym and fitness suite.

Lifeguards also work as teachers, ensuring that people adhere to safe bathing areas and other rules, monitoring the water for incidents, taking part in rescues, giving first aid and liaising with other authorities such as the police or local coastguard.

Entry, qualifications and training

Formal academic qualifications are not essential for this work. To be a swimming pool attendant or lifeguard you must be aged 16 and to work as a beach lifeguard you must be aged 18. In both cases you must be physically fit and be a good swimmer. To work at a swimming pool you have to have one of the Royal Lifesaving Society (RLSS) lifesaving qualifications – see their website for details. They also offer national qualifications for beach lifeguarding work. All qualifications have to be reviewed every two years, when you must have both your swimming and your first-aid skills checked. Local swimming pools and swimming clubs can provide a lot of helpful information on qualifying.

Personal attributes

Apart from your swimming skills, you must have excellent 'people' skills, be friendly and approachable but also calm, confident and authoritative at times. You should be very observant and good at making quick and very important judgements.

Earnings

Pay starts at around the minimum wage to £14,000 a year, but many lifeguards and pool attendants work part time and are paid an hourly rate. Full-time work is more common in large leisure centres, where pool attendants have a wider range of responsibilities and duties and pay can be up to £29,000.

Info

SkillsActive
033 0004 0005
www.skillsactive.com

Swimming Teachers Association (STA)
01922 645097
www.sta.co.uk

Royal Lifesaving Society UK (RLSS)
www.rlss.org.uk

Royal National Lifeboat Institute (RNLI)
0300 300 9990
www.rnli.org

STATISTICIAN

Monitoring the effectiveness of a new drug, measuring trends in air pollution, predicting the performance of pension plans, or analysing the results of consumer surveys for predicting the future demand for particular products and services are just some of the problems with which statisticians work. Their work can be concerned with scientific, psychological, social or commercial issues and questions.

Statisticians design experiments and surveys. They analyse the results of these and use their findings in many different ways. They work for all kinds of organisations, from central and local government, local authorities and the NHS to private industry and commerce in many sectors.

Entry, qualifications and training

For most trainee positions you need a good honours degree in a highly numerate discipline, e.g. maths or economics. If you are working in medical statistics you will probably need a degree or postgraduate qualification in medical or life science. The Civil Service offers a range of training schemes for statisticians with a good honours degree in a numerate subject. Some employers consider applicants with a degree in social science and psychology, particularly if that degree has covered statistical methods in some detail and if work is going to be linked to these specific areas. Training is on the job, though many statisticians work for postgraduate qualifications on a part-time basis.

Personal attributes

In addition to having proven ability with numerical and scientific data, statisticians have to be creative thinkers, good problem solvers and excellent communicators. As a statistician you often need to report your findings and analysis in clear, everyday language to non-mathematical colleagues or clients. You also have to be a good team worker.

Earnings

Trainees earn between £24,000 and £30,000. With a few years' experience salaries rise to £30,000 to £60,000. In general, business and industry pay higher salaries than central and local government and science and medicine.

Info

Royal Statistical Society
020 7638 8998
www.rss.org.uk

SURVEYING

While many of us are familiar with the role of the surveyor who comes to value our property, or to assess any structural problems with a property that we might wish to purchase, there are several other types of surveyor – some with highly specialised roles.

Building surveying

Building surveyors carry out structural surveying of properties and report on their condition and valuation. They advise on necessary repairs and maintenance, and prepare plans and specifications for alterations and improvements. Local and central government employ a large proportion of qualified building surveyors, although many are in private practice. Qualifications in this area are available from the Association of Building Engineers (ABE), The Chartered Institute of Building (CIOB) Faculty of Architecture and Surveying (FAS) and the Royal Institution of Chartered Surveyors (RICS).

Commercial/residential property surveyor

This includes auctioneering, estate agency, valuation and estate management. People working in this area are responsible for the selling or letting, surveying, valuation and management of both urban and rural property. Qualifications in general practice are offered by the ABE, the FAS and the RICS.

Hydrographic surveying

The hydrographer surveys and charts underwater areas such as ports and harbours and offshore areas where drilling for oil takes place. Hydrographic surveying qualifications are offered by the FAS and the RICS.

Land geomatics surveying

The land surveyor measures and charts the earth's physical features so that maps can be drawn. This area of work has become more technical and draws on many disciplines and so the term land geomatics is more widely used now than simply 'land' surveyor. The Royal Institute of Chartered Surveyors (RICS) describes geomatics as the science and study of spatially related information, particularly the collection, interpretation/analysis and presentation of the natural, social and economic geography of the natural and built environments. Geomatics information and analysis are important in a diverse range of sectors, including: construction; property; cartography; offshore engineering and exploration; geographic information systems.

Minerals surveying

Minerals surveyors assist in the design, development and surveying of quarries and underground mines, ensuring safety for the workers as well as optimum profitability for the company extracting the minerals. They also value mineral workings for rating and taxation, and therefore need to be all-rounders with knowledge of geology, the management of mineral workings, taxation and planning legislation. This area of surveying is unique in having its qualifications and duties laid down by law. Minerals surveyors must hold the surveyor's certificate granted on behalf of the Secretary of State for Industry by the Mining Qualifications Board. They must be at least 21 and have at least four years' practical experience (including 2,000 hours underground) in order to sit the exam for this certificate. Further qualifications are provided by the RICS and the FAS.

Planning and development surveying

Surveyors specialising in this area work on a range of projects connected with development, redevelopment and regeneration. They oversee projects such as regenerating a rundown housing area, new developments on brownfield sites or the conservation of rural properties. Their work involves looking at the viability of planning proposals, considering different planning options and monitoring developments that are agreed to ensure that they are adhering to the original proposals and plans.

Quantity surveying

In private practice quantity surveyors work with an architect to draw up design specifications in line with the client's budget. When the finished design is agreed, the quantity surveyor draws up a bill of quantities, detailing the materials and labour that will be needed. Building contractors work on this bill of quantities in preparing their tender for the job; they will use their own quantity surveyors to estimate their costs. Quantity surveyors also monitor costs as the work progresses and is completed. If they train for this work while employed by construction contractors, they usually take the qualification of the RICS. Professional qualifications are also offered by the The Chartered Institute of Building's (CIOB) Faculty of Architecture and Surveying (FAS).

Rural practice surveying

This is often combined with land agency, and concerns the use and development of agricultural land. The qualifying bodies in this area are the FAS and the RICS.

Technical surveying

Technical surveyors, often referred to as surveying technicians, support the work of chartered surveyors. The work includes drawing up plans, estimating costs for projects, and gathering data and information that may form part of plans or reports. The work is often similar to that of a chartered surveyor and includes valuation of land and property and organising the sale of assets. Technical surveyors work in many branches of the profession, including commercial and residential property, rural practice, land geomatics and minerals surveying.

Entry, qualifications and training

The RICS offers a range of qualifications in the different areas of surveying. Normally entrants need three A levels or equivalent for entry into a RICS-approved degree or diploma course. An alternative is undertaking an HND or HNC in a related surveying discipline, which can give advanced entry to those courses. On successful completion of a RICS-approved degree or diploma, graduates enrol onto the Assessment of Professional Competence (APC), which is two years' practical training while in employment, concluding with a RICS professional assessment interview. Various degree backgrounds are valuable for surveying; one-year full-time and two-year part-time postgraduate conversion courses are available.

Technicians need a relevant HNC/HND or NVQ level 4 followed by the Assessment of Technical Competence. This is two years' RICS structured training while working, which concludes with the RICS technical assessment interview. Those who have gained technical membership of the RICS can take a bridging course to become a chartered surveyor.

Personal attributes

Logical and orderly thinking, ability in figure work and detailed drawings are called for in this precision work. Communication skills and business acumen are essential. Good oral and written English is an asset, and some areas may require specialised mathematical ability.

Earnings

Trainee surveyors earn between around £16,500 and £20,000. Newly qualified surveyors earn between around £21,000 and £27,000. Experienced surveyors earn between £27,000 and £43,000. Senior chartered surveyors working for large companies can earn more than £50,000. Some surveying work, especially general practice, building or quantity surveying, is sensitive to the general economic climate. Salaries may not rise so fast when the property market is sluggish.

Info

Royal Institute of Chartered Surveyors (RICS)
024 7686 8555
www.rics.org

University College of Estate Management
0800 019 9697
www.ucem.ac.uk

The Chartered Institute of Building's (CIOB) Faculty of Architecture and Surveying (FAS)
www.ciob.org.uk/topics/foaas

The Chartered Institution of Civil Engineering Surveyors
0161 972 3100
www.cices.org

The Chartered Association of Building Engineers (CABE)
01604 404121
www.cbuilde.com/the-cabe

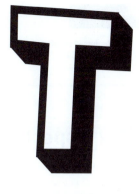

TAXATION WORK

Working in taxation involves either administering the collection of taxes to provide revenues for government, or advising those who pay tax to calculate how much they should pay.

Tax adviser/technician

Tax advisers/technicians work for private firms or independently, offering assistance to other firms/individuals who need guidance through the complications of the tax laws. A tax adviser is able to advise clients on how to plan and present their taxable income so that they legally pay the least tax possible.

Tax technicians work for firms of accountants or solicitors, in clearing banks and for consultancy firms that offer a complete tax service to their clients. However, the largest area of work involves corporate tax in organisations that have their own tax department to prepare corporate tax and VAT returns on behalf of the company

Entry, qualifications and training

There are two routes into this profession. If you choose direct entry then you apply to become a taxation trainee with a firm of accountants or the tax department of an industrial or commercial or other large organisation. You can then take the Association of Taxation Technicians (ATT) examination. If you pass this you are eligible to take the Chartered Tax Adviser (CTA) examination and become a member of the Chartered Institute of Taxation. You do not need a degree for direct entry, but some applicants do have degrees in business studies, accountancy or mathematics. Accountancy firms and other employers set their own entry requirements, but you must have good numeracy skills. The alternative route into this profession is to qualify first as an accountant, solicitor or barrister and then apply to take the CTA examination. This route is quite popular with graduates.

Personal attributes

You have to be a logical thinker and a good communicator. You need the ability to translate complex financial information into something that is readily understood by someone without a financial background. You also have to be an imaginative problem solver with good business and commercial awareness.

Earnings

In training, earnings are between £18,000 and £26,000. Newly qualified tax technicians earn between £27,000 and £37,000. Tax advisers with a few years' experience or in senior positions can earn £40,000 to £60,000.

Info

Chartered Institute of Taxation (CIOT)
020 7340 0550
www.tax.org.uk

Association of Taxation Technicians (ATT)
020 7340 0551
www.att.org.uk

Tax inspector

Tax inspectors (also referred to as senior tax professionals) work for HM Revenue & Customs (HMRC). It is the government department responsible, under the direction of the Treasury, for the efficient administration of income tax, tax credits, corporation tax, capital gains tax, petroleum revenue tax, inheritance tax, National Insurance contributions and stamp duties. Inspectors are responsible for the tax affairs of businesses and individuals, ensuring that they pay the right amount at the right time, and helping them to obtain their entitlements and meet their obligations. Inspectors detect and deter non-compliance and encourage voluntary compliance by carrying out enquiry work.

Entry, qualifications and training

If you wish to join HMRC as a trainee tax inspector you need either a good degree (at least 2.1) in any subject, or a professional accountancy qualification. With a degree you can join the Tax Professionals Graduate Programme. With a professional accounting qualification you can apply for the Tax Professionals Programme. Competition for places on either scheme is fierce. There is a three-stage selection process, starting with an online application form and tests, followed by a half day at a regional centre and a one day assessment centre. If you do not have the appropriate qualifications, you can join HMRC as an administrative assistant (GCSEs grades 9–4 in maths and English), or an administrative officer (five GCSEs grades 9–4). HMRC may be prepared to offer you an administrative job without the appropriate GCSEs if you pass an aptitude test. After some experience you can then apply to join the Tax Professionals Development Programme, which lasts four years and includes on-the-job training and further examinations.

Personal attributes

You must be very good at analysing large quantities of information and data. You must be a creative problem solver with an open, enquiring mind. Good written and spoken English, numeracy and IT skills are also essential. You must be a good communicator, calm, fair and able to interpret and apply rules.

Earnings

Graduate trainees on the Tax Professionals Graduate Programme earn around £31,000 with an additional amount for working in London. You will be promoted to a Grade 7 post on completion of the programme, earning £51,000 (national), or £57,000 in London.

Info

HM Revenue & Customs (HMRC)
www.hmrc.gov.uk

Working for the Civil Service
www.gov.uk/government/organisations/civil-service/about/recruitment

TEACHING

Imparting knowledge, teaching skills, preparing students for assessments and inspiring an enthusiasm for learning are what teaching is concerned with. Teaching takes place in many settings and with many different age groups – from young children to mature adults.

Lecturer – further education

Lecturers in this field may teach one or more subject(s) in many educational settings including sixth form colleges, further educational colleges, universities, adult education and community colleges, prisons or work-based learning. The students they teach will be aged at least 16, and lecturers will find themselves teaching adults of all ages. The range of courses on which they teach is diverse, from academic subjects to business, technical and other vocational courses – from basic numeracy and literacy to advanced cookery or conversational foreign language courses.

Lecturer – higher education

Lecturers in universities and other higher education institutions (HEIs) teach mainly undergraduates. As well as teaching, many carry out research, write articles and books, and give outside lectures and broadcasts. Competition is fierce and it is unlikely that a new graduate would be able to enter higher education as a first job.

Entry, qualifications and training

You can work as a lecturer in further education without specific qualifications, especially if you are teaching on a vocational course where you have relevant experience. However your prospects for career enhancement will be much better if you do have a qualification. There is a wide range of qualifications available; including level 3 certificates, level 4 awards and level 5 diplomas, and the majority of these can be worked towards through part-time study.

To lecture in higher education (HE) you normally need a degree and often a postgraduate degree related to the subject(s) you wish to teach. Sometimes it is possible to do some part-time teaching while you are studying for a postgraduate qualification. On more vocational courses it may be possible to lecture without these qualifications if you have plenty of experience in an appropriate area of business or technology. Many HE institutions also expect you to study part time for formal qualifications in HE lecturing. Institutions often provide in-house courses on management, curriculum development, IT and administration.

Personal attributes

At all levels you need a compelling and communicable interest in the subject you are teaching. You also need an in-depth knowledge of that subject. You need to be able to plan and develop materials and be a well-organised administrator. You need excellent communication skills, and to be confident when delivering a lecture in a large lecture theatre, but equally good working one-to-one or with small groups of students. If you are working in higher education, you may also need good research skills.

Earnings

In further education, unqualified lecturers earn £18,000 to £22,000 – qualified lecturers/teachers earn between £24,000 and £35,000. Higher education lecturers on full-time contracts earn between £33,000 and £55,000. Lecturers with considerable management responsibility or other special roles can earn more.

Info

FE Advice	**University and College Union**
0300 303 1877	020 7756 2500
www.feadvice.org.uk	www.ucu.org.uk
Higher Education Academy	**Society for Education and Training**
www.heacademy.ac.uk	www.set.et-foundation.co.uk

Teacher

Teachers work in all schools in the state and independent sectors, including free schools and academies. The state sector is by far the larger. The teacher's role is to help pupils acquire particular knowledge and understanding of a subject. Teachers plan lessons, set and mark assignments, help pupils who are having difficulty and maintain a good working atmosphere in the classroom.

Whether teachers cover one or several subjects depends on the age range they train and qualify to teach. The different options are: nursery or early years, teaching pupils aged three to five; primary, teaching pupils aged five to 11; secondary, teaching pupils aged 11 to 18; and special educational needs teaching, working with pupils of all ages who have special needs associated with disability, psychological or behavioural issues.

Other work can include supervising pupils in various activities, attending parents' evenings and other functions, and doing all the administrative work and record keeping associated with pupils' assessments and progress.

Entry, qualifications and training

There are different routes to qualifying to teach. Usually people work towards Initial Teacher Education Training (ITET) through either a university-led degree course, a postgraduate award route or through a school-led route. In both instances you will need GCSEs grades 9–4 in English and maths and a GCSE in science if you are to teach science. You need to pass ITET literacy and numeracy tests before you commence training and you need to have an enhanced background check by the Disclosure and Barring Service (DBS). You will also need experience of working with young people, this can be either paid or voluntary work. You could, for example, volunteer to help at a local school or youth club.

Degree courses can lead to BA, BSc or BEd awards but the key point to check is that they are Qualified Teacher Status (QTS). If you wish to do a postgraduate teacher training qualification, your initial degree must be in a subject that forms part of the National Curriculum.

There are several different types of school-led courses and which of these suits you will depend on what experience you have already gained, as well as what academic qualifications you have achieved. There is a programme to help people leaving the armed services become teachers – this is called Troops to Teachers.

Some independent and free schools may not require you have have completed one of the Qualified Teacher Status training routes, but the vast majority of teachers will have this qualification.

Personal attributes

Teachers must enjoy working with the age group they teach. They must be excellent communicators and able to motivate and encourage their students. They have to have great self-confidence, be able to handle difficult situations and discuss issues with parents as well as students. They must be able to work under considerable pressure, be well-organised administrators and come up with imaginative solutions to problems.

Earnings

New entrants in England and Wales begin on a salary of £24,000. In Inner London it is £30,500. You earn more for taking on extra responsibility or for working in challenging areas. A headteacher in a large school earns up to £100,000. Salaries in the independent sector can be higher or lower than in the state sector.

Info

Department of Education – Teaching
getintoteaching.education.gov.uk

UCAS Teacher training
www.ucas.com/ucas/teaching-in-the-uk

Department of Education Northern Ireland (DENI)
028 9127 9279
www.education-ni.gov.uk

Teach in Scotland
www.teachinscotland.scot

Teacher – English as a Foreign Language (EFL teacher)

Teaching English to people from all over the world and in many different countries is referred to as Teaching English as a Foreign Language (TEFL). Adults and children undertake short English language courses for many reasons – to improve business communication, to increase educational opportunities, to prepare for study in the United Kingdom or other English-speaking countries, or simply for social and leisure reasons. There are language centres and schools throughout the United Kingdom and in many other countries employing EFL teachers.

Entry, qualifications and training

You do not need to be a qualified teacher to train as an EFL teacher. While this work may be open to anyone with a good level of education and an excellent command of English, it is increasingly becoming a graduate-entry career. A degree in English, a modern language or education is particularly useful. You then study for an appropriate certificated course; this usually amounts to 100 hours, including teaching practice. Suitable courses include the CELTA (Certificate in English Language Teaching to Adults) run by Cambridge University Examinations and the CertTESOL (Trinity College London Certificate in Teaching English to Speakers of Other Languages). Note that to work in some countries you will need Qualified *Teacher* Status (see *Teacher*) and you may also need a work permit.

Personal attributes

You need to be confident, imaginative, lively and highly communicative. You have to be able to work with groups of people of all ages, from teenagers upwards, and you also have to have the understanding and patience to work with people of different abilities and varying prior levels of knowledge of English. You have to be able to make classes fun and clear and have the organisational skills to plan your workload. You need to be able to maintain order in a classroom, especially if working with excitable teenagers on their first trip abroad.

Earnings

Based on working full time in the United Kingdom, salaries are between £14,000 and £35,000 a year. However, many jobs are not full time – you are often paid an hourly or monthly rate that equates to the figures above. Much of the work is seasonal too. Working abroad there is an enormous range in salaries, but often accommodation is provided in addition to your salary.

Info

University of Cambridge ESOL Exams
http://uk-ireland.cambridgeesol.org/exams

British Council
0161 957 7755
www.britishcouncil.org

International Association of Teachers of English as Foreign Language (IATEFL)
www.iatefl.org

TEFL Teaching jobs
0845 652 0807
www.tefl.com

Teaching assistant

Teaching assistants or classroom assistants provide help and support for qualified teachers in the classroom. They can work in any school, but most are employed at primary school level helping younger children with reading, writing and mathematics. They often provide particular support to children with special needs or whose first language is not English. They also help prepare lesson materials.

If a job advertisement describes the post as 'learning support assistant' rather than a classroom or teaching assistant, the work involves supporting an individual child who has particular special needs, such as a sensory impairment, or a physical or psychological disability.

Entry, qualifications and training

At present, this varies from LEA (local education authority) to LEA, although the government does plan to introduce a standard training model. Many LEAs do not ask for any formal qualifications, but some ask for GCSEs in English and mathematics. You could also consider Supporting Teaching and Learning qualifications at Level 2 and 3, a Level 3 Diploma in Childcare and Education, or a T level in Education.

Personal attributes

Teaching assistants must be able to build good relationships with children and have a lot of common sense. They should be able to work well as part of a team, and being imaginative and creative is also useful.

Earnings

Salaries range between minimum wage and £23,000. Teaching assistants are often paid on an hourly rate and this is sometimes close to the minimum wage. A lot of the work is part time and available only during term time.

Info

Department For Education
www.gov.uk/government/organisations/
department-for-education

Adverts in local press and online

THEATRE

(see Performing arts)

THERAPY SPECIALISMS (ARTS-BASED)

There are many different therapists working in the NHS and for independent health and social care providers. Occupational therapy, physiotherapy and speech and language therapy are covered elsewhere. The therapies described in this section are art, dance, music and drama. They are all based on activities that help people to feel better, gain in confidence and find new ways to express their feelings. While they can be used with many patients, they are used predominantly in mental health and learning disability, rehabilitation and palliative care settings.

Most arts-based therapists work in hospitals, some in special schools and child guidance clinics, and some in prisons, detention centres and community homes. As posts are often part time, therapists usually work for more than one institution within an area.

Art therapist

Art therapists use art to treat psychological and emotional disorders. Drawing, painting, modelling and sculpture are among the creative activities employed.

Dance/movement therapist

Dance therapists use movement and dance as a way of helping people to engage creatively in a process of growth and personal integration. Dance movement therapists work with individuals and groups in health, education and social service settings. Their clients include people who are emotionally disturbed or have learning difficulties, and those who want to use this therapy for personal growth.

Drama therapist

Drama therapists work with people of all ages who are experiencing emotional or psychological problems, especially in communicating and understanding their own feelings. Drama therapists help people to express their feelings through role-play and other drama-based exercises. They encourage clients to be creative and to use their imaginations. Drama therapists work closely with psychologists, social workers and other members of the social and healthcare team.

Music therapist

Music therapists help people to express their thoughts and feelings by listening to music, singing, or playing musical instruments. The therapist uses live, improvised music to draw the client into an interactive musical relationship. Therapists work with people of all ages in a wide variety of settings, including special schools, psychiatric hospitals, hospices, day centres and residential homes. Music therapy is used in many clinical areas, including communication disorders, developmental delay, learning disabilities, mental health problems, physical difficulties, emotional problems, challenging behaviour and terminal illness.

Entry, qualifications and training

Although each of these four professions has its own requirements, they all follow a very similar pattern. You need a degree relevant to the therapeutic area that interests you, e.g. art for art therapist, music for music therapist, etc. If you do not have a relevant degree, but you do have a degree in psychology or a background in health or social care, it is worth contacting the relevant professional body for guidance as to the best way into your chosen profession. Once you have graduated you need to take a further course approved by the relevant professional body.

Art therapists then take a diploma or Master's in art therapy approved by the British Association of Art Therapists. Dance/movement therapists need a postgraduate qualification in dance movement. The University of Roehampton and Goldsmiths College both offer this qualification. The main qualification for drama therapists is a postgraduate diploma or Master's course approved by the British Association of Drama Therapists (BADth). Music therapists take a postgraduate diploma course lasting between one and two years. Some courses offer a part-time option.

In all cases, if you wish to work in the NHS or social services departments you have to register with the Health and Care Professions Council (HCPC).

Personal attributes

You must have great skill in your own field of art, drama, music or dance and be able to combine this with excellent communication skills. You have to be sensitive, responsive and encouraging. You must be creative and imaginative – if one approach does not work with someone, try something else. You should be able to work with groups or individuals and you should also be able to work closely with other members of healthcare and social service teams.

Earnings

In the NHS, all the various therapy professionals are paid on the same scale. The differences in pay relate to how long you have worked, your level of experience and your responsibilities rather than to the therapy specialism in which you practise. Newly qualified therapists are paid on band 5 of the NHS pay scales, which ranges from £24,200 to £30,100. Therapists with more management or other special responsibilities are paid on band 7, from £37,600 to £43,800. In inner London staff earn an additional 20 per cent and an additional 15 per cent in outer London. In the independent healthcare sector, salaries for new entrants may be a little higher than those in the NHS, but the gap closes at management level. Working for charitable organisations, as many art therapy professionals do, salaries can be a little lower than in the NHS.

Info

NHS Careers
0345 60 60 655
www.healthcareers.nhs.uk

British Association of Arts Therapists (BAAT)
020 7686 4216
www.baat.org

British Association of Dramatherapists (BADth)
07923 299453
www.badth.org.uk

Health and Care Professions Council (HCPC)
0300 500 6184
www.hcpc-uk.org

British Association for Music Therapy (BAMT)
020 7837 6100
www.bamt.org

Therapy support worker

Therapy support workers, sometimes referred to as assistants, work across the many different health professions allied to medicine. They assist therapists in their work with patients and help patients to carry out the activities that therapists have designed for them. What you might actually be doing varies according to your particular role. With an art therapist, you might be helping prepare materials and equipment as well as working with patients. If you are working with an occupational therapist, you might accompany him or her and a patient on a home visit to see what adaptations to the home might be necessary. If you are working with a physiotherapist, perhaps you will be supervising some exercises, helping a patient get ready for a session in the hydrotherapy pool, or taking a patient's blood pressure. In whatever role you are working, you are likely to have a great deal of contact with patients and work closely with other members of the healthcare team.

Entry, qualifications and training

There are no standard entry requirements, but each hospital and each therapy specialism may set its own requirements. Most will want a minimum of four GCSEs grades 9–4; sometimes one of these will need to be a science, for physiotherapy for example, whereas for art therapy an art and design subject would be more usual. Often the most important thing is to have had some experience of working with people. Training is provided on the job, but you may have opportunities to attend short courses and to work towards NVQs.

Personal attributes

Although some of these may vary according to which healthcare profession you are supporting, there are many skills and qualities that apply in all situations. You will have to be very good at working with people, understanding, sensitive and good at explaining procedures or treatments. You will need to be good at working as part of a team and you may need to have practical, IT or administrative skills as well.

Earnings

There is considerable variation, but many support staff are paid on NHS bands 3 and 4. This range is from around £18,800 to £20,800 for band 3 posts and £21,100 to £23,800 for band 4 support workers. The NHS Careers website gives more detail on exact salaries.

Info

NHS Careers
0345 60 60 655
www.healthcareers.nhs.uk

Skills for Health
020 7388 8800
www.skillsforhealth.org.uk/nsahealth

TOWN AND COUNTRY PLANNER

Town and country planners are concerned with reconciling the needs of the population for buildings, shopping centres, schools and leisure centres with the necessity of preserving and enhancing the natural and built environment. They collect information about the present use of land and the position of roads and other features, as well as drawing up plans for new schemes. Planners in development control ensure that buildings or developments intended for a particular area are suitable and do not conflict with existing buildings or the surrounding environment. Planners work for local and central government, environmental agencies, and to an increasing extent in private practice. There are also varied opportunities for planning support staff.

Entry, qualifications and training

To become a town planner you must complete a course accredited by the Royal Town Planning Institute (RTPI). You can either do a four-year degree course in town and country planning or a postgraduate diploma course if you already have a degree in surveying or another relevant subject. There is also an option to qualify through a distance-learning course if you are already working in planning but not as a qualified town planner. The RTPI website contains a list of all accredited courses.

Planning support staff normally require GCSEs grades 9–4 in English, maths and perhaps geography and IT. Some employers prefer applicants to have A levels – again geography and IT are particularly useful.

Personal attributes

Town planners and support staff need to have a knowledge of many subjects: economics, sociology, architecture and geography. Planners must be able to work in a team and cooperate with experts in other subjects. Planners need to take advice and opinions from many different people, and therefore need to be able to reconcile the conflicting views of various interest groups. They must be good communicators and have imagination, and an interest in and understanding of both people and the environment.

Earnings

Planning support staff earn £16,000 to £18,500, while newly qualified planners earn between £20,000 and £29,000. Senior planners earn between £30,000 and £40,000. Team leaders and managers earn between £35,000 and £45,000, and with experience can pay up to £80,000.

Info

Royal Town Planning Institute (RTPI)
020 7929 9494
www.rtpi.org.uk

Local government jobs
www.lgjobs.com

TRADING STANDARDS OFFICER

Trading standards officers are employed by local authorities and are responsible for enforcing a range of legislation aimed at protecting consumers and traders. Laws relate to food and consumer product safety, credit, descriptions of goods and services, prices, animal health and welfare. While most operations are carried out through random inspections, officers are also required to investigate complaints and, where appropriate, take matters to court.

Entry, qualifications and training

The essential qualification for trading standards officers is the Diploma in Consumer Affairs and Trading Standards (DCATS). The usual way to obtain this qualification is to take a degree in consumer protection or a postgraduate qualification approved by the Chartered Trading Standards Institute (CTSI); people then apply for trainee trading standards officer posts with a local authority. If you have a lot of previous experience in consumer affairs you may not have to have a degree or postgraduate qualification. Some local authorities may offer sponsorship to applicants interested in doing a degree in consumer protection. Without a degree or relevant experience you can apply for posts as an enforcement officer or consumer adviser in trading standards departments and study for the Foundation Certificate in Consumer Affairs and Trading Standards. The CTSI has developed a range of modular courses for trading standards workers at all levels. For all of these you must undergo on-the-job training and submit a portfolio of your work activities.

Personal attributes

You need a broad mix of skills to work in trading standards. You must be a good communicator, confident and persistent, but also patient and tactful at times. You should be able to handle technical equipment and complex technical information. Good IT and numeracy skills and an interest in the law are also important. You should be happy working as an effective member of a team, but also able to work on your own.

Earnings

Trainees earn between £19,000 and £24,000; once qualified, salaries range from £25,000 to £35,000, and £40,000 to £45,000 for management roles. Many trading standards officers move to work with private sector employers or with organisations that look after consumer interests in relation to utilities or the communications industry. These posts are normally paid at equivalent to or higher than management roles in local government trading standards departments.

Info

Chartered Trading Standards Institute (CTSI)
01268 582200
www.tradingstandards.uk

Local government jobs
www.lgjobs.com

TRAFFIC WARDEN

Traffic wardens, also referred to as civil enforcement officers, are civilians who work in conjunction with local police forces. They check parking meters and penalise drivers parking on double yellow lines or in other illegal places. They may also be required to do school crossing patrols or traffic control duty, as well as receiving vehicles towed into the police pound.

Entry, qualifications and training

Each Police Authority sets its own entry requirements, but there is no need to have formal educational qualifications; instead you have to pass a written test, which includes maths and English. Training is on the job, sometimes being supervised by a police officer, and many areas send you on a short, introductory course.

Personal attributes

You need to be calm, confident and possess a degree of common sense to do this work. You should be a good communicator and able to deal with aggression without becoming aggressive yourself.

Earnings

There is some variation between localities, but generally starting pay is between £16,000 and £35,000 – the highest salaries are paid in London. In most cases, you can earn more through shift allowances.

Info

British Parking Association
01444 447 300
www.britishparking.co.uk

TRAVEL AND TOURISM

(see also Civil aviation)

Travel and tourism include many jobs connected with transport, hospitality, recreation management, marketing and administration. There has also been a growth in IT work linked to travel and tourism as the number of people making their own travel and holiday arrangements via the internet has increased.

Below are some of the key jobs that are specific to the tourism and travel industry.

Resort representative

The role of a resort representative is often very similar to that of a tour manager (see below), but resort representatives are usually based in one centre and work for one tour operator. They have to receive each party of holidaymakers as they arrive at airports and seaports. They accompany them to hotels and run welcome meetings to tell them about tours and activities on offer. They make sure they are available at regular times to deal with queries and in many cases they also accompany parties on tours and trips, or at least take the bookings for these events.

Tour manager

Tour managers (sometimes referred to as tour directors) organise and accompany parties of holidaymakers on a wide variety of tours and excursions. They are often involved in the planning and the marketing of these tours. Another key part of their role is to deal with any problems that holidaymakers have, from losing a passport to being taken ill, or simply wanting further information about a particular activity or destination.

Tourist guide

Tourist guides or couriers accompany groups of tourists on visits to places of interest. These could be castles, museums, art galleries, city centres or places of natural wonder. Your main role as a tour guide is to give detailed and interesting information about these sites. In some cases you will need to have a really good knowledge of your area, as with special-interest tours, where your customers have real knowledge and enthusiasm for art or history, for example.

Entry, qualifications and training

To work as a tour manager, tourist guide or resort representative you do not need formal academic qualifications, although many applicants do have good GCSE results, A levels and a degree in a subject such as education, tourism, geography, history or marketing. Being able to speak the language in the country in which you work is a big advantage. A background in customer care, hospitality or other work in travel and tourism is a big plus for all these jobs. You could also consider a college course such as a Level 4 Diploma in Tourism Management, which may assist you in finding a role; a travel consultant advanced apprenticeship is also an option to consider.

Personal attributes

You need to have excellent interpersonal skills, being friendly, helpful and calm. You also need excellent organisational skills and to be a tour manager or resort rep you often need good marketing skills too. Tourist guides need to have a genuine interest in the sites and objects they are describing and a flair for conveying information in a lively and informative way.

Earnings

Resort representatives and tour managers earn £16,000 to £25,000, but they get board and lodging in addition to a salary. Some tour managers are self-employed, even though they are allocated work by tour operators. Tourist guides are mostly self-employed and the work is often seasonal or part time. The Association of Professional Tourist Guides can offer guidance on what fees you should charge.

Info

Institute of Travel and Tourism
0844 4995 653
www.itt.co.uk

International Association of Tour Managers (IATM)
020 8942 4338
www.iatm.co.uk

Association of Professional Tourist Guides
aptg.org.uk

People 1st
020 3074 1222
www.people1st.co.uk

Tourist information assistant/manager

Tourist information assistants and managers provide information and advice to members of the public about accommodation, leisure activities, amenities, visitor attractions, special events and transport in a particular location and also nationwide. Most tourist information centre staff are employed by local authorities, but some private visitor attractions and organisations such as national parks employ people in this role. Much of the day-to-day work as an assistant is answering questions from visitors to the centres, on the telephone or by e-mail, on all the subjects just listed. Your work is also likely to involve booking events, journeys or accommodation for visitors. Tourist information officers also have many items for sale – books, postcards and gifts – so you will also be selling these items. Part of the job includes collecting appropriate brochures, leaflets and display information for the centre and making sure that they are well displayed and that all information is up to date. As a manager of a centre you have responsibility for choosing and purchasing items to be sold, training and recruiting staff, and ensuring that the centre is presentable, welcoming and efficient.

There are also some opportunities to work with national or regional tourist organisations. In these roles there may be less dealing directly with the public and more involvement with marketing, promotional and publicity work.

Entry, qualifications and training

There are no specific entry requirements for this work, although a good standard of education is important. Many local authorities and other employers expect you to have three or four GCSEs, including maths and English. You could also consider a college course such as a Level 2 Award in the Principles of Customer Service in Leisure, Travel and Tourism, or a Level 3 Applied Certificate in Tourism. To join directly as a manager, it may be useful if you have a qualification in marketing, travel and tourism, or business, but this is not essential. Having some background experience in retailing or other jobs working directly with the public is a big advantage for both assistant and manager posts.

Personal attributes

You need to be very good at dealing with people – friendly, approachable and able to give information in a clear and precise way. You should be well organised, and good at sorting and updating information. You need basic computer skills, and some creative flair is useful for organising window or other displays. Working as a manager, you have to be good at motivating people, and good at guessing what products and ideas are likely to do well. All staff must be good at working as part of a team.

Earnings

Assistants start on around the minimum wage to £18,000; managers earn £18,000 to £30,000.

Info

Institute of Travel and Tourism 0844 499 5653 www.itt.co.uk	**Britain Express** www.britainexpress.com
People 1st 020 3074 1222 www.people1st.co.uk	

Travel agent

Travel agents sell tickets for travel by air, land and sea on behalf of transport organisations. They make hotel bookings for individual travellers, business people and holidaymakers. Some travel companies deal only with business travel, and are also involved in arranging conferences and trade fairs. However, travel agents are best known for selling package holidays on behalf of tour operators. Many travel agents will also advise travellers on visas, foreign currency and necessary injections. Travel agents face a lot of competition from people booking their own holidays via the internet, so are having to concentrate on marketing and on services that might give added value to customers. An example of this is developing special-interest packages, e.g. holidays focused on painting, sailing, horse-riding or ancient history.

Entry, qualifications and training

Apprenticeships and NVQ qualifications are available. No specific qualifications are asked for, but GCSEs in maths, English and geography are an advantage. Computer literacy is also useful.

Personal attributes

Travel agents must enjoy dealing with the general public; have a responsible attitude regarding the accuracy of information given; and good administrative and ICT skills.

Earnings

On the administrative side, earnings start at around the minimum wage to £16,000. Once you take on more sales work, salaries go up to £15,000 to £25,000, with an average of around £21,000. Many sales consultants are also paid commission on holidays or other products sold. Travel agency staff may also get discounts on holidays or flights.

Info

People 1st 020 3074 1222 www.people1st.co.uk	**Careers That Move** www.careersthatmove.co.uk

UNDERTAKER

(see Funeral director)

UNDERWRITER

(see Insurance)

UPHOLSTERER

(see Furniture and furnishing)

VETERINARY SCIENCE

(see also Animals)

Veterinary science is concerned with the care of animals, including both farm animals and domestic pets.

Veterinary nurse

Veterinary nurses (VNs) assist vets during operations and X-rays, sterilise instruments, look after animals recovering from surgery, and keep the animals and their cages clean. After qualification, the work of a VN can include practice management, staff supervision, teaching and training other nurses or support staff. Some VNs choose to work outside veterinary practice in research establishments, colleges, zoos and breeding or boarding kennels.

Entry, qualifications and training

The Royal College of Veterinary Surgeons (RCVS) administers a nationally recognised veterinary nurse training scheme. To train as a VN you must be aged 17 or over and have five GCSEs grades 9–4, including English, maths and two science subjects. You must also be employed by a practice registered to offer training. You can get details of practices approved to provide training from the RCVS website or from the British Veterinary Nursing Association (BVNA). If you particularly want to work with horses you can do specialised training as part of your qualification, but you must be working for a practice that takes on equine work.

If you do not have the required GCSEs and are working for an approved practice, you can take a day-release or distance-learning level 2 Certificate for Animal Nursing Assistants. As an alternative to the VNs there are several degree and HND courses available in veterinary nursing. If you consider this route, ensure that the course you choose is approved by the RCVS. You could consider a college course such as a Level 3 Diploma in Veterinary Nursing or an apprenticeship such as a veterinary nursing advanced apprenticeship.

During training, veterinary nurses can specialize in small animal or equine work. There is no opportunity to choose farm veterinary work as a training route, but this is likely to change in the near future.

Personal attributes

You have to love animals and be calm, kind and patient when handling them. You have to be able to deal with sad or distressing situations and you must be able to communicate with people as well as their pets. You need to be practical, with an interest in science, and you can't be the least bit squeamish.

Earnings

Trainees earn from around £15,000. Qualified VNs earn around £23,000. Senior VNs in large practices may earn £27,000. There are sometimes opportunities for overtime through working weekends or evening and night shifts, or for being available to support on-call vets.

Info

Lantra
02476 696996
www.lantra.co.uk

British Veterinary Nursing Association (BVNA)
01279 408644
www.bvna.org.uk

Royal College of Veterinary Surgeons (RCVS)
020 7222 2001
www.rcvs.org.uk

British Equine Veterinary Association (BEVA)
01638 723555
www.beva.org.uk

Veterinary surgeon

Most vets work in private practice, usually starting out as a veterinary assistant and working their way up into a partnership or into their own business. Some specialise in small-animal treatment, including pets such as dogs, cats and birds, while others work with farm animals, horses or more exotic zoo animals. Other vets work in research or industry. The Department for Environment, Food and Rural Affairs, for instance, employs a substantial number to work on disease control, monitoring such epidemics as foot and mouth or swine vesicular disease. Others are employed by animal welfare organisations, such as the People's Dispensary for Sick Animals (PDSA), in animal hospitals. Vets are also needed in the food-processing industries, where their job is concerned with checking that conditions are humane and hygienic.

Entry, qualifications and training

A veterinary surgeon must hold a degree from a veterinary school in the United Kingdom. Universities offering the course set their own entrance requirements but all demand an extremely high standard of A level passes or equivalent. Chemistry is essential, and other useful subjects are physics, maths, biology and zoology. The course lasts five years (six at Cambridge), and covers a formidable amount of academic and practical work, comparable to that needed to be a doctor. There is currently a shortage of farm vets, but strong competition for positions in small animal or equine work.

Personal attributes

Vets need to be sympathetic but detached. They must be excellent communicators, explaining to and reassuring pet owners and farmers. Patience, calmness and, later on, a good business sense and problem-solving skills are also important.

Earnings

Newly qualified vets earn around £32,000, but with a few years' experience this rises to £45,000 to £50,000. Senior vets in large practices can earn £60,000 to £90,000.

Info

Lantra
02476 696996
www.lantra.co.uk

Royal College of Veterinary Surgeons (RCVS)
020 7222 2001
www.rcvs.org.uk

British Veterinary Nursing Association (BVNA)
01279 408644
www.bvna.org.uk

British Equine Veterinary Association (BEVA)
01638 723555
www.beva.org.uk

WAREHOUSE WORK

Warehouses play a key role in the supply chain, for retail, wholesale and online delivery companies. All kinds of goods pass through warehouses, from components for manufacturers, to fresh and frozen foods, wine, furniture and electronic goods. In fact anything you buy or own has probably spent some of its life in a warehouse somewhere.

Warehouse manager

Working as a warehouse manager you would be responsible for every aspect of the operation. You would have to negotiate with suppliers and customers to ensure the appropriate goods were stored and dispatched at the right time. You would have to allocate storage space for goods. You would have to pay great attention to the health and safety of other staff, but also be responsible for safe storage of various types of goods (perishable foods or hazardous chemicals for example). It would often be part of your role to recruit other warehouse staff, and you would almost certainly be involved in staff training, even if recruitment were part of some central head office operation.

Warehouse operative

In this role you could work on any or all of the warehouse operations. This could include unloading and checking goods as they arrive, particularly checking for damaged packaging or goods, moving stock to the appropriate storage areas, collecting and loading goods to be dispatched and keeping records of stock and stock movements. You might also have to clean and tidy work areas and carry out basic checks on equipment.

Entry, qualifications and training

You may not necessarily need formal qualifications to work as a warehouse operative, although good basic English and maths would be required by most employers and some would expect you to have three or four GCSEs. Many warehouse managers start as operatives, work their way up through supervisory roles and then into management. Some managers enter this work with relevant HND or foundation degree qualifications. It is then possible to work for professional qualifications with the Chartered Institute of Logistics and Transport. You could also consider a supply chain warehouse operative intermediate apprenticeship or an intermediate apprenticeship in warehousing and storage.

Personal attributes

Managers will have to have excellent leadership and planning skills, backed up by good maths and IT skills. All warehouse staff have to be good at working as part of a team, working under pressure and being flexible. Warehouse operatives must be good at keeping paperwork or electronic records up to date and be physically fit and practical. Everyone must be prepared to pay close attention to health and safety.

Earnings

Warehouse operatives earn the minimum wage to £17,000 and in supervisory roles this can rise to £27,000. Warehouse managers earn £20,000, to £30,000 – up to £40,000 in very large operations.

Info

Chartered Institute of Logistics and Transport (CILT)
01536 740100
www.ciltuk.org.uk

Skills for Logistics
0117 927 8800
www.skillsforlogistics.co.uk

WATCH AND CLOCK MAKER/REPAIRER

Watch and clock makers make timepieces by hand, sometimes to a design of their own.

Repairers receive watches and clocks from customers for servicing and repair. They must be able to examine a timepiece thoroughly for worn-out parts, clean and regulate a watch or clock, and repair or replace faulty parts. The work involves the use of precision tools and electronic equipment. Restoration is carried out on antique clocks and watches.

Entry, qualifications and training

You may be able to get a trainee position without qualifications and gain qualifications part time. There are also several courses accredited by the British Horological Institute (BHI), including certificates at preliminary, intermediate and final level. You can study for these at the University of Central England in Birmingham and through distance-learning modules. The University of Central England also offers a degree in horology. You may be able to complete courses specialising in restoring and conserving antique clocks and watches. Some local colleges offer part-time courses in clock and watch servicing and repair, and this could be a useful way to get started.

Personal attributes

A real interest in watches, clocks and mechanical devices is a good starting point. You need excellent manual dexterity, to be able to work on intricate, delicate and detailed devices and to maintain a level of careful concentration. You need mathematical skills and you may also need drawing skills. You must be able to deal with clients and customers and, if you work for yourself, you need all the skills of running a business – bookkeeping, marketing your services, managing your own time, etc.

Earnings

New entrants earn around £15,000. Experienced repairers can earn £25,000 to £30,000 – some of the highest rates are paid in restoration and conservation work. If you are self-employed there is a lot of variation in earnings, depending on how much work you do, but £20,000 may be a reasonable average.

Info

British School of Watchmaking
www.britishschoolofwatchmaking.co.uk

British Horological Institute (BHI)
www.bhi.co.uk

Worshipful Company of Clockmakers
020 7998 8120
www.clockmakers.org

WELFARE ADVICE WORKER

Welfare advice workers are employed by local authorities, Citizens Advice and various charities and voluntary organisations. Advice workers answer questions and offer confidential advice and practical help, for example help with filling in a form to members of the public. Some work with specific client groups, rather than the general public, such as students at a college or tenants of a housing association. The work often involves advocacy work, taking up an issue on behalf of a client or dealing with bureaucracy on their behalf. Some advice workers are generalists, offering advice on many different problems; working for the CAB is a good example of this. Other welfare advisers specialise in issues such as debt management, housing questions, consumer concerns, education and career decisions or discrimination of some kind.

Entry, qualifications and training

Although there are no formal entry qualifications, many advice workers are graduates in sociology, psychology or similar subjects. They have often had experience of working with people and many advice workers begin their advice careers in a voluntary capacity. There is a variety of part-time courses available at NVQ levels 2, 3 and 4 in advice and guidance work – many people undertake these once they are working in this field.

Personal attributes

You must be very good at listening to people and at explaining documents or rules patiently and carefully. You need good information research skills and good powers of persuasion if your role involves advocacy work of any kind. You need to be well organised and flexible, with good written communication skills.

Earnings

Earnings are from around £16,000 up to £27,000 – although few posts pay at the top of this range. If you work for a local authority or an academic institution, your salary is likely to be higher than if you work for a voluntary body or charity.

Info

Advice UK
0300 777 0107
www.adviceuk.org.uk

Citizens Advice
www.citizensadvice.org.uk

WINDOW CLEANER

Window cleaning can be much more involved than doing a round in a residential area cleaning house windows for individual customers. Window cleaners clean the windows, doors and other glass surfaces of large buildings including tower blocks and tall commercial premises. Window cleaners working in these high environments work either on special platforms which attach to buildings or on abseiling harnesses. Some operate special water-fed long poles to avoid having to climb up ladders. Some window cleaners are self-employed, building up local rounds for themselves, others work for cleaning contractors.

Entry, qualifications and training

There are no formal academic requirements to do this work. You need a driving licence and if you work for a contractor you might take NVQ level 2 certificates in cleaning processes and in working at heights. You may be able to do an apprenticeship in window cleaning and each employer sets their own entry requirements for applicants. You may need to complete training in rope access work or operating a mobile platform in order to work as a window cleaner on tall buildings.

Personal attributes

You have to be physically fit and not afraid of heights. You should be very aware of safety issues. You should have good people skills, especially if you are working with residential customers, aiming to build up a business. You also need to have some business sense, able to market your services and manage your finances. If you aim to be a contractor yourself, you will need people management skills too.

Earnings

Earnings for self-employed window cleaners vary widely, depending on how much work you generate and the geographical region in which you work. Contract window cleaners earn between £16,000 and £23,000.

Info

British Institute of Cleaning Science (BICSc)
01604 678710
www.bics.org.uk

WINE TRADE

(see also Hospitality and Catering for Publican/licensee and Retailing)

The wine trade has grown and changed significantly in recent years, increasing opportunities in wine retailing, buying, importing and marketing. Wine specialists work for supermarkets, for off-licence chains, for specialist wine traders and for online wine retailers and wine markets. Opportunities exist in sales (including telephone sales), management, marketing and importing. To work as a wine buyer, you need extensive experience and knowledge. Wine merchants who do not employ their own buyers may use wine brokers who work with growers and select the kinds of wine in which a particular merchant is interested. There are now many English vineyards springing up, creating some further marketing opportunities.

Entry, qualifications a training

On the retail management side, entry requirements vary – some ask for A levels, some prefer graduates, and you must be over 18 to sell wine to customers. To get into wine brokerage or wine buying, you normally have to have worked in the trade and also completed wine tasting courses. The Wine and Spirit Education Trust (WSET) runs a wide range of courses for professionals as well as amateurs; check the website for further details.

Personal attributes

You need good people skills, whether dealing directly with customers or working with growers from all parts of the world. You need to have a flair for business, good organisational skills and the ability to work as part of a team and to motivate others.

Earnings

Junior managers earn between £15,700 and £20,000. Managers of larger wine and spirit retailers may earn £25,000. Sales staff marketing home delivery wine services earn between £15,000 and £20,000, with possibilities to earn more through commissions on sales. Experienced wine buyers may earn £40,000.

Info

People 1st
020 3074 1222
www.people1st.co.uk

National Skills Academy for Food & Drink
0845 644 0558
www.nsafd.co.uk

Wine and Spirit Education Trust (WSET)
020 7089 3800
www.wsetglobal.com

WRITER

(see also Journalism)

For writers other than journalists, making a living purely from writing can be very difficult, so many writers, especially before they are established, have other careers as well. There are few who become successful fiction writers or writers of really popular non-fiction such as biographies. There are some jobs for writers-in-residence with theatre companies and regional arts organisations, prisons or university departments, but many of these posts are temporary contracts.

Technical authors write user manuals and instruction books for anything from washing machines to computer software, and there are writers who specialise in writing textbooks and other teaching materials. Technical authors are often on permanent or at least more secure contracts. Many writers of textbooks have other jobs in education.

Entry, qualifications and training

There are no formal entry qualifications, although most writers have a good level of education, especially in English or other subjects where a good command of the language is important. There are many creative writing courses that can teach the technical aspects of writing, but creativity is not something you can learn. If your goal is to work in film, radio or television, it might be worth considering a script-writing course.

Technical authors come from a wide range of academic disciplines, but science, technology and engineering are particularly useful backgrounds. Although there are no specific entry requirements for this work, it is very much a graduate profession.

Personal attributes

Being a brilliant communicator of the written word is the key to your success. While creative writers have to have imagination, flair and a way of drawing the reader in, technical authors must be able to make complex material accessible. All writers have to be determined, self-disciplined, highly motivated and able to cope with rejection. Technical authors have to have a very thorough and careful approach to their work.

Earnings

Earnings vary. For creative writers the average income is only around £5,000 a year and more than half of all creative writers have additional jobs, many in teaching or lecturing. Technical authors earn between £18,000 and £30,000.

Info

Association of British Science Writers
www.absw.org.uk

Institute of Internal Communication (IoIC)
01908 232168
www.ioic.org.uk

Creative & Cultural Skills
020 7015 1800
www.ccskills.org.uk

The Poetry Society
020 7420 9880
www.poetrysociety.org.uk

Screen Skills
020 7713 9800
www.screenskills.com

The Writers' Guild of Great Britain
020 7833 0777
www.writersguild.org.uk

YOUTH OFFENDING TEAM OFFICER

Youth offending team officers (YOTs) work for local authorities. Their work is concerned with trying to stop young people committing crimes or to prevent those who have already committed offences from reoffending. The work is very varied and YOTs work with young offenders right from the stage where they may have to appear in court through to supporting them after they have been released from secure institutions. As a YOT you might have to prepare sentence reports for the courts. You could be supervising young offenders who have received non-custodial sentences, which they must serve in the community. You could be involved in mediation between victims and offenders in restorative justice programmes. Part of your role would be to help young people to get back into education or training or to find work after serving a sentence. Sometimes you would work on a one-to-one basis with your clients, on other occasions you would work with groups. You would also work closely with other agencies, such as those involved in drug rehabilitation programmes.

Entry, qualifications and training

Many YOTs have a background in other relevant work such as social work, the probation service or youth work. Youth offending teams also employ young offending team support workers who work with lower-risk offenders and do not have to have the same background qualifications. The Youth Justice Board website gives further details of specific requirements. Training is through a combination of on-the-job training and short professional development courses. You may also get the opportunity to work towards a foundation degree in youth justice.

Personal attributes

You need to be a really good communicator, able to be understanding but also clear and assertive. You need to be confident and calm when dealing with clients who might be hostile to you and your ideas. You also need to be good at motivating people. You must be very good at keeping records, managing a caseload and writing clear reports.

Earnings

Qualified YOTs earn from £20,000 to £30,000, but can earn up to £38,000 depending on experience. Support staff in the team earn around. £16,000 to £20,000.

Info

Skills for Justice
www.sfjuk.com

Youth Justice Board
020 3334 5300
https://www.gov.uk/government/organisations/
youth-justice-board-for-england-and-wales

YOUTH WORKER

Youth workers support young people aged 13 to 19 – occasionally younger, 11 and 12, or older, up to aged 25. Youth workers are employed by local authority social services departments or by Connexions services, but some work for charities and other community organisations.

The work of individual advisers depends on their clients' needs. Most of an adviser's time is spent in direct contact with young people. You could be organising activities such as sports or games, mentoring individuals, facilitating discussions or setting up meetings with other agencies. Your clients may have many problems: drug or alcohol abuse, difficult family backgrounds, problems coping with school. As a youth worker you might be based at a youth club or a drop-in centre of some kind. You might also do outreach work, going into the community to identify young people who might be facing difficulties and be in need of support.

Entry, qualifications and training

All youth workers need a professional qualification in youth work approved by the National Youth Agency (NYA). This can be either a three-year full-time degree course or a one-year postgraduate course, if you have a degree in another subject. Both of these courses are also offered part time. You can also join a service as a youth support worker and work towards NVQ levels 2 and 3 and then study for a degree part time. At whatever level you join, much of the training is on the job. Other options include a Level 2 or 3 Diploma in Youth Work Practice, and an advanced apprenticeship in youth work.

Relevant experience is a really important part of the selection process. You need to have worked either in a paid or voluntary capacity with young people or in the community in some way.

Personal attributes

Youth workers need strong communication and relationship-building skills to engage the trust and respect of young people. They need to be able to listen carefully and respond appropriately; a non-judgemental approach is essential. Youth workers need to empathise with young people's concerns while maintaining professional and emotional detachment. A sense of humour, reliability, flexibility, good time management and team-working skills are also important.

Earnings

Youth support workers earn £15,000 to £17,500; qualified youth workers earn £23,000 to £30,000, and up to £37,000 depending on experience – there is some geographical variation. Recent government cuts in funding have resulted in a reduction in the number of youth worker jobs available.

Info

National Youth Agency (NYA)
0116 242 7350
www.nya.org.uk

Local Government Jobs
www.lgjobs.com

Youth Council for Northern Ireland
www.youthcouncilni.org

British Youth Council
www.byc.org.uk

ZOOLOGY

Zookeeper

(see Animals)

Zoologist

Zoologists work in either research or teaching. Zoologists study the anatomy, physiology, classification, distribution, behaviour and environment of all kinds of creatures, from insects to elephants. When working in zoos they usually coordinate conservation breeding programmes, collection planning and general conservation strategies. A small number find jobs in industry, mainly in pharmaceutical and animal foodstuff companies. Research zoologists work for governments, non-government organisations and wildlife conservation bodies looking at such issues as species under pressure from climate change or human activity, or preservation and understanding of habitat and ecology.

Entry, qualifications and training

A few universities offer degrees in zoology, and this is normally the only way to pursue a career as a zoologist. Often this is followed by postgraduate study in a specialised area such as mammalian behaviour, migration or birds, breeding cycles of insects, the changing populations of fish in our oceans – these are a few typical examples or possible topics.

Personal attributes

Zoologists should have a scientific mind and an interest in research. They should also have keen powers of observation and be patient and confident.

Earnings

New graduates working as research or technical assistants earn around £21,000. With experience, zoologists can earn up to £48,000. Zoologists in research posts earn up to £30,000.

Info

Zoological Society of London
www.zsl.org/science

Index